THE STRUCTURE
OF LEARNING PROCESSES

Edited by

Jaan Valsiner
Technische Universität Berlin

and

Hans-Georg Voss
Technische Hochschule Darmstadt

ABLEX PUBLISHING CORPORATION
NORWOOD, NEW JERSEY

Printed in the United States of America

Library of Congress Cataloging-in-Publication Data

The structure of learning processes / edited by Jaan Valsiner and Hans
  -Georg Voss.
    p.   cm.
    Includes bibliographical references and indexes.
    ISBN 0-89391-981-0. -- ISBN 1-56750-253-9
    1. Learning, Psychology of.   I. Valsiner, Jaan,   II. Voss, Hans
  -Georg, 1944–
    BF318.S78   1996
    153.1´5--dc20   95-26811
                                                  CIP

Ablex Publishing Corporation
355 Chestnut Street
Norwood, New Jersey 07648

Contents

General Introduction.
The Structured Nature of Learning:
History Revisited

Jaan Valsiner   Hans-Georg Voss

Learning has been a widely studied topic in psychology—and yet we know very little about it. This paradoxical situation is partially explainable by the variety of uses of the term *learning* in our psychological discourse. It is a term easily usable as an attribution (as in such claims as "students' performance is due to their learning"), and it can be used in ways that emphasize contrasts between various explanations ("children's knowledge of the properties of their minds develop either by learning or by maturation"). In both of these attributional uses of the term, the function of the given use is to create a "black box" explanation (in Bateson's sense—see Bateson, 1972). Such explanations proliferate in psychology, but they may constitute a danger for further understanding, as has been pointed out by a fervent critic of psychologists' reasoning:

> The psychologist takes conditioning as the principle of learning, and accepting this principle as not subject to further analysis, not requiring ultimate investigation, he endeavors to apply it to everything and to explain all the individual features of learning as one and the same process. (Pavlov, 1932, pp. 91—in response to Guthrie, 1930)

Much of the discourse about learning in psychology can be seen as an effort to explain relevant phenomena by the application of the explanatory concept of learning, and (equally widely) to demonstrate experimentally new phenomena that are explained by the same concept (see review by Stevenson, 1970). This is obviously the legacy that the dominance of behavioristic ideology in (mostly) North American psychology has left behind and with which the discipline must wrestle.

Psychology is highly fashion dependent. Together with the disappearance of behavioristic ideology (or its becoming a clandestine operation), the preoccupation with learning can be seen to have diminished in the recent decades (see Langley & Simon, 1981). It has given way to the use of other popular labels (e.g., *knowledge acquisition* and its strategies—see also Brown, 1982). The change from the behavioristic orthodoxy to the "cognitive revolution" has brought with it a wider use of permissible concepts, but not necessarily a greater clarity in the explanations of learning processes. As Estes has explicitly stated:

> Because of the disjointness of the research settings, the kinds of subjects customarily studied, and the descriptive vocabularies employed in research on conditioning and learning on the one hand and cognitive psychology and information processing on the other, one may well get a distorted impression of the degree of novelty of the concepts and principles that have become current in the latter areas. Emphasizing differences rather than correspondences doubtless serves a protective function, helping investigators in either tradition by classifying as irrelevant much literature outside a given investigator's specialty. . . . There is a possible cost of indulging in this protective mechanism, of course, in the form of a lack of perspective that may encourage superficiality and shut off potentially stimulating or catalyzing inputs to the investigator's theoretical efforts. (Estes, 1978, p. 277)

Indeed, theoretical superficiality and obsession with empirical details psychology (the "error of the third kind"—Mitroff & Featheringham, 1974) are rampant in psychology. Contemporary cognitive psychology continues along those lines, as did its predecessor—with a behavioristic fixation on details of learning, paired with the lack of theoretical explanation of learning processes. However, issues of learning cannot disappear from our sphere of interest. This is hardly surprising, as the social and biological sciences need to conceptualize the unavoidable aspect of change in the biological, social, and (nowadays) computer systems, and the concept of learning (or its synonyms) affords such use.

What, then, is *learning?* In the most general terms, the question of learning is predicated upon the whole conceptual issue of change (or "permanent modifiability"—Thorndike, 1913, p. 171) and therefore is rooted in the cultural history. The very first metatheoretical issues about learning that guide the use of that concept is the construction of its opposition with other terms (as in learning *or* instinct/maturation), and the form the particular opposition takes (i.e., the specific meaning of the disjunction *or,* as in the contrast between learning *versus* instinct as separate from learning *and* instinct). The contrast that is captured by the two meanings of *or* (i.e., the disjunctive disjunction of *either . . . or,* and the conjunctive disjunction of *and*) is at the core of the distinction between associationistic and structuralistic approaches to learning, as we will encounter them below.

Learning is an eternal problem for human minds. It is therefore not surprising that traces of thinking about learning can be found in any ancient philosophical system (e.g., in Aristotle—see Ogden, 1930). Psychology's concern with issues of learning can be seen to emerge from the 19th-century discourse about the contrasts between free will and determinism (Daston, 1982). It can be argued that learning occupies a middle position between viewing organisms as preprogrammed *automata* (i.e., instinct-based adaptations to the world) on the one hand, and the extreme vicissitudes of voluntarism on the other. In the case of learning, the permanent change is lawful as it takes place (i.e., it is deterministic—e.g., Thorndike, 1917), while what is being learned is open to choice (the voluntaristic facet). From the perspective of this analysis, it becomes understandable why early learning theorists were adamant about positing *laws* of learning but did not proceed further to explain these laws themselves. Their main concern was to make learning phenomena similar to the ideal of mechanistic determinism, rather than to let it be used as a showcase for the proof of the free will mentality.

The Ordinary Language: Its Meanings for *Learning*

Like most of our psychological concepts, notions of modifiability are encoded into the history of human common language use. Analysis of the semantic fields of the terms of ordinary languages that cover the domain of phenomena of learning is instructive in a number of ways. First, it constitutes a *fossilized* form (to borrow Vygotsky's term) of cultural organization of human self-reflection. The history of the multiple uses of the given language term cannot be traced easily from the present state of the term. The users of different languages all around the world, and over the history of the human species, have encoded the phenomena of learning in different (but to a large extent overlapping) ways. Psychology has been largely a hostage to the common language use (Molenaar, 1986; Smedslund, 1978; Valsiner, 1985), and as such it has imported many nuances of the common language into its theorizing. Whereas it goes without saying that the common language serves as a rich resource for human self-reflection (including that of theoretical self-understanding by psychologists—see Siegfried, 1994), its outer boundaries set blinders for reaching a general understanding of psychological kind. If psychological theorizing is to lead to general knowledge about psychological phenomena, it needs to transcend the limits of the common language meanings by generating a metalevel perspective that is equally appreciative and inclusive of each and every language's constructions of the phenomena.

Even a very simple look at the meanings of the verb *to learn* in the English language (Webster's Third New International Dictionary, 1981, p. 1286) reveals interesting evidence. That verb is reported to possess the following meanings:

1.1. to gain knowledge, understanding, or skill by study, instruction, or experience;

1.2. to develop an ability or readiness by practice, training, or repeated experience;

1.3. to become aware;

1.4. to acquire (as a skill or habit or a modification of an existing habit) through experience, practice, or exercise;

1.5. to commit to memory;

1.6. to teach;

1.7. to inform (a person) of something;

1.8. to find out.

There are similar connotations in German language. The famous *Deutsches Wörterbuch* of the brothers Grimm from 1885 (Grimm & Grimm, 1885), and the latest edition of The Duden (1989) list the following meanings:

2.1. to become more experienced with the passage of time (*erfahren werden*) and in the course of life (*Lebenserfahrung*);

2.2. the passive form of teaching (actually, the concept "teaching" (*lehren*) appeared quite earlier in history; then in 16th century there was a mixed form of lehrnen, which is the active form *lehren* and the passive form lernen taken together;

2.3. a technical term that signifies the graduation of skilled manual workers (*auslernen*);

2.4. to acquire knowledge or special skills (in art, in language);

2.5. to learn from life, to form special attitudes and beliefs, often in a negative sense ("I have learned the bitter lesson of obedience");

2.6. to become acquainted with a person (*kennen lernen*);

2.7. used metaphorically as in the sentence "*die Uhr lernt gehen*" (the clock is learning to function) or the sentence "*meine Beine lernen wieder zu gehen*" (my legs will learn to walk again);

2.8. to exercise (*üben*), which also has the stronger form of "going through" a text or an action by exercising (*durchexerzieren*);

2.9. to train or to optimize a skill that is already there;

2.10. there may be also a negative connotation of learning: if someone learns too much in terms of the time being spent, he or she is called a *Streber,* which refers to a kind of opportunistic behavior.

The very first noteworthy aspect of these meanings is the commonality that unites all of them under the assumption of the active person who learns. Thus, the usual contrast of learning with pregiven or passively assumed characteristics in psychologists' discourse is well supported by the common language system. The second relevant aspect of this semantic field is the trace of connectedness of teaching with learning (see meanings 1.6 and 2.2). In the history of the English language these two sides of the learning process were not differentiated until the 19th century (Weekley, 1967, p. 834), and they remain interdependent in many other languages in our time. For example, the case of *obuchenie* in Russian refers to a complex of the process of teaching and learning, assuming both the active learner and the goal-directed teacher (Valsiner, 1988, pp. 162–164). Likewise, in the Maori language, the word *ako* refers to both "to learn" and "to teach" (Metge, 1984, p. 2). Thus, learning as a concept in normal language spans a broad range of connotations, from functional processes in the organism (human or animal) such as memory formation or knowledge aquisition, to the expression of societal values (see meanings 2.5 and 2.10) and the circumscription of cultural practices (see meaning 2.3).

Psychologists' Understanding of Learning

There exist all too many viewpoints on learning in psychology—so that efforts at classifying different theories can produce some order in that domain (Heinen, Sherman, & Stafford, 1990). Learning is obviously related to the notion of development, but it is not reducable to it (see a conceptual analysis by Van Geert, 1986, pp. 23–28; and also Voss, in this volume). Learning has been addressed in varied ways, depending upon the general theoretical background of the addresser. As in psychology as a whole, the two major world views— atomistic (associationistic) combinatorialism and structural holism (see Valsiner, 1987, 1989)—can be seen to clash intensely on how to explain learning. The problem of learning emerges as having been embedded in 19th-century thought about biological evolution and the modifiability of animal and human beings.

Roots of Learning—Jean Baptiste Lamarck's Philosophy of Nature

It would be quite revealing to discover a theory in learning in the oft-mentioned (but rarely read) classic *Zoological Philosophy* (Lamarck, 1809/1984). As a major founder of the intellectual movement for the modifiability of a being's nature, Lamarck surely can qualify as the first modern learning theorist. The principal idea of modification of the existing form of the organism (and its intergenerational transmission) is present not only in Lamarck's two laws of evolution (Lamarck, 1809/1984, p. 113), but also in his account of psychological development:

> To regard certain propensies which have become altogether dominant as innate in the human species, is not only a dangerous belief but also a genuine mistake. We may no doubt possess at birth special tendencies transmitted from the organization of our parents, but it is certain that if we did not strongly and habitually exercise the faculties favoured by these tendencies, the special organs concerned would never have developed. (pp. 369–370)

Lamarck's emphasis on the exercising of faculties in ontogeny was later matched by Thorndike's laws of use, disuse, exercise, and effect (Thorndike, 1913; also see O'Donohue & Krasner, 1988). Furthermore, Lamarck's founding of modern learning perspectives becomes obvious in his emphasis on the supportive and constraining role of the environment in the process of modification—a central point of modern ecological psychology (Johnston & Pietrewicz, 1985).

The Main Contrast: Associationistic and Gestalt Perspectives

Accounts of learning have usually been known to belong to the associationistic traditions of psychology. Surely the great physiologists Ivan Pavlov and Vladimir Bekhterev, whose contributions to the study of mechanisms of learning are physiological classics, relied on the associationistic world views (Bechterev, 1932; Pavlov, 1906; Windholz, 1984; Windholz & Lamal, 1986). The importation of their ideas to other countries rendered their ideas even more associationistic and reductionistic than the original corpus of knowledge (see Skinner, 1981). The overwhelming majority of empirical elaborations of behavioristic learning perspectives have taken their associationistic roots (Thorndike, 1913) and axioms for granted, and gone on to study details of a process that is construed on the basis of these axioms. For example, consider the following effort to explain that learning is:

> the change in a subject's behavior or behavior potential to a given situation brought about by the subject's repeated experiences in that situation, provided that the behavior change cannot be explained on the basis of the subject's native response tendencies, maturation or temporary states of the subject (e.g., fatigue, drunkenness, drives, and so on). (Bower & Hilgard, 1981, p. 11)

A careful analysis of this effort reveals both the ideological commitment and the basic common-sensical differentiation of meanings that are used here. First, behaviorists' pet terminology (*behavior* or *behavior potential*) is utilized. The term *behavior* is probably the least well defined (and most widely used) in the brand of psychology that follows the behavioristic belief system of objectivity of behavior. Secondly, the explanation evokes the common-sense contrast of learning *versus* a list of supposedly fixed phenomena (*native response tendences, maturation*), and separates learning from temporary states of the learner. In contrast with the picture painted by Lamarck, the behavioristic views of learning have taken a step backward by eliminating the organismic (intrasystemic) consideration of the learning process and its interdependence with the environmental task demands. In other terms—the behavioristic focus on learning has overlooked the basics of development (see also criticisms in Johnston, 1985; Revusky, 1985).

It is therefore only too realistic to find structuralistic developmentalists (e.g., Piaget and Vygotsky—see Van der Veer & Valsiner, 1991), ecologically oriented developmental biologists (Johnston, 1981; Johnston & Turvey, 1980; Johnston & Pietrewicz, 1985), and Gestalt psychologists (e.g., Koffka, 1925; Ogden,

1930; as well as hybrids of behaviorism and Gestalt psychology like Tolman, 1951) united in their opposition to the behavioristic accounts of learning. Interestingly, social learning theory joins that enterprise (Bandura, 1991, Bandura & Walters, 1963).

The Gestalt psychological tradition has always emphasized the need to view learning processes as structurally organized holistic entities. Hence it is no surprise that we can trace alternative concepts to learning in the work of Gestaltists. Thus, to reiterate Koffka:

> we find at the beginning, in our most elementary reactions, even at the level of reflexes and instincts and again in training and in intelligent performances, unitary, articulate, meaningful wholes; to which we apply the name of Gestalt, configuration, structure. Development starts, not with chaos or with multitude of mental elements without order or meaning, but with structures. Gradually, by a number of smaller or larger leaps and bounds, we achieve different orders, different articulations, different meanings. (1925, pp. 672–673)

The Gestalt position on learning denied the assumption of elements as starting points in constructing the learned knowledge structure, and rather emphasized learning as transformation of structure from one state to another. There is an attempt made in this volume (the chapter by Voss) to define learning in terms of a process by which dynamical developmental systems will pass through the parameter space designed to characterize the dimensions of the system. The basic Gestalt position on learning was shared by other psychologists of structuralist underpinnings, including William Stern (1938) and Jean Piaget (1971; see also Sinclair, 1973). In fact, any developmental perspective on learning is necessarily structural-dynamic, since it has to explain the emergence of novelty in specified parts of the whole. In other terms (those of Driesch, 1927, p. 9) "every unbiased psychologist must be a Gestalt psychologist"—since psychological phenomena are context-dependent wholes.

Why such sudden renewal of the role of Gestalt psychology? After all, the question of learning was never a central one for Gestalt psychology, and there is a tradition in contemporary psychology to underestimate the role of the discipline's history for inventing new directions. However, it is exactly in the old discussions of holistic issues in psychology that we may regain a perspective on learning. After all, Gestalt psychology arose in protest against a scientific world view in which there was no room for meanings or values, and that tried to reduce human functioning to those of automata (Henle, 1985). This protest has produced many misconceptions about Gestalt psychology, as its major figures and their ideas migrated from Europe to North America (see analyses of those in Arnheim, 1985; Henle, 1984; Sokal, 1984). Most importantly, the Gestalt-psychological focus of structural organization and transformation of holistic units remains a central issue for any adequate learning theory to embrace. Learning is essentially the formation and modification of gestalts (Tolman, 1951, p. 389). Koffka's work is particularly relevant among other Gestalt psychologists for efforts to reinterpret phenomena of learning within a structuralist framework (Koffka, 1980).

The contemporary ecological perspective on learning (Johnston, 1981; Johnston & Pietrewicz, 1985) is in many ways an outgrowth of the dispute between the associationistic and Gestalt perspectives on the acquisition of novelty. Furthermore, the ethology movement (from 1930s onwards) in the study of animal behavior in its natural habitats has set up the conditions for efforts to link the study of learning in few species of (laboratory-adjusted) animals with a wider evolutionary view of learning phenomena as means of adaptation to real environments. The emphasis on the limiting conditions that the species—environments conditions set up for learning have fascinated a great number of researchers (Galef, 1990; Gould & Marler, 1987; Hinde, 1973; Seligman, 1970). However, the *given/acquirable* dichotomy that has been part and parcel of the issues of learning throughout the history of psychology continues in the thinking of ethologists. Zing-Yang Kuo has summarized it in a concise way:

> While the current ethologists may differ among themselves in certain details, the dichotomy between innate and learned or acquired responses still remains a most outstanding principle of ethology . . . the fact remains that the fundamental assumptions of ethology are based on the theoretical conceptions of (1) uniformity of behavior and (2) uniformity of environment. *As no ethologist is prepared to abandon the view of species-specificity of behavior and its survival value for the species as a result of natural selection, it would be a contradiction in terms were he to stress the extreme variability of behavior and environment.* (1970, p. 182; emphasis added)

The ecological approach productively and forcefully does away with the dichotomy, and hence opens the possibility of considering the variability of both the organism and its environment in terms of their variability over time (Magnusson, 1988; Valsiner, 1984, 1987). The roots of the ecological approach go back to the theoretical biology of the turn of the 20th century (e.g., Jakob von Uexküll's *Umweltlehre*—see von Uexküll, 1928, 1957), as well as to the field-theoretic and personalistic notions that were widespread in Germany between the two wars (e.g., Ash, 1985; Duncker, 1935; Heider, 1960; Jaeger, 1990; Muchow, 1930; Stern, 1938).

The family of developmental epigenetic theoretical perspectives in contemporary psychology (see Gottlieb, 1976, 1992; Kuo, 1970; Lickliter, in this volume; Miller, 1985; Schneirla, 1966) relates the developing organisms with their environments during the course of their lives, allowing for different forms of interdependence between the structure of behavior of the organism and that of the environment. The same general ethos can be seen in a number of perspectives on human development (Brent, 1984, Bronfenbrenner, 1979; Cairns, 1986;

Lerner, 1984; Magnusson, 1988; Piaget, 1971; Rogoff, 1990; Valsiner, 1987, 1989; Wapner & Kaplan, 1983). An additional line of thought that has fed into the advancement of the psychology of organism—environment relationships is the ecological perspective of James Gibson (1979), which is also known to have direct Gestalt-psychological roots (Hoffmann, 1985).

All in all, the contemporary ecological perspective on learning begins to chart out the complexity of the learning processes that take place in organisms—environment interaction contexts (Johnston, 1982). Learning ceases to be a phenomenon that is prey to theoretically narrow laboratory research that overlooks the life-course of the learner. The open-systemic nature of the learning processes begins to be acknowledged and verified. Thus, Shaw and Alley have summarized the properties of learning functions in three propositions:

1. Learning functions are *cumulative* (on the average, they increase monotonically).
2. The cumulative nature of such functions is, in general, positively (or negatively for aversive conditioning) *constrained by hereditary influences* on analogy to dissipative parameters.
3. The generic learning functional most likely will prove to be *nonlinear,* with linearity being a special, if important, case. (1985, p. 287)

In this quotation, the tentative approach of modern learning specialists to the complexity of psychological development is still obvious. While the emphasis on species-specific (phylogenetic and ontogenetic) constraining is obvious, the exact nature of that (as shown in proposition 2) remains undefined. The primacy of nonlinearity of learning processes (proposition 3) is explicitly recognized—yet it remains paired with the faith in the cumulative nature of learning (even if that latter is qualified to take place "on the average"—proposition 1). This brings modern learning researchers back to the reality—in which no "average learning curves" exist (see Skinner, 1950; Valsiner, 1986) and where individual learners construct novelty on the basis of their experiences, and by way of a variety of nonlinear time-dependent processes (see Van Geert, 1991; Voss, this volume). Furthermore, learning becomes to be understood as *a process for generating adaptations* (rather than being an adaptation itself—see Plotkin & Odling-Smee, 1982), which would make it possible to approach the issue of microgenetic processes that are mechanisms for ontogenetic development. Developmentally oriented psychology cannot get by without an explicit understanding of learning, but that understanding does not amount to proving (or disproving) that one or another preconceived general model of learning fits the whole complexity of context-dependent learning phenomena. That complexity calls for a more sophisticated approach, rudiments of which can be seen to emerge in our contemporary science.

The Structure of the Learning Processes: The Goals of This Book

In this book, we are bringing together a variety of contemporary approaches to learning that by and large follow along the structuralist path to understand learning. This path is both ecological and dynamic—we are interested in viewing the learning processes as those take place in the course of person—environment relationships. It is our intention to reintroduce to psychologists' discourse on learning the focus of learning *processes* on the one hand, and the *structural organization* of those processes on the other. Hence the present title—*The Structure of Learning Processes.* Different contributions to this volume cover a vast range of issues under that general title—from rethinking traditional Skinnerian behaviorism in new terms, to social co-construction of roles in the context of children's play. All these contributions are geared towards overcoming the difficulties of traditional views on learning.

In Part I (Theoretical Foundations) we find different contributors looking for different metalevel perspectives on issues of learning. The ecological perspective is clearly visible in these efforts. In Part II (Structure of Learning and Structure of Environment), the issue of environmentally based learning is dealt with in intricate detail. Social and co-constructionist perspectives on learning are elaborated by the contributors to Part III (Discourse and the Structure of Learning: The Process of Co-Construction in Human Development), and in the last part of the book (Prospective Conceptual Orientations) we find some elaborations of both old and new themes in the mindscape of learning. All in all, the contributions to the present volume are united in their effort to find new ways to approach the very old problem of the modifiability of living organisms by experience.

REFERENCES

Arnheim, R. (1986). The two faces of Gestalt psychology. *American Psychologist, 41* (7), 820–824.

Ash, M.G. (1985). Gestalt psychology: Origins in Germany and reception in the United States. In C. Buxton (Ed.), *Points of view in the modern history of psychology* (pp. 295–344). Orlando, FL: Academic Press.

Bandura, A. (1991). Social cognitive theory of self-regulation. *Organizational Behavior and Human Decision Processes, 50,* 248–287.

Bandura, A., & Walters, R.H. (1963). *Social learning and personality development.* New York: Holt, Rinehardt & Winston.

Bateson, G. (1972). Metalogue: What is instinct? In G. Bateson, *Steps to an ecology of mind* (pp. 38–58). New York: Ballantine Books.

Bechterev, V.M. (1932). *General principles of human reflexology.* New York: International Publishers.

Bower, G.H., & Hilgard, E. (1981). *Theories of learning* (5th ed.). Englewood Cliffs, NJ: Prentice-Hall.

Brent, S.B. (1984). *Psychological and social structures*. Hillsdale, NJ: Erlbaum.

Bronfenbrenner, U. (1979). *The ecology of human development*. Cambridge, MA: Harvard University Press.

Brown, A.L. (1982). Learning and development: The problem of compatibility, access, and induction. *Human Development, 25*, 89–115.

Cairns, R.B. (1986). A contemporary perspective on social development. In P.S. Strain, M.J. Guralnick, & H.M. Walker (Eds.), *Children's social behavior* (pp. 3–47). Orlando, FL.: Academic Press.

Daston, L.J. (1982). The theory of will versus the science of mind. In W.R. Woodward & M.G. Ash (Eds.), *The problematic science: Psychology in Nineteenth-century thought* (pp. 88–115). New York: Praeger.

Driesch, H. (1927). Critical remarks on some modern types of psychology. *Pedagogical Seminary, 34*, 3–13.

Duncker, K. (1935). Lernen und Einsicht im Dienst der Zielerreichung. *Papers read to the X International Congress of Psychology ar Copenhagen, 1932* (pp. 77–82). The Hague: Martinus Nijhoff.

Estes, W.K. (1978). On the organization and core concepts of learning theory and cognitive psychology. In W.K. Estes (Ed.), *Handbook of learning and cognitive processes. Vol. 6. Linguistic functions in cognitive theory* (pp. 235–292). Hillsdale, N.J.: Erlbaum.

Galef, B.G. (1990). A historical perspective on recent studies of social learning about foods by Norway rats. *Canadian Journal of Psychology, 44* (3), 311–329.

Gibson, J.J. (1979). *The ecological approach to visual perception*. Boston: Houghton-Mifflin.

Gottlieb, G. (1976). The roles of experience in the development of behavior and the nervous system. In G. Gottlieb (Ed.), *Neural and behavioral specificity* (pp. 25–54). New York: Academic Press.

Gottlieb, G. (1992). *Individual development & evolution*. Oxford: Oxford University Press.

Gould, J.L. & Marler, P. (1987). Learning by instinct. *Scientific American, 256* (1), 74–85.

Grimm, J., & Grimm, W. (1885). *Deutsches Wörterbuch. Vol. VI*. Leipzig: Hirzel.

Guthrie, E.R. (1930). Conditioning as principle of learning. *Psychological Review, 37*, 412–428.

Heider, F. (1960). The Gestalt theory of motivation. In M.R. Jones (Ed.), *Nebraska symposium on motivation* (Vol. 8, pp. 145–172). Lincoln, NE: University of Nebraska Press.

Heinen, J.R.K., Sherman, T.M., & Stafford, K.R. (1990). Role of learning theory in educational psychology. *Psychological Reports, 67*, 763–774.

Henle, M. (1984). Robert M. Ogden and Gestalt psychology in America. *Journal of the History of the Behavioral Sciences, 20*, 9–19.

Henle, M. (1985). Rediscovering Gestalt psychology. In S. Koch & D.E. Leary (Eds.), *A century of psychology as science* (pp. 100–120). New York: McGraw-Hill.

Hinde, R.A. (1973). Constraints on learning—an introduction to the problems. In R.A. Hinde & J. Stevenson-Hinde (Eds.), *Constraints on learning* (pp. 1–19). London: Academic Press.

Hoffman, R.R. (1985). A "Gestalt" on Gibson. In J. Sanches-Rosa (Ed.), *Proceedings of the XXIII International Congress of Psychology*. Amsterdam: North Holland.

Jaeger, S. (1990). *Gestaltpsychologie—Wolfgang Köhler und seine Zeit*. Berlin: Universitetsbibliothek der Freien Universität Berlin.

Johnston, T.D. (1981). Contrasting approaches to a theory of learning. *Behavioral and Brain Sciences, 4*, 125–173.

Johnston, T.D. (1982). Learning and the evolution of developmental systems. In H.C. Plotkin (Ed.), *Learning, development, and culture* (pp. 411–442). Chichester UK: Wiley.

Johnston, T.D. (1985). Conceptual issues in the ecological study of learning. In T.D. Johnston & A.T. Pietrewicz (Eds.), *Issues in the ecological study of learning* (pp. 1–24). Hillsdale, NJ: Erlbaum.

Johnston, T.D. & Pietrewicz, A.T. (Eds.). (1985). *Issues in the ecological study of learning*. Hillsdale, NJ: Erlbaum.

Johnston, T.D., & Turvey, M.T. (1980). A sketch of an ecological metatheory for theories of learning. In G.H. Bower (Ed.), *The psychology of learning and motivation* (Vol. 14, pp. 147–205). New York: Academic Press.

Koffka, K. (1925). Mental development. *Pedagogical Seminary, 32*, 659–673.

Koffka, K. (1980). *Growth of the mind*. New Brunswick, NJ: Transaction Books.

Kuo, Z.-Y. (1970). The need for coordinated efforts in developmental studies. In L.R. Aronson, E. Tobach, D.S. Lehrman & J. Rosenblatt (Eds.), *Development and evolution of behavior* (pp. 181–193). San Francisco: W.H. Freeman.

Lamarck, J.B. (1984). *Zoological philosophy*. Chicago: University of Chicago Press. (Original work published 1809)

Langley, P., & Simon, H. (1981). The central role of learning in cognition. In J.R. Anderson (Ed.), *Cognitive skills and their acquisition* (pp. 361–380). Hillsdale, NJ: Erlbaum.

Lerner, R.M. (1984). *On the nature of human plasticity*. Cambridge, UK: Cambridge University Press.

Magnusson, D. (1988). *Individual development from an interactional perspective: A longitudinal study*. Hillsdale, NJ: Erlbaum.

Metge, J. (1984). *Learning and teaching—He tikanga Maori*. Wellington: New Zealand Department of Education.

Miller, D.B. (1985). Methodological issues in the ecological study of learning. In T.D. Johnston & A.T. Pietrewicz (Eds.), *Issues in the ecological study of learning* (pp. 73–95). Hillsdale, NJ: Erlbaum.

Mitroff, I., & Featheringham, T.R. (1974). On systemic problem solving and the error of the third kind. *Behavioral Science, 19*, 383–393.

Molenaar, P.C.M. (1986). Issues with rule-sampling theory of conservation learning from a structuralist point of view. *Human Development, 29*, 137–144.

Muchow, M. (1930). Zur Frage einer lebensraum- und epochaltypologischen Entwicklungspsychologie des Kindes und Jugendlichen. *Beihefte zur Zeitschrift für angewandte Psychologie, 59*, 185–202.

O'Donohue, W., & Krasner, L. (1988). The logic of research and the scientific status of the law of effect. *Psychological Record, 38*, 157–174.

Ogden, R.M. (1930). The Gestalt psychology of learning. *Journal of Genetic Psychology, 38*, 280–286.

Pavlov, I.P. (1906). The scientific investigation of the psychical faculties or processes in the higher animals. *Science, 24* (No. 620), 613–619.

Pavlov, I.P. (1932). A reply of a physiologist to psychologists. *Psychological Review, 39*, 91–127.

Piaget, J. (1971). *Biology and knowledge*. Chicago: University of Chicago Press.

Plotkin, H.C., & Odling-Smee, F.J. (1982). Learning in the context of a hierarchy of knowledge gaining processes. In H.C. Plotkin (Ed.), *Learning, development, and culture* (pp. 443–471). Chichester, UK: Wiley.

Revusky, S. (1985). The general process approach to animal learning. In T.D. Johnston & A.T. Pietrewicz (Eds.), *Issues in the ecological study of learning* (pp. 401–432). Hillsdale, NJ: Erlbaum.

Rogoff, B. (1990). *Apprenticeship in thinking*. Oxford: Oxford University Press.

Schneirla, T.C. (1966). Behavioral development and comparative psychology. *Quarterly Review of Biology, 41*, 283–302.

Seligman, M.E.P. (1970). On the generality of the laws of learning. *Psychological Review, 77*, 5, 406–418.

Shaw, R.E., & Alley, T.R. (1985). How to draw learning curves: their use and justification. In T.D. Johnston & A.T. Pietrewicz (Eds.), *Issues in the ecological study of learning* (pp. 275–304). Hillsdale, NJ: Erlbaum.

Siegfried, J. (Ed.). (1994). *The role of common sense in psychology*. Norwood, NJ: Ablex.

Sinclair, H. (1973). Some remarks on the Genevan point of view on learning with special reference to language learning. In R. Hinde & J. Stevenson-Hinde (Eds.), *Constraints on learning* (pp. 397–415). London: Academic Press.

Skinner, B.F. (1950). Are theories of learning necessary? *Psychological Review, 57*, 4, 193–216.

Skinner, B.F. (1981). Pavlov's influence on psychology in America. *Journal of the History of the Behavioral Sciences, 17*, 242–245.

Smedslund, J. (1978). Bandura's theory of self-efficacy: A set of common-sense theorems. *Scandinavian Journal of Psychology, 19*, 1–14.

Sokal, M.M. (1984). The Gestalt psychologists in behaviorist America. *American Historical Review, 89*, 4–5, 1240–1263.

Stern, W. (1938). *General psychology*. New York: MacMillan.

Stevenson, H.W. (1970). Learning in children. In P.H. Mussen (Ed.), *Carmichael's manual of child psychology* (3rd ed., Vol. 1, pp. 849–938). New York: Wiley.

The Duden. (1989). *Deutsches Universalwörterbuch*. Mannheim: Dudenverlag.

Thorndike, E.L. (1913). *Educational psychology. Vol. 1. The original nature of man*. New York: Teachers' College Press.

Thorndike, E.L. (1917). The psychology of thinking in the case of reading. *Psychological Review, 24*, 220–234.

Tolman, E.C. (1951). *Purposive behavior in animals and men*. Berkeley, CA: University of California Press.

Valsiner, J. (1984). Two alternative epistemological frameworks in psychology: The typological and variational modes of thinking. *Journal of Mind and Behavior, 5* (4), 449–470.

Valsiner, J. (1985). Common sense and psychological theories: The historical nature of logical necessity. *Scandinavian Journal of Psychology, 26*, 97–109.

Valsiner, J. (Ed.). (1986). *The individual subject and scientific psychology*. New York: Plenum.

Valsiner, J. (1987). *Culture and the development of children's action.* Chichester, UK: Wiley.

Valsiner, J. (1988). *Developmental psychology in the Soviet Union.* Brighton, UK: Harvester Press.

Valsiner, J. (1989). *Human development and culture.* Lexington, MA: D.C. Heath.

Van der Veer, R., & Valsiner, J. (1991). *Understanding Vygotsky: A quest for synthesis.* Oxford: Basil Blackwell.

Van Geert, P. (1986). The concept of development. In P. van Geert (Ed.), *Theory building in developmental psychology* (pp. 3–50). Amsterdam: North-Holland.

Van Geert, P. (1991). A dynamic systems model of cognitive and language growth. *Psychological Review, 98,* 1, 3–53.

von Uexküll, J. (1928). *Theoretische Biologie.* Berlin: Julius Springer.

von Uexküll, J. (1957). A stroll through the worlds of animals and men. In C.H. Schiller & K.S. Lashley (Eds.), *Instinctive behavior* (pp. 5–80). New York: International Universities Press.

Wapner, S., & Kaplan, B. (Eds.). (1983). *Toward a holistic developmental psychology.* Hillsdale, NJ: Erlbaum.

Weekley, E. (1967). *An etymological dictionary of modern English.* New York: Dover.

Windholz, G. (1984). Pavlov's little-known primate research. *The Pavlovian Journal of Biological Science, 19* (1), 23–31.

Windholz, G., & Lamal, P.A. (1986). Pavlov and the concept of association. *The Pavlovian Journal of Biological Science, 21* (1), 12–15.

PART I

Theoretical Foundations

CHAPTER 1

Learning, Development, and Synergetics

Hans-Georg W. Voss

Institut für Psychologie
Technische Hochschule Darmstadt
Darmstadt, Germany

Learning is a biological characteristic of all living organisms. The universality of learning both across species and individuals has let early Anglo-Saxon theorists (e.g., Hull, 1943; Skinner, 1938) think of learning in terms of a uniform phenomenon that may apply to the study of animals, children, and adults. Under these circumstances, the most effective way of studying learning phenomena would be the experimental laboratory approach in which all factors were said to be completely under the control of the experimenter. The sterile atmosphere of the laboratory allowed for a more adequate study of the processes of learning in terms of systematically linking variation in stimulus conditions and variation in responses, and simultaneously controling for "error effects" such as interindividual differences, unwanted fluctuations in both the respondents' and the experimenters' behavior, unexpected events occurring in the situation, and so on. In these "in vitro" analyses, learning refered to an elementary bonding process through which environment and behavior became attached to each other. The S–R bond was supposed to represent the basic unit of analysis, and interactions among these elements would make up more complex kinds of cognitive activities as problem solving, transfer phenomena, or discrimination learning. According to this view, children—as was the case with both adults and, for example, pigeons—were considered to be passive organisms receiving stimulation from the environment and responding in a more or less stereotyped manner.

There was no reason for including children in the learning paradigm except for the fact that children could somehow be placed in the middle of a scale of organisms' complexity ranging from the *mus norvegicus* to the matured adult.

This led early reviewers of the learning literature to conclude that "the investigations on learning theory in children have failed" (Munn, 1954, p. 449) or, in an even stronger statement, that "no learning theory has ever been constructed from studies of children or been specifically directed towards them—strictly speaking, there is no learning theory in child psychology" (White, 1970, pp. 667–668). Nevertheless, children do learn, and there is of course a large body of research on children's learning in different environmental contexts (among them, the family, the kindergarten, and the school) as well as numerous practical attempts to teach normal children in a diversity of educational settings. Many of these studies have been extensively reviewed in the sequel volumes of *Carmichael's Manual of Child Psychology* (Brown, Bransford, Ferrara, & Campione, 1983; Munn, 1954; Stevenson, 1970; 1983; White, 1970). These authors have also characterized the major trends in the overlapping fields of learning and development and have argued for a merge of different theoretical approaches based on different assumptions about the nature of the learner–context interaction. For example, White (1970) contrasted the learning theory approach predominantly expressed in American psychology to that of the "genetic point of view" advocated by European schools of developmental psychology. The latter tradition was partly rooted in the evolutionism of Spencer, Darwin, and Galton; the other part was represented by the philosophical traditions of vitalism (Driesch, Bergson) and the philosophy of Ganzheit (the German term being *Genetische Ganzheitspsychologie*) of the so-called second Leipzig school of psychology (Krueger, 1926, 1948; Wellek, 1950, 1954). Most prominent in those days was a holistic view of learning and development that stressed the qualitative rather than the quantitative nature of growth processes in living organisms, allowing, at the same time, a comparison of different species on such common basic principles as Heinz Werner's "orthogenetic principle" of development. This movement, however, remained apart from mainstream American psychology (or, at least, it was not a central issue in psychology textbooks) because it did not fit the positivistic thinking of the majority of researchers outside the European continent. Thus, in 1970, White still came to the conclusion that "transcription of the genetic point of view in a rigorous and tough-minded program for maintaining and containing research . . . never took place, and has not yet taken place" (White, 1970, p. 663). While this statement was true and still is true, it also offers a false alternative: Associationism (or empiricism) and "genetic" (or biological evolutionistic) thinking refer to different epistemological paradigms, and it would not make any sense trying to transform one into the other. Besides this "monadic" view (Leibniz), there were more pragmatic reasons for the advent of the learning theory approach in the sense White mentioned it: Except for a neat demonstration of behavioral change under isolated conditions and most often of only short duration, experimental learning theory could not account for the complexities of knowledge acquisition in everyday settings or learning environments such as the classroom or the family.

The experimental paradigm waned with the beginnings of the '70s; we now look back over a period of cognitivistic thinking and theorizing in which learning processes were treated under the labels of *memory formation, remembering, metacognition, knowledge acquisition, self-regulated learning,* and so on. Brown et al. (1983) have characterized the major trends in research and theory between 1970 and 1980 in terms of a shift in emphasis to the learner's side of the learner–context interaction, or the activities and behavior strategies of the organism when adapting to a changing environment. Besides this general shift, these authors have also diagnosed a change in the type of materials that children were set to learn, away from isolated bits of information such as color/form stimuli, single words and pictures, or nonsense syllables, towards more complex materials that forced the learner to apply or to develop organizing rules or strategies of optimizing the informational flow. At the same time, researchers in the field of learning and cognition became more willing to include a developmental view into their theorizing; that is, rather than conceptualizing a progression of cognitive gains across the individual's life course as a manifestation of learning, learning phenomena were to be understood in terms of a microgenetic process of knowledge acquisition and memory formation. This leads us to a closer inspection of the two interrelated concepts of learning and development.

LEARNING AND DEVELOPMENT

Logically stated, learning and development can be put together into three ways: as being identical and used synonymously, as excluding each other, and as being interdependently related. All three have been discussed by Vygotsky (1935). The first position is compatible with the general belief held by proponents of the experimental learning tradition mentioned above, namely, that learning can be conceptualized in terms of a "purely" external process that is not actively involved in development. Although change is the essence of development (Wohlwill, 1973), behavioral change in many instances does not signal development. As is also mentioned by Vygotsky, Piagetian thinking is in line with the view of an independence of learning and development, because there exist intellectual operations that must mature first, before learning can take place. Thus, development is always a prerequisite for learning. From a closer inspection of this statement, however, and from a more detailed analysis of the meanings of the concepts of learning and development in this context, one may notice that to a large extent *development* has been treated synonymously with *maturing,* and *learning* with *teaching.*[1] Thus, there may be a general agreement

---

[1] Reference is made here to Vygotsky's collection of essays entitled "Ustvennoie razvitie detei v protsesse obuchenia," published posthumiously in 1935, where the term *obuchenia* means both learning as well as teaching (see also editors' introduction to this volume).

with the notion that teaching a child special skills is always dependent on the extent to which the child's corresponding mental functions have already matured.

The second theoretical position entails that learning and development coincide in the sense that the two processes occur simultaneously. This view is principally held by experimental learning theorists of the Hull-Spence tradition who claim that the formation of habit hierarchies through mechanisms of S–R learning is only an alternative expression for the developmental process. There is an interesting temporal aspect in notions of learning–development identity: given that the formation of conditional reflexes or habits, respectively, is most often of a relatively short duration (that is, learning often takes place here within a series of short-time trials) the analysis of the developmental process can be largely reduced to an inspection of events occurring in a narrow time interval. With this it becomes possible to observe learning actually taking place within an individual over time. This *microgenetic* approach may be most valuable in describing essential elements in both adults' and children's learning. I would like to emphasize, however, that a microanalytical strategy of defining development in terms of "bits of learning" does not necessarily limit our understanding of learning and development to the submolar level of reflexive and conditioned behavioral tendencies.

A third major theoretical position mentioned by Vygotsky (1935) refers to a combination of the two concepts of learning and development. These are not identical but form a unity in which the former is embedded in the latter. For example, the acquisition, or learning, respectively, of the meaning of a word of spoken language allows the child to use this word instrumentally and thus adds to the growth of competence in a variety of social contexts. One may therefore conceptualize a learning sequence in terms of a microdevelopmental process that is both a function of the developmental level already reached and a prerequisite for further development. From this point of view, "learning is not development; however, properly organized learning results in mental development and sets in motion a variety of developmental processes that would be impossible apart from learning" (Vygotsky, 1935; quoted in Cole, John-Steiner, Scribner, & Souberman, 1987, p. 90). The question of how learning must be organized in order to optimize developmental processes then arises. The answer lies, according to Vygotsky, in what he calls the *zone of proximal development,* which circumscribes a theoretical construct that expresses the distance between a child's current level of development and the next level that potentially can be reached by the child when he or she is guided by another person or works in collaboration with more capable individuals (as will be seen later in this chapter).

It may have become obvious from our brief discussion that the nature of relationships between learning and development might be a matter of definition rather than a more profound theoretical problem. Accordingly, learning, when placed on a microgenetic scale, may well fit the definition of a short-interval developmental process and at the same time may also be compatible with the notion of learning versus maturation/development. Both positions can be combined into a general framework of development when placed on different locations of the micro–macro scale of developmental processes.

One may also think of learning sequences as being embedded in larger sequences of ontogenetical change that directly correspond to manifestations of organism–environment interaction. The special adaptations and affordances involved in this complex interaction will define the developmental tasks that must be solved, or the content of learning, respectively. Bronfenbrenner and Crouter (1983) have referred to this as a *person–process–context model.* Developmental processes, in this model, are assumed to vary as a joint function of biological and environmental factors, and there are cumulative developmental effects on both sides of the organism–environment equation. More recently, Bronfenbrenner has elaborated his ecological concept of development in the sense that there is now a closer account of the synergism taking place between the self-organized developmental potentials of the person and the "developmentally instigative" factors of the social and physical context (Bronfenbrenner, 1989). The concept of synergism is of central importance here, and the treatment of our topic may benefit from a closer look at synergetics.

SYNERGETICS AND DYNAMICAL SYSTEMS

Synergism refers to "acting together" interdependently; that is, there exists a system in which two or more parts can produce, by their cooperation, a new quality of the whole system. Whereas the concept of synergism can be traced back to the ancient philosophies of dynamical systems (Heraclitus) and has also had its proponents in theological discourse in the 16th century (the "synergistic struggle" of Luther against Melanchthon on religious conversion), synergistic models of complex systems have been developed in more recent times in the fields of thermodynamics, chemical kinetics, and biological self-organization (Haken, 1977; Nicolis & Prigogine, 1977; Prigogine, 1961). Synergistic thinking was also prevalent in Gestalt theoretical formulations of pattern formation in which complex structures originate in the system's own dynamics and order is created spontaneously as a result of the organism's autonomous activities (Köhler, 1920; for more details see Stadler & Kruse, 1990).

A new field of interdisciplinary research called *synergetics* (Haken, 1977) has emerged out of these ideas, and there is general reference to this research program in terms of a metatheoretical approach to the dynamics of complex systems, rather than in terms of a well-established theory of behavior of physical and biological systems. In the following section, I shall briefly sketch the most basic concepts of synergetics and complex dynamical systems and then try to pose a synergistic view of the learning-development topic.[2]

Dynamical Systems

Dynamical systems are composed of active elements that are mutually effective and that influence other dynamic systems or are influenced by them. Systems of this kind evolve in time according to well-defined rules. These rules can be mathematically expressed by nonlinear equations describing the evolution of the system in time and space. The (observable) variables of the system constitute an abstract "space," which is generally called the *phase space* of the dynamical system. Dynamical systems differ in terms of their complexity, which mainly depends on the number of variables, or degrees of freedom, needed to describe the system. Therefore, the *dimension* of the phase space is determined by the number of degrees of freedom. According to the geometry of the phase space, a point in this space represents the momentarily state, and a line or curve signifies a movement of the system through time and space, called *trajectory.* There may be many trajectories for a special system, but most often, there is "order" in that there exists a typical set of trajectories, or *phase portrait.*

Take, for instance, a very simple dynamical system, the undampened pendulum: its phase space reduces to a phase plane, since there only exists one degree of freedom (there are but two dimensions: the angular displacement of the pendulum from the vertical, and one generalized momentum). The phase portrait of the simple pendulum equals a closed trajectory, which can generally be represented by a circle centered in the origin of the two (orthogonal) dimensions. The radius of the circle will vary according to different amounts of energy (impulse) of the system. It is important to note that the simple pendulum is an idealized *perpetuum mobile* that uniformly swings in all times, permanently oscillating between minima and maxima of kinetic potential energy. This brings us to the more general distinction of conservative and dissipative dynamical systems. Dynamical systems are called *conservative* when there is no flow of energy or substance beyond the borders of the system and when the coordinates of the phase space remain unchanged. Thus, the term conservative

---

[2] There is now easy access to both basic principles and applications of synergetics in a wide array of scientific disciplines, including as diverse topics as chemical dynamics, brain sciences and cognition, economic behavior, and psychotherapy, to name a few. There is also the Springer Series in Synergetics (up to now 47 volumes). According to its principal editor, Herman Haken, "synergetics, an interdisciplinary field of research, is concerned with the cooperation of individual parts of a system that produces macroscopic spacial, temporal or functional structures. It deals with deterministic as well as stochastic processes" (Haken, 1983, p. 6; see also Haken, 1977). For a more detailed analysis of complex systems, I would like to refer to Nicolis and Prigogine (1987), and Schuster (1985).

refers to a constancy of the energy and the preservation of the phase space volume (Campbell, 1989). As everybody knows, an activated pendulum eventually will come to a rest in the vertical position with its bob down.

There is a loss (or a dissipation) of energy due to the dampening of the pendulum. In *dissipative* dynamical systems—which are by far the most normal case in nature—energy is not preserved and there are special features of particular initial motions that damp out. In terms of its trajectories, this process allows the system to approach a restricted region (which may also be a fixed point in the case of the pendulum) called an *attractor.* The restricted region of the phase space to which various initial conditions may be attracted is called the *basin of attraction.* There may be more than one attractor for a dynamic system, each with its own basin of attraction. In this case, the conditions that govern the journey of the systems across different basins of attractor become an important object of study. Note that there is always at least one irreversible process (for example, the transaction of temperature and diffusion, as well as biological evolution) in a dissipative dynamical system, and only in this case there may be an attractor becoming operant on a long-time scale. Dissipation that is comparable to one-way traffic of system-specific components towards the system environments (which represents a dynamical system, too) is indeed the most basic condition for evolutionary processes of different kinds. Thus, development can only occur within dissipative (open) dynamical systems.

Evolution of dynamical systems. Evolution means lawful change of a system from an initial towards an end state. There is general agreement among scientists that all systems—be they the one-cell organism or the universe—share the same fate of increasing entropy. This is expressed by the second law of thermodynamics (Nicolis & Prigogine, 1987), which simply states that the amount of entropy, or the opposite of order, gradually increases up to a point where any single element of the system is randomly distributed in space and all effects among elements have become perfectly unpredictable. This statement is expressed by the differential expression $dS/dt \geq 0$, where S refers to the entropy. A convenient example for this is given by the extension of two gases that have been initially separated within a closed container. After taking away the separating device, a homogenious fluidum of the two gases will soon be established. Obviously, the end state is less structured than the initial state. This may characterize the behavior of a closed system when there is no exchange with an environment. For an open system, however, conditions are slightly different, since there is exchange of energy and substance. Nicolis and Prigogine (1987) therefore made the assumption that there exist two subcategories of entropy, which sum up to an overall entropy. Accordingly, the differential equation becomes $dS/dt = d_iS/dt + d_eS/dt$, where d_iS and d_eS refer to the *production* of entropy within the system and the flow of entropy between system and environment (or another system). From what has been said earlier, it becomes clear that for a closed system $d_eS = 0$; as long as d_iS is strictly positive, there exist irreversible processes, which also means that dissipation occurs. Nicolis and Prigogine further stress the fact that no physical law exists for determining the sign of the entropy flow d_eS in a nonclosed system; thus, it may depend on the kind of system whether the sign becomes negative or positive. There is an important conclusion so far: according to the flow of entropy in open dynamical systems, overall entropy of a specific system may become less, which means that order will be generated rather than destroyed.

According to the terminology introduced earlier, there may be at least one attractor that determines the trajectory of the system under certain conditions. Metaphorically, evolution then means time-irreversible movement through one or several basins of attraction. For linear dissipative systems with one degree of freedom, fixed points are the only possible attractors, the system then being stationary (unmoved) and balanced. Another case is exemplified by the final thermodynamic balanced state. Natural systems, however, may never—in this sense—become stationary, since there always exists some disturbance in terms of error variables that may cause an instability of the system or fluctuations in its behavior. In the expression $X(t) = X_s + x(t)$, according to Nicolis and Prigogine (1987), the actually occurring state of a system $X(t)$ is a function of a specific reference state X_s (or balanced state) and the disturbance $x(t)$. For instance, the actual state of a driven pendulum such as a grandfather clock is normally in very close neighborhood to the reference state that equals a regular oscillator (sinus characteristic), since there may only be very small disturbances in terms of such environmental conditions as temperature, humidity, aerial movements, and so on. Of more interest here is the ability of a dynamical system to gradually eliminate disturbances and to return to the reference state, which may be asymptotically approached. The opposite may also be true: There is an instability of the reference state, which leads to an exponential growth of the disturbance. Another case refers to a more complex form of instability—a disturbing influence may gradually exceed a critical level in strenght and then may force the system to leave its current basin of attraction and move to another one. This description is identical with the notion of *phase transitions,* which means that the system passes regions of instability (where relatively small influences have a strong effect) on its way to more attracting areas (where relatively strong influences have minor effects). To give an example that is not drawn from physics—horses will exert different kinds of motorical patterns with increasing speed, from walking, through trotting, to galloping (Hoyt & Taylor, 1981). This may also demonstrate that there are both local instabilities with respect to the specific movement pattern, each representing an attractor, and global stability, since the different movement patterns serve the function of maintaining energy costs at a minimum level. Speed of movement, in this case, may better be called a *control parameter* than a disturbance. Other instances of control parameters are the degree of excitation in laser technology, or temperature of fluids, and, as will become more obvious later on in this chapter, instruction in learning processes. More formally, the evolution of a dissipative system can be expressed by the differential equation

$$dX_i/dt = F_i(\{X\}p)$$

in which F_i refers to complex mathematical functions of a set of variables $\{X\}$ that characterizes the system; the term p refers to a control parameter, which may be a macroscopic (observable) variable. It can be shown that this equation leads to a linear solution under certain restrictions, whereas in most cases of dynamical systems the solutions will become nonlinear (and rather complicated). (The equation can also be elaborated in order to distinguish between control parameters and disturbances x(t); hence it is written as $dX_i/dt = F_i(\{X\}, p) + x(t)$.) As the examples given here show, the dynamics of a system is mainly governed by *order parameters* according to specific macroscopic variables of the system (for example, motorical behavior patterns, movement, mental images, and even thoughts and other mental operations).

The *evolution equation* of a system given above, which states that the change of a system is a function of the system itself (and a disturbance parameter added), is also an expression of the self-organization of the system. Self-organization means that there exist forces inherent in the system that act on structural and functional properties of the system without a direct reference to the environment. However, because according to General Systems Theory each system is a part in a larger one, self-organization is in itself a relational term in the sense that it only holds true under specific conditions, that is, when the larger surrounding system will remain unchanged or when there is a constant influence (for example, temperature in fluids, degree of excitation of atoms in laser light, space for living, family structure, and so on). Forces acting upon systems can be described in terms of control parameters; these are unspecific to the system—that is, they do not constitute the system but nevertheless may change its internal structure and functioning. It is important to note that systems maintain stability through *adaptive self-stabilization* (this term was used by Laszlo, 1972) or through autocatalytic processes to a considerable extent. This holds even more true for larger biological and social systems such as insect populations and ethnic groups, which may be put high on a level of plasticity when facing an ever-changing environment (Cairns, 1979).

Through control parameters, a system may become unstable and the values of its order parameter may oscillate within a well-defined range. With respect to cognitive processes, this phenomenon has been described in connection with perceptual ambiguity, multistability of images, and spontaneous figure–ground reversions (see Kruse & Stadler, 1990). With increasing effectiveness of a control parameter, the system may depart from an ordered state (regular fluctuations) and become *chaotic*, as has been observed in a large variety of mathematical models and natural phenomena, among them movement patterns in many types of fluid flows (Libchaber & Maurer, 1980), laser light waves (Haken, 1985), fluctuations in population size (May, 1976), cardiac arhythmias (Goldberger & Rigney, 1987), and neural dynamics of odor perception in rabbits (Skarda & Freeman, 1987). Contrary to a common belief, chaos is a rather healthy state in physiological parameters, and regularity may indeed indicate a pathological condition; for example, in some anemias and leukemias, densities of red and white blood cells become periodic, whereas normally there are chaotic oscillations (Campbell, 1989). There is also the paradox of a *deterministic chaos*, which means that the present state of a dynamical system is unpredictable but nevertheless may be described by nonlinear mathematical equations.

Dynamical Systems and Development

Developmental psychology deals with a changing organism in a changing environment. As true as this statement may be, it does not offer a clear answer to the question of how both entities act together and how this synergism gives way to the complexities of developmental phenomena. Behavioristic approaches to this problem have conceptualized organism and environment in terms of physical properties such as body movements and stimuli. Both organism and environment have been treated here as separated entities of reality, and unidirectional functional relationships have been used for describing developmental phenomena. Although this tactic has been valuable, resulting conceptualizations of developmental processes have been unduly narrow. An advancement had been made with the invention of context (for environment), in order to express both the structural as well as the functional relationships that exist between organism and environment: the individual is a part in a larger context (containing also many other entities), and it is also embedded functionally in this context in that both interact in a reciprocal manner. Nevertheless, the heritage of behaviorism is still alive in conceptualizations where organism and context are independently defined and said to be independently observed.

In approaches such as this, context stays conceptualized in terms of a separate variable being defined independently of the individual's actions and the analysis-of-variance model being the main tool for analyzing interindividual differences. A remarkable shift in metatheory occurred with the invention of ecological ideas into the field of psychology, giving rise to a *transactional* view of development. In the case of cognitive development, the following passage from a chapter entitled "Integrating Context and Cognitive Development" by Barbara Rogoff may best illustrate what I think is the current state of the art in developmental psychology:

> The contextual event or transactional approach views the context and the person's activities as jointly producing psychological events. Neither the context nor the person's activity can ultimately be defined independently, as their meanings derive

from their integration in the psychological event. The contextual event approach assumes that events are structured such that no constituent can be adequately specified apart from the specification of the other constituents. (Rogoff, 1982, p. 132).

This statement reads like a translation of synergistic formulations into the theoretical context of developmental psychology. How then should we conceptualize our theoretical terms in the field of development (and learning) in order to fit the synergistic view? It should be noted that this question calls for a constructivistic treatment of the topic under consideration. By this I mean relativistic thinking with respect to defining the concepts we have to deal with: within a theoretical or metatheoretical framework, the heuristical value of theoretical terms not only depends on the actual or potential amount of empirical evidence being gathered; it also depends on the structural properties of the theory itself and whether these terms prove to be meaningful when they are applied in the context of a specific discipline. In other words, there exist no systems per se, although many researchers would readily accept the notion that "the" organism and "the" environment may well fit a systems definition. Sometimes, to do so may prove to be meaningful—and sometimes not.

The cognitive system. Psychological systems are most often hypothetical in nature, and both order and control parameters in general refer to theoretical constructs or hypothetical variables. For example, models of information processing share at least some theoretical constructs, such as short and long term memory, attention-getting and attention-holding processes, rehearsal mechanisms, and so on. The hardware may be seen to be represented in structural and functional properties of the brain such as neurons, synapses, "cell assemblies," and gating mechanisms. There is a considerable body of research now on synergetics of the brain (Basar, Flohr, Haken, & Mandell, 1983), and a large portion of it addresses the problem of learning in the context of connectionistic models of brain functioning (e.g., Brousse & Smolensky, 1990; McNaughton, 1989). In these models, vast numbers of neurons are linked into coupled dynamical systems that "behave" according to the existence of such alternative attractors as associative memories (Hopfield, 1982). In models of parallel-processing neural networks, learning can be interpreted in terms of alterations in synaptic weight among the model neurons (Rummelhart & McClelland, 1986); that is, learning may be a kind of fundamental ordering principle by which chaotic attractors in neural networks will be converted to orderly ones (Kauffman, 1989a). Skarda and Freeman (1987) have studied information processing in the olfactory system of the rabbit and have demonstrated the usefulness of synergistic chaos in the learning of new odors. Their suggestion rests on the idea that chaotic background activity (measured in terms of EEG activity and bulbar unit activity) "provides the system with a deterministic 'I don't know' state within which new activity patterns can be generated . . . (the) 'chaotic well' enables the system to avoid all of its previously learned activity patterns and to produce a new one" (Skarda & Freeman, 1987, p. 171). As in physiology, chaotic behavior may be quite useful in instances where a regular behavior would be damaging. A well-known case where active and strong desynchronization is highly recommended concerns the case of a platoon of soldiers crossing a bridge: periodic behavior such as marching in ranks might set the bridge into destructive resonant oscillations (Garfinkel, 1987). I also would like to mention that chaotic behavioral patterns as can be found in trial-and-error learning do well fit the notion of clearing the system in order to give way for the establishment of new connections. Phenomenological evidence comes also from Gestalt theoretical descriptions of the problem-solving process or productive thinking: subjects often experience a state of confusion that is most often depressed beneath the level of awareness (incubation), giving way to a sudden "insight." These examples (see also Stadler & Kruse, 1990) may suffice here in order to demonstrate the usefulness of the chaotic attractor metaphor in the operation of different kind of dynamical systems.

So far, I have sketched the synergistic view applied to the "cognitive system" represented by physiological brain mechanisms. Developmental systems may be located on a more macroscopical level. They serve as interfaces between the physiological, social, and ecological components of the whole system and therefore share some common features such as the rules governing the use of specific behavioral systems (including language, body movements, behavioral styles, and customs) in context. Gibson (1979) has used the concepts *affordances of the environment* and *effectivity of the organism* to describe the mutuality in functional relationships between organism and environment. In developmental terms, a person can only become effective (or competent) when his or her activity meets with specific conditions of the environment that provide opportunities for orientation and meaning generation (Kreitler & Kreitler, 1976). Cognitive theories in developmental psychology in general, and ecological approaches in specific, stress the view of the basically active organism. Its proponents prefer to talk about cognitive structures as something the person does rather than something the person possesses (Michaels & Carello, 1981). The concept of activity is also most prevalent in such Russian thinkers as Vygotsky and his followers Leont'ev (1981) and Luria (1973), and the description and analysis of children's actions in cultural context (Valsiner, 1987) has currently become a *via regia* of developmental research. Such theoretical terms as *activity, action, cultural practice* (Laboratory of Comparative Human Cognition, 1983), or *cognitive event* (Rogoff, 1982, 1990) share the common feature of inseparability of organism and environment on a theoretical and methodological level.

In conclusion, rather than treating the organism as separated from the context, there is mutuality in the sense that both form a Ganzeheit (wholeness) that in itself is synergistically linked to larger contexts such as the societal system or the specific culture.

This brings us back to the terminology introduced earlier, and for the remainder of this chapter I would like to discuss how learning and development may be implemented in a general theory of dynamical systems and how research may profit from this effort.

LEARNING: AN ADAPTIVE WALK THROUGH
THE DEVELOPMENTAL LANDSCAPE[3]

Development, in the cognitive sphere, occurs according to a dynamical system far from equilibrium, which follows a developmental trajectory in a complex phase space. Learning refers to a process by which the system moves to another attractor by experiencing a transient state that resembles a chaotic attractor. The evolution of the system is self-organized and follows a nonlinear course.

The concept of *developmental landscape* has been borrowed here from the metaphor of *epigenetical landscape* introduced by the embryologist Waddington (1957). Waddington used a three-dimensional physical space analogy, the epigenetic landscape, in order to illustrate genetic control of growth trajectories and the relative degree of canalization of these trajectories. There is a ball moving down the slope of valleys of an imaginary landscape. The contour of the landscape is determined by the genotype; the ball represents the system (organism or species) being equipped with a multiplicity of genetic determinants. The movement of the ball through the valleys represents the developmental process and the slope or the velocity of the movement, respectively, stand for the speed of change or the steepness of developmental functions.

The pathways represent a buffering or stabilizing function in that they allow the ball to fluctuate laterally according to the wideness or narrowness of the valley. For example, a narrow floor with steep walls represents a strong canalizing effect where environmental forces have only little impact. Waddington's main concern was the study of control systems in developmental genetics. The epigenetic landscape metaphor might be called an "empty metaphor" in that this idea may have provided "impediments to thinking clearly about the need for conceptual and empirical analysis at all levels of the developmental systems hierarchy" (Gottlieb, 1991, p. 7). Gottlieb (1970) has criticized the limited validity of the landscape metaphor in terms of a "predetermined conception of epigenesis," being correctly defined as "the emergence of new structures and functions during the course of individual development" (Gottlieb, 1991, p.7). For a closer approximation to what I have referred to earlier in this chapter, I

---

[3] By using the metaphor "adaptive walk" here, I am indebted to Kauffman (1989b) who used the phrase "adaptive walks in parameter space to `good' attractors" in order to discuss an idea expressed by Ashby (1960). *Ashby's paradigm* reads: "Wire up an autopilot backwards and have the system fix itself before the airplane crashes" (quoted in Kauffman, 1989b, p. 634).

would like to broaden the perspective of epigenesis to the level of development in general and thus refer to a *developmental landscape* that indeed parallels the logic of dissipative dynamical systems' movement through a multidimensional parameter space. Kauffmann (1989b) has elaborated Waddington's landscape analogy theoretically to include a synergistic conception of developing systems. In his analogy, which leans on similar formulations offered by Maturana and Varela (1980), "the idea of basins of attraction and steady-state point attractors is essentially the same as a mountainous region, with hills, ridges and valleys and a water drainage system. The 'lakes' correspond to attractors; the drainage basin corresponds to the basin of attraction" (Kauffmann, 1989b, p. 628).

Development is characterized by a sequence of qualitative changes that are induced by the system itself. It is important to note that the transitions that systems undergo occur far from equilibrium, because order is generated rather than destroyed. On the other hand, there is local stability being reached by a system in certain regions of the phase portrait. The existence of plateaus in learning curves of complex motor skills may serve as illustrating examples. Many properties of dynamical systems have been described and extensively reviewed throughout the literature, among them wholeness and order, adaptive self-stabilization, adaptive self-organization, and hierarchical structuring (Laszlo, 1972; Sameroff, 1983). These principles can easily be incorporated into the theoretical framework of synergetics, and they have been applied to cognitive theories of development, most often the one proposed by Piaget (e.g., Piaget, 1952; see also Sameroff, 1983; An der Heiden, 1990). If we deal with complex systems the question of how to select the relevant order parameters that govern the behavior of the system arises. Nobody has ever counted the number of dimensions of a dynamical system such as the human brain or has decomposed the complex transactional structure of a person–environment system (given that this ever would be possible). There is, however, a good message: most often, only a few order parameters govern the dynamics of the whole configuration that might be composed of a large number of parts. The age dimension in developmental psychology serves as a good example, since it traditionally is effective as a source of strong constraints on the dimensionality of the developmental system. Another example of an order parameter of a higher theoretical value may be maturation (Gesell, 1929). Order parameters may force the system to approach an attractor of a noticeably low dimensionality. This attractor may even be strange or chaotic, as in the case of rodents' odor behavior (Skarda & Freeman, 1987; see above).

Piaget (1970) has held the position that the construction of structures is mainly the work of a basic mechanism called *equilibration,* which means self-regulation of the organism rather than a balancing between opposite forces. *Progressive equilibration* then might be the order parameter that governs the sequencing of stages of the cognitive system, whereas the organizational structure of several stages may (theoretically) correspond to a hierarchy of attractors.

Brainerd (1978) has pointed out that Piagetian research is mainly aimed at studying the cognitive products of person–environment interaction in terms of a general learning process. With respect to validity, Charlesworth (1981) has criticized empirical investigations in this domain (Piaget's own classical observational studies being an exception) as almost exclusively focusing on the logic of cognitive structures and thus missing "ecological representativeness of the test items used to tap cognitive structures or the possible adaptive value of the cognitive structures measured" (Charlesworth, 1981, p. 143). The criticism may be refuted by Piaget's (1970) notion that learning is an active enterprise and that there is mutuality in learner–environment interaction. But nevertheless, there remains some deficit in this formulation when referring to an understanding of the ecological rather than the logical structure of tasks included in cognitive developmental analyses. With respect to animal learning, Johnston (1981) has pointed out that it may be a fallacy to assume a general learning process (or processes) supposed to be unaffected by content, that is, what the animal is learning to do. According to the discussion of learning–development relationships given above, and from conceptions of learning in terms of a *cognitive event* (Rogoff, 1982), it becomes obvious that from an ecological point of view, the study of learning involves a taxonomy of learning objectives. This will not necessarily mean, however, ending up with a catalog of learning tasks (for example, a child has to learn how to climb a tree, how to solve a puzzle, how to master arithmetics). Only in artificially designed learning situations such as the school is a learner exposed to or placed in opposition to specific tasks or problems. Natural learning will occur permanently without formal goals and most often without formal instruction. Since both organism and environment are abstractions when considered as two poles of a continuum of mutuality, the same holds true for both task descriptions (in terms of environmental constraints) and ability prescriptions (on the organism's side). I agree with Alley and Shaw, who have criticized the ecological approach to learning (Johnston, 1981) and have concluded that: "learning, like perception and action, is construed as an activity *of an ecosystem* rather than as an activity *by an animal in an ecosystem*" (Alley & Shaw, 1981, p. 140). A statement such as this would make it hard to give an account of what the tasks are that humans are exposed to. Rather, there may be "developmental milestones" to be observed in the ontogenesis of a species that are representative of specific transitions in the developmental process aimed at optimizing the adaptational success of the whole system. Nevertheless, the ecological view is most valuable in stressing the natural context of living organisms as a main source for the constitution of learning phenomena. It may be noticed, however, that for humans, a natural environment is highly artificial in that humans create their own environments to a high degree.

For children, there are many instances of "ordinary," socialized, functional, and adventurous learning (Paris & Cross, 1983), where learning processes occur informally in everyday contexts such as the home and the playground. Rather than being formally designed by adults or by experts, such as teachers, *learning tasks* for children are embedded in *cultural practices* (Laboratory of Comparative Human Cognition, 1983) that refer to *systems of activity* in a given culture. Activity here mainly refers to social interactional processes among the members of the group, and credit is also given to the view that so called physical objects are social in the sense that they carry social-cognitive meanings to the actor. Thus, the *phase space* of learning and development mainly refers to dimensions of socially (or culturally) defined activities and learning. In this context, it resembles a process of mirroring or reconstructing primarily given social-cultural phenomena on the individual level.

A main topic of this chapter is to conceptualize the learner–environment functional unit as a dynamical system or, in what perhaps might be the better term, a *dynamical learning system.* Following this line of thinking, one can take advantage of the principles of synergetics or general dynamical systems theory. Learning refers here to the establishment of relatively stable states (or attractors) of the system (a child will become able to undress/dress herself without the help of an adult). Both the type of attractor (narrow, broad, ordered, chaotic) and the profile of the trajectory of the system (sequence of steps in the parameter space) will depend on the specific order variables (for example, dependence/independence) and control parameters (social pressure towards obedience, or maturational level). In this model, learning refers to the maintaining of a *status quo* in system's dynamics; that is, learning results in a state of self-maintained stability in the system, which may only be temporary but may be reestablished under the influence of control parameters. The very conservative nature of learning is exemplified in such circumscriptions as *habit formation,* acquiring skills and knowledge, memory formation, establishing firm action tendencies, reaching goals, solving problems or tasks, and so on.

A strict analogy between general learning principles (in terms of biological fitness and adaptation) and the laws of physics (general conservation principles), which are both governed by conservation conditions, has also been mentioned by Alley and Shaw (1981). On the other hand, the term *development* is used here when referring to an irreversible (symmetry-breaking) process of successive stages or transitions governing the trajectories of the system (or the special matrix of correlated landscapes). An illustration of the status of learning and development as sketched here can be given by the following quotation from Plotkin and Odling-Smee:

> Development is characterized by a high degree of irreversibility, whereas learning is characterized by a high degree of reversibility. It is possible, of course, for prior development to be compensated for by subsequent development, but compensation is not the same thing as reversibility. Similarly, although no learner can ever return fully to some original, prelearning state, thereby indicating that the reversibility of learning is limited, we would still argue that the reversibility of

learning makes it *qualitatively different* from development. (1981, pp. 154–155, emphasis added; see also Plotkin & Odling-Smee, 1979)

This view fits also the cumulative nature of learning (see the introduction to this volume).

Irreversibility of developmental process can be taken as an alternative expression for symmetry breaking in the development of dynamical systems, which in turn is to be expressed by nonlinear mathematical functions. The question of what kinds of order parameters are involved in dynamical learning systems can be raised. In terms of the so-called sociohistorical approach to development and learning (which best fits the "ordinary learning" view addressed earlier), this question can also be formulated as a corollary to Vygotsky's "general law of cultural development"; that is, how the social-to-psychological transformation of cognitive functions can be realized. Vygotsky has referred to this in terms of a general principle of developmental steps called the *zone of nearest development* (Vygotsky, 1935). I shall not discuss this concept here in length, since there exist more comprehensive treatments of the topic elsewhere (Brown & Ferrara, 1985; Campione, Brown, Ferrara, & Bryant, 1984; Day, 1983; McLane, 1987; Valsiner & Van der Veer, 1992). According to Valsiner (1984), the zone of proximal development (ZPD) "denotes the range of possible nearest-future transformations of the present psychological processes" (Valsiner & Van der Veer, 1992). Since the ZPD is originally mentioned to represent a descriptive concept that carries important implications for developmental processes on several levels of reference (for example, the social-to-individual level, the intraindividual learning potentials levels, and the learning-through-teaching level, among others), it also fits well a synergistic conception of learning and development in that it may describe a system's self-organized activities that indicate a change in order parameters and thus may allow the system to approach a new basin of attraction for further learning. In terms of dynamical systems theory, the ZPD denotes a region in parameter space where a system reaches a point of instability where the dynamic of the system is governed by relatively few order parameters and where a small perturbation (a signal or a surprising event) "causes the system to leave its initial state and to acquire a totally new state" (Haken, 1983, p. 14). In periods of systems evolution such as this, the outcome is often unpredictable and the system is driven to a temporary state of being chaotically organized. Such periods in development have often been described as crises on both the micro and the macro levels of developmental changes. As Valsiner and Van der Veer (1992) point out, Vygotsky's ideas about crisis periods in human ontogeny are mentioned to describe major changes in large-scale development, that is, on the plane of the individual life course (newborn, first, third, seventh, thirteenth and seventeenth year), representing the relevant periods of development, "as the ontogenetic progression takes a catastrophic form and resembles revolutionary breakthroughts" (Vygotsky, 1933/1984, p.249; quoted in Valsiner & Van der Veer, 1992). I would like to guess that there is a parallel in dynamics of developmental process on the microgenetic level, where periods of chaotic organization (or crisis centered around instability points) are indications for chaotic attractors that serve the function of reorganizing cognitive structures in order to give rise to novel functions. Under conditions of stress—for example, when exposed to dangerous stimuli, when a laboratory animal is trapped in a cage—coping often takes the form of trial-and-error learning, which means that different behaviors are shown in a disorganized, chance-like manner. Another example is the form of creative problem solving known as brainstorming. There is also evidence of disorganized temporary states in exploratory learning sequences (Voss, 1987). The beginning of exploratory activity is often characterized by the execution of a broad array of actions, and there is a relatively high proportion of irrelevant manipulations of the novel object. The system then changes to a level of more integrated, purposive actions, which eventually may result into a newly formed concept of meaning (Voss, 1987; see also Greif, this volume).

In the next part of the chapter, I shall give an example for learning (in terms of dyadic problem solving) that serves the function of illustrating the microgenetic evolution of a dynamical learning system.

THE MOTHER–CHILD DYAD AS A DYNAMICAL LEARNING SYSTEM: AN ILLUSTRATION

The mother–child dyad is defined here in terms of a dynamical learning system—there is coordinated behavior of interacting partners in a task-oriented situation, where a certain goal has to be reached through the mastering of successive stages of a problem-solving process. The paradigm of the mother–child dyad as a problem solver has been introduced into the research literature by Vygotskyan researchers, especially by Wertsch and his co-workers (Wertsch, 1978; Wertsch, McNamee, McLane, & Budwig, 1980; Wertsch, Minick, & Arns, 1984; Wertsch & Hickmann, 1987) and is also present in the event (activity) approach used by Rogoff (1982, 1986, 1990). I use this paradigm here for the sake of demonstrating the applicability of dynamical systems theory to the phenomenon of jointly interacting mother and child in a constrained situation that is relatively unaffected by external control variables.[4]

Wertsch et al. (1980) have conducted a study on how mothers and their children (18 mother–child dyads that were divided into three groups of six dyads each on the basis of the child's age) were mutually engaged in mastering a puzzle that had to be assembled in accordance with a model. The interaction was

---

[4] Research reported here is part of a study to be published elsewhere (Voss, 1993).

videotaped and scores were computed from both the mother's and the child's utterances, gestures, and handling of the pieces, as well as the child's gazes towards the mother or towards the units of the task (model, copy, pile of pieces). The authors were mainly interested in the distribution of the child's self-regulated and other-regulated gazes. A gaze was classified as other-regulated if it was contingent upon the mother's pointing to the model or upon an utterance of the mother that explicitly mentioned an aspect of the task. Main results of this study "support the notion of an ontogenetic transition from other-regulation to self-regulation in connection with a crucial strategic step [looking at the model] in our task setting" (Wertsch et al., 1980, p. 1221). There was only partial evidence for a microgenetic progress from other-regulated to self-regulated gazes at the model, occurring in individual cases.

According to synergistic formulations of the mother–child dyad, the focus here is on a demonstration of the relative weight of the monitoring activity of the mother as opposed to the self-reliant actions of the child, which both are instances for order parameters governing the evolution of the system across several age levels. (It may be noted that the study is designed cross-sectionally rather than longitudinally.) The result of the study easily can be "transcribed" into the language of synergetics: other-initiated and self-initiated gazes both refer to two modes of a collective variable (or order parameter), and they compete (rather than cooperate) when considered on a large-scale developmental process; in other words, there is a "win" of self-initiated gazes over other-initiated ones for this special type of dyadic system, the latter ones being "slaved" by the former ones (Haken, 1983). The developmental change in the order parameter governing the system, which is the same as a phase transition in dyadic behavioral regulations, cannot be observed directly here due to the cross-sectional data presented by Wertsch et al. (1980). The study had also not been designed for demonstrating stabilizing effects, which may allow an interpretation of the results in terms of learning. It may therefore be useful to design a study in which the evolution of the system can be evaluated directly.

DESIGN OF THE STUDY

The study was originally designed in order to evaluate microgenetic changes in behavioral regulations of a mother and child who are jointly engaged in a problem-solving situation. The problem consisted of a mechanical puzzle that resembled an automatic candy dispenser (Figure 1-1). A container holding chewing gum balls was placed on top of a base unit to which a horizontally movable lever was attached. The lever was formed according to a slot that corresponded in size to a slot at the base unit. The slots had to be matched in order to allow a coin to fit. When the coin was inserted, a piece of gum would be released from the container. There were exactly four steps in the sequence if the

Figure 1.1.   The gum-ball machine used in the study by Voss (1993).

apparatus was to be handled successfully: (a) moving the lever from its start-ing position at the left corner of the base unit to the right corner, where the two slots could be matched; (b) inserting the coin; (c) moving the lever backwards, which was only possible by overcoming a counterforce posed by a hidden spring mechanism; and (d) pushing the lever to the right side again, which resulted in the desired release of the gum.

Sixteen mother–child dyads took part in this investigation. The mean age of the children was 40.6 months (age span was 40.06–41.56 months), and the mean age of the mothers was 30 years (age span 26–38 years). Mother and child were seated in a comfortable position allowing both face-to-face and side-by-side interaction. The apparatus (together with a coin) was introduced to mothers as a play-object, and mothers were encouraged to engage in mutual play. No specific instructions concerning the mechanics and the "affordances" of the object were given; all dyads clearly saw the apparatus as something that had to be manipulated if gum were to be released. Videotaped behaviors were coded according to a larger array of categories ranging from manipulative acts of both partners to verbal and vocal utterances and emotional reactions (for details, see Voss, 1993). There were three trials, each defined in terms of actu-al success in releasing the gum. Since the report here is on the "dialogue struc-ture" (Schaffer, 1979) of mother–child interaction, as well as on how the dynamical learning system will develop in the course of action, only a small amount of information will be considered.

The question of which one of the several variables considered best describes the dynamics of the system can be raised. As in the Wertsch at al. (1980) study, a candidate for a collective variable (or order parameter) would be the number of self-initiated versus the number of other-initiated behaviors. It may often be difficult, however, to infer a cause for or a prompting of a problem-solving activity from both the occurrence of a certain behavior as well as the time or event structure (critical intervals, transitional probabilities). I thus chose the number of "help-seeking behaviors" of the child, and its complement, the number of "help-giving responses" of the mother, to represent a collective variable that might account for the time profile of the system's activities. This decision was made according to the assumed greater competence of mothers in handling the object. Help or information seeking consisted of the child's gazes to the mother, most often coupled with a break in manipulative acts or with utterances that indicated a question (in terms either of literally asking a question or of asking a "prosodic question" by changing level of intonation in a characteristic manner). Some children also touched the mother's hand and tried to initiate manipulative acts. In a few cases a child would stop action and remain relatively unaffected by the task; in all cases where mothers provided special hints about the manipulation of the object, action stops were also coded as help-seeking behaviors. It should be noted, however, that coding help seeking was not conditionally linked to the occurrence of a help-providing response of the mother. There were many instances where help was not given. And vice versa, coding of help giving was not linked to a preceding help-seeking behavior of the child; in many cases, mothers gave information concerning the functioning of the object without any obvious relation to the child's questioning or imperative acts.

In Figure 1-2, the magnitudes of both classes of behavior across time segments of 15 seconds each are represented for a selected case. The dialogue structure represented by Figure 1-2 offers some interpretation in terms of dynamical systems theory. Throughout the first two minutes, dyadic interaction in this category of behavior is relatively uncoordinated. Since the object is new to both partners, this segment of systems evolution may be characterized as relatively "chaotic" in terms of a match between help-seeking and help-giving behaviors. Synchronicity in interaction is already evident from about 150 seconds on until the end of the sequence where the solution is attained. There is also clear evidence for asymptotic stability in the dynamic of the system, since amplitudes of sinuslike curves decrease in time. If one takes into account that there are fluctuations (or noise) in the system, a good fit of the diagram with conventional graphical representations of a dissipative system such as the dampened pendulum could be gained. The term *asymptotic stability* is also another expression for the approaching of a point attractor, since phase space trajectories will converge against the attractor in the course of the system's evolution (see Figure 1.3).

The evolution of the dyadic learning system (after the first minute) can also be mathematically described by a derivate of the *general logistic map* (Verhulst map), which reads $X_{t+1} = px_t(1 - x_t)$ and which was used by Verhulst in 1845 to describe population growth (May, 1976). The parameter p refers to a growth

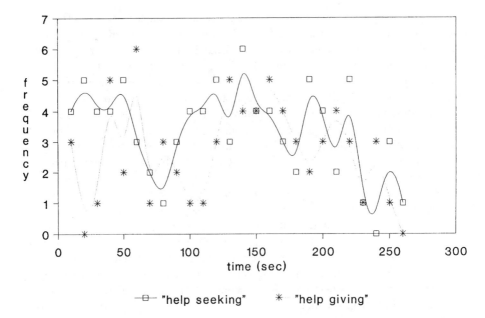

Figure 1.2. Child's help-seeking behavior and maternal support (frequency of responses of one mother-child dyad across a time span of 390 seconds. (Note: fitted polygons.)

parameter. As has been pointed out by Kriz (1990), communication patterns occurring in social situations are characterized by a high degree of mutuality, and therefore a description of individual behavior in mathematical terms must include a statement of the other person. This has been discussed under the rubric of *symbiosis,* and there are equations available that take into account the permanent influence of the other (Haken, 1983; Kriz, 1990).

FINAL REMARKS

In this chapter, I have tried to familiarize the reader with basic ideas underlying the synergistic perspective. Synergetics and dynamical systems theory have been widely used synonymously here because of a large commonality in both theoretical terms and assumptions. Synergistic thinking has been successfully applied to a large variety of phenomena, including the laser beam, horse gait, coordinated finger movements in humans, optical illusions, thinking and memorizing, and psychotherapy, to name a few. Learning is among the concepts that will certainly get more attention in the near future. Learning can easily be embedded in the theoretical framework of synergetics, and there are a few studies on this topic that are addressed mainly to the question of how learning phe-

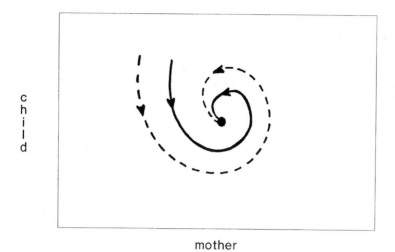

c
h
i
l
d

mother

Figure 1.3. Graphic representation of asymptotic stability (approaching a point attractor) in the evolution of mother–child interaction.

nomena would meet with special implications of human brain models and neural net conceptions (McNaughton, 1989; Palmer, 1989). That learning might relate to phase transitions in the parameter space of some behavioral system is very well demonstrated (Kelso, 1990), and the occurrence of deterministic chaos in memory processes and learning is now becoming better understood (Kauffman, 1989b; Nicolis, 1983; Skarda & Freeman, 1987).

Developmental psychologists are well familiar with general systems theory (von Bertalanffy, 1968), which has advanced to become a kind of universal viewpoint in the field. Nevertheless, synergistic thinking is not very prevalent in developmental psychological publications and often still is considered as an exotic branch of outmoded physicalistic thinking in psychology. Among the first who related synergism and developmental systems was Bronfenbrenner (1979, 1989), and dynamical systems theory was explicitly mentioned in a chapter of Mussen's "handbook" by Sameroff (1983).[5]

I have treated synergetics and dynamical systems theory here as metatheoretical concepts for the study of development and learning processes, rather than as a theory of learning and development. It is my guess that the synergistic view meets very well with developmental theories of learning that stress the importance of social interaction and principles of ordinary learning such as mutuality

---

[5] Developmentally oriented approaches have been also presented by An der Heiden (1990) and Bischof (1990). After working on this chapter, I also became aware of an article by Schmidt-Denter (1992).

in action patterns, natural environments, learning by discovery (Shulman & Keisler, 1966), or learning in terms of a permanent problem-solving process. There is also much space for students of learning and development to utilize general dynamical systems theory or synergetics in order to pursue a fascinating idea: Approaches such as this represent metatheoretical devices for implementing and understanding complex systems in a variety of scientific disciplines.

REFERENCES

Alley, T.R., & Shaw, R.E. (1981). Principles of learning and the ecological style of inquiry. *Behavioral and Brain Sciences, 4,* 139–141.

An der Heiden, U. (1990). Three worlds interactions and developmental psychology: Perspectives of the synergetic approach. In H. Haken & M. Stadler (Eds.), *Synergetics of cognition* (pp. 453–360). Berlin: Springer.

Ashby, W.R. (1960). *Design for a brain.* New York: Wiley.

Basar, E., Flohr, H., Haken, H., & Mandell, A.J. (Eds.). (1983). *Synergetics of the brain.* Berlin: Springer.

Bertlanffy, L. von (1968). *Organismic psychology theory.* Barre, MA: Clark University with Barre Publishers.

Bischof, N. (1990). Phase transitions in psychoemotional development. In H. Haken & M. Stadler (Eds.), *Synergetics of cognition* (Vol. 45, pp. 361–378). Berlin, Heidelberg: Springer-Verlag.

Brainerd, C.J. (1978). The stage question in cognitive-developmental theory. *The Behavioral and Brain Sciences, 1,* 173–213.

Bronfenbrenner, U. (1979). *The ecology of human development: Experiments by nature and design.* Cambridge, MA.: Harvard University Press.

Bronfenbrenner, U. (1989). Ecological systems theory. In R. Vasta (Ed.), *Six theories of child development* (pp. 185–246). Greenwich, CT.: JAI Press.

Bronfenbrenner, U., & Crouter, A.C. (1983). The evolution of environmental models in developmental research. In P.H. Mussen (Ed.), *Handbook of child psychology* (4th ed., Vol. I, pp. 357–414). New York: John Wiley & Sons.

Brousse, O., & Smolensky, P. (1990). Connectionist generalization and incremental learning in combinatorial domains. In H. Haken & M. Stadler (Eds.), *Synergetics of cognition* (Vol. 45, pp. 70–80). Berlin, Heidelberg: Springer-Verlag.

Brown, A.L., Bransford, J.D., Ferrara, R.A., & Campione, J.C. (1983). Learning, remembering, and understanding. In P.H. Mussen (Ed.), *Handbook of child psychology* (4th ed., Vol. III, pp. 77–166). New York: Wiley.

Brown, A.L., & Ferrara, R.A. (1985). Diagnosing zones of proximal development. In J.V. Wertsch (Ed.), *Culture, communication, and cognition: Vygotskyan perspectives* (pp. 273–305). Cambridge, UK: Cambridge University Press.

Cairns, R. (1979). *Social development: The origins and plasticity of interchange.* San Francisco: Freeman.

Campbell, D. (1989). Introduction to nonlinear phenomena. In D.L. Stein (Ed.), *Lectures in the sciences of complexity* (Vol. I, pp. 3–105). Redwood City, CA: Addison-Wesley.

Campione, J.C., Brown, A.L., Ferrara, R.A., & Bryant, N.R. (1984). The zone of proximal development: Implications for individual differences and learning. *New Directions for Child Development, 23,* 77–91.

Charlesworth, W.R. (1981). An ecological approach toward a unified theory of learning. *Behavioral and Brain Sciences, 4,* 142–143.

Cole, M., John-Steiner, V., Scribner, S., & Souberman, E. (Eds.) (1978). *L.S. Vygotsky: Mind in society.* Cambridge, MA: Harvard University Press.

Day, J.D. (1983). The zone of proximal development. In M. Pressley & J.R. Levin (Eds.), *Cognitive strategy research* (pp. 155–175). New York: Springer.

Garfinkel, A. (1987). The virtues of chaos. *Behavioral and Brain Sciences, 10,* 178.

Gesell, A. (1929). Maturation and infant behavior patterns. *Psychological Review, 36,* 307–319.

Gibson, E.J. (1979). *The ecological approach to visual perception.* Boston: Houghton Mifflin.

Goldberger, A.L., & Rigney, D.R. (1987). Defending against sudden death: Fractal mechanisms of cardiac stability. *Proceedings of 9th Annual IEEE/EMBS Conference, 1,* 313.

Gottlieb, G. (1970). Conceptions of prenatal behavior. In L.R. Aronson, E. Tobach, D.S. Lehrman, & J.S. Rosenblatt (Eds.), *Development and evolution of behavior* (pp. 111–137). San Francisco: Freeman.

Gottlieb, G. (1991). Experiential canalization of behavioral development: Theory. *Developmental Psychology, 27,* 4–13.

Haken, H. (1977). *Synergetics.* Berlin: Springer.

Haken, H. (1983). Synopsis and introduction. In E. Basar, H. Flohr, H. Haken, & A.J. Mandell (Eds.), *Synergetics of the brain* (Vol. 23, pp. 3–25). Berlin, Heidelberg: Springer-Verlag.

Haken, H. (1985). *Light. Vol. 2, Laser Light Dynamics.* Amsterdam: North-Holland.

Hopfield, J.J. (1982). Neural networks and physical systems with emerging collective computational ability. *Proceedings of the National Academy of Sciences, 83,* 1847.

Hoyt, D.F., & Taylor, C.R. (1981). Phase transitions in horse gait. *Nature, 292,* 239–240.

Hull, C.L. (1943). *Principles of behavior.* New York: Appleton-Century-Crofts.

Johnston, T. (1981). Contrasting approaches to a theory of learning. *The Behavioral and Brain Sciences, 4,* 125–173.

Kauffman, S.A. (1989a). *Origins of order: Self-organization and selection in evolution.* Oxford, UK: Oxford University Press.

Kauffman, S.A. (1989b). Principles of adaptation in complex systems. In D.L. Stein (Ed.), *Lectures in the sciences of complexity* (pp. 619–712). Redwood City, CA: Addison-Wesley.

Kauffman, S.A. (1989c). Adaptation on rugged fitness landscapes. In D.L. Stein (Ed.), *Lectures in the sciences of complexity* (pp. 527–618) Reading, MA: Addison-Wesley.

Kelso, J.A.S. (1990). Phase transitions: Foundation of behavior. In H. Haken & M. Stadler (Eds.), *Synergetics in cognition* (pp. 249–268). Berlin: Springer.

Koehler, W. (1920). *Die physischen Gestalten in Ruhe und im stationären Zustand.* Braunschweig: Vieweg.

Kreitler, H., & Kreitler, S. (1976). *Cognitive orientation and behavior.* New York: Springer.

Kriz, J. (1990). Synergetics in clinical psychology. In H. Haken & M. Stadler (Eds.), *Synergetics of cognition* (pp. 393–405). Berlin: Springer.

Krueger, F. (1926). Über psychische Ganzheit. *Neue Psychologische Studien, 1* (1), 101–121.

Krueger, F. (1948). *Lehre von dem Ganzen.* Bern, Switzerland: Huber.

Kruse, P., & Stadler, M. (1990). Stability and instability in cognitive systems: Multistability, suggestion, and psychosomatic interaction. In H. Haken & M. Stadler (Eds.), *Synergetics of cognition* (pp. 201–217). Berlin: Springer.

Laboratory of Comparative Human Cognition. (1983). Culture and cognitive development. In P.H. Mussen (Ed.), *Handbook of child psychology.* (W. Kessen, Vol. ed.) (4th ed., Vol. I, pp. 295–356). New York: Wiley.

Laszlo, E. (1972). *Introduction to systems philosophy: Toward a new paradigm of contemporary thought.* New York: Harper & Row.

Leontiev, A.N. (1981). The problem of activity in psychology. In J.V. Wertsch (Ed.), *The concept of activity in Soviet psychology.* White Plains, NY: Sharpe.

Libchaber, A., & Maurer, J. (1980). Une experience de Rayleigh-Benard de geometrie reduite: Multiplication, accrochage, et demultiplication de frequences. *Journal de Physique, 41,* 51.

Luria, A.R. (1973). *The working brain.* London: Penguin.

Maturana, H. & Varela, F. (1980). *Autopoesis and cognition: The realization of the living.* Boston: Houghton & Mifflin.

May, R.M. (1976). Simple mathematical models with very complicated dynamics. *Nature, 261,* 263–268.

McLane, J.B. (1987). Interaction, context, and the zone of proximal development. In M. Hickmann (Ed.), *Social and functional approaches to language and thought* (pp. 267–285). Orlando, FL Academic Press.

McNaughton, B.L. (1989). The neurobiology of spatial computation and learning. In D.L. Stein (Ed.), *Lectures in the sciences of complexity* (Vol. I, pp. 389–437). Reading, MA: Addison-Wesley.

Michaels, C.F., & Carello, C. (1981). *Direct perception.* Englewood Cliffs, NJ: Prentice-Hall.

Munn, N.L. (1954). Learning in children. In L. Carmichael (Ed.), *Manual of child psychology* (2nd ed.). New York: Wiley.

Nicolis, G., & Prigogine, I. (1977). *Self-organization in nonequilibrium systems.* New York: Wiley.

Nicolis, G., & Prigogine, I. (1987). *Die Erforschung des Komplexen.* München: Piper.

Nicolis, J.S. (1983). The role of chaos in reliable information processing. In E. Basar, H. Flohr, H. Haken, & A.J. Mandell (Eds.), *Synergetics of the brain* (pp. 330–344). Berlin: Springer.

Palmer, R. (1989). Neural nets. In D.L. Stein (Ed.), *Lectures in the sciences of complexity* (pp. 439–462). Redwood City, CA: Addison-Wesley.

Paris, S.G., & Cross, D.R. (1983). Ordinary learning: Pragmatic connections among children's beliefs, motives, and action. In J. Bisanz, G. L. Bisanz, & R. Kail (Eds.), *Learning in children: Progress in cognitive development research* (pp. 137–169). New York: Springer.

Piaget, J. (1952). *The origins of intelligence in children.* New York: International Universities Press.

Piaget, J. (1970). Piaget's theory. In P.H. Mussen (Ed.), *Carmichael's manual of child psychology.* (3rd ed., vol. I, pp. 703–732). New York: Wiley.

Plotkin, H.C., & Odling-Smee, F.J. (1979). Learning, change, and evolution: An inquiry into the teleonomy of learning. *Advances in the Study of Behavior, 10,* 1–41.

Plotkin, H.C., & Odling-Smee, F.J. (1981). Is an ecological approach radical enough? *The Behavioral and Brain Sciences, 4,* 154–155.

Prigogine, I. (1961). *Introduction to thermodynamics of irreversible processes.* New York: Wiley.

Rogoff, B. (1982). Integrating context and cognitive development. In M.E. Lamb & A.L. Brown (Eds.), *Advances in developmental psychology* (Vol. 2, pp. 125–170). Hillsdale, NJ: Erlbaum.

Rogoff, B. (1986). Adult assistance of children's learning. In T.E. Raphael (Ed.), *The contexts of school-based literacy* (pp. 27–40). New York: Random House.

Rogoff, B. (1990). *Apprenticeship in thinking.* New York: Oxford University Press.

Rummelhart, D.E., McClelland, J.L., and the PDP research group (1986). *Parallel Distributed Processing: Explorations in the microstructure of cognition* (2 vols.). Cambridge, MA: Bradford.

Sameroff, A.J. (1983). Developmental systems: Contexts and evolution. In P.H. Mussen (Ed.), *Handbook of child psychology.* (4th ed., Vol. I, pp. 237–294). New York: Wiley.

Schaffer, H.R. (1979). Acquiring the concept of the dialogue. In M.H. Bornstein & W. Kessen (Eds.), *Psychological development from infancy* (pp. 279–305). Hillsdale, NJ: Erlbaum.

Schmidt-Denter, U. (1992). Chaosforschung: Eine neue physikalische Herausforderung an die Psychologie. *Psychologie in Erziehung und Unterricht, 39,* 1–16.

Schuster, H. (1985). *Deterministic chaos.* Weinheim: Physik-Verlag.

Shulman, L.S., & Keisler, E.R. (Eds.) (1966). *Learning by discovery: A critical appraisal.* Chicago: Rand McNally.

Skarda, C.A., & Freeman, W.J. (1987). How brains make chaos in order to make sense of the world. *The Behavioral and Brain Sciences, 10,* 161–195.

Skinner, B.F. (1938). *The behavior of organisms: An experimental analysis.* New York: Appleton-Century-Crofts.

Stadler, M., & Kruse, P. (1990). The self-organization perspective in cognition research: Historical remarks and new experimental approaches. In H. Haken & M. Stadler (Ed.), *Synergetics of cognition* (Vol. 45, pp. 32–52). Berlin, Heidelberg: Springer-Verlag.

Stevenson, H.W. (1970). Learning in children. In P.H., Mussen (Ed.), *Carmichael's manual of child psychology* (3rd ed., Vol. 1, pp. 849–938). New York: John Wiley & Sons.

Stevenson, H.W. (1983). How children learn—the quest for a theory. In P.H. Mussen (Ed.), *Handbook of child psychology* (4th ed., Vol. I, pp. 213–236). New York: John Wiley & Sons.

Turvey, M.T., & Shaw, R.E. (1979). The primacy of perceiving: An ecological reformulation of perception for understanding memory. In L.-G. Nilsson (Ed.), *Perspectives on memory research* (pp. 167–222). Hillsdale, NJ: Erlbaum.

Valsiner, J. (1984). Construction of the zone of proximal development in adult-child joint action. *New Directions in Child Development, 23,* 65–76.

Valsiner, J. (1987). *Culture and the development of children's action.* Chichester: Wiley.

Valsiner, J., & Van der Veer (1992). The encoding of distance: The concept of the "zone of proximal development" and its interpretations. In R.R. Cocking & K.A. Renninger (Eds.), *The development and meaning of psychological distance* Hillsdale, NJ: Erlbaum.

Voss, H.G.W. (1987). An empirical study of exploration-play sequences. In D.Görlitz, & J.F. Wohlwill (Eds.), *Curiosity, imagination, and play* (pp. 151–178). Hillsdale, NJ: Erlbaum.

Voss, H.G.W. (1993). Zur Synergistik der Mutter-Kind-Dyade als Problemlöser. Technical Report, 93–5, Institute of Psychology, Institute of Technology, Darmstadt.

Vygotsky, L.S. (1935). *Umstvennoie razvitie detei v protsesse obuchenia.* Moscow-Leningrad: Gosudarstvennoie Uchebnopedagogicheskoie Izdatel'stvo.

Vygotsky, L.S. (1984). Problema vozreasta. In L.S. Vygotsky (Ed.), *Sobranie sochinenii. Volume 4: Detskaia psikhologia* (pp. 244–268). Moscow: Pedagogika. (Original work published 1933)

Waddington, C.H. (1957). *The strategy of the genes.* London: Allen and Unwin.

Wellek, A. (1950). *Die Polarität im Aufbau des Charakters.* Bern, Switzerland: Franke.

Wellek, A. (1954). Die Genetische Ganzheitspsychologie. *Neue Psychologische Studien XV* (Whole No. 3).

Wertsch, J.V. (1978). Adult-child interaction and the roots of meta-cognition. *Quarterly Newsletter of the Institute for Comparative Human Development, 1,* 15–18.

Wertsch, J.V., & Hickmann, M. (1987). Problem solving in social interaction: A microgenetic analysis. In M. Hickmann (Ed.), *Social and functional approaches to language and thought* (pp. 251–266). Orlando, FL: Academic Press.

Wertsch, J.V., McNamee, G.D., McLane, J.B., & Budwig, N.A. (1980). The adult-child dyad as a problem-solving system. *Child Development, 51,* 1215–1221.

Wertsch, J.V., Minick, N., & Arns, F. (1984). The creation of context in joint problem solving. In B. Rogoff & J. Lave (Eds.), *Everyday cognition.* Cambridge, MA: Harvard University Press.

White, S.H. (1970). The learning theory tradition and child psychology. In P.H. Mussen (Ed.), *Carmichael's manual of child psychology.* (3rd ed., Vol. I, pp. 657–701). New York: Wiley.

Wohlwill, J.F. (1973). *The study of behavioral development.* New York: Academic Press.

CHAPTER 2

Reflexivity and Learning: Problems, Perspectives, and Solutions

Ursula Christmann

University of Heidelberg

Norbert Groeben

University of Köln

THE RESEARCH PROGRAM SUBJECTIVE THEORIES AS AN ALTERNATIVE TO THE INFORMATION-PROCESSING APPROACH

During the last 25 years a theoretical change has taken place in many areas of psychology, which can be characterized by the sloganlike term *cognitive turn*. In opposition to the behaviorist research tradition, this term refers to the ever-increasing consideration given to internal, mental aspects of human information processing. Psychology has become cognitive insofar as mental structures and internal processes have become the focus of theory development.

The cognitive turn has become manifest in particular in the form of those cognitive models of knowledge, thinking, and learning, and so on, which have been developed within the information-processing approach. What those different theoretical models all have in common is that they all take the cognitive constructivism of Bartlett (1932) as a starting point and so do not regard information processing as passive reception, but as an active process of construction; in the course of this process the individual actively incorporates new information into his or her knowledge structure. This assumption can be regarded as sufficiently confirmed at least in the field of verbal learning. Studies within the psychology of memory on the organization and integration of linguistic items (chunking; Miller, 1956) and processes of clustering (Bousfield, 1953), as well as on subjective organization processes in recall of unrelated words (e.g., Tulving, 1962), can count as corresponding evidence. In the area of sentence and text learning, the studies by Bransford and coworkers (e.g., Bransford & Franks, 1971) in particular have demonstrated that in information processing, subjects go beyond the immediately given semantic input and construct a holistic description of situations/events on the basis of general world knowledge. Taken in all, these studies demonstrate that processing verbal information involves constructive inferences that transcend the information given.

The assumption of the cognitive construction of meaning has led to a radical change of those core assumptions that were taken as obligatory prior to the cognitive turn: universalist instead of connectionist, holistic instead of reductionist, intentionalistic instead of mechanistic, introspectionistic instead of empiristic (cf. Anderson & Bower, 1973, p. 41). In our opinion, however, these assumptions cannot—or can only in a reductive way—be translated into the system-theoretic language game of the information-processing approach. Within system theory human behavior is described as an output of systems; this type of description does not permit conceptualizing the human being as an intentionally acting, reflexive subject without getting involved in inadmissible con-taminations of actor language on the one hand and system language on the other (T. Herrmann, 1982). In addition, the system theoretical description of cognitions by algorithmic rules for the execution of operations, and the experimental control and manipulation of conditions for the use of these rules, generally has mechanistic implications that are likewise not compatible with the conceptualization of the human being as an intentionally acting subject. Thus, in case of inconsistencies in the cognitive system (contradictory conceptual relations), a set of rules has to be applied in a fixed sequence until consistency is achieved (T. Herrmann, 1985, pp. 186ff.). Escaping from this fixed rule system, as is for instance necessitated by creative acts, cannot (or can in a very uneconomical manner only) be handled. These types of mechanistic implications in the information-processing approach cast doubt on whether it is really justified to speak of a *cognitive turn.* For it is precisely this type of mechanistic implication that is characteristic of the behaviorist research tradition that the information-processing approach claims to have overcome. Under this perspective the contents of research may have changed from the behaviorist concentration on observable behavior to the information theoretical concentration on internal mental processes, but the structure of research methodology and the implied "model of man" certainly have not (Groeben, 1986, pp. 370ff; 1990). The core assumption of cognitive constructivity surmounting behaviorism, which implies the conceptualization of the human being as a reflexive subject, has in our opinion been consistently applied neither in theory development nor in the research process of the information processing approach, and can in fact not be thus applied in a nonreductionist way for the above reasons. The system theoretical modelling of cognitive constructivism (by the information-processing approach) must hence be criticized as "formalistic, functionalistic and descriptivistic" (Vorderer, 1987).

In order to arrive at a consistent (and hence constructive) theoretical modelling of the cognitive constructivity of the human being, in our opinion it would consequently seem appropriate as a heuristic to go back to the core assumptions of behaviorism that have to be overcome: starting with the reconstruction of these core assumptions, those (antipodal) central assumptions can be elaborated that may permit a more coherent (and hence, in the final analysis, action theoretical) modelling of cognitive constructivity.

For this heuristic recourse both the conceptualization of science and the understanding of the subject matter of behaviorism have to be taken into account. The behaviorist research program has conceptualized the scientific process of knowledge acquisition according to the model of the classical natural sciences and correspondingly has taken precision as its most important methodological criterion, to which the definition of the subject matter of research has de facto been subordinated (Skinner, 1948, 1973; Westmeyer, 1973, pp. 12ff.). Thus, only those processes are accepted as subject matter of scientific research that become manifest in observable behavior and hence satisfy the preordinated precision criterion (Groeben & Scheele, 1977, pp. 9ff.). The subject matter of behaviorist research has been external, observable human behavior. The first main point of criticism concerning this conception of science relates to the question of whether the scientific criteria of the natural sciences can be transferred to the social sciences (Habermas, 1968). Whereas the natural sciences are based on the assumption of a fundamentally fixed subject–object relation (the researcher is the conceiving subject; and the subject matter, that is, the human being upon whom research is conducted, is the object), in the social sciences this relation has to be regarded as fundamentally open; here it is human beings who are the objects of research, who through self-knowledge are just as capable of knowledge as the research subject. This neglect of the research object's potential capacity for knowledge has on the level of the subject matter of research led to a radical limitation of the behaviorist research paradigm. On the one hand the human being has been considered as being under the exclusive control of the environment; on the other, his or her specifically human dimension of reflexivity has been reduced to the point of insignificance.

On the level of the subject matter of research, this critique of behaviorism may be condensed in the form of the argument of self-application: While the research object in behaviorism is conceptualized as passive, reactive, and totally determined by the environment, the research subject in his or her experimental acting takes on an actively constructive role that allows him or her to control the environment. In other words, the behaviorist cannot explain his or her own research activity on the basis of those scientific concepts he or she himself or herself has provided (Groeben & Scheele, 1977, p. 15).

In contrast to this behaviorist conceptualization of science and subject matter we propose a research paradigm that starts out precisely from the two points of criticism set out above: On the methodological level, we assume a subject–object relation that is in principle open (the research object by means of self-knowledge is just as capable of knowledge as the research subject); on the level of the subject matter of research, we consider the reflexive dimensions of human beings as central. In contrast to the behaviorist reactive "model of man," we base our paradigm on an epistemological model that conceptualizes the human being as (fundamentally) capable of language, communication, and action, an autonomous and potentially rational subject. These goal characteristics are met by the research program subjective theories (RPST) that were developed during the 1970s in German-speaking countries (Laucken, 1974; Groeben & Scheele, 1977), and elaborated in a first step on the metatheoretical and object-theoretical level during the '80s (Dann, 1990; Groeben, 1986, 1990; Scheele & Groeben, 1988a; Groeben, Wahl, Schlee, & Scheele 1988), and applied on various subject matters in the 1990s (c.f. alcoholism: Barthels, 1991; second language research: Grotjahn, 1991; teaching: Dann, 1992b; argumentational integrity: Christmann & Groeben, 1991, 1993; Christmann & Scheele, 1995; achievement evaluation: Mischo & Groeben, 1995).

We conceptualize subjective theories as cognitions of the everyday psychologist relating (on the content level) to the self and the world, whose structure and function are to be seen as parallel to the structure and function of objective theories for the scientist (cf. Kelly's conception of "man the scientist"; Kelly, 1955), that is, those of explanation, prediction, and technology. In order to be able to fulfill these functions, the concepts have to be connected to form an at least implicit argumentational structure, so that—as the concept of theory already implies—inferential procedures become possible. Accordingly subjective theories are, in a first attempt, defined as

- cognitions relating to the self and the world
- constituting a complex aggregate with an (at least implicit) argumentational structure
- that also fulfills functions parallel to those of objective theories
- that is those of explanation, prediction, and technology. (Groeben, 1988a, p. 19)

These defining attributes are constitutive for the so-called broad variant of the construct *subjective theories*—broad because it allows the subsumption of an entire set of theoretical approaches within cognitive psychology, as for instance: personal construct theory (Kelly, 1955), implicit personality theory (Bruner & Tagiuri, 1954), and attribution theory (Kelley, 1967; Jones, Kanouse, Kelley, Nisbett, Valins, & Weiner, 1971), as well as research on metacognition which is relevant to the explanation of learning and retention (see next section). What these approaches have in common is that in theory development they all focus on the cognition aggregates of the reflexive subject and assume these aggregates to be connected so as to form an implicit argumentational structure. In personal construct theory, this structure consists of correlative relations, in implicit personality theory of inferences, and in attribution theory of the causal attribution of events (Groeben, 1988a, pp. 19ff.).

In this explication of the broad variant of the concept of subjective theories, the integration potential of the RPST becomes manifest. The attributes of the

above conceptualization of science and the resulting "model of man" can, however, be applied in an even more radical manner. From the assumption of a
structural parallel between objective and subjective theories it follows, on the
one hand, that the reflections of the research object that, in the optimal case,
will be rational are to be judged according to their adequacy to reality; it is further to be tested whether they can be accepted as objective knowledge. On the
other hand, it follows (from the goal attributes of the epistemological "model
of man") that the research object's capacity for language and communication
not only be taken into account but further put to constructive use; the most
effective way of accomplishing this is by means of direct communication
between the research subject and object. For the assessment of subjective theories this implies that they are to be reconstructed in a dialogue together with
the object of research; this dialogue is to ascertain for a reconstruction adequate
description of the subjective theories. Thus the consensus-in-dialogue is introduced as a hermeneutical criterion of truth. It is (following the Frankfurt
School; e.g., Apel, 1964/1965; Habermas, 1968) a procedure to ascertain that
intersubjectivity that requires a process of coming to an agreement between the
subject and object of research. The dialogue consensus thus constitutes a procedure for ascertaining understanding, which is to guarantee that the
researcher's reconstruction of what is verbalized by the research object does
indeed correspond to the research object's intended meaning (Groeben, 1986,
pp. 124ff.). On the basis of these two strong conditions the following narrow
explication of the concept of subjective theories is proposed:

- Cognitions relating to the self and the world
- which can be actualized and reconstructed in dialogue-consensus
- as a complex aggregate with an (at least implicit) agrumentational structure
- that also fulfills functions parallel to those of objective theories
- that is those of explanation, prediction, and technology
- whose acceptability as objective knowledge is to be tested. (Groeben, 1988a,
  pp. 22)

On the methodological level, a two-phase research structure results from this
conceptualization: (a) the communicative validation phase, and (b) the phase of
explanatory validation. In the first phase, that of communicative validation, the
researcher in dialogue with the research object reconstructs his or her subjective theory. This reconstruction includes the assessment of the subjective theory by means of the self-report of the reflexive subject as well as the more precise and elaborate formulation of the everyday reflections in scientific language.
The adequacy of this reconstruction (in the sense of an adequate rendering of
the research object's inner view and its adequate verbal description) is guaran-
teed by the research object's agreement (dialogue consensus criterion of truth).
This first phase of communicative validation can thus be characterized as a

phase of description by understanding. It accomplishes the consensus on a correct rendering of the research object's inner view as well as the consensus on a verbal representation that can function as a description of the construct assessed. The fact that the communicative phase is preordinated results from the attributes of the epistemological "model of man" on which the RPST is based, and among these from the attributes of reflexivity and rationality in particular. The potential rationality of the research object's self-interpretative inner view that manifests itself in concrete actions permits the use of this potential in the development of objective theories.

The potentiality of this rationality is at the same time the decisive reason why the description by understanding by itself does not yet suffice. A decision as to the adequacy of the research object's inner view of reality must be made with the aid of external observation (a question of the explanatory function of action constructs). That is, it has to be tested whether the actor's inner view is indeed adequate to reality; that is, whether the reasons given by the actor do in fact become operatively effective. Such a test is indeed necessary because in the area of human experience and acting cases in which the research object's inner view is in fact inadequate to reality also occur; this applies in particular to intransparent situations (to give an extreme example) in which because of emotional stress the subject is unable adequately and comprehensively to process information that is present in the situation. Likewise situations can be conceived of in which cognitions adequate to reality are present but do not become operatively effective; addiction would probably be a paradigmatic example (Scheele & Groeben, 1988b). This question of the explanatory function of the research object's inner view is tested in the second phase of the research structure (explanatory validation). It is superordinated to the phase of communicative validation for the very reason that it alone permits a decision as to the operative efficacy of the reasons given.

So far (with regard to the subject matter of learning and education), it has been teachers' subjective theories in particular that have been investigated within the RPST (e.g., Dann, Humpert, Krause, Kügelgen, Rimele, & Tennstädt, 1982; Treutlein, 1984; Wahl, Schlee, Krauth, & Mureck, 1983). In these studies, the subjective theories of teachers on their own teaching methods formed the basis for the diagnosis of problematic teaching strategies and their replacement by more adequate strategies, such as for instance increasing the social competence of teachers in dealing with aggressive students (Konstanz Training Model: Humpert & Dann, 1988). As an example of such a subjective theory, a teacher's cognitive action structure in dealing with aggressive student behavior that has been assessed by means of a dialogue consensus procedure is given in Figure 2.1. (The teacher's actions are shown in their temporal sequence; the figure starts with the aggressive student behavior and ends at that point where the teacher continues his or her regular teaching.)

In principle, however, learning theories can also be dealt with within the

RPST. For the area of subjective learning theories, there are good reasons to assume that individuals have knowledge with regard to factors that are relevant to learning processes, which is partially parallel to objective theories and can be actualized in dialogue consensus (see below).

To summarize: As the central assumption of cognitive constructivity (overcoming behaviorism) is being consistently applied neither in the theory development nor in the research process of the information processing approach, and for the above reasons in fact cannot be so applied without significantly reducing the cognitive constructivity of the reflexive subject, we conceive of the RPST as an action theoretical alternative to the (system theoretical) information-processing approach; because the RPST shapes the modelling of theories as well as the empirical research process in agreement with the core assumptions of constructivity, reflexivity, and potential rationality of the human being. As a consequence, there results on the one hand an integration potential of the RPST with regard to those approaches of cognitive psychology dealing with complex cognition aggregates within an action theoretical conceptualization (among others) (see below); on the other hand an innovation potential results with regard to the assessment of these cognition aggregates (in form of subjective theories) by means of dialogue-consensus methods (see below).

THE RPST AS AN INTEGRATIVE THEORETICAL FRAMEWORK FOR METACOGNITIVE RESEARCH PERSPECTIVES

So far reflexivity in learning has mainly been dealt with in the context of research on metacognition; the explication of metacognition as "knowledge about" necessarily presupposes the component of reflexivity. A reconstruction of metacognition within the RPST might, in our opinion, contribute towards a solution of some of the permanent problems that have been besetting research on metacognition. As this reconstruction according to our knowledge has not yet been put forward explicitly, we must here limit ourselves to demonstrating the possibility of subsuming the metacognitive approach under the RPST and the usefulness of a reconstruction of metacognitions within the RPST on the basis of some examples that typically count as problematic in traditional research on metacognition.

The term *metamemory* (later *metacognition;* Flavell & Wellman, 1977) initiated by Flavell (1970) refers on the one hand to the knowledge about memory and learning processes in general and on the other hand to the knowledge about the efficiency of one's own memory/learning. The most prominent and most frequently used system for the classification of the content of this knowledge (Flavell & Wellman, 1977) distinguishes a sensitivity as well as a variable category. *Sensitivity* refers to the knowledge about the necessity of acting in a strategic and planful manner in specific learning situations. The *variable* cate-

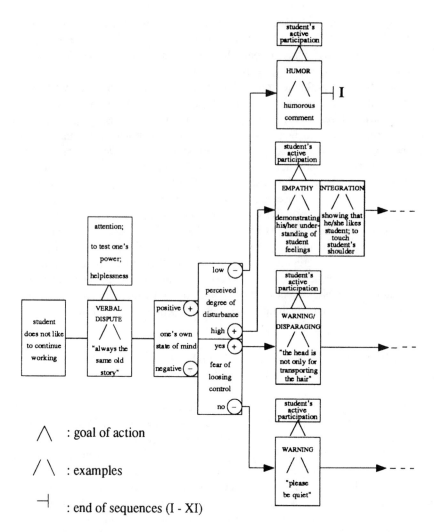

Figure 2.1.   (Unpublished) example of a teacher's Subjective Theory on an aggressive conflict situation in the classroom (for a discussion see Dann 1990).

gory comprises knowledge about factors that influence learning and memory performance, such as, for instance, knowledge about the person variable (containing a declarative and a procedural monitoring component), knowledge about the task variable (such as task difficulty), and knowledge about strategies (that can be used in concrete learning situations) as well as knowledge about the interaction of the above variable categories (such as differential use of strategies depending on task and person variables).

While Flavell focuses on the declarative aspect of metaknowledge, in her

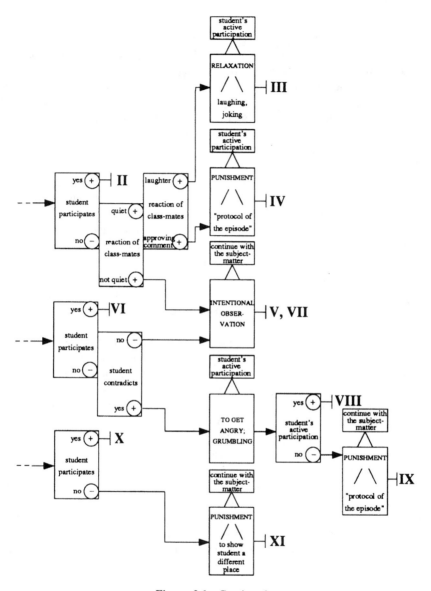

Figure 2.1. Continued

elaboration of the construct of metacognition Brown (1977) accentuates the executive aspect of metacognitive knowledge (in the sense of monitoring one's own learning activity). She distinguishes the constructs of metacomprehension (as the ability to be aware of one's own knowing or nonknowing), prediction, planning, monitoring, testing, and evaluation. In contrast to declarative metaknowledge that counts as knowledge that is stable over time, is conscious, and can be verbalized, executive metaknowledge is conceptualized as task and situation specific and hence changeable—as knowledge, that is, which is not necessarily conscious and not necessarily amenable to verbalization.

Declarative knowledge is mainly collected by questionnaires on the efficacy of one's own memory (cf., for example, D.J. Herrmann, 1984) or by means of largely standardized interviews (Kreutzer, Leonard, & Flavell, 1975). Executive knowledge is frequently assessed by means of prediction of one's own learning and memorizing capacity, the allocation of learning time and learning intensity, the sensitivity for the adequacy of learning material and learning structure, and the identification of main ideas in study texts, as well as the retrospective evaluation of learning results. The data are collected either before, during, or after the learning task. Recently the attempt has been made to link metacognition to the information-processing approach; in this context some additional indicators of metacognition based on physiological measures have been introduced (e.g., attention focusing; for a survey cf. Schneider, 1985; Knopf, 1987).

These explications of metaknowledge have stimulated an abundance of research, which on the whole concentrated on demonstrating the influence of metacognitive knowledge on learning and memory in children (e.g., Campione & Brown, 1977) as well as in adults (e.g., Perlmutter, 1978). The data, however, are somewhat ambiguous. While Cavanaugh and Perlmutter (1982) in their research survey report only small or no correlations for the relationship between metaknowledge and memory/learning performance, Wellman (1983) cites studies that demonstrate a satisfactory correlation between metamemory and memory performance. Closer inspection of these studies shows, however, that the studies Wellman refers to focused on the testing of the executive aspects of metamemory, while the studies quoted by Cavanaugh and Perlmutter concentrated primarily on the influence of declarative knowledge on memory performance (Schneider, 1985, pp. 58ff.). In a metaanalysis based on 27 studies (47 correlations, 2,231 subjects), Schneider (1985) could confirm this trend: Studies referring to the executive aspect of metaknowledge on average show higher correlations than studies that test the influence of task and strategy knowledge on learning/memory performance (even in this type of study, however, medium correlations could be demonstrated). The overall correlation coefficient between metacognition and memory was .41. An updating of this metaanalysis taking into account more recent studies employing improved methods of data collection (60 publications, 123 correlations, 7,097 subjects) yielded the same overall total correlation of .41 (Schneider & Pressley, 1989, pp. 112ff.). Only the standard deviation could be reduced from .18 to .14. On the basis of the height of the correlations the following rank order results for the types of studies that had been subjected to metaanalysis: Memory monitoring/text processing (.44); memory monitoring/training studies (.40); memory monitoring/lab tasks (.39); organizational strategies/training studies (.37); organizational strategies/clustering (.33) (Schneider & Pressley 1989, p. 113). One should not be deluded, however, by these comparatively high correlations: The data are highly inconsistent—or, to put it in the authors' own words: "Sometimes there are associations between metamemory and memory behavior, and sometimes there are not" (Schneider & Pressley, 1989, p. 120).

The data concerning the question of which indicators of metacognition can be considered the most valid are just as inconsistent. The results are highly dependent on the measures used as well as the indicatorization. Knopf (1987, p. 241), for instance, reports that in a series of studies conducted by the Max Planck Institute, different indicatorizations of prediction accuracy led to different results for the same data. The results presently available thus permit only the deduction of hypotheses which do, however, require closer empirical testing: (a) Indicators collected in temporal proximity to the learning result are more valid than temporally distal indicators. (b) Indicators measuring situation-specific activated knowledge are more valid than indicators referring to the beliefs that are stable in time. (c) Indicators measuring task-specific learning and memory performance are more valid than indicators measuring task-independent performance (Knopf, 1987, pp. 241ff.).

This incoherence and inconsistency presently characterizing research on metacognition is presumably caused by the fact that the relation between metamemory and performance varies depending on population as well as task difficulty; hence correlations cannot be expected to be stable (Weinert, 1984, p. 16). In addition, reasons immanent to the theory, as well as more technical reasons relating to the methods of data collection, probably also contribute to this situation.

First of all, the lack of precise defining characteristics for the metaconcept on the level of theoretical explication obviously should be criticized—the relation between cognition and metacognition remains open. As a consequence it remains unclear which indicators of metacognition do in fact measure metacognitive abilities and which indicators measure merely cognitive abilities (Brown, 1984, p. 62). In the meantime it could be demonstrated empirically (Knopf, 1987, p. 263) that these indicators cannot, as had originally been assumed, all be considered equally valid. A homogenous construct of metacognition is nowhere in sight. The ambiguity of the concept of metacognition has probably been a factor contributing to the heterogeneity and relative arbitrariness of the indicators used. If even measures of reaction time are acceptable as indicators for metacognition (Lachman & Lachman, 1980), this clearly shows that the component of reflexivity originally connected with the concept of metacognition is now being increasingly neglected (Knopf, 1987, p. 62). At present, the concept of metacognition has been expanded to such an extent that it permits the subsumption of a veritable deluge of partially totally heterogenous studies. As a consequence, researchers on metacognition on the one hand now plead for a narrowing of the concept—either by concentrating on those knowledge phenomena that are based on consciousness and reflexivity (Yussen, 1985) or by integration of the concept into the information processing approach (Knopf, 1987); on the other hand, they are beginning to wonder on quite a fundamental level whether a precise definition of the concept is possible at all (Weinert, 1984). In our opinion, however, a solution to this problem cannot be found by concentrating on those indicators of metamemory that empirical research has shown to be valid. First of all, what is to be measured by these indicators and what they claim to measure must be clarified.

In view of these shortcomings and problems of theory explication, a reconstruction of metacognition within the RPST appears promising. In the first instance, this kind of reconstruction would be entirely compatible with the defining attributes of subjective theories. In principle all metacognitive constructs can be subsumed under the broad variant of the RPST: The constructs, in a broad sense, all refer to the efficiency of memory/learning in general as well as the efficiency of one's own memory/learning; thus they constitute phenomena relating to the self and the world of the reflexive subject (first defining attribute of subjective theories). (Thus the construct "person knowledge" sensu Flavell comprises knowledge of the limited capacity of memory altogether as well as knowledge of individual capacities and difficulties—having a good memory for numbers or a bad memory for names, and so on.)

The second defining attribute of the construct subjective theories demands that the cognitions relating to the self and the world constitute complex aggregates with an at least implicit argumentational structure; that is, the thematic cognitions must (in structural analogy to scientific theories) be connected so as to permit the drawing of conclusions. This presupposes that these structures be relatively stable over time. The interaction of person, task, and strategy variables sensu Flavell, for instance, can thus be reconstructed.

The third and fourth defining attributes of subjective theories accentuate the functions of explanation, prediction, and technology (in parallel to objective theories). Explanation, prediction, and technology constitute indicators of metacognition central to research in this field, whose validity allows conclusions as to the quality of the metaknowledge: According to Flavell, for instance, establishing a relation between person, task, and strategy knowledge functions as an explanation for the reflexive subject of his or her actions in performance situations; likewise performance prediction constitutes one of the most frequently used indicators within executive metaknowledge.

In our opinion, the decisive advantage of a reconstruction of metacognitions within the RPST is made by the assumption of an at least partially implicit argumentational structure (the second defining attribute of subjective theories). In general, this implicit argumentational structure consists in the connection between different metacognitive knowledge elements (declarative aspect) which constitute a condition for metacognitive procedures and monitoring processes (executive aspect). The manner in which metacognitions are connected and refer to each other, and the types of conclusions about one's own learning ability and actions drawn on this basis, should be of greater importance to the question of the relation between metaknowledge and actual learning performance than scores on isolated indicators of metacognition for the very reason that this kind of argumentation structure permits an explicitly statement of the conditions for the use of strategies depending on person and task variables.

At the same time, the assumption of an argumentational structure allows a theoretical consideration of the reasons why one would or would not attribute a certain quality to one's own metaknowledge. And this constitutes the second decisive advantage of a reconstruction of metacognitions within the RPST. Under this perspective, combining metacognition and attribution theory (Kelley, 1967) is facilitated or might even be said to become unavoidable. Attribution theory could act as the basis for formulating an explicit argumentational structure in the sense of a subjective causal attribution. On the content level, self-enhancing and self-derogatory attributional patterns would presumably become relevant; this could in fact be empirically shown for attributional patterns in connection with the constructs hope for success and fear of failure, learned helplessness, and external or internal locus of control, as well as high/low self-concept (Heckhausen, 1984). Thus the evaluation of cognitive processes can count as a main factor within Brown's approach. Evaluations of this kind cannot as a rule be attributed solely to the objective result of an action; instead the result must be seen in relation to individual competences (self-concept of one's own ability) as well as the situation and task-specific determinants of performance (individual attributional style). In the case of fear of failure, for example, subjects who tend to precipitatively attribute their failure at a task to a general lack of their own abilities (Abramson, Seligman, & Teasdale 1978), might distort the evaluation of their own performance in a manner inadequate to reality; the prediction of own performance (a frequently used indicator of metacognition) presumably does not remain untouched by this distortion. Here questions arise that have so far not been asked, let alone been dealt with. From research on attribution, for instance, it is known that information on identical performance leads to different self-evaluations and expectancies of success depending on individual attributional styles. How do these different convictions as to one's own capacities effect metacognitive knowledge, and what are the consequences resulting for the relation between metacognitions and performance? Immediate practical consequences, for instance, would result for so-called training programs in metacognition that interindividually lead to different effects. Thus Borkowski and Krause (1985), in testing different training programs (strategy training, metacognition training, combined training), found that those participants profited most who attributed their learning success to their own efforts. The result of this study can be taken to indicate that in training of metacognitive strategies, one ought to make sure whether it would not be advisable at the same time to aim for a modification of attributional style.

The close interrelation between metacognitive structures and patterns of causal attribution has already been pointed out by several authors (e.g., Borkowski, Carr, Rellinger, & Pressley, 1990; Borkowski & Krause, 1985; Groteluschen, Borkowski, & Hale, 1990; Knopf, 1987; Weinert, 1984). Thus variables relevant to attribution theory, such as "self-concept of one's own ability" and "individual attributional style" are comparable to metacognitive variables such as "knowledge about own competence" and "metacognitive evaluation of performance determinants" (Weinert, 1984, p. 17). Relevant research, however, only rarely takes this interconnection into account—as is being lamented, for example, by Schneider and Pressley (1989); how essential it in fact is, has been shown in a study conducted by Hasselhorn, Hager, and Barving (1989). The authors dealt with the question of whether there is in fact any point in investigating metacognition without also taking into account motivational and attributional variables. Starting on the one hand from the largely parallel design for the testing of executive metaknowledge (performance prediction), and the testing of the level of aspiration on the other, they investigated the potential confounding of the two variables. The hypothesis that in students who have "hope for success" additional achievement motivation significantly improves performance prediction could be confirmed. (Performance motivation was effected by induction of failure, assuming that people who have "hope for success" will attribute failure to a lack of effort and will hence increase their readiness to make an effort.) The study at least demonstrates the importance of attributive elements when evaluating one's own learning/memory performance. In our opinion, however, a solution to this problem cannot—as expected by the authors of the above study—consist in experimentally controlling for motivational/attributional factors. In our opinion it would be more promising to instead follow up the question of which attributions accompany which outcomes of actions and how these actions are then evaluated.

For combining attribution theory and research on metacognition the RPST provides that theoretical framework which at the moment can count as the most promising. The construct of subjective theories permits an integrative theoretical modelling of the reasons that an individual considers to be causal for the outcome of an action, as well as the consequences that can be derived from this for the prediction, planning, and execution of future actions. The reconstruction of these reasons had best be carried out employing dialogue-consensus methods (see below).

In addition to the lack of precision characterizing the construct of metacognition and the related problems in operationalizing, the procedures employed in the assessment of metacognitions also contribute to the relatively divergent nature of the findings. In this context the assessment of declarative as well as executive metaknowledge is to be criticized from the perspective of the goal characteristics of the epistemological "model of man" set forth above (see above: capacity for language use and communication, reflexivity, and potential rationality).

The assessment of metaknowledge by means of questionnaires and standardized interviews is generally aimed at collecting "correct" elements of knowledge (in the sense of expert knowledge) while "wrong" elements of knowledge are neglected (Knopf, 1987, pp. 42ff.). The method used for data collection thus has the effect of at least partially concealing the research object's reflexivity, his or her reflection space, that is. A large part of the knowledge potentially guiding the individuals actions is thus not even taken into account. In our opinion, however, problems also arise with respect to that part of knowledge covered by the respective questionnaire: the answers given by the subjects are precipitatively accepted as adequate to reality and valid. Whether they do indeed guide the actions of the individual, however, is not tested (Groeben, 1986, pp. 116ff.). It is perfectly possible that individuals have so-called correct knowledge but, for whatever reasons, do not put it to use in actual performance situations. In addition, having at one's disposal correct elements of knowledge about the efficiency of memory as well as learning strategies does not yet imply that incorrect knowledge is recognized as such. Knopf (1987, p. 259), for example, could empirically demonstrate that knowledge of positive learning strategies by no means implies knowledge of unfavorable and hence to-be-avoided learning strategies. Finally the research object in his or her replies is limited to the scientist's language choice in constructing the questionnaire; quite possibly different individuals will interpret these language choices in different ways and hence differ in their replies on this basis (Groeben, 1986, pp. 117ff.). Due to this partial individuality of reflections, questionnaires and standardized interviews are generally relatively unsuitable for the investigation of actions.

The assessment of executive knowledge we also consider as problematic. Here metacognitive knowledge is not measured directly; instead, conclusions are drawn retrospectively on the basis of reports on one's own cognitive functioning in working on various tasks. In the case of classic designs for the investigation of executive metaknowledge, for instance, retrospective conclusions are drawn as to metacognitive planning activities, if the subjects are able to provide adequate performance predictions. In our opinion, indicators of this kind indicate rather the degree to which individuals are experienced in/accustomed to specific learning situations and learning materials than knowledge about adequate planning and execution of learning tasks. In addition, measures frequently are not suitable for differentiating between reflexive processes and simple cognitive processing; hence they are rather inextricably intertwined with or in fact even constitutive for the learning process itself.

Consequently, in our opinion, methods used for data collection in more recent research can also be further improved. Thus, for instance, in their research on metacognition in Germany the Max Planck Group investigated metaknowledge only in an indirect manner; while they succeed in integrating the two components of metamemory that have so far only been investigated seperately (declarative knowledge sensu Flavell and executive knowledge sensu Brown), and in addition to the classical indicators of metamemory they investigated a multitude of further indicators that were then systematically related to learning/memory performance at different types of tasks (e.g., Knopf, 1987; Körkel, 1987), yet they collect (declarative) metaknowledge exclusively by means of questionnaires that are construed on the basis of expert judgements (concerning correctness/incorrectness of knowledge elements) or employing standardized interviews. Although the techniques for the assessment of declarative metaknowledge in particular have been improved considerably as well as elaborated (Schneider, Körkel, & Vogel, 1987) by comparison to the classical Kreutzer interview (Kreutzer et al., 1975) in the sense of the multiple-assessment approach (collection of metaknowledge employing various procedures) propagated by Cavanaugh and Perlmutter (1982), this does still not solve the basic problem of data collection set forth above: The reflections of the research object are not covered in their totality. Recent research on metacognition does recognize this problem; a solution, however, in our opinion cannot only consist in concentrating one's research efforts on developing ever more sophisticated questionnaires (cf. Schneider & Pressley, 1989).

A more comprehensive and direct assessment of metacognitive reflections in our opinion can be effected through the reconstruction of metacognition by means of dialogue-consensus-based procedures (as provided within the narrow variant of the RPST: for a survey on different dialogue-consensus-based procedures, cf. Scheele & Groeben, 1988a, as well as Groeben, Wahl, Schlee, & Scheele, 1988; Dann 1992b). In contrast to questionnaire-based procedures, the reconstruction by means of a dialogue consensus procedure does not only yield information about strategy and task knowledge, but in particular information about which strategies are used for which reason in which situation and task context, why the subject is convinced of the efficiency of a certain strategy, and about how exactly he or she intends to use it in a learning situation (for greater detail cf. below).

In addition, reconstructing metacognitions in this way as subjective theories allows for the possibility of connection and exchange between objective and subjective theories; this is important for educational applications in particular. This possibility of an exchange is based on the assumption of structural analogy between objective and subjective theories programmatic to the RPST. As a consequence, the imparting of objective (scientific) knowledge in order to optimize learning processes can take the research objects' subjective theories on their knowledge about learning and memory as an immediate starting point. Thus the gap between what the reflexive subjects already know, and learning and processing strategies derived from objective theories can be closed. The failure to close this gap constitutes the neuralgic spot of current learning strategy programs (e.g., Dansereau, 1979) whose lack of efficacy can partially be attributed to the fact that they fail to take into account the self-reflexive processes of the research object. (That is, the training programs were conducted without considering the respective individual knowledge and action-related learning prerequisites and needs—Fischer & Mandl, 1981.) This further comprises the following suggestion for overcoming this deficit: optimization of the training programs by including executive metaknowledge—developing planning, monitoring, and self-evaluation competencies (Fischer & Mandl, 1981; Brown, 1984; Campione, 1984). This is supported by the fact that knowledge of self-diagnostic strategies is not much advanced in learners: In an empirical study on the learning habits and learning activities of extramural students it could be shown that they have their greatest deficit in self-diagnostic processes (Fischer & Mandl, 1980). The lack of such evaluation procedures is obviously the cause of the phenomenon that already existing skills are nevertheless not put to use (production deficit sensu Flavell & Wellman, 1977).

In conducting metacognitive trainings it has been attempted to take into account some of the above critical aspects. Thus greater training efficiency (stability and transfer) could be achieved by employing a more elaborate instruction demonstrating why and in what situations a strategy would be efficient (Campione, 1984). Likewise training efficacy (in children) could be increased by use of active feedback as well as the teaching of task independent self-monitoring strategies (Campione, 1984). (Increase of training efficiency by means of integrative teaching of task-specific as well as general strategies to be expected; Pressley, 1985). Those new training concepts, however, still do not sufficiently take into consideration the *individual* learning situations and prerequisites. For measuring the baseline prior to the training phase by means of current questionnaires at best provides information about what person, task, and strategy knowledge is available to the learners, but not about whether and under what conditions they put this knowledge to use.

Within the RPST, by contrast, the dialogical reconstruction of metacognitions as subjective theories already would constitute a constructive condition for an optimal exchange between subjective and objective theories. This subjective knowledge of the reflexive subject can act as a starting point for the teaching of objective knowledge by for instance transferring implicit into explicit knowledge, completing insufficient metaknowledge about certain strategies and their efficiency, and building up knowledge about person, task, and strategy variables in order to permit a complete consciously planful use of these strategies in a manner adequate to reality. This is based upon the assumption that this exchange between subjective and objective theories takes place stepwise and includes testing phases. For effecting such a stepwise modification of subjective theories Schlee (in Groeben et al., 1988, pp. 300ff.) has proposed the following phases: (a) establishing a sense of psychological security and trust (ascertaining transparency of the situation); (b) attention and contemplation (supportive strategies for the concentration on the reflexive subject's inner perspective); (c) making the implicit explicit; (d) testing the rationality of one's own subjective theory (by comparing it to the objective theory); (e) restructuring or newly developing the subjective theory; (f) testing and veridicality (testing in actual real-life and training situations); (g) degree to which the subjective theory permits effective action (compatibility with other effective points of view). In our opinion, these phases can be put into practice within interactive learning settings, as has in a first step been done within the project "Autonomous Learners" (Beck, 1989). Here, strategies of cognitive and metacognitive action are not taught in the traditional sense of a training, but are generated and tested by the students themselves in cooperation with the teachers (for detail see below).

The problems of research on metacognition discussed above, and the advantages of the reconstruction of metacognitions within the RPST, can hence be summarized as follows: (a) Because a unified concept of metacognition is nowhere in sight and there furthermore exist no precise definition criteria as to what exactly *metacognition* is supposed to mean, we suggest that metacognitions be reconstructed as subjective theories about one's own learning/knowledge. The constructs elaborated in metacognition research can be subsumed under the broad variant of the RPST. (b) The advantage of a reconstruction of metacognitions as subjective theories consists in the assumption and correspondingly the reconstruction of an (at least implicit) argumentational structure that permits us to establish connections between different metacognitions and thus to explicitly model, for instance, the use of strategies depending on person and task characteristics. In our opinion this constitutes a progress by comparison to the way in which research on metacognition is traditionally conducted—isolated assessment of metacognition variables. The second advantage of a reconstruction of metacognitions within the RPST we see in the combination of metacognition and attribution theory, the latter potentially constituting the basis for an explicit argumentational structure. A linking of motivational/attributional variables and metacognitions can count as a desirable next step of theory elaboration within this area of research. (c) The assessment of metacognitions by traditional procedures such as questionnaires and standardized interviews is to be regarded as problematic in two respects: On the one hand, the reflexive subject's reflection space is only partially tapped; on the other hand, it remains unclear what exactly it is that the indicators of metcognition are supposed to measure. Assessing metacognitions by means of the dialogic methods of reconstruction provided by the RPST would take into consideration the reflexivity of the research objects in a more comprehensive manner and at the same time permit the investigation of those reasons that potentially guide the reflexive subjects' actions. (d) In addition, a reconstruction of metacognitions using dialogical procedures optimally provides the prerequisites for an exchange between subjective and objective theories, which constitutes an educationally constructive alternative to traditional training programs.

EXKURSUS: THE SURMOUNTING OF FALSE COMPETITIONS BETWEEN THEORIES AS SUPERCEDING THE CONSTRUCTIFICATION FALLACY

Apart from the integration of different theories through subsumption on an object-theoretical level (see above), the RPST also provides the possibility of surmounting false competitions between theories by means of partially metatheoretical integration—under recourse to the component of reflexivity, that is. The fact that the (currently predominating) information-processing approach does not consistently realize the implications resulting from the cognitive constructive perspective on the explanation of human information processing on the theoretical as well as the empirical level constitutes one reason among others for the development of such false competitions between theories. What is especially being neglected is the possibility of reflexive choices (available to the research object), which is already inherent in the construct of cognitive constructivity. Within the information-processing approach, this aspect is neither sufficiently discussed nor accounted for methodologically—in particular because knowledge is modeled and investigated in isolation from its subjective context of usage. Instead the question of the formal functioning of information processing in terms of a system theoretical input–output model (see above) is central. Below, we will attempt to show on the basis of concrete research examples that when reflexivity in the sense of a situation-specific choice of processing strategies is consistently taken into account, it is possible to disentangle false competitions between theories.

In the area of verbal learning in particular, the neglect of reflexivity as the possibility of consciously choosing processing strategies has led to a series of basically unnecessary, partially even absurd, competitions between theories. This includes, for example, the question of the choice of the organizational core in sentence processing. Within the basic research on psychology of memory it has been unanimously shown (e.g., Bock, 1978) that the processing of language items on the word, sentence, and textual level can be described by means of the recoding principle (organization and integration of bits of isolated information into comprehensive units) developed by Miller (1956). On the word level, integration is effected, for instance, by the summarizing of separate concepts into a generic term (which may be generated according to subjective preferences), which then functions as an organizational core (e.g., Bower, Clark, Lesgold, & Winzenz, 1969; Mandler, 1967). Which word on the sentence level is the one to function as the organizational core is, however, controversial. While propositional approaches that take Fillmore's (1968) casus theory, focusing the sentence predicate as a starting point, assume that this part is played by the verb (e.g., Kintsch, 1974), and the psychological relevance of verb dominance could be experimentally confirmed in a series of studies (e.g., Raue & Wilczok, 1973;

Engelkamp, 1977), approaches also exist which assume that it is the sentence subject that functions as organizational core (Bock, 1978). Thus for instance a higher reproduction probability could be demonstrated for the sentence subject (followed by object, adjective, and verb: e.g., Clark, 1966; Blumenthal, 1967), assuming that the sentence subject is (semantically) processed more intensively. While Bock (1978, p. 43), after reviewing a multitude of studies, comes to the conclusion that in sentence processing it is clearly the subject that functions as organizational core, in our opinion the data do not permit such a straightforward interpretation. Instead we believe that it is in fact quite probable that the recipient can choose among different processing strategies depending on the stimulus material (Groeben, 1982, p. 31).

This in our opinion also applies to the problem of forgetting syntactic and semantic information in sentence processing. The frequently quoted study by Sachs (1967) could demonstrate that syntactic information is forgotten more rapidly than semantic information (in comparing a syntactically or semantically deviation from a previously heard sentence, syntactic changes were recognized as such only if the original and the test sentence immediately followed each other; by contrast, semantic changes were also recognized after a longer time interval). Together with other studies (e.g., Engelkamp, 1973; Fillenbaum, 1966) this study constitutes the basis for the coining of the phrase of the dominant part of semantics in sentence processing. However, studies exist that have yielded contrary results—that semantic information is forgotten more rapidly than syntactic information if the attention of the subjects is directed towards syntactic aspects (e.g., Graesser & Mandler, 1975; Luther & Fenk, 1984). On the basis of these discrepant results, the possibility of the differential use of processing strategies depending on the respective task suggests itself.

In the area of semantic memory, competition between network and feature models is frequently observed. The decisive difference between the two consists in the fact that network models make the additional assumption of a hierarchic organization of memory structure. This assumption could be confirmed in so-called verification tasks for the understanding of language items. Sentences such as "A canary can sing" are verified more rapidly than sentences such as "A canary can fly"—because *singing* is more directly linked to the concept of *canary* than is *flying* (Collins & Quillian, 1969). This result is compatible with the principle of cognitive economy postulated by network models, by which attributes are encoded on the highest possible concept level. Not compatible with this principle, however, are findings of studies conducted within feature theory (Smith, Shoben, & Rips, 1974). The feature model distinguishes between defining and characteristic concepts of a category. The exemplars (robin, duck) of a category (bird) may have the same defining attributes but differ with regard to the characteristic attributes and thus have a greater or smaller distance to the respective category. It could in fact be empirically demonstrated that sentences such as "A robin is a bird" are verified more rapidly than sentences such as "A duck is a bird." This result can not be predicted on the basis of network mod-els because robin and bird are situated on the same level of the network hier-archy (Bredenkamp & Wippich, 1977, p. 113). The competition between the two models can again be surmounted by recourse to the strategy concept. In case of language material that is organized in a logical and hierarchical man-ner, processing takes place via hierarchical analysis. In case of material that shows an inner differentiation on one level only, processing (presumably) takes place via analysis on the basis of characteristic features (Groeben, 1982, p. 36).

Data concerning the question of the processing of metaphors are also inco-herent. It is controversial whether the processing of a metaphorical expression is more time consuming than the processing of a literal expression. While cur-rent theories of metaphor, such as the interaction theory of Black (1979) or the three-stage model of metaphor comprehension by Searle (1979), postulate that it takes longer to understand a metaphor than a nonmetaphor, the proponents of the information-processing approach (e.g., T. Herrmann, 1985; Rumelhart, 1979) assume that metaphors are processed just as rapidly as literal expressions. According to the three-stage model by Searle (1979), in the first step a literal interpretation of the respective utterance is attempted; in the second step the adequacy of this interpretation to the respective context is tested. If context ade-quacy is lacking, in a third step a metaphorical expression is inferred. Going through these phases makes the processing of metaphors more time consuming than the processing of normal language expressions. This hypothesis could be empirically confirmed in a study by Janus and Bever (1985; replication of a study by Ortony, Schallert, Reynolds, & Antos, 1978). Verbrugge and McCar-rell (1977) presented (more indirect) evidence in favor of this hypothesis: On the basis of the assumption that a prolonged processing time in the compre-hension of metaphors is due to additional inference processes that are necessary for the decoding of the metaphor, they could show that such additional infer-ence processes in metaphor comprehension do indeed take place (the ground of a metaphor to be inferred constitutes an effective retrieval cue for the metaphor itself). In contrast, the proponents of the information processing approach assume that metaphors are understood directly—that is, not against the back-ground of their literal meaning—and that for this reason the processing time is not increased by comparison to literal expressions (T. Herrmann, 1985). Accordingly it is assumed that there is no qualitative difference between the comprehension of a metaphor and a nonmetaphor (Rumelhart, 1979). Indeed some findings are incompatible with the "literal first" thesis. Thus Ortony et al. (1978) found that the comprehension of metaphors does not require additional processing steps provided that there is sufficient context information for the lis-tener to build up expectations concerning the meaning of a metaphor. The find-ings by Glucksberg, Gildea & Bookin (1982) also contradict the literal first the-sis: In a verification task the metaphoric expression was verified more rapidly than the literal meaning as long as the expression was plausible if taken as a metaphor but wrong if taken literally. These conflicting findings (see the long-lasting debate on this issue between Dascal, e.g. 1987 and Gibbs, e.g. 1989) can in our opinion also be resolved by taking recourse to the concept of the possibility of choosing between alternative strategies. Whether a metaphor requires longer processing time than a literal equivalent would then depend on which of the listener's reference systems is actually activated. Metaphors that are conventional or familiar in relation to the listener's reference system (or that he or she wants to understand in a conventional way) certainly do not require more processing time than nonmetaphorical expressions. However, metaphors that are new against the background of the listener's reference system presumably require more time to be processed. Presumably the listener himself or herself can choose the depth at which the expression is to be processed: conventional metaphors also allow for a nonconventional interpretation (Groeben, 1993); unconventional metaphors can be mistaken for nonsense expressions.

In all these cases, competing theories are involved that can be overcome by recourse to the complementary problem of the reification fallacy, which we shall call *constructification fallacy*. The methodological norm of the avoidance of reification decrees that it is inadmissible to equate theoretical constructs (as constructions on observable processes taking place in reality) with what is directly observable (Holzkamp, 1964; McCorquodale & Meehl, 1948). Tolman's assumption, for instance, that rats "have at their disposal cognitive maps" even in case of a metaphorical reading of the concept map clearly will refer to a construct only; hence it would be nonsensical and inadmissible to impute the real existence of such maps in the heads of the experimental animals. This, however, presupposes that a clear decision as to the existence/nonexistence of a reification is possible. This, however, is problematic if the possibility of reflexivity and hence self-knowledge is attributed to the research object as well. In this case, one must at least in principle act upon the assumption that the possibility of arriving at knowledge is approximately equal for both the subject and object of research; in this case constructs generated by the research subject would be identical with the observable reality. The constructs are real in the sense that they are present in the knowledge of the research object and guide his or her actions (Groeben, 1994). Theoretical constructs or models of psychology that (at least partially) refer to the reflexivity of human beings hence frequently constitute cases in which no decision on reification is possible. But if no safe decision whatsoever can be made about whether a specific theoretical assumption constitutes a construct (exclusively) on the level of scientific theorizing or perhaps also on the level of (subjective) reflections of the research object (with regard to the possibility of choosing ways of cognitive processing), it would make little sense to regard contradictory or competing assumptions in this respect as competition to scientific theories. For this constitutes by explication a competition on the objective theoretical level *only:* a competition *about* the area of research, not *in* the area of research. In cases where it is not possible to decide on the question of reification, this competition—better: alternativity—likewise can occur on the level of the subject matter—in the reflexivity of the subjective everyday psychologist. In this case, the assumption of competition between theories implies so to speak the complementary category error to that of the reification fallacy. While in the reification fallacy the purely theoretical construct explication is projected onto the level of the scientific subject matter, in the complementary error a distinction existing in the area of the scientific subject matter is regarded a purely theoretical one: For this complementary type of error, we suggest the term *constructification fallacy*. These two complementary category errors do, by the way, have approximately the same effect; that is, an unnecessary reduction of the flexibility of scientific theorizing. In case of the reification fallacy, the flexibility is limited by erroneously assuming that the respective construct refers to reality itself; in case of the constructification fallacy, an exaggerated claim to validity is made without taking into account that the reflexive human being himself or herself—depending on specific antecedents—can choose among processing alternatives corresponding to supposedly competing approaches. This impossibility of making decisions about the question of reification, and the consequent danger of constructification for scientific theorizing, presumably occur whenever the research object has an at least implicit knowledge about possible alternative processing strategies and thus at the same time the possibility of choosing between different strategies depending on situational factors, plans, and goals. The concept of strategy already implies that the research object has at least intuitive explanatory concepts concerning their efficacy available and is thus able to intentionally employ those strategies.

In our opinion, more recent models of learning, language comprehension, and memory in particular increasingly generate constructs that imply that the object of research may be capable of reflections leading to self-knowledge, and for which the question of reification can hence not be decided. Within more recent schema theoretical developments this includes, for instance, the plot–unit model (Lehnert, 1981), which provides an explanation-driven coherence structure between plots; likewise the source–goal–plan model (Abbott & Black, 1986), which in generating story units takes recourse to the goal-directed reasons and motives of the actors involved. This also includes the conceptualization of comprehension processes within mental models (e.g., Johnson-Laird, 1985), which assumes that the research object can employ different strategies in generating a coherent mental model. A particularly striking example is constituted by the modification of the concept of coherence within the research on text processing: While earlier approaches of text processing conceptualized coherence as a property of the text (e.g., Kintsch, 1974), more recent approaches concede (e.g., van Dijk & Kintsch, 1983) that in explicating the concept of coherence, the flexibility of potential processing strategies of the research object has to be taken into account. The choice of the processing strategy used is taken to depend on the reception goal and the recipient's knowledge.

If theories relating to the same area of research are in competition, and there are for that area of research good reasons for the assumption that the research object has at least an intuitive knowledge of processing strategies, these only apparent competitions can be resolved by recourse to the methodological level where a decision as to the question of reification cannot be made (by assuming a possibility of strategy choice on the level of the scientific subject matter). If the reflexivity of the research object is taken into account to permit the research object to choose from a reservoire of available strategies that he or she considers to be suitable to a concrete task, theories that claim that only one of those strategies exists or is effective can only be regarded as an inadmissible constructification. The assumption that the individual thus is able to employ strategies flexibly is supported on the one hand by the findings of research on metacognition. On the other hand, it could be demonstrated empirically, especially for the area of language comprehension, that the manner of processing is strongly determined by task demands (e.g., Bobrow & Bower, 1969) and the experimental material (e.g., Mistler-Lachman, 1972; for a comprehensive discussion of the concept of strategy within the psychology of language, see Hörmann, 1976). Within psychology of memory the results on strategy use depending on task demands found within the levels of processing approach can count as evidence in favor of the above assumption (Craik & Lockhart 1972).

Because of the focal role it ascribes to human reflexivity as a central attribute of the research object, the RPST is especially well suited to resolve potential constructification fallacies in former research. For what happens in constructification is that certain assumptions are located, so to speak, one level too high—that is, on the level of scientific theorizing—while really—in order to be more empirically fruitful—they are to be situated on the scientific object level. Theoretical models that suffer in this way from the constructification fallacy hence never will be able to adequately reconstruct and explain the plasticity and constructivity of human information processing and of human learning in particular. In a first step, the contribution of the RPST will consist in resolving those cases in which earlier research has erroneously underestimated the cognitive flexibility of its object as far as this is possible and makes sense. A next step would be to systematically elaborate which exactly are the conditions determining the choice of a processing strategy; that is, which specific situational conditions must be implemented in order to resolve the competition in the above examples. In our opinion, this can be achieved by the dialogical reconstruction procedures provided within the RPST. The integration potential of the RPST thus manifests itself, on the one hand, in the surmounting of fruitless and unnecessary theory competitions, and, on the other, in its innovation potential in the elaboration of new interaction hypotheses.

INNOVATIVE GOAL PERSPECTIVES FOR RESEARCH
AND METHODOLOGY

If one takes metacognition research as a starting point, knowledge about one's own knowledge (deficiencies, competences, conscious use of strategies) always presupposes reflexivity and potential self-knowledge. Although empirical research in this area has not consistently succeeded in demonstrating a positive influence of metaknowledge on learning performance (see, however, the problems of assessing metacognitions discussed earlier), in our opinion one ought to hold on to reflexivity as a goal for optimizing learning processes on metatheoretical as well as object-theoretical grounds.

In our opinion, reflexivity constitutes a prerequisite for that rationality that the human being potentially is able to attain. We regard this potential for rationality as a very fundamental constructive potential of the reflexive subject (Groeben & Scheele, 1977, pp. 65ff.). Against the background of the above assumptions resulting from the epistemological "model of man," we assume that a conceptualization of psychology within the social sciences ought to focus on this constructive potential of human beings from reflexivity to rationality. This is not to say that subjective reflections are always rational; instead, rationality constitutes a prescriptive–descriptive criterion for evaluating the quality of the research object's reflections (for an explication of criteria for the evaluation of subjective rationality, see Groeben, 1988b, pp. 97ff.). The recourse to subjective reflections on one's own learning is necessary for the diagnosis of suboptimal rationality as well as the improvement of the research object's reflections on self-knowledge. For it is to be expected that research objects differ with regard to the degree to which their reflections are differentiated, complete, and adequate to reality—objects of research differ to the extent to which they have explicit knowledge of their own learning—and depending on the respective level of explicitness, differential didactic procedures have to be employed in order to suitably deal with that knowledge (for a research example see Christmann & Groeben, 1993). Positive results on autonomous learning that under the perspective of educational application can count as the optimal case of learning as such, in our opinion constitute sufficient evidence to conclude that an improvement of reflections relating to the self might in turn lead to an improvement of learning performance. According to studies within the expert–novice paradigm, it is a characteristic of autonomous learners that they have at their disposal a repertoire of different strategies to guide their thinking and acting that they can employ in a conscious and planful manner; typically they are also capable of self-observation; able to reflect on their own learning and performance, to draw conclusions, and to put these to a constructive use in the restructuring of problems and generating of new strategies (for a survey cf. Beck, 1989; Glaser & Bassok, 1989). What is characteristic for such learners is the flexible use of strategies depending on situation and task variables. For the building up of the capacity of autonomous learning reflexivity does, however, constitute an indispensable prerequisite.

This is also demonstrated, for instance, by the integrated manuals for the procedural management of text learning developed by Weltner (1974, 1978). In relation to the subject matter to be covered by the learner, these manuals contain strategies for the individual planning and setting of learning goals and concrete instructions for the initiation of learning activities; in addition they also prepare for potential learning problems. Their main focus is on the diagnosis of learning states and deficits, and the offering of aid for compensating these deficits. In addition, the manual contains a series of reliably effective learning techniques as well as strategies for self-motivation and self-control. The processes of self-evaluation that are initiated by the respective strategies and presuppose reflexive processes constitute a decisive factor in this program. The efficacy of the integrated manual by comparison to textbooks and classroom teaching could be empirically confirmed (measurement of learning increase).

Likewise the positive experiences with metacognition trainings by comparison to simple trainings of learning strategies demonstrate the importance of giving an even greater weight to the component of reflexivity in order to optimize learning processes (Campione, 1984; Hasselhorn, 1987). Metacognition trainings are conducted according to the principle that the efficacy of strategy use and procedures of self-control be explained and thus made transparent to the learner under recourse to his or her own cognitive system, and that conditions for the use of strategies be specified. The success of this way of proceeding decisively depends on whether the learner, by means of suitable didactic measures, can be made to become conscious of himself or herself and his or her own cognitive potential, and to reflect thereon (Bromme, 1992). At the same time these findings demonstrate the necessity of building up declarative as well as executive metaknowledge in combination with task-specific knowledge and of putting them in relation to each other. In our opinion, dialogic teaching–learning models are better suited to the initiation and amplification of reflexive processes than traditional teaching models, as they concentrate on comprehending individual learning processes and match the strategies to be imparted with individual needs/problems. The manner in which individual comprehension processes can be taken into account in building up declarative and executive metaknowledge is demonstrated, for instance, by the studies conducted within the project "Autonomous Learners" (Bachmann, Guldimann, Niedermann, & Zutavern 1990); at the same time they constitute a first step towards approximating the goals to be pursued within the RPST. In this research project strategies are not imparted through training, but the students themselves generate the cognitive and metacognitive strategies that they regard as suitable. This is done in interaction with teachers and other students who function as models as well as by self-observation, reflection, and evaluation of their own learning (see above). This approach has already been used in text writing, mathematical problem solving, and learning from texts. The authors try to realize two central goals: On the one hand, they want to systematically observe whether in school the students' already existing capacities for problem solving and their reflections on their own learning are taken into consideration; on the other hand, they want to improve students' self-reflections and their application to learning in cooperation with the teachers (Bachmann et al., 1990, p. 1).

Under the first of the above goal perspectives they assume that students do in fact "have at their disposal a network of knowledge on explanation and strategies with regard to their learning activities for which in turn they are able to give reasons" (Bachmann et al., 1990, p. 3); they further assume that this knowledge is not yet as closely interconnected as for instance in the case of experts. Hence, their central question is whether school teaching contributes towards "making this cognitive network more dense" (p. 3). They have attempted to find an answer to this question by means of interviews and questionnaires, in particular by comparing results obtained from fourth and seventh graders. In relation to the efficacy of school teaching for instance in the area of composition the results are frustrating. Metacognitive aspects of knowledge on text production and its teachability in particular are extremely poor, rather stereotyped, and represent only mechanically learned knowledge; in particular there is hardly any progress from fourth to seventh grade, as the following comparison of answers to the question "Are you satisfied with your text?" demonstrates:

Fourth grade:
• Yes. Because there are some good things in it.
• Not really, because it's too short.
• Yes. Because it's a sad story and hard to write down.
• Yes. Because there are some good sentences in it, and sometimes there aren't.
• Yes. Because it's a good text and has some detailed description.
• Not quite. There's too little description.
Seventh grade:
• Yes. It's not long, but there's something in it.
• Well—it's always sort of the same words and no good choice of words.
• Yes, it's a bit short and not so personal.
• I think so, yes. It describes a bit of everything.
• No, not really. I should have written more and in greater detail.[1] (Bachmann et al., 1990, p. 5)

According to Bachmann et al., one possible explanation for these negative results might be that the students would like to evaluate their text production autonomously but come into conflict with the teacher's evaluation on whom

---

[1] Quotations on pages 71 and 72 were translated by M. Schreier and U. Christmann.

they are dependent. In any case the conclusion that school normally does not take students' subjective learning theories as a starting point seems justified (p. 6).

Improving this state of affairs is the second explicit goal of the project. For this purpose, the following intervention strategies are used that are supposed to permit the students to individually take recourse to as well as to further develop their subjective learning theories:

- observation and selective imitation of models (modelling);
- self observation and written documentation of one's own cognitions (monitoring);
- analysis of experience gained with the learning partner (evaluating);
- exchange of results and amplification of one's repertoire of strategies in group meetings (conferencing);
- retrospective reflection on what has been learnt (reflecting). (Beck, 1989, p. 3)

First results demonstrate that this procedure does indeed lead to greater differentiation and specification of the students' subjective learning theories. Thus, for instance, even a student who was regarded by the teacher as a poor learner was able to record the following self-instruction in his exercise book:

> I should more often approach a new task more spontaneously, solve it by myself, battle my way through, and achieve results . . . .
> Under no circumstances must I present aloud something I didn't get even when reading it slowly. If I read it aloud, it will be even faster, and the others won't get it anyway. I'll present only things which I found easy to understand.[1] (Bachmann et al. 1990, p. 9)

In our opinion, this project is of interest for the very reason that it indeed starts out in a nondirective way from those reflections the students themselves contribute. The subjective reflections on one's own learning, as well as a reconstruction of the structure of those reflections as it is provided by the dialogue–consensus procedures developed within the RPST, is, however, not systematically assessed (see below).

Such a systematic reconstruction of subjective theories about one's own learning processes already constitutes the first step towards the initiation and amplification of reflections about one's own learning. By assessing subjective learning theories in dialogue, implicit knowledge, for instance, is definitely rendered more explicit. Further improvement of reflections relating to the self can then start out from this explicit knowledge of the research object.

By reconstructing subjective learning theories new perspectives for asking research questions can be elaborated; at the same time possibilities for the solution of old problems of metacognitive training research can be developed.

The fruitfulness of proceeding in this way is demonstrated in a first step by the study conducted by Bereiter and Scardamalia (1989) on the comparison of naive learning theories of children to those of adults. According to this study, adults regard learning as a problem-solving process in the service of superordinated goals and accordingly also give strategies for achieving these goals. Children, on the contrary, regard learning and knowledge acquisition as an activity that is not directed towards long-term goals. When asked about their learning, they accordingly mention only routine procedures. It also emerged that children have unrealistic expectations as to how rapidly they will be able to learn something. At the same time the interview protocols showed that children do have an at least implicit knowledge about some aspects of learning that are relevant in objective theories. Thus, for instance, they differentiate between declarative and procedural knowledge, know about the hierarchical structuring of knowledge, and are also aware of the possibility of approaching different types of knowledge from different cognitive perspectives. These studies illustrate, on the one hand, that even children already have an implicit knowledge about learning processes, and, on the other hand, that it might not be indicated to impart to children an entire arsenal of learning strategies, as they do not think in terms of long-term goal–means schemata; hence it would be more advisable to first amplify their reflexivity with regard to the importance of learning per se—particularly for achieving long-term goals—and to thus establish a basis for the later imparting of learning strategies.

From this the following particularly fruitful questions can be derived for a reconstruction of subjective learning theories within a corresponding elaboration of the RPST:

- What is the position and what is the subjective meaning of learning in the everyday life of students?
- Is a connection established between everyday experience and learning in school?
- Are there desirable learning goals for students, and what are the means they use for attaining those goals?
- How do students view the process of knowledge acquisition and knowledge incorporation?
- What are the metacognitive and cognitive strategies learners have at their disposal, and what are the conditions under which they are employed?
- How is the efficacy of these strategies to be explained according to the learners' opinion?
- What are the convictions students have regarding their own learning capacity in different fields? How do they explain these different capacities?
- Are students at all interested in improving their own learning, and what means do they use towards such an improvement?
- How do they deal with negative experience and failure?

In taking these perspectives into account it becomes possible to assess the state of learners' reflections on knowledge and convictions in much greater detail than is currently done by global diagnoses on the basis of testing procedures. This might at the same time solve a problem central to metacognitive training approaches. Research in this field has been facing the fundamental difficulty that the trainings have interindividually different effects. The general and specific knowledge of the learners count as the central predictor for the efficacy of the trainings; this, however, cannot be assessed sufficiently by means of the traditional testing procedures as well as the more sophisticated knowledge diagnoses of the information-processing approach (Hasselhorn, 1987). Here a reconstruction of subjective learning theories might yield differential indicators for the use of trainings precisely because they start out from the individual structures of knowledge and beliefs. Before strategy knowledge is imparted through training, we would, however, suggest that the reflections of the research object be individually amplified, supplemented, or completed under recourse to objective theories (for an exchange between subjective and objective theories, see above).

A reconstruction of subjective theories as complex units of an action-theoretical conceptualization of psychology in our opinion cannot take place within the traditional experimental methodology. For experimental methodology the systematic control and manipulation of variables is constitutive. Hence it must of necessity miss out on the arising of "natural spontaneous intentionality" as a central attribute of the action-theoretical approach. The research object's reflexive processes are—as long as they are not relevant to the issue in question—either kept constant or eliminated as interfering variables (Groeben, 1986, pp. 252ff.). Research on the social psychology of the experiment has been able to clearly demonstrate the potentially resulting distortions and artefacts (e.g., Bungard, 1980).

The questionnaire method, which is excessively used in psychology, is likewise not optimal for the reconstruction of subjective theories, because the questionnaire items refer to a reality already given and prestructured with regard to content by the researcher. Whether the research object shares this point of view remains at least partially open, and for this reason it can in principle not be decided whether the classical methodological criterion of internal validity is in fact met (Scheele in Groeben et al., 1988, p. 129). In addition, the questionnaire method does not optimally take into account the capacity of the research object for language and communication; instead the questionnaire items are worded in the language of the subject, not of the object of research, and hence presupposes the researcher's view of reality. This procedure does, however, by no means guarantee the desired intersubjectivity, since subjects understand and differentially interpret given language items depending on contextual factors. Likewise, premolded language templates would hardly be suitable for the assessment of the cognitive belief system of the intentionally acting subject, as it becomes manifest in subjective theories in particular. In our opinion, this does, however, require the recourse to the everyday language of the research object (Birkhan, 1992; Gigerenzer, 1981; Obliers, 1992; Scheele, 1992).

Accordingly we propose for the reconstruction of subjective learning theories a methodology that in accordance with the goal characteristics of the epistemological "model of man" starts out from the research object's capacity for language and communication: the assessment of the reconstruction adequacy in dialogue–consensus (first phase of the two-phase research structure, see above). For the implementation of this procedure Scheele (in Groeben et al., 1988) has, under recourse to a speech act theoretical framework, elaborated concrete methodological criteria whose realization should provide for the possibility of an undistorted reconstruction of subjective reflections. In critically discussing the problem of whether cognitive processes are accessible to introspection (Nisbett & Wilson, 1977; Wilson & Nisbett, 1978), she maintains that the research object is in principle capable of verbalizing internal processes. It is, however, to be assumed that knowledge about cognitive processes is frequently only implicit. Accordingly the criteria she elaborated for the "ideal speech situation" (I actualization; II communication; III equality of the partners in communication; IV argumentativeness of communication; V readiness to confront the issue; VI insightful acceptance of arguments) are aimed at creating those conditions that allow for the surmounting of the problem of the implicitness of internal processes. In order to meet these criteria, certain cognitive and motivational prerequisites must be realized on the part of the research object, which it is the researcher's task to stabilize (I motivation to make one's cognitions explicit and accessibility of those cognitions; II capacity for verbalization; III motivation for verbalization; IV capacity for argumentation; V motivation for self-knowledge; VI motivation for meaning and trust in making one's cognitions explicit. For a more detailed explication of this speech act theoretical framework, cf., e.g., Scheele in Groeben et al., 1988, pp. 142ff.).

The dynamics for making the implicit explicit inherent in dialogic reconstruction procedures has the effect that the method at least partially modifies the research object; and this is an aspect in which dialogic procedures fundamentally differ from traditional assessment procedures. To put it more specifically, this means that subjective theories become more explicit, precise, and coherent. This does, however, constitute an intended consequence of the "model of man" on which the RPST is based: the effecting of changes in the human being with regard to his or her positive potential for further development (Groeben, 1994; Scheele, 1988, p. 140).

Presently there exist several dialogue–consensus variants for the reconstruction of subjective theories (Dann, 1992b; Groeben et al., 1988; Scheele & Groeben, 1988a). The principle according to which the assessment is conducted (keeping structure and content separate) is the same for all these variants (Groeben, 1992) and will here, as an example, be demonstrated for the Heidelberg Structure Formation Technique (SFT), a procedure for the reconstruction of medium range subjective theories (Scheele & Groeben, 1984). The reconstruction of subjective theories by SFT takes place in two separate steps (one at a time). In the first step, the content of the subjective theory is assessed by means of a semistandardized interview. In the second step, the structure of the subjective theory is reconstructed by means of a structure formation game. This game contains a structure formation manual as well as formal relations for definition and explanation; with the aid of these relations a structure is formed containing the central concepts of the subjective theory. Following the interview, the research object studies the structure formation manual, which in the following session enables him or her to form a structure of his or her subjective theory containing those concepts extracted from the interview by the researcher and judged by the research object as to their adequacy. This structure formed by the research object is compared to a structure formed by the interviewer (which shows the interviewer's understanding of the research object's verbalizations). The final structure is determined in dialogue between research subject and object, the view of the research object being decisive in cases of disagreement. A first advantage of this dialogue–consensus method thus lies in the fact that the explication support (of the ideal speech situation) helps to make even those parts of the research objects' metacognitive knowledge—which in everyday acting might possibly be and remain merely implicit—accessible to (conscious) verbalization; secondly—and this constitutes yet another advantage of this method—an explicit structure is formed by which the individual reflexive statements are interconnected which offers an optimal starting point for testing the operative efficacy (the extent to which the subjective theory does in fact guide the reflexive subject's actions) as well as the degree to which the subjective theory is modified through the exchange with objective scientific theories.

The subjective theories reconstructed in the above manner are in a first step analyzed idiographically, in particular with regard to the coherence and completeness of their structure. A nomothetical analysis is, however, also possible by concentrating on the formal characteristics of the structure of subjective theories (coherence, empty slots, differentiation, degree of structuring) as well as in combination with procedures such as content and text analysis (Scheele & Groeben, 1988a; for procedures allowing to nomothetically summarize subjective theories, cf. Obliers & Vogel, 1992; Stössel & Scheele, 1992; for a computer-aided analysis, c.f. Oldenbürger, 1992; Mischo & Groeben, 1995; Oldenbürger & Schreier, 1995). As we pointed out at the beginning (see above), this method has so far only been used with adults, for instance teachers with regard to their subjective theories on teaching and their profession in general. The assessment of subjective learning theories, at least those of children and teenagers, necessitates further simplification and adaptation. A more flexible, adaptive dialogue-consensus variant that provides an everyday translation of the formal relations used in the classical variants was developed by Scheele, Groeben, and Christmann (1992). It allows the assessment of subjective theories of children and, in general, of persons who are not accustomed to the use of formal relations.

The reconstruction of subjective theories by dialogue–consensus achieves an understanding by description of the research object's inner knowledge and beliefs. Whether this description is indeed adequate to reality and operatively effective must always be empirically tested during the second phase (explanatory validation). This testing relates to the question of whether the reasons the subjective theoretician gives for his or her actions are indeed operatively effective; that is, whether they can count as causes of his or her actions for an external observer. In the correspondance of the inner and the outer perspective on the reflexive subject's knowledge and beliefs, the adequacy to reality of the actor's subjective theory, and hence his or her rationality, becomes manifest. Such a correspondance between reasons and causes certainly constitutes the optimal case. But even if the research object is wrong with regard to his or her self-reflections, it is of eminent importance to know these reflections in order to be able to explain and by modification of his or her subjective theories to possibly improve the reflexive subject's carrying out as well as abstaining from acting (cf. above: the problem of metacognitive knowledge not put to use, that is the problem of the lack of knowledge of inadequate strategies).

Current psychology, however, has so far mostly limited itself to the explanatory phase of research exclusively. In our opinion, this implies a reduction of the object of psychological research in the sense that the reflexivity and potential rationality of the reflexive subject could not be dealt with. The two-phase structure of research in our opinion realizes a conceptualization of psychology that deals with the subject matter of psychological research in an unreduced manner. The phase of understanding by description takes into account the capacity for reflexivity with regard to the world in which the human being lives; the phase of explanation by observation tests the degree to which the reflexive subject's inner perspective is adequate to reality. A testing of the correspondance between inner and outer perspective can only be achieved by means of the combination of these two phases—and this is to say by means of the integration of hermeneutics and empirics in the sense of an understanding–explanative conceptualization of psychology (Groeben, 1986).

To summarize: We consider a reconstruction of subjective learning theories within the RPST to be innovative and progressive for the following reasons: (a) For an optimization of learning processes, the improvement and amplification of reflexions on self-knowledge (especially in the sense of furthering the constructive potential for development of the human being) can count as a goal perspective on metatheoretical as well as object-theoretical grounds. (b) The realization of this goal perspective cannot be achieved within the current experimental methodology in psychology, as this does not permit to reconstruct the component of reflexivity in an adequate, comprehensive, and unreduced manner. The RPST, as an action-theoretical conceptualization of psychology, by contrast, conceptualizes the research process so as to consistently be in accordance with the core assumptions of rationality, reflexivity, and the capacity for language and communication of the human being, and is consequently especially suited to comprehensively take into consideration subjective reflexions. (c) A reconstruction of subjective learning theories within the RPST can and ought to be achieved by means of a dialogue–consensus procedure which distinguishes between content and structure of subjective theories. The advantage of a reconstruction of subjective learning theories by consensus in dialogue consists in the fact that parts of metacognitive knowledge that normally remain implicit by means of this method are made accessible to verbalization. The explicit knowledge thus depicted in form of a structure constitutes the starting point for an improvement of reflexions on self-knowledge and the testing of the operative efficacy of subjective theories. (d) The amplification and modification of subjective reflections on one's own learning can on this basis be achieved by an exchange between "objective" and subjective learning theories.

REFERENCES

Abbott, V., & Black, J.B. (1986). Goal-related differences in comprehension. In J.A. Galambos, R.P. Abelson, & J.B. Black (Eds.), *Knowledge structures* (pp. 123–142). Hillsdale, NJ: Erlbaum.

Abramson, L.Y., Seligman, M.E.P., & Teasdale, J.D. (1978). Learned helplessness in humans: Critique and reformulation. *Journal of Abnormal Psychology, 87,* 49–74.

Anderson, J.R., & Bower, G.H. (1973). *Human associative memory.* Washington, DC: Winston.

Apel, K.D. (1964/65). Die Entfaltung der "sprachanalytischen Philosophie" und das Problem der "Geisteswissenschaften". *Philosophisches Jahrbuch, 72,* 240ff.

Bachmann, T., Guldimann, T., Niedermann, R., & Zutavern, U. (1990). *Schülertheorien über Lernen.* Forschungsstelle der pädagogischen Hochschule St. Gallen.

Barthels, M. (1991). *Subjektive Theorien über Alkoholismus.* Münster: Aschendorff.

Bartlett, F. (1932). *Remembering. A study in experimental and social psychology.* Cambridge, UK: Cambridge University Press.

Beck, E. (1989). *Eigenständige Lerner.* Beiträge, Informationen 89, Pädagogische Hochschule St. Gallen.

Bereiter, C., & Scardamalia, M. (1989). Intentional learning as a goal of instruction. In L.B. Resnick (Ed.), *Knowing, learning, and instruction.* Essays in honor of Robert Glaser (pp. 361–392). Hillsdale, NJ: Erlbaum.

Birkhan, G. (1992). Die (Un-)Brauchbarkeit der klassischen Testgütekriterien für Dialog-Konsens-Verfahren. In B. Scheele (Ed.), *Struktur-Lege-Verfahren als Dialog-Konsens-Methodik* (pp. 231-293). Münster: Aschendorff.

Black, M. (1979). More about metaphor. In A. Ortony (Ed.), *Metaphor and thought* (pp. 19–45). Cambridge, UK: Cambridge University Press.

Blumenthal, A.L. (1967). Prompted recall of sentences. *Journal of Verbal Learning and Verbal Behavior, 6,* 203–206.

Bobrow, S.A., & Bower, G.H. (1969). Comprehension and recall of sentences. *Journal of Experimental Psychology, 80,* 455–461.

Bock, M. (1978). *Wort-, Satz-, Textverarbeitung*. Stuttgart: Kohlhammer.

Borkowski, J.G., Carr, M., Rellinger, E., & Pressley, M. (1990). Self-regulated cognition. An interdependence of metacognition, attribution, and self-esteem. In B.F. Jones & L. Idol (Eds.), *Dimensions of thinking and cognitive instruction* (pp. 53–92). Hillsdale, NJ: Erlbaum.

Borkowski, J.G., & Krause, A.J. (1985). Metacognition and attributional beliefs. In G. D'Ydewalle (Ed.), *Cognition, information processing, and motivation* (pp. 557–568). Elsevier: North Holland.

Bousfield, W.A. (1953). The occurrence of clustering in the recall of randomly arranged associates. *Journal of General Psychology, 49,* 229–240.

Bower, G.H., Clark, M.C., Lesgold, A.M., & Winzenz, D. (1969). Hierarchical retrieval schemes in recall of categorized word lists. *Journal of Verbal Learning and Verbal Behavior, 8,* 323–343.

Bransford, J.D., & Franks, J.J. (1971). The abstraction of linguistic ideas. *Cognitive Psychology, 2,* 331–350.

Bredenkamp, J., & Wippich, W. (1977). *Lern- und Gedächtnispsychologie,* (Vol. I.). Stuttgart: Kohlhammer.

Bromme, R. (1992). *Der Lehrer als Experte. Zur Psychologie des professionellen Wissens.* Bern: Huber.

Brown, A.L. (1979). Theories of memory and the problems of development: Activity, growth, and knowledge. In L.S. Cermak & F.I.M. Craik (Eds.), *Levels of processing in human memory* (pp. 225–258). Hillsdale, NJ: Erlbaum.

Brown, A.L. (1984). Metakognition, Handlungskontrolle, Selbststeuerung und andere, noch geheimnisvollere Mechanismen. In F.E. Weinert & R.H. Kluwe (Eds.), *Metakognition, Motivation und Lernen* (pp. 60–109). Stuttgart: Kohlhammer.

Bruner, J.S., & Tagiuri, R. (1954). The perception of people. In G. Lindzey (Ed.), *Handbook of Social Psychology* (Vol. II, pp. 634–654). Cambridge, MA: Addison-Wesley.

Bungard, W. (Ed.). (1980). *Die "gute" Versuchsperson denkt nicht. Artefakte in der Psychologie.* München: Urban & Schwarzenberg.

Campione, J.C. (1984). Ein Wandel in der Instruktions forschung mit lernschwierigen Kindern. Die Berücksichtigung metakognitiver Komponenten. In F.E. Weinert & R.H. Kluwe (Eds.), *Metakognition, Motivation und Lernen* (pp. 109–132). Stuttgart: Kohlhammer.

Campione, J.C., & Brown, A.L. (1977). Memory and metamemory development in educable retarded children. In R.V. Kail & J.W. Hagen (Eds.), *Perspectives on the development of memory and cognition* (pp. 367–406). Hillsdale, NJ: Erlbaum.

Cavanaugh, J.C., & Perlmutter, M. (1982). Metamemory: A critical examination. *Child Development, 53,* 11–28.

Christmann, U., & Groeben, N. (1991). *Argumentationsintegrität (VI):* Subjektive Theorin über Argumentieren und Argumentationsintegrität—Erhebungsverfahren, inhaltsanalytische und heuristische Ergebnisse. Arbeiten aus dem SFB 245 "Sprechen und Sprachverstehen im sozialen Kontext," Bericht Nr. 34. Heidelberg/Mannheim.

Christmann, U., & Groeben, N. (1993). *Argumentationsintegrität (XI):* Retrognostische Überprüfung der Handlungsleitung Subjektiver Theorien über Argumentationsintegrität bei Kommunalpolitikern/innen. Arbeiten aus dem SFB 245 "Sprache und Situation," Bericht Nr. 64. Heidelberg/Mannheim.

Christmann, U., & Scheele, B. (1995). Subjektive Theorien über (un-)redliches Argumentieren. Ein Forschungsbeispiel für die kommunikative Validierung mittels Dialog-Konsens-Hermeneutik. In E. König & P. Zedler (Eds.), *Bilanz qualitativer Forschung*. Weinheim: Deutscher Studien Verlag.

Clark, H.H. (1966). The prediction of recall patterns in simple active sentences. *Journal of Verbal Learning and Verbal Behavior, 5,* 99–106.

Collins, A.M., & Quillian, M.R. (1969). Experiments on semantic memory and language comprehension. In L.W. Gregg (Ed.), *Cognition in learning and memory* (pp. 117–137). New York/London/Toronto: Wiley.

Craik, F.I.M., & Lockhart, R.S. (1972). Levels of Processing. A framework of memory research. *Journal of Verbal Learning and Verbal Behavior, 11,* 671–684.

Dann, H.-D. (1990). Subjective theories: A new approach to psychological research and educational practice. In G.R. Semin & J. Gergen (Eds.), *Everyday understanding: Social and scientific implications* (pp. 227-243). London: Sage Publications.

Dann, H.-D., Humpert, W., Krause, F., Kügelgen, T., Rimele, W. & Tennstädt, K.-Ch. (1982). *Arbeits- und Ergebnisbericht des Projekts "Aggression in der Schule."* Zentrum für Bildungsforschung, SFB 23. Universität Konstanz.

Dann, H.-D. (1992a). Subjective theories and their social foundation in education. In M. v. Cranach, W. Doise, & G. Mugny (Eds.), *Social representations and the social bases of knowledge* (pp. 161–168). Lewiston, NY: Hogrefe & Huber.

Dann, H.-D. (1992b). Variationen von Lege-Strukturen zur Wissensrepräsentation. In B. Scheele (Ed.), *Struktur-Lege-Verfahren als Dialog-Konsens-Methodik* (pp. 3–41). Münster: Aschendorff.

Dansereau, D.F., Collins, K.W., McDonald, B.A., Holley, Ch.D., Garland J., Drekhoft, G., & Evans, S.H. (1979). Development and evaluation of a learning strategy training program. *Journal of Educational Psychology, 71,* 64–73.

Dascal, M. (1987). Defending literal meaning. *Cognitive Science, 11,* 259–281.

Engelkamp, J. (1973). *Semantische Struktur und die Verarbeitung von Sätzen.* Bern: Huber.

Fillenbaum, S. (1966). Memory for gist: Some relevant variables. *Language and Speech, 9,* 217–227.

Fillmore, C.J. (1968). The case for case. In E. Bach & R.T. Harms (Eds.), *Universals in linguistic theory* (pp. 1–88). New York: Holt, Rinehart & Winston.

Fischer, P.M., & Mandl, H. (1980). *Selbstwahrnehmung und Selbstbewertung beim Lernen. Metakognitive Komponenten der Selbststeuerung beim Lernen mit Texten.* Deutsches Institut für Fernstudien an der Universität Tübingen, Forschungsbericht Nr. 10.

Fischer, P.M., & Mandl, H. (1981). *Metakognitive Regulation von Textverarbeitungsprozessen—Aspekte und Probleme des Zusammenhangs von metakognitiven Selbstaussagen und konkretem Leistungsverhalten.* Deutsches Institut für Fernstudien an der Universität Tübingen. Forschungsbericht Nr. 15.

Flavell, J.H. (1970). Developmental studies of mediated memory. In H.W. Reese & L.P. Lipsitt (Eds.), *Advances in child development and behavior* (pp. 181–211). New York: Academic Press.

Flavell, J.H., & Wellman, H.M. (1977). Metamemory. In R.V. Kail & J.W. Hagen (Eds.), *Perspectives on the development of memory and cognition* (pp. 3–33). Hillsdale, NJ: Erlbaum.

Gibbs, R.W. (1989). Understanding and literal meaning. *Cognitive Science, 13,* 243–251.

Gigerenzer, G. (1981). *Messung und Modellbildung in der Psychologie*. München/Basel: Reinhardt.

Glaser, R., & Bassock, M. (1989). Learning theory and the study of instruction. *Annual Review of Psychology, 40*, 631–666.

Glucksberg, S., Gildea, P. & Bookin, H.B. (1982). On understanding non-literal speech. Can people ignore metaphors? *Journal of Verbal Learning and Verbal Behavior, 21*, 85–98.

Graesser, A.C., & Mandler, G. (1975). Recognition memory for the meaning and surface structure of sentences. *Journal of Experimental Psychology: Human Learning and Memory, 104*, 238–248.

Groeben, N. (1982). *Leserpsychologie: Textverständnis—Textverständlichkeit*. Münster: Aschendorff.

Groeben, N. (1986). *Handeln, Tun, Verhalten als Einheiten einer verstehend-erklärenden Psychologie*. Tübingen: Francke.

Groeben, N. (1988a). Explikation des Konstrukts 'Subjektive Theorie'. In N. Groeben et al., Kap.2.2. (pp. 17–24). Tübingen: Francke.

Groeben, N. (1988b). Bewertung subjektiver Rationalität. In N. Groeben et al., Kap.3.3. (pp. 97–125). Tübingen: Francke.

Groeben, N. (1990). Subjective theories and the explanation of human action. In G.R. Semin & J. Gergen (Eds.), *Everyday understanding: Social and scientific implications* (pp. 19–44). London: Sage Publications.

Groeben, N. (1992). Die Inhalts-Struktur-Trennung als konstantes Dialog-Konsens-Prinzip?! In B. Scheele (Ed.), *Struktur-Lege-Verfahren als Dialog-Konsens-Methodik* (pp. 42–89). Münster: Aschendorff.

Groeben, N. (1993). Nicht-/Wörtlichkeit als Ästhetik von Alltagskommumikation. *SPIEL (Siegener Periodikum zur Internationalen Empirischen Literaturwissenschaft), 12,2*, 252–275.

Groeben, N. (1994). Humanistic models of human development. In T. Husen & T.N. Postlethwaite (Eds.), *International Encyclopedia of Education* (Vol. 5, 2nd ed., pp. 2689–2692). Oxford: Pergamon.

Groeben, N., & Scheele, B. (1977). *Argumente für eine Psychologie des reflexiven Subjekts*. Darmstadt: Steinkopff.

Groeben, N., Wahl, D., Schlee, J. & Scheele, B. (1988). *Forschungsprogramm Subjektive Theorien. Eine Einführung in die Psychologie des reflexiven Subjekts*. Tübingen: Francke.

Groteluschen, A.K., Borkowski, J.G., & Hale, C.H. (1990). Strategy instruction is often insufficient: Addressing the interdependency of executive and attributional processes. In T.E. Scruggs & B.Y.L. Wong (Eds.), *Intervention research in learning disabilities* (pp. 81–101). New York: Springer.

Grotjahn, R. (1991). The research programme Subjective Theories. *SSLA, 13*, 187–214.

Habermas, J. (1968). *Erkenntnis und Interesse*. Frankfurt: Suhrkamp.

Hasselhorn, M. (1987). Lern- und Gedächtnisförderung bei Kindern: Ein systematischer Überblick über die experimentelle Trainingsforschung. *Zeitschrift für Entwicklungspsychologie und Pädagogische Psychologie, 19,2*, 116–142.

Hasselhorn, M., Hager, W., & Barving, L. (1989). Zur Konfundierung metakognitiver und motivationaler Aspekte im Prädiktionsverfahren. *Zeitschrift für Experimentelle und Angewandte Psychologie, 36,1*, 31–41.

82   CHRISTMANN & GROEBEN

Heckhausen, H. (1984). Attributionsmuster für Leistungsergebnisse—individuelle Unterschiede, mögliche Arten und deren Genese. In F.E. Weinert & R.H. Kluwe (Eds.), *Metakognition, Motivation und Lernen* (pp. 133–163). Stuttgart: Kohlhammer.

Herrmann, D.J. (1984). Questionnaires about memory. In J.E. Harris & P.E. Morris (Eds.), *Everyday memory, actions and absent-mindedness* (pp. 133–151). London: Academic Press.

Herrmann, T. (1982). Über begriffliche Schwächen kognitivistischer Kognitionstheorien: Begriffsinflation und Akteur-System-Kontamination. *Sprache und Kognition, 1,* 3–14.

Herrmann, T. (1985). *Allgemeine Sprachpsychologie. Grundlagen und Probleme.* München/Wien/Baltimore: Urban & Schwarzenberg.

Holzkamp, K. (1964). *Theorie und Experiment in der Psychologie.* Berlin/New York: de Gruyter.

Hörmann, H. (1976). *Meinen und Verstehen. Grundzüge einer psychologischen Semantik.* Frankfurt: Suhrkamp.

Humpert, W., & Dann, H.-D. (1988). *Das Beobachtungssystem BAVIS. Beobachtungsverfahren zur Analyse von aggressionsbezogenen Interaktionen im Schulunterricht.* Göttingen: Hogrefe.

Janus, R.A., & Bever, T.G. (1985). Processing of metaphoric language: An investigation of the three-stage-model of metaphor comprehension. *Journal of Psycholinguistic Research, 14,* 473–487.

Johnson-Laird, P.N. (1985). *Mental models. Towards a cognitive science of language, inference, and consciousness.* Cambridge, UK: Cambridge University Press.

Jones, E.E., Kanouse, D.E., Kelley, H.H., Nisbett, R.E., Valins, S. & Weiner, B. (1971). *Attribution. Perceiving the causes of behavior.* Morristown, NJ: General Learning Press.

Kelley, H.H. (1967). Attribution theory in social psychology. *Nebraska Symposion on Motivation, 15,* 192–241.

Kelly, G.A. (1955). *The psychology of personal constructs* (Vol. I/II). New York: Norton.

Kintsch, W. (1974). *The representation of meaning in memory.* Hillsdale, NJ: Erlbaum.

Knopf, M. (1987). *Gedächtnis im Alter. Empirische Studien zur Entwicklung des verbalen Gedächtnisses bei älteren Menschen.* Berlin/Heidelberg/New York/London/Paris/Tokyo: Springer.

Körkel, J. (1987). *Die Entwicklung von Gedächtnis- und Metagedächtnisleistungen in Abhängigkeit von bereichsspezifischen Vorkenntnissen.* Frankfurt: Lang.

Kreutzer, M.A., Leonard, C., & Flavell, J.H. (1975). *An interview study of childrens' knowledge about memory.* Monographs of the Society for Research in Child Development, 40, 1. Serial No. 159.

Lachman, J.L., & Lachman, R. (1980). Age and the actualization of world knowledge. In L.W. Poon, Fozard, J.L., Cermak, L.S., Ahrenberg, D., & Thompson, L.W. (Eds.), *New directions in memory and aging* (pp. 285–312). Hillsdale, NJ: Erlbaum.

Laucken, U. (1974). *Naive Verhaltenstheorie.* Stuttgart: Klett-Cotta.

Lehnert, W.G. (1981). Plot-units and narrative summarization. *Cognitive Science, 4,* 293–331.

Luther, P., & Fenk, A. (1984). Wird der Wortlaut von Sätzen zwangsläufig schneller vergessen als ihr Inhalt? *Zeitschrift für Experimentelle und Angewandte Psychologie, 31,* 101–123.

Mandler, G. (1967). Organization and memory. In K.W. Spence & J.T. Spence (Eds.), *The Psychology of learning and motivation* (Vol. 1, pp. 327–372). New York: Academic Press.

McCorquodale, K., & Meehl, P.E. (1948). On a distinction between hypothetical constructs and intervening variables. *Psychological Review, 55,* 95–107.

Miller, G.A. (1956). The magical number seven plus or minus two: Some limits on our capacity for processing information. *Psychological Review, 63, 2,* 81–97.

Mischo, C., & Groeben, N. (in press). Bezugsnormorientierung: Warum sich LehrerInnen unterscheiden? *Empirische Pädagogik.*

Mistler-Lachman, J.L. (1972). Levels of comprehension in processing of normal and ambigious sentences. *Journal of Verbal Learning and Verbal Behavior, 11,* 614–623.

Nisbett, R.E., & Wilson, T. (1977). Telling more than we can know: Verbal reports on mental processes. *Psychological Review, 84, 3,* 231–259.

Obliers, R. (1992). Die programmimmanente Güte der Dialog-Konsens-Methodik: Approximation an die ideal Sprechsituation. In B. Scheele (Ed.), *Struktur-Lege-Verfahren als Dialog-Konsens-Methodik* (pp. 198-230). Münster: Aschendorff.

Obliers, R., & Vogel, G. (1992). *Subjektive Autobiographie-Theorien als Indikatoren mentaler Selbstkonfigurationen.* In B. Scheele (Ed.), *Struktur-Lege-Verfahren als Dialog-Konsens-Methodik* (pp. 296–332). Münster: Aschendorff.

Oldenbürger, H.-A. (1992). *Netz-Werk-Zeug 1. Zählwerk für beliebige Variablenkombinationen.* Göttingen.

Oldenbürger, H.-A., & Schreier, M. (in press). *Netzwerkzeug 1. Ein Programm zur Auszählung beliebiger Variablen-Kombinationen und seine Anwendung bei der Aggregierung Subjektiver Theorie-Strukturen.*

Ortony, A., Schallert, D.D., Reynolds, R., & Antos, S. (1978). Interpreting metaphors and idioms. Some effects of context on comprehension. *Journal of Verbal Learning and Verbal Behavior, 17,* 465–477.

Perlmutter, M. (1978). What is memory aging the aging of? *Developmental Psychology, 14,* 330–345.

Pressley, M. (1985). Review of Borkowski's insights. In S.R. Yussen (Ed.), *The growth of reflection in children* (pp. 145–148). New York: Academic Press.

Raue, B., & Engelkamp, J. (1977). Gedächtnispsychologische Aspekte der Verbvalenz. *Archiv für Psychologie, 129,* 157–174.

Rumelhart, D.E. (1979). Some problems with the notion of literal meanings. In A. Ortony (Ed.), *Metaphor and thought* (pp. 78–90). Cambridge, UK: Cambridge University Press.

Sachs, J.S. (1967). Recognition memory for syntactic and semantic aspects of connected discourse. *Perception and Psychophysics, 2,* (9) 437–442.

Scheele, B. (1988). *Rekonstruktionsadäquanz: Dialog-Hermeneutik.* In N. Groeben, D. Wahl, J. Schlee, & B. Scheele, Kap. 4.1. (pp. 126–179). Tübingen: Francke.

Scheele, B. (Ed.) (1992). *Struktur-Lege-Verfahren als Dialog-Konsens-Methodik.* Münster: Aschendorff.

Scheele, B., & Groeben, N. (1984). *Die Heidelberger Struktur-Lege-Technik (SLT)*. *Eine Dialog-Konsens-Methode zur Erhebung Subjektiver Theorien mittlerer Reichweite*. Weinheim.

Scheele, B., & Groeben, N. (1988a). *Dialog-Konsens-Methoden zur Rekonstruktion Subjektiver Theorien*. Tübingen: Francke.

Scheele, B., & Groeben N. (1988b). *Probleme bzw. Gegenstandsbereiche ohne (direkten) Lösungsanspruch*. In N. Groeben, D. Wahl, J. Schlee, & B. Scheele, Kap. 3.1. (pp. 35–46). Tübingen: Francke.

Scheele, B., Groeben, N., & Christmann, U. (1992). Ein alltagssprachliches Struktur-Lege-Spiel als Flexibilisierungsversion der Dialog-Konsens-Methodik. In B. Scheele (Ed.), *Struktur-Lege-Verfahren als Dialog-Konsens-Methodik* (pp. 198-230). Münster: Aschendorff.

Schlee, J. (1988). *Anwendung und Forschung: Das Beispiel 'Modifikation'*. In N. Groeben, D. Wahl, J. Schlee, & B. Scheele, Kap. 7.1. (pp. 292–310). Tübingen: Francke.

Schneider, W. (1985). Developmental trends in the metamemory-memory behavior relationship: An integrative review. In D.L. Forrest-Pressley, G.E. MacKinnon, & T.G. Waller (Eds.), *Cognition, metacognition, and human performance* (Vol. 1, pp. 57–109). New York.

Schneider, W., & Pressley, M. (1989). *Memory development between 2 and 20*. New York/Berlin/Heidelberg/London/Paris/Tokyo: Springer.

Schneider, W., Körkel, J., & Vogel, K. (1987). Zusammenhänge zwischen Metagedächtnis, strategischem Verhalten und Gedächtnisleistungen im Grundschulalter: Eine entwicklungspsychologische Studie. *Zeitschrift für Entwicklungspsychologie und Pädagogische Psychologie, 19*, 99–115.

Searle, J.R. (1979). Metaphor. In A. Ortony (Ed.), *Metaphor and thought* (pp. 92–123). Cambridge, UK: Cambridge University Press.

Skinner, B.F. (1948). *Walden two*. New York: Macmillan.

Skinner, B.F. (1973). *Jenseits von Freiheit und Würde*. Hamburg: Rowohlt.

Smith, E.E., Shoben, E.J., & Rips, L.J. (1974). Structure and process in semantic memory: A featural model for semantic decisions. *Psychological Review, 81*, 214–241.

Stössel, A., & Scheele, B. (1992). Interindividuelle Integration Subjektiver Theorien zu Modalstrukturen. In B. Scheele (Ed.), *Struktur-Lege-Verfahren als Dialog-Konsens-Methodik* (pp. 333–385). Münster: Aschendorff.

Treutlein, G. (1984). *Abschlußbericht für das Forschungsprojekt 'Methoden zur Erfassung handlungssteuernder Kognitionen bei Lehr- und Lernprozessen im Sport'*. Pädagogische Hochschule Heidelberg.

Tulving, E. (1962). Subjective organization in free recall of "unrelated" words. *Psychological Review, 69*, 344–354.

van Dijk, T.A., & Kintsch, W. (1983). *Strategies of discourse comprehension*. New York: Academic Press.

Verbrugge, R.R., & McCarrell, N.S. (1977). Metaphoric comprehension. Studies in reminding and ressembling. *Cognitive Psychology, 9*, 494–533.

Vorderer, P. (1987). Perspektiven für eine ideologiekritische Konzeption von Wissenspsychologie. In P. Vorderer & N. Groeben (Eds.), *Textanalyse als Kognitionskritik? Möglichkeiten und Grenzen ideologiekritischer Inhaltsanalyse* (pp. 226–254). Tübingen: Narr.

Wahl, D., Schlee, J., Krauth, J. & Mureck, J. (1983). *Naive Verhaltenstheorie von Lehrern.* Abschlußbericht eines Forschungsvorhabens zur Rekonstruktion und Validierung subjektiver psychologischer Theorien. Oldenburg.

Weinert, F.E. (1984). Metakognition und Motivation als Determinanten der Lerneffektivität: Einführung und Überblick. In F.E. Weinert & R.H. Kluwe (Eds.), *Metakognition, Motivation und Lernen* (pp. 9–22). Stuttgart: Kohlhammer.

Wellman, H.M. (1983). Metamemory revisited. In M.T.H. Chi (Ed.), *What is memory development the development of? A look after a decade* (pp. 31–51). Basel: Karger.

Weltner, K. (1974). Individualisierung von Lernprozessen durch Förderung von Selbstinstruktionstechniken. In: R. Schwarzer (Ed.), *Lernerfolg und Schülergruppierung* (pp. 62–75). Düsseldorf: Schwann.

Weltner, K. (1978). *Autonomes Lernen.* Stuttgart: Klett-Cotta.

Westmeyer, H. (1973). *Kritik der psychologischen Unvernunft.* Stuttgart: Kohlhammer.

Wilczok, K. (1973). Satzbildungs- und Satzverarbeitungsprozesse mit unterschiedlich spezifizierten Verben. Unpublished diploma thesis. Psychologisches Institut der Ruhr-Universität Bochum.

Wilson, T.D., & Nisbett, R.E. (1978). The accuracy of verbal reports about the effects of stimuli on evaluation and behavior. *Social Psychology, 41,* 118–131.

Yussen, S.R. (1985). The role of metacognition in contemporary theories of cognitive development. In D.L. Forrest-Pressley, G.E. MacKinnon, & T.G. Waller (Eds.), *Cognition, metacognition, and human performance* (Vol. 1, pp. 253–284). New York: Academic Press.

CHAPTER 3

Structured Organisms and Structured Environments: Developmental Systems and the Construction of Learning Capacities

Robert Lickliter

Virginia Polytechnic Institute and State University

Even though everyone recognizes its futility, the nature–nurture debate continues because there does not seem to be any other alternative.

R. C. Bolles (1988)

Some 25 years ago, a number of investigators began to argue against the then-prevalent *general process* approach to learning and proposed what has become known as the *biological boundaries* approach to learning (see Johnston, 1981; Domjan & Galef, 1983, for historical and conceptual reviews). This more recent approach to the study of learning was initially fueled by the results of several studies of taste aversion, which contradicted the principle of equivalence of associability of stimuli (see Seligman, 1970, for a review) and was further supported by work concerned with defense reactions, navigation and homing, imprinting, and song learning. The varied results from these lines of investigation led a number of authors to argue that learning capacities are best thought of as specialized adaptations to the specific demands of the environment inhabited by different animal species (Bolles, 1970; Hinde & Stevenson-Hinde, 1973; Rozen & Kalat, 1971; Seligman & Hager, 1972; Shettleworth, 1972). Although certainly not embraced by all learning theorists (e.g., Domjan, 1983; Logue, 1979; Rescorla & Holland, 1976; Revusky, 1977, 1985), the biologically bounded view of learning nonetheless served to question the arbitrariness of the general process approach to learning and promoted an increased consideration of the ecological adaptations and evolutionary history of animal species (see Shettleworth, 1983).

One result of the emphasis on ecological adaptation and evolutionary history is that the biological boundaries approach to learning has generally offered a dichotomous view of the causal factors underlying animals' learning capacities. Put simply, most biological views of learning hold that the specific features of learning capacities in any organism are determined by either (a) events that occurred earlier in the development of the organism, or (b) preontogenetic factors that operated on the ancestors of the organism (see Garcia, Brett, & Rusiniak, 1989; Gould & Marler, 1984, 1987; Lorenz, 1965, 1969; Schwartz, 1978; Seligman, 1970; Seligman & Hager, 1972). For example, Seligman and Hager (1972) proposed that:

> what an organism learns in the laboratory or in his natural habitat is the result of not only the contingencies which he faces and has faced in his past but also of the contingencies which his species faced before him—its evolutionary history and genetic outcome. (p. 7)

This way of thinking about ontogeny and phylogeny as alternative means by which information is made available to developing individuals has a long history in both biology and psychology, and continues to be widespread in both disciplines (see Oyama, 1985, 1989; Lickliter & Berry, 1990, for critical reviews). When applied to theories of learning this view of causality assumes that the learning capacities of an organism can be divided into those that are programmed by the genes and those that depend on individual experience (see Marler, 1990). In other words, learning capacities are shaped by either historical or "evolutionary" events that designed the organism's "genetic program" or by events that act upon the organism during its own ontogeny. This dichotomous way of thinking is based on the underlying assumption that genes and environment are related to each other only in the sense that the contribution of one source is *added* to the contribution of the other to provide for the realization of phenotypic outcomes. A recent quote from Suboski (1990) serves to illustrate how this view is applied to theories of learning:

> Responses that are biologically appropriate in both form and direction are pre-programmed to occur in the presence of particular releasing stimuli. Then, transfer of control over release and stimulus direction of such responses provided a mechanism whereby learned changes in the occurence of released responses can be acquired. (p. 273)

This conceptual framework, which explicity distinguishes between inherited (genetic) capacities and acquired (environmental) ones, is an example of what I have previously termed the *phylogeny fallacy* (Lickliter & Berry, 1990). This perspective clearly implies a form of genetic predeterminism, in that phylogenetic information is believed to be somehow encoded or preprogrammed into the genes and then unfolded during the course of maturation. Plotkin and Odling-Smee (1979) captured the extreme form of this view when they wrote: "All learning is a function of innate mechanisms of adaptability which are both provided and primed by phylogenesis with respect to some specific primary referent" (p. 36). Even a cursory review of the animal learning literature reveals that the phylogeny fallacy is common, if not prevalent, in the biological boundaries approach to learning and is also a component (albeit not often discussed) of more traditional, behavioristic approaches to learning theory (i.e., Skinner, 1966).

DEVELOPMENTAL SYSTEMS AND LEARNING CAPACITIES

In contrast to the causal framework common to most views of learning, this chapter presents an alternative, developmental systems approach to the study of learning capacities. On this view, boundaries or constraints on learning are understood not simply as the result of genetic programs or environmental events, but rather as outcomes emerging from the underlying dynamics of the organism-environment system. *Constraints on learning do not pre-exist developmental processes; rather, they are constructed by them.* Learning capacities, like all other phenotypic outcomes, are thus always a product of development, not prior programs or precoded instructions. Indeed, there are no programs or instructions, only processes comprised of a complex array of endogenous (including genetic) and environmental components. An organism's learning capacity thus depends on its developmental context as profoundly as it does on its genome. The illusion of some learning capacities being "inherited" and some "acquired" stems from inadequate attention to and appreciation of this processual nature of behavioral development (see Johnston, 1987, for further discussion of this point).

   The conceptual shift in thinking offered by the developmental systems approach presented in this chapter emphasizes this processual character of development (see Dent, 1990; Oyama, 1989; Thelen, 1989, for recent examples) and appreciates that any phenotypic trait or character (including learning capacities) is always the result of complex developmental interactants (including organic, organismic, and environmental) coacting throughout the course of individual ontogeny (Gottlieb, 1976, 1987; Lickliter & Ness, 1990; Oyama, 1985). As we shall see, this insight requires investigators to adopt a much broader view of the mechanisms responsible for the achievement of learning capacities. In particular, it necessitates a commitment to programmatic investigation beyond the boundaries of the organism. Such a concern is lacking in most of the work on which our current understanding of learning capacities is based, due in large part to the fact that descriptions and empirical analyses of environments have historically not been a major focus of psychological inquiry. Indeed, one can argue that much of our psychological tradition has encouraged researchers to separate learning from the organism and the organism from its environment (Alberts, 1987; Johnston & Turvey, 1980).

The Organism–Environment System

Traditionally the study of the relationship between an organism and its environment has been relegated to the biological discipline of ecology. As some authors have pointed out (Allen & Starr, 1982; O'Neill, DeAngelis, Waide, & Allen, 1986), although ecology is a particularly diverse discipline with many and varied approaches, it can nonetheless be generally characterized as the study of process within systems. For example, the biologist Jessop (1970) writes that:

> The individual organism is an inextricable component of an organism–environment complex consisting of itself, other members of its species, creatures of other types, and physio-chemical factors of the abiotic environment. It is senseless in its broadest context to consider adaptation outside the frame of reference of the total complex. (p. 114)

Perhaps as a result of this type of perspective, it has been primarily biologists who have emphasized the importance of examining and interpreting behavior (including learning) from an ecological or systems framework much more than have psychologists (e.g., Humphrey, 1933; King, 1968; Klopfer & Hailman, 1965; Mason & Langenheim, 1957; Morse, 1980). Traditional psychological theories have, for the most part, been theories about organisms and their capacities rather than theories about the relationship between organisms and their environments.

However, over the course of the last several decades a growing number of psychologists have argued for a consistently ecological approach to the study of behavior, an approach that explicitly emphasizes a focus on the organism–environment relationship (e.g., Bronfenbrenner, 1979; Bronfenbrenner & Crouter, 1983; Brunswik, 1952, 1956; Gibson, 1966, 1979; Gottlieb, 1971, 1976, 1983; Johnston, 1982, 1985; Lehrman, 1970; Oyama, 1985, 1989; Valsiner, 1987, 1989). For example, James Gibson (1979) advocated an ecological approach to the study of perception in which the researcher is explicitly concerned with the structure of the environment, of how the organism moves about in it, and of what sorts of information the environment affords the perceiving organism. This approach holds much promise for the investigation of complex organism–environment systems (see Reed, 1991).

A key point that is emerging from the increasing appreciation of organism–environment reciprocity is that the contributions of organism and environment to the development of behavioral competencies (such as learning) are *interdependent* and *transactional* (Hazen & Pick, 1985; Lickliter & Berry, 1990; Lickliter & Ness, 1990; Miller, 1988), rather than simply additive or interactive. In other words, the organism and its environment form a functional unit within which neither has privileged status or causal priority in effecting phenotypic development. From this view, an organism and its environment are not casually paired, but constitute a system whose parts are complementary and coimplicative (Dewey & Bentley, 1949; Johnston & Turvey, 1980; Johnston, 1982; Oyama, 1985, 1989). As a result, such behavioral processes as learning are best studied and understood as developmental outcomes of a system (organisms and their ecological niche) rather than simply as an activity of an animal (Germana, 1989; Miller & Blaich, 1984).

From this perspective, Johnston (1985) has characterized learning as "the modification or maintenance of the behavioral relationship between an animal and its environment as a result of individual experience." Germana (1989) has described learning as "a primary system process which promotes certainty in the behavioral relationship between organism and environment." As we shall see in subsequent sections of this chapter, these similar definitions of learning, incorporating the organism–environment system, imply several important strategies for the study of learning. These include an empirical concern with the species-specific environments of learning (the "ecology" of learning) and a focus on the developmental analysis of learning capacities. In the general sense, these strategies involve assessing the kinds of stimuli to which animals are normally exposed in the course of development and determining experimentally the particular aspects of the available stimulus array to which the developing organism is sensitive and responsive (Miller, 1981, 1985). The goal is to explain the nature and pattern of learning capacities not as properties of genes or even organisms, but rather as phenotypic characters emerging from the underlying dynamics of the organism–environment system.

STRUCTURED ORGANISMS AND STRUCTURED ENVIRONMENTS

To illustrate and further develop this developmental systems approach, I briefly review recent research both from my laboratory and from other comparative laboratories operating from this conceptual framework. Despite the diversity of topics and species studied, results from these varied research programs demonstrate that the physical, biological, and social contexts of the developing animal are essential components in the achievement of species-typical behavior, including learning capacities. These findings serve to underscore the central theme of this chapter, that the organism–environment relationship is one that is structured on both sides. That is, it is a relation between a structured organism *and* a structured environment. The organism inherits not only its genetic complement, but also the structured organization of the environment into which it is born. In this expanded view of inheritance, neither the genes nor the environment can be viewed as more fundamental than the other for any trait or character; each is completely tied to the other at all stages of development. Thus, the mere passing on of a genetic complement cannot serve as a sufficient explanation for the achievement of learning capacity, although it is certainly a necessary one. What is passed on from one generation to the next is not just genes, but a host of other necessary influences and interactants as well (Oyama, 1985; West & King, 1987). Although extragenetic inheritance is often overlooked or undercharacterized in both the biological and psychological literature (but see West & King, 1987a; West, King, & Arberg, 1988), most organisms are just as likely to inherit stable and reliable environments as they are copies of their parents' genes.

Interestingly, much of the work that provides evidence for this expanded perspective of phenotypic development comes from the study of behaviors that also initially gave rise to the biological boundaries approach to learning. These behaviors include imprinting (species identification), song learning, and feeding behavior.

Imprinting and Species Identification

Since the well-known work of Konrad Lorenz over 50 years ago, the study of imprinting has been an important source of concepts relating to the early development of behavior. In fact, imprinting represents one of the most extensively studied phenomena in the field of behavioral development. Over the last 50 years, research concerned with the nature of imprinting and species identification has generated a large and diverse literature and has influenced thinking within several disciplines about the mechanisms and processes underlying early social attachment (see Bateson, 1966; Bolhuis, 1991; Hess, 1973; Sluckin, 1973; Smith, 1962, for reviews). How did the study of imprinting achieve such status? While there are a number of possible answers to this interesting question, one prominent reason for the longstanding interest in imprinting is that it demonstrates features of learning that cannot be easily explained by traditional theories built in accordance with behavioristic and associationistic schemes (but see Hoffman & Ratner, 1973; Moltz, 1960; Rajecki, 1973, for opposing views). For example, imprinting appears to occur without the presence of any obvious reinforcement, is achieved relatively rapidly and during restricted periods, and often shows enduring stability. These features have led a number of investigators to conclude that the learning processes underlying imprinting are somehow unique and are preprogrammed into the organism (that is, that they are "genetically determined"—see Eibl-Eibesfeldt, 1970; Gould, 1982; Lorenz, 1965; Suboski, 1990).

As a result of its predominantly organismic emphasis, most of the research concerned with imprinting has not concerned itself with the physical, biological, or social context in which the young animal normally displays its early filial behavior. For example, almost all studies of imprinting have employed highly artificial objects such as lights, balls, or balloons as maternal surrogates. In addition, subjects typically have been reared in social isolation and visual isolation from hatching through the course of the experiment. This isolation rearing is, of course, in marked contrast to the process of imprinting as it must occur in the natural environment of the young bird. The natural ecological and social context in which social preferences are formed by young animals is clearly more complex than the design of conventional imprinting experiments would imply.

Interestingly, when investigators began to turn their attention away from artificial conditions and to employ more ecologically valid methods of investigation, a different and more complicated story of the process of species identification began to emerge. Contrary to the widely held view that imprinting must be innate or preprogrammed, an ecological approach to the study of imprinting has revealed that subtle, often nonobvious forms of experience are necessary for the development and maintenance of early perceptual and social preferences underlying early species identification (Gottlieb, 1971, 1973; Lickliter, Dyer, & McBride, 1993).

For example, several studies have shown that social interaction with siblings (broodmates) in the period following hatching is an important organizer of young ducklings' ability to learn the visual characteristics of a maternal hen (Johnston & Gottlieb, 1985; Lickliter & Gottlieb, 1985, 1986). Furthermore, the timing of social experience with siblings appears to determine its effectiveness in contributing to visually controlled maternal imprinting. Specifically, it was found that social interaction with broodmates must occur *after* initial exposure to a maternal hen in order to be effective; social experience with siblings *prior* to exposure to the maternal hen was found to be without apparent effect (Lickliter & Gottlieb, 1987). A subsequent study demonstrated that to successfully learn a visually imprinted preference for a maternal hen, young ducklings must be allowed social interaction with broodmates of their own species. Social experience with other birds, even ducklings of another species, was found insufficient to support the emergence of the ability to learn species-specific visual cues (Lickliter & Gottlieb, 1988).

The ecological approach to imprinting has also served to demonstrate that as the young animal develops, the nature of its relationship to its surroundings changes, so that the developmentally relevant features of its structured environment (its effective environment) also change. For example, the young of many different species of birds and mammals show the ability to learn the individually distinctive vocal characteristics of their parents' voices shortly before or after birth or hatching (DeCasper & Fifer, 1980; Epsmark, 1971; Evans, 1982; Shillito Walser, Walters, & Hague, 1982). Gottlieb (1988) recently examined the ability of mallard duckling embryos and hatchlings to learn individual mallard maternal calls. He found that both embryos and hatchlings are able to learn acoustic differences in individual maternal calls based upon only 12 min of exposure to the calls. However, whereas hatchlings could both learn and remember a familiar call for an additional day after exposure, embryos could only learn to recognize an individual call if tested shortly after exposure to the call; embryos could not remember the familiar call if tested on the day after initial exposure. An additional difference between the auditory learning capacity of embryos and hatchlings was that hatchlings (but not embryos) were able to learn the acoustic features of an individual maternal call even if it was pulsed at different repetition rates during the exposure period and the subsequent test for recognition. The embryo's lack of retention and its inability to learn the acoustic features of maternal calls based on different repetition rates demonstrates that learning and retention capacities develop at different rates, and the hatchling is more competent than the embryo at both.

Of course, under normally occurring circumstances, avian hatchlings receive stimulation in both the auditory and visual modalities. Lickliter and Virkar (1989) investigated the nature of the relationship between auditory and visual stimulation in establishing a species-specific maternal preference in young bobwhite quail chicks. Results revealed a hierarchy in the functional priority of the auditory and visual systems in the days immediately following hatching. At one and two days of age, species identification in quail hatchlings was found to depend on the auditory component of maternal stimulation. Later in development (at three and four days of age), combined auditory-visual stimulation was necessary to control filial behavior. However, even at these later stages of development, the auditory modality remained dominant over the visual in eliciting responsiveness to the maternal hen. These findings conform well to what is known about the neuroembryological development of the sensory systems, in that the auditory system of birds (and mammals) develops in advance of the visual system (Gottlieb, 1968, 1971). This prenatal sequence of sensory system development thus appears to influence the nature of early postnatal perceptual preferences in young avian hatchlings and has important implications for the processing of sensory information in the postnatal period and in turn for the ways in which the young bird learns the specific features of its social and physical environment.

One of the heuristic values of the construct of the "developmental system" is that it affords a perspective that leads to a keener methodological awareness of the context of phenotypic development (e.g., Miller, Hicinbothom, & Blaich, 1990; Ness & Franchina, 1990). For example, recent evidence from work with both avian and mammalian infants indicate that the stimulation histories of the sensory systems during both prenatal and early postnatal development play an important role in the organization of the sensory systems and in the processing of sensory information underlying early learning abilities. Gottlieb, Tomlinson, and Radell (1989) report that duckling embryos who received premature visual stimulation concomitantly with exposure to an individual maternal call failed to learn that maternal call, whereas control embryos who were not exposed to unusually early visual experience during exposure to the call did learn the individual maternal call. In a similar vein, recent work from my lab has demonstrated that unusually early (prenatal) visual stimulation alters bobwhite quail chicks' auditory and visual responsiveness to species-specific maternal cues in the days immediately following hatching (Lickliter, 1990 a,b). Specifically, chicks that received premature visual experience as embryos exhibited a more rapid decline in auditory responsiveness to the bobwhite maternal call than did normally reared chicks. In addition, chicks allowed unusually early visual experience could utilize visual cues to direct their filial preferences earlier in postnatal development than did hatchlings who had not experienced premature visual stimulation (Lickliter, 1990 b).

Taken together, the results of the studies discussed above indicate that we require surprisingly detailed information about the experiential stimulation present during the course of development if we are to successfully design experiments to understand that development. Given that phenotypic development always depends on transactions involving the organism and its context, the task of defining the relevant developmental features of an organism's environment, of delineating the actual physical, biological, and social aspects of the structured surround with which the developing organism interacts, becomes a necessary step in any systematic description or analyses of the development of behavior, including learning (see Johnston 1981, 1985, for a more in depth discussion of the role of environmental description and analyses in the study of learning). Recent work concerned with the development of vocal learning in birds also serves to illustrate the value of this developmental systems approach to the study of learning capacities.

Avian Song Development

As is well known to most students of behavior, the study of bird song has been an important focus of research in comparative psychology and animal behavior for many years (e.g., Marler, 1963, Thorpe, 1958, 1961). Indeed, as Konishi (1985) has pointed out, the study of song learning has not only generated a large and influential literature, it has also achieved major significance in the study of animal behavior in recent years; for example, some of the best examples of sensitive periods come from songbird research (Kroodsma & Pickert, 1980). Although advances are certainly being made in the study of bird song and our understanding of the underlying processes involved in song development is growing rapidly, much of the work in this area remains based on inadequate conceptual foundations. Put simply, the study of song learning in birds has and continues to be influenced by the phylogeny fallacy articulated in the previous sections of this chapter; most contemporary theories of song learning have been directed by the dichotomous view that elements of bird song development can be attributed to either preontogenetic (that is, genetic) information *or* ontogenetic (environmental) experience (see Johnston, 1988, for a recent review and critique).

For example, it is well documented that the young of a number of songbird species are able to pick out species-typical song patterns from their auditory environment and then use those species-specific patterns as the basis for subsequent song learning (Konishi, 1978). This selective auditory responsiveness in songbirds to sounds of their own species has led a number of investigators to propose the existence of "genetically encoded specifications" (Searcy & Marler, 1987; Thorpe, 1964) or "innate blueprints" (Konishi, 1978; Marler & Sherman, 1985) for avian song-learning capacities. However, recent work with several songbird species suggests that this willingness to assign information for development to a genetic program or blueprint can result in aspects of the organism–environment system that actually contribute to song development being overlooked or remaining unanalyzed. In particular, the view that mechanisms of song-learning development are dependent on innate or preprogrammed information has led a number of investigators to overlook the role of the naturally occurring context in which song learning normally takes place. As was the case with much of the imprinting research of the last several decades, the song-learning literature is rich with examples of studies that have tended to ignore or obscure the importance of the developing animal's structured environment to the achievement of species-typical behavioral outcomes.

A seemingly inconsequential research method commonly employed in song-learning research serves to illustrate this shortcoming. Until very recently, most song-learning research typically utilized taped recordings to present song stimuli to avian subjects. Although this method of presenting previously recorded songs was chosen for a number of practical reasons (it ensured both the experimenter's control of the stimulus input and control of stimulus quality), the prevalent choice of a single method to present song stimuli has resulted, at least in some cases, in an incomplete (and inaccurate) view of song learning mechanisms (see Petrinovich, 1988, 1990, for reviews). For example, recent results obtained from work with white-crowned sparrows, a species previously thought capable of learning only conspecific song (Marler, 1970), demonstrate that they are also capable of learning non-conspecific song *if it is sung by a live tutor* (Baptista & Petrinovich, 1984, 1986). The presence of a live song tutor also serves to markedly extend the sensitive period for song learning in this species (Petrinovich & Baptista, 1987). Similar work with zebra finches (Slater, Eales, & Clayton, 1988) has likewise demonstrated the pronounced effects of social context on the process of song learning. Clearly, the developmental context in which song learning normally takes place is far more complex (and influential) than the traditional design of song learning experiments would imply (see also Logan, 1983; Kroodsma, 1989, for similar critiques). Some of the ecological factors that appear to contribute to differences in learning abilities include migratory habits, photoperiod, density of other avian species, and the bioacoustics of the song learner's environment, to name but a few (Kroodsma, 1983).

Work from West and King's (King & West, 1983, 1984, 1987; West & King, 1985, 1988) laboratory concerned with the development of vocal learning in cowbirds, a species in which females lay their eggs in the nests of other species and the resulting young are then raised by members of that species, illustrates how considering the influence of social context can pay unexpected dividends in the study of learning capacities. In particular, their systematic research program demonstrates how remarkably "structured" the organism's structured environment actually is (see also Gottlieb, 1982; Hofer, 1978, 1987, for other examples). In a series of related studies, West and King have documented that male cowbirds require social guidance to develop a repertoire of songs that female cowbirds will respond to. In other words, males require social feedback (from both other males and females) to identify and learn the songs most effective in attracting potential mates. This sensitivity to social influences and the resulting vocal flexibility of cowbirds serves to make the point that what is transmitted between generations is not programs or blueprints but developmental means (Oyama, 1985; West & King, 1987 a,b). These developmental means certainly include genetic factors but also include the larger developmental context, including parents, siblings, and other conspecifics.

Applying a developmental systems framework to vocal learning in birds thus requires an empirical concern for the "experience of experience" (King & West, 1987 b). That is, the task of defining the relevant experiential features of an organism's environment necessarily becomes an explicit empirical problem for systematic description and analyses. As many of the studies discussed above affirm, viewing learning capacities not as genetically or environmentally predetermined but as *constructed* by species-typical developmental systems sets the stage for the empirical analysis of the organic, organismic, and environmental components necessary for development to occur.

METHODOLOGICAL STRATEGIES OF A DEVELOPMENTAL SYSTEMS APPROACH

The studies of imprinting and song learning briefly reviewed in the preceding sections of this chapter have an important methodological characteristic in common. Namely, all have utilized controlled developmental analysis involving the imposition of varying degrees of species-atypical conditions on developing organisms to experimentally identify the experiential requirements of normal or species-typical development. A number of comparative and developmental psychologists have discussed and described methodological approaches appropriate to the developmental analysis of behavioral traits or characteristics in recent years, including Petrinovich (1979, 1981), Miller (1981, 1985), Gottlieb (1977,

1983), and Valsiner (1987). These authors have all acknowledged that systematic analysis of phenotypic development first requires the collection of a normative data baseline, founded on naturalistic observation across developmental contexts. This crucial step affords a documentation of species-typical experiences and developmental trajectories associated with the organism's normally occurring context and illuminates the range of behavioral capacities and developmental outcomes characteristic of the organism-context transaction process. This critical starting point is then followed by the second step, experimental intervention and manipulation designed to uncover the means and interactants necessary and sufficient for normal phenotypic development to occur.

Gottlieb (1977) and Miller (1981, 1985) have identified five basic experiential manipulations commonly employed in the experimental analysis of developmental systems. *Experimental attenuation,* the most widely used, involves withholding or preventing the organism from encountering normally occurring, species-typical experiences. This procedure is exemplified by the so-called "deprivation" experiment advanced by Lorenz (1965). In contrast, *experimental enhancement* involves the presentation of increased amounts of normally occurring, species-typical experience. In this procedure, the organism is subjected to more stimulation than it would normally encounter during the course of development (see Lickliter & Stoumbos, 1991, for an example). *Experimental transposition* involves shifting, moving, or somehow rearranging normally occurring events and/or experiences. That is, the experimenter reconfigures aspects of the normal surround in an attempt to unpack the specificity of the organism–environment relationship. Emlen's (1970, 1972, 1975) elegant work on the development of migratory orientation in selected bird species, in which he reconfigured aspects of the night sky in a planetarium setting, illustrates the dividends of employing this type of procedure. As its name implies, *experimental substitution* encompasses removing a normally occurring event or experience and replacing it with some different form of stimulation. The work of Mason and his associates (Mason, 1978; Mason & Capitanio, 1988; Mason & Kenny, 1974) using dogs as surrogate mothers for rhesus macaque infants to explore the nature of early social attachments illustrates this approach. Finally, *experimental displacement* manipulates the temporal occurence of species-typical experiences by shifting stimulus events either forward or backward in time in relation to their usual presentation or occurrence. Turpin, Johnston, and Fulk's (1988) displacement of social stimulation to hamster pups, and Pfister, Cramer, and Blass's (1986) displacement of rat pups' access to lactating dams, demonstrate the value of this experimental procedure in discovering the nature of the interactants necessary for the development and maintenance of species-typical behavior.

The important point is that by not separating the organism from its environment and by not thinking of the organism's environment as simply posing problems to which the organism must adapt (Lewontin, 1982; Gray, 1987), a developmental systems approach allows investigators to characterize both the genes and the stimulative developmental context as equal partners in providing the basic, necessary elements for development. This theoretical context sets the stage for the empirical analysis of the organic, organismic, and environmental factors necessary for development to occur. A brief overview of the contemporary animal feeding and foraging literature serves to illustrate some consequences of this conceptual shift.

Animal Feeding and Foraging

As is well known, members of any given animal species tend to seek out and eat similar kinds of foods. In keeping with the phylogeny fallacy, many investigators of animal feeding behavior have assumed that such consistency in diet and food choice is determined by either genetically encoded and transmitted predispositions or individual experience over the course of ontogeny (Galef, 1977; Gould, 1987; Young, 1968). For example, Gould (1987, p.480) argues that "learning and instinct both play essential roles in the process of foraging." This way of thinking about the determinants of feeding behavior can be found in research drawn from animal behavior, behavioral ecology, and comparative psychology and is clearly evident in *optimal foraging* theory that directs much of the work concerned with the relationship between learning capacities and feeding and foraging behavior (see Kamil, 1983; Kamil & Roitblat, 1985; Kamil & Sargent, 1981, for examples). In the general sense, optimal foraging theory assumes that organisms are somehow designed by natural selection to fit their particular, species-specific environments; as demonstrated by the above quote from Gould (1987), this assumption often includes the notions of predetermined instincts or genetic programs.

However, positing such preontogenetic explanations for aspects of feeding and foraging behavior does not explain how feeding and foraging capacities are actually realized by any individual organism, nor do they describe the conditions, circumstances, or interactants necessary for such phenotypic outcomes to occur. Instead of assuming that an optimal foraging phenotype has evolved (and invoking the notion of a preformed genetic program to explain animals' feeding and foraging capacities), the developmental systems approach views the development of feeding and foraging behavior as an ontogenetic process involving a wide range of factors present in the organism–environment system (see Gray, 1987, for a detailed and compelling discussion of this view). These include an array of morphological and physiological factors, but also include such factors as chemical traces from parental foraging (Corbet, 1985; Galef & Henderson, 1972), gut microorganisms (Jones, 1983), olfactory cues (Galef, 1990), social experience and interaction (Galef & Clark, 1971, 1972), and social tradition (Galef, 1976), to name but a few.

The point here is that a developmental systems view of the learning capacities underlying feeding and foraging behavior makes the animal-context transaction process the explicit object of study. This emphasis on the ontogenetic construction of learning capacities effectively eliminates the opposition between inherited and acquired determiners of learning capacities and in so doing offers a view of phenotypic development than can potentially integrate genetic, physiological, psychological, and social levels of analysis within a developmental framework (see Alberts & Cramer, 1988; Lickliter & Ness, 1990).

CONCLUSION

To ask better and more appropriate questions, it is sometimes necessary to step back from our empirical concerns and explore the theoretical context in which our research is organized. In this light, Kantor (1973) argued that "progress in science is dependent upon the constant improvement in the axioms or assumptions guiding investigation and research (p.451)." In the present chapter, I have attempted to critically evaluate the underlying but often unexamined causative assumptions that guide most "biological" approaches to learning capacity. Specifically, the idea that learning capacities can be attributed to either genetic *or* environmental determinants (the phylogeny fallacy) was targeted for scrutiny. An alternative, developmental systems approach was articulated and explored. On this view, phenotypic traits or characters are not transmitted in the genes, nor are they contained in features of the organism's environment. Rather, traits or characters are always constructed by the complex coaction of organic, organismic, and environmental factors operating during individual ontogeny. This expanded, systematic view of phenotypic development serves to eliminate the need for the dichotomization of explanations of learning capacity into inherited and acquired and directs research attention to the organism–transaction process, thereby including a large class of factors and variables often omitted from preontogenetic explanations of learning capacity. In particular, an appreciation of an organism's developmental system necessarily leads to systematic investigation beyond the boundaries of the organism in order to understand the organism fully (Gottlieb, 1991; Oyama, 1989).

It seems important to emphasize again that the conception of the developmental system does not deny that genes play a significant and necessary role in phenotypic development. Rather, this approach proposes that what is passed on or made available in reproduction is both a structured genome and a structured segment of the world. As a result, the function of the genes or any other influence on phenotypic development can be understood only in relation to the developmental system of which they are a part. This view thus emphasizes the interdependent rather than the co-relational nature of the link between the genes and the organism's developmental context and results in a specific empirical concern with the physical, biological, and social aspects of the surround with which the developing organism actually interacts. Thus, the appropriate focus of studies of learning capacity becomes the nature of the relation between the organism and its environment, rather than simply the organism itself. This focus serves to redefine the traditional scope of psychological inquiry and can direct future research attention to the important but often overlooked question of *how* learning possibilities and constraints emerge in process.

REFERENCES

Alberts, J.R. (1987). Early learning and ontogenetic adaptation. In N.A. Krasnegor, E.M. Blass, M.A. Hofer, & W.P. Smotherman (Eds.), *Perinatal development: A psychobiological perspective* (pp. 11–37). New York: Academic Press.

Alberts, J.R., & Cramer, C.P. (1988). Ecology and experience. In E.M. Blass (Ed.), *Handbook of behavioral neurobiology* (Vol. 9, pp. 1–39). New York: Plenum Press.

Allen, T.F.H., & Starr, T.B. (1982). *Hierarchy: Perspectives for ecological complexity.* Chicago: University of Chicago Press.

Baptista, L.F., & Petrinovich, L. (1984). Social interaction, sensitive phases and the song template hypothesis in the white-crowned sparrow. *Animal Behaviour, 32,* 172–181.

Baptista, L.F., & Petrinovich, L. (1986). Song development in the white-crowned sparrow: Social factors and sex differences. *Animal Behaviour, 34,* 1359–1371.

Bateson, P.P.G. (1966). The characteristics and context of imprinting. *Biological Reviews, 41,* 177–220.

Bolhuis, J.J. (1991). Mechanisms of avian imprinting: A review. *Biological Reviews, 66,* 303–345.

Bolles, R.C. (1970). Species-specific defense reactions and avoidance learning. *Psychological Review. 77,* 32–48.

Bolles, R.C. (1988). Nativism, naturalism, and niches. In R.C. Bolles & M.D. Beecher (Eds.), *Evolution and learning* (pp. 1–15). Hillsdale, NJ: Erlbaum.

Bronfenbrenner, U. (1979). *The ecology of human development: Experiments by nature and design.* Cambridge, MA: Harvard University Press.

Bronfenbrenner, U., & Crouter, A.C. (1983). The evolution of environmental models in developmental research. In P.H. Mussen (Ed.), *Handbook of child psychology* (Vol. 1, pp. 357–414). New York: Wiley.

Brunswik, E. (1952). *The conceptual foundations of psychology.* Chicago: University of Chicago Press.

Brunswik, E. (1956). *Perception and the representative design of experiments in psychology.* Berkeley, CA: University of California Press.

Corbet, S.A. (1985). Insect chemosensory responses: A chemical legacy hypothesis. *Ecological Entomology, 10,* 147–153.

Decasper, A.J., & Fifer, W.P. (1980). Of human bonding: Newborns prefer their mothers' voices. *Science, 208,* 1174–1176.

Dent, C.H. (1990). An ecological approach to language development: An alternative functionalism. *Developmental Psychobiology, 23,* 679–704.

Dewey, J., & Bentley, A.F. (1949). *Knowing and the known.* Boston: Beacon Press.

Domjan, M. (1983). Biological constraints on instrumental and classical conditioning 10 years later: Implications for general process theory. In G.H. Bower (Ed.), *The psychology of learning and motivation* (Vol. 17, pp. 215–277). New York: Academic Press.

Domjan, M., & Galef, B.G. (1983). Biological constraints on instrumental conditioning: Retrospect and prospect. *Animal Learning and Behavior, 11*, 151–161.

Eibl-Eibesfeldt, I. (1970). *Ethology: The biology of behavior.* New York: Holt, Rinehart and Winston.

Emlen, S.T. (1970). Celestial rotation: Its importance in the development of migratory orientation. *Science, 170*, 1198–1201.

Emlen, S.T. (1972). The ontogenetic development of orientation capabilities. In S.R. Galler, K. Schmidt-Koenig, G.J., Jacobs, & R.F. Bellesville (Eds.), *Animal orientation and navigation* (pp. 191–216). Washington, DC: NASA (SP-262).

Emlen, S.T. (1975). Migration: Orientation and navigation. In D.S. Farner & J.R. King (Eds.), *Avian biology* (Vol. 5, pp. 129–219). New York: Academic Press.

Epsmark, Y. (1971). Individual recognition by voice in reindeer mother-young relationship: Field observations and playback experiments. *Behaviour, 60*, 295–301.

Evans, R.M. (1982). The development of learned auditory discriminations in the context of postnatal filial imprinting in young precocial birds. *Bird Behaviour, 4*, 1–6.

Galef, B.G. (1976). The social transmission of acquired behavior: A discussion of tradition and social learning in vertebrates. *Advances in the Study of Behavior, 6*, 77–100.

Galef, B.G. (1977). Mechanisms for the social transmission of acquired food preferences from adult to weanling rats. In L.M. Barker, M.R. Best, & M. Domjan (Eds.), *Learning mechanisms in food selection* (pp. 123–148). Waco, TX: Baylor University Press.

Galef, B.G. (1990). An adaptionist perspective on social learning, social feeding, and social foraging in Norway rats. In D.A. Dewsbury (Ed.), *Contemporary issues in comparative psychology* (pp. 55–79). Sunderland, MA: Sinaver.

Galef, B.G., & Clark, M.M. (1971). Social factors in the poison avoidance and feeding behavior of wild and domesticated rat pups. *Journal of Comparative and Physiological Psychology, 75*, 341–357.

Galef, B.G., & Clark, M.M. (1972). Mother's milk and adult presence: Two factors determining initial dietary selection by weanling rats. *Journal of Comparative and Physiological Psychology, 78*, 220–225.

Galef, B.G., & Henderson, P.W. (1972). Mother's milk: A determinant of the feeding preferences of weaning rat pups. *Journal of Comparative and Physiological Psychology, 78*, 213–219.

Garcia, J., Brett, L.P., & Rusiniak, K.W. (1989). Limits of Darwinian conditioning. In S.B. Klein & R.R. Mowrer (Eds.), *Contemporary learning theories* (pp. 181–204). Hillsdale, NJ: Erlbaum.

Germana, J. (1989). The biological significance of behavioral learning from a systems view. *Behavioral Science, 34*, 228–237.

Gibson, J.J. (1966). *The senses considered as perceptual systems.* Boston: Houghton-Mifflin.

Gibson, J.J. (1979). *The ecological approach to visual perception.* Boston: Houghton-Mifflin.

Gottlieb, G. (1968). Prenatal behavior of birds. *Quarterly Review of Biology, 43,* 148–174.

Gottlieb, G. (1971). *Development of species identification in birds.* Chicago: University of Chicago Press.

Gottlieb, G. (1973). Neglected variables in the study of species identification in birds. *Psychological Bulletin, 79,* 362–372.

Gottlieb, G. (1976). The roles of experience in the development of behavior and the nervous system. In G. Gottlieb (Ed.), *Neural and behavioral specificity* (pp. 25–54). New York: Academic Press.

Gottlieb, G. (1977). The development of behavior. In K. Immelmann (Ed.), *Grzimek's encyclopedia of ethology* (pp. 579–606). New York: Van Norstrand Reinhold.

Gottlieb, G. (1982). Development of species identification in ducklings: IX. The necessity of experiencing normal variations in embryonic auditory stimulation. *Developmental Psychobiology, 15,* 507–517.

Gottlieb, G. (1983). The psychobiological approach to developmental issues. In P.H. Mussen (Ed.), *Handbook of child psychology* (Vol. 2, pp. 1–26). New York: Wiley.

Gottlieb, G. (1987). The developmental basis of evolutionary change. *Journal of Comparative Psychology, 101,* 262–271.

Gottlieb, G. (1988). Development of species identification in ducklings: XV. Individual auditory recognition. *Developmental Psychobiology, 21,* 509–522.

Gottlieb, G. (1991). Experimental canalization of behavioral development: Theory. *Developmental Psychology, 27,* 35–39.

Gottlieb, G., Tomlinson, W.T., & Radell, P.L. (1989). Developmental intersensory interference: Premature visual experience suppresses auditory learning in ducklings. *Infant Behavior and Development, 12,* 1–12.

Gould, J.L. (1982). *Ethology: The mechanisms and evolution of behavior.* New York: W.W. Norton.

Gould, J.L. (1987). The role of learning in honey bee foraging. In A.C. Kamil, J.R. Krebs, & H.R. Pulliam (Eds.), *Foraging behavior* (pp. 479–496). New York: Plenum Press.

Gould, J.L., & Marler, P. (1984). Ethology and the natural history of learning. In P. Marler & H.S. Terrace (Eds.), *The biology of learning* (pp. 47–74). New York: Springer-Verlag.

Gould, J.L., & Marler, P. (1987). Learning by instinct. *Scientific American, 256,* 62–73.

Gray, R.D. (1987). Faith and foraging: A critique of the "paradigm argument from design." In A.C. Kamil, J.R. Krebs, & H.R. Pulliam (Eds.), *Foraging behavior* (pp. 69–140). New York: Plenum Press.

Hazen, N., & Pick, H.L. (1985). An ecological approach to development of spatial orientation. In T.D. Johnston & A.T. Pietrewicz (Eds.), *Issues in the ecological study of learning* (pp. 201–244). Hillsdale, NJ: Erlbaum.

Hess, E.H. (1973). *Imprinting.* New York: Van Nostrand Reinhold.

Hinde, R.A., & Stevenson-Hinde, J. (1973). *Constraints on learning: Limitations and predispositions.* New York: Academic Press.

Hofer, M.A. (1978). Hidden regulatory processes in early social relationships. In P.P.G. Bateson & P.H. Kleffer (Eds.) *Perspectives in ethology* (Vol. 3, pp. 135–166). New York: Plenum Press.

Hofer, M.A. (1987). Early social relationships: A psychobiologist's view. *Child Development, 58,* 633–647.

Hoffman, H.S., & Ratner, A.M. (1973). A reinforcement model of imprinting: Implications for socialization in monkeys and men. *Psychological Review, 80*, 527–544.

Humphrey, G. (1933). *The nature of learning in its relation to the living system*. London: Kegan Paul.

Jessop, N.M. (1970). *Biosphere: A study of life*. Englewood Cliffs, NJ: Prentice-Hall.

Johnston, T.D. (1981). Contrasting approaches to a theory of learning. *Behavioral and Brain Sciences, 4*, 125–173.

Johnston, T.D. (1982). Learning and the evolution of developmental systems. In H.C. Plotkin (Ed.), *Learning evolution and culture* (pp. 411–442). New York: Wiley.

Johnston, T.D. (1985). Conceptual issues in the ecological study of learning. In T.D. Johnston & A.T. Pietrewicz (Eds.), *Issues in the ecological study of learning* (pp. 1–24). Hillsdale, NJ: Erlbaum.

Johnston, T.D. (1987). The persistence of dichotomies in the study of behavioral development. *Developmental Review, 7*, 149–182.

Johnston, T.D. (1988). Developmental explanation and the ontogeny of birdsong: Nature/nurture redux. *Behavioral and Brain Sciences, 11*, 617–663.

Johnston, T.D., & Gottlieb, G. (1985). Effects of social experience on visually imprinted maternal preferences in Peking ducklings. *Developmental Psychobiology, 18*, 261–271.

Johnston, T.D., & Turvey, M.T. (1980). A sketch of an ecological metatheory for theories of learning. In G.H. Bower (Ed.), *The psychology of learning and motivation* (Vol. 14, pp. 147–205). New York: Academic Press.

Jones, G.G. (1983). Microorganisms as mediators of resource exploitation. In P.W. Price, C.N. Slobodchikoff, & W.J. Gand (Eds.), *A new ecology: Novel approaches to interactive systems* (pp. 53–99). New York: Wiley.

Kamil, A.C. (1983). Optimal foraging theory and the psychology of learning. *American Zoologist, 23*, 291–302.

Kamil, A.C., & Sargent, T.D. (1981). Foraging behavior: *Ecological, ethological and psychological approaches*. New York: Garland STPM Press.

Kamil, A.C., & Roitblat, H.L. (1985). The ecology of foraging behavior: Implications for animal learning and memory. *Annual Review of Psychology, 36*, 141–169.

Kantor, J.R. (1973). System structure and scientific psychology. *The Psychological Record, 23*, 451–458.

King, A.P., & West, M.J. (1983). Epigenesis of cowbird song: A joint endeavor of males and females. *Nature, 305*, 704–706.

King, A.P., & West, M.J. (1984). Social metrics of vocal learning. *Learning and Motivation, 15*, 441–458.

King, A.P., & West, M.J. (1987). Different outcomes of synergy between song perception and song production in the same subspecies *(Molothrus ater ater)*. *Developmental Psychobiology, 20*, 177–187.

King, J.A. (1968). Species specificity and early experience. In G. Newton & S. Levine (Eds.), *Early experience and behavior* (pp. 42–64). Springfield, IL: Charles C. Thomas.

Klopfer, P.H., & Hailman, J. (1965). Habitat selection in birds. *Advances in the Study of Behavior, 1*, 279–303.

Konishi, M. (1978). Auditory environment and vocal development in birds. In R.D. Walk & H.L. Pick (Eds.), *Perception and experience* (pp. 29–48). New York: Plenum.

Konishi, M. (1985). Birdsong: From behavior to neuron. *Annual Review of Neuroscience, 8*, 125–170.

Kroodsma, D.E. (1983). The ecology of avian vocal learning. *Bioscience, 33*, 165–171.

Kroodsma, D.E. (1989). Suggested experimental designs for song playbacks. *Animal Behaviour, 37*, 600–609.

Kroodsma, D.E., & Pickert, R. (1980). Environmentally dependent sensitive periods for avian vocal learning. *Nature, 288*, 477–479.

Lehrman, D.S. (1970). Semantic and conceptual issues in the nature-nurture problem. In L.R. Aronson, E. Tobach, D.S. Lehrman & J.S. Rosenblatt (Eds.), *Development and evolution of behavior* (pp. 17–52). San Francisco: W. Freeman.

Lewontin, R.C. (1982). Organism and environment. In H.C. Plotkin (Ed.), *Learning, development, and culture* (pp. 151–170). New York: Wiley.

Lickliter, R. (1990 a). Premature visual stimulation accelerates intersensory functioning in bobwhite quail neonates. *Developmental Psychobiology, 23*, 15–27.

Lickliter, R. (1990 b). Premature visual experience facilitates visual responsiveness in bobwhite quail neonates. *Infant Behavior and Development, 13*, 487–496.

Lickliter, R., & Berry, T.D. (1990). The phylogeny fallacy: Developmental psychology's misapplication of evolutionary theory. *Developmental Review, 10*, 332–348.

Lickliter, R., Dyer, A.B., & McBride, T. (1993). Perceptual consequences of early social experience in precocial birds. *Behavioral Processes, 30*, 185–200.

Lickliter, R., & Gottlieb, G. (1985). Social interaction with siblings is necessary for the visual imprinting of species specific maternal preference in ducklings. *Journal of Comparative Psychology, 99*, 371–378.

Lickliter, R., & Gottlieb, G. (1986). Visual imprinted maternal preference in ducklings is redirected by social interaction with siblings. *Developmental Psychobiology, 19*, 265–277.

Lickliter, R., & Gottlieb, G. (1987). Retroactive excitation: Post-training social experience with siblings consolidates maternal imprinting in ducklings. *Journal of Comparative Psychology, 101*, 40–46.

Lickliter, R., & Gottlieb, G. (1988). Social specificity: Interaction with own species is necessary to foster species specific maternal preference in ducklings. *Developmental Psychobiology, 21*, 311–321.

Lickliter, R., & Ness, J. (1990). Domestication and comparative psychology: Status and strategy. *Journal of Comparative Psychology, 104*, 211–218.

Lickliter, R., & Stoumbos, J. (1991). Enhanced prenatal auditory experience facilitates species-specific visual responsiveness in bobwhite quail chicks. *Journal of Comparative Psychology, 105*.

Lickliter, R., & Virkar, P. (1989). Intersensory functioning in bobwhite quail chicks: Early sensory dominance. *Developmental Psychobiology, 22*, 651–667.

Logan, C.A. (1983). Biological diversity in avian vocal learning. In M.D. Zeiler & P. Harzen (Eds.), *Advances in analysis of behaviour* (Vol. 3, pp. 143–176). New York: Wiley.

Logue, A.W. (1979). Taste aversion and the generality of the laws of learning. *Psychological Review, 86*, 276–296.

Lorenz, K. (1965). *Evolution and modification of behavior.* Chicago: University of Chicago Press.

Lorenz, K. (1969). Innate bases of learning. In K. Pribram (Ed.), *On the biology of learning* (pp. 13–93). New York: Harcourt, Brace and World.

Marler, P. (1963). Inheritance and learning in the development of animal vocalizations. In R.G. Busnel (Ed.), *Acoustic behavior of animals* (pp. 228–243). Amsterdam: Elsevier.

Marler, P. (1970). A comparative approach to vocal development: Song learning in the white-crowned sparrow. *Journal of Comparative and Physiological Psychology Monograph, 71,* 1–25.

Marler, P. (1990). Innate learning preferences: Signals for communication. *Developmental Psychobiology, 23;* 557–568.

Marler, P., & Sherman, V. (1985). Innate differences in singing behaviour of sparrows reared in isolation from adult conspecific song. *Animal Behaviour, 33,* 57–71.

Mason, H.L., & Langenheim, J.H. (1957). Language analysis and the concept environment. *Ecology, 38:* 325–340.

Mason, W.A. (1978). Social experience and primate cognitive development. In G.M. Burghardt & M. Bekoff (Eds.), *The development of behavior: Comparative and evolutionary aspects* (pp. 233–251). New York: Garland Press.

Mason, W.A., & Capitanio, J.P. (1988). Formation and expression of filial attachment in rhesus monkeys raised with living and inanimate mother substitutes. *Developmental Psychobiology, 21,* 401–430.

Mason, W.A., & Kenny, M.D. (1974). Redirection of filial attachments in rhesus monkeys: Dogs as mother surrogates. *Science, 183,* 1209–1211.

Miller, D.B. (1981). Conceptual strategies in behavioral development: Normal development and plasticity. In K. Immelmann, G.W. Barlow, L. Petrinovich, & M. Main (Eds.), *Behavioral development* (pp. 58–82). Cambridge, UK: Cambridge University Press.

Miller, D.B. (1985). Methodological issues in the ecological study of learning. In T.D. Johnston & A.T. Pietrewicz (Eds.), *Issues in the ecological study of learning* (pp. 73–95). Hilldale, NJ: Erlbaum.

Miller, D.B. (1988). Beyond interactionism: A transactional approach to behavioral development. *Behavioral and Brain Sciences, 11,* 641–642.

Miller, D.B., & Blaich, C.F. (1984). Alarm call responsivity of mallard ducklings: The inadequacy of learning and genetic explanations of instinctive behavior. *Learning and Motivation 15,* 417–427.

Miller, D.B., Hicinbothom, G., & Blaich, C.F. (1990). Alarm call responsivity of mallard ducklings: Multiple pathways in behavioral development. *Animal Behaviour, 39,* 1207–1212.

Moltz, H. (1960). Imprinting: Empirical basis and theoretical significance. *Psychological Bulletin, 57,* 291–314.

Morse, D.H. (1980). *Behavioral mechanisms in ecology.* Cambridge, MA: Harvard University Press.

Ness, J.W., & Franchina, J.J. (1990). Effects of prenatal alcohol exposure on rat pup's ability to elicit retrieval behavior from dams. *Developmental Psychobiology, 23,* 85–99.

O'Neill, R.V., DeAngelis, D.L., Waide, J.B. & Allen, T.F.H. (1986). *A hierarchical concept of ecosystems.* Princeton, NJ: Princeton University Press.

Oyama, S. (1985). *The ontogeny of information: Developmental systems and evolution.* Cambridge, UK: Cambridge University Press.

Oyama, S. (1989). Ontogeny and the central dogma: Do we need the concept of genetic programming in order to have an evolutionary perspective? In M.G. Gunnar & E. Thelen (Eds.), *Minnesota symposia on child psychology* (Vol. 22, pp. 1–34). Hillsdale, NJ: Erlbaum.

Petrinovich, L. (1979). Probabilistic functionalism: A conception of a research method. *American Psychologist, 34,* 373–390.

Petrinovich, L. (1981). A method for the study of development. In K. Immelmann, G.W. Barlow, L. Petrinovich, & M. Main (Eds.), *Behavioral development* (pp. 90–130). Cambridge, UK: Cambridge University Press.

Petrinovich, L. (1988). The role of social factors in white-crowned sparrow song development. In T.R. Zentall & B.G. Galef (Eds.), *Social learning: Psychological and biological perspectives* (pp. 255–278). Hillsdale, NJ: Erlbaum.

Petrinovich, L. (1990). Avian song development: Methodological and conceptual issues. In D.A. Dewsbury (Ed.), *Contemporary issues in comparative psychology* (pp. 340–359). Sunderland, MA: Sinauer.

Petrinovich, L., & Baptista, L.F. (1987). Song development in the white-crowned sparrow: Modification of learned song. *Animal Behaviour, 35,* 961–974.

Pfister, J.F., Cramer, C.P., & Blass, E.M. (1986). Suckling in rats extended by continuous living with dams and their preweanling litters. *Animal Behaviour, 34,* 425–430.

Plotkin, H.C., & Odling-Smee, F.J. (1979). Learning, change, and evolution: An enquiry into the teleonomy of learning. *Advances in the Study of Behavior, 10,* 1–41.

Rajecki, D.W. (1973). Imprinting in precocial birds: Interpretation, evidence, and evaluation. *Psychological Bulletin, 79,* 48–58.

Reed, E.S. (1991). The intention to use a specific affordance: A conceptual framework for psychology. In R. Wozniak & K. Fischer (Eds.), *Children's thinking: The effects of specific environments.* Hillsdale, NJ: Erlbaum.

Rescorla, R.A., & Holland, P.C. (1976). Some behavioral approaches to the study of learning. In M.R. Rosenweig & E.L. Bennett (Eds.), *Neural mechanisms of learning and memory* (pp. 165–192). Cambridge, MA: MIT Press.

Revusky, S. (1977). Learning as a general process with an emphasis on data from feeding experiments. In N.W. Milgram, L. Krames, & T.M. Alloway (Eds.), *Food aversion learning* (pp. 1–51). New York: Plenum Press.

Revusky, S. (1985). The general process approach to animal learning. In T.D. Johnston & A.T. Pietrewicz (Eds.), *Issues in the ecological study of learning* (pp. 401–432). Hillsdale, NJ: Erlbaum.

Rozen, P., & Kalat, J.W. (1971). Specific hungers and poison avoidance as adaptive specializations of learning. *Psychological Review, 78,* 459–486.

Schwartz, B. (1978). *Psychology of learning and behavior.* New York: W.W. Norton.

Searcy, W.A., & Marler, P. (1987). Response of sparrows to songs of deaf and isolation-reared males: further evidence for innate auditory templates. *Developmental Psychobiology, 20,* 509–519.

Seligman, M.E.P. (1970). On the generality of the laws of learning. *Psychological Review, 77,* 406–418.

Seligman, M.E.P. & Hager, J.L. (1972). *Biological boundaries of learning*. New York: Appleton, Century and Crofts.

Shettleworth, S.J. (1972). Constraints on learning. *Advances in the Study of Behavior, 4*, 1–68.

Shettleworth, S.J. (1983). Function and mechanism in learning. In M.D. Zeiler & P. Hazzem (Eds.), *Advances in analysis of behavior* (Vol. 3, pp. 1–39). New York: Wiley.

Shillito Walser, E., Walters, E., & Hague, P. (1982). Vocal communication between ewes and their own and alien lambs. *Behaviour, 81*, 140–151.

Skinner, B.F. (1966). The phylogeny and ontogeny of behavior. *Science, 153*, 1205–1213.

Slater, P.J.B., Eales, L.A., & Clayton, J.J. (1988). Song learning in zebra finches: Progress and prospects. *Advances in the Study of Behavior, 18*, 1–34.

Sluckin, W. (1973). *Imprinting and early learning*. Chicago: Aldine.

Smith, F.V. (1962). Perceptual aspects of imprinting. *Journal of the Zoological Society of London, 8*, 171–191.

Suboski, M.D. (1990). Releaser-induced recognition learning. *Psychological Review, 97*, 271–284.

Thelen, E. (1989). Self organization in developmental processes: Can systems approaches work? In M.G. Gunnar & E. Thelen (Eds.), *Minnesota symposia on child psychology* (Vol. 22, pp. 77–118). Hillsdale, NJ: Erlbaum.

Thorpe, W.H. (1958). The learning of song patterns by birds, with special reference to the song of the chaffinch. *Ibis, 100*, 535–570.

Thorpe, W.H. (1961). *Bird song*. Cambridge, UK: Cambridge University Press.

Thorpe, W.H. (1964). The isolate song of two species of *Emberiza*. *Ibis, 106*, 115–118.

Turpin, B., Johnston, T.D., & Fulk, K.R. (1988). Sibling inhibition of hoarding in postweaning hamster pups. *Developmental Psychobiology, 21*, 467–476.

Valsiner, J. (1987). *Culture and the development of children's action*. Chichester, UK: Wiley.

Valsiner, J. (1989). *Human development and culture*. Lexington, MA: D.C. Heath.

West, M.J., & King, A.P. (1985). Social guidance of vocal learning by female cowbirds: Validating its functional significance. *Zeitschrift fur Tierpsychologie, 70*, 225–235.

West, M.J., & King, A.P. (1987 a). Settling nature and nurture into an ontogenetic niche. *Developmental Psychobiology, 20*, 549–562.

West, M.J., & King, A.P. (1987 b). Coming to terms with the everyday language of comparative psychology. In D.W. Leger (Ed.), *Nebraska symposium on motivation* (Vol. 35, pp. 51–89). Lincoln, NE: University of Nebraska Press.

West, M.J., & King, A.P. (1988). Visual displays of female cowbirds affect the development of song in males. *Nature, 334*, 244–246.

West, M.J., King, A.P., & Arberg, A.A. (1988). The inheritance of niches. In E.M. Blass (Ed.), *Handbook of behavioral neurobiology* (Vol. 9, pp. 41–62). New York: Plenum Press.

Young, P.T. (1968). Evaluation and preference in behavioral development. *Psychological Review, 75*, 222–241.

PART II

Structure of Learning and Structure of Environment

CHAPTER 4

Observation and Learning: Theoretical Paradoxes of Observational Learning

Toni Goodyear

University of North Carolina at Chapel Hill

The relationship of observation to learning in nonhuman species has generated theoretical controversy among psychologists for nearly a century. The controversy has hinged on the problem of determining the observer's mental state as the modeled behavior is performed for the first time: Is the observer's action purposeful, the result of having discerned, by watching, the cause/effect relationship embodied in the activity; or is it an unintentional, uninformed response that subsequently leads to learning by operant or trial and error methods?

The *intentional versus unintentional* dichotomy was posed by the earliest researchers of observational learning in animals. Lloyd Morgan drew a distinction between *instinctive* imitative behavior (i.e., social facilitation effects) and *voluntary* or *intelligent* imitation, which embodies an understanding of the reason for the action (Lloyd Morgan, 1896; see also Baldwin, 1897/1902). Washburn distinguished between "inferential imitation" and instinctive response by describing the former as an instance "where an animal, watching another one go through an action and observing the consequences, is led to perform a similar act from a desire to bring about the same result" (Washburn, 1908, p. 239). Thorpe's (1963) distinctions are perhaps the most pervasive in the field today. He distinguished between social facilitation, local enhancement effects (that is, the enhancement of the stimulus, Spence, 1937) and *true imitation*. True imitation involves the "*intent to profit by another's experience*" (Thorpe, 1963, p. 135; emphasis added). Thorpe's distinctions seem to suggest a family resemblance between true imitation and Koehlerian insight learning (Koehler, 1925); the learner's first correct performance of a task is informed and intentional and guided by a preexisting hypothesis. In contrast, social facilitation effects can involve an increase in arousal levels (Zajonc, 1965), a biasing toward certain aspects of the learning situation,

111

autoshaping and mindless copying behavior (mindless in the sense of no personal knowledge of the reason for the activity). *True imitation* is generally regarded as the true parallel to human capability, and attempts to investigate the generality of this capability across species have been numerous.

The Bandurian position has carried on the classic contention that preperformance knowledge constitutes true observational learning. It postulates that learning by observation is a fundamental cognitive process separate from the mechanisms involved with learning by conditioning (Bandura, 1986; Hilgard & Bower, 1966; John, Chesler, Bartlett, & Victor, 1968). In this view, organisms have (or do not have) a capacity to cognitively grasp a cause/effect relationship *while* observing an individual perform an action. *Vicarious reinforcement* is seen to play a critical motivational role, but response merely serves to maintain or alter what has already been learned (that is, experiencing successful or unsuccessful consequences).

This simple and strongly intuitive argument—that organisms learn *by* watching others—became a major theoretical contest in behaviorally oriented American psychology by suggesting that no response is necessary for learning to occur. Bypassing the definition of learning *as behavior,* and suggesting that one was distinct from the other, it rekindled age-old mentalistic controversies recast in behaviorist vs. cognitive terms. Many investigators still contend that observation serves only as a shaping device via the mechanisms of social facilitation and local enhancement of the stimulus. The essence of these arguments is that observation of a model biases the observer toward certain aspects of the environment; therefore modeling increases the probability that a correct response will happen to occur. The task itself is learned by the consequences of initially uninformed performance, consistent with operant principles.

EMPIRICAL DILEMMAS

Despite the extensive efforts to resolve the controversy empirically, the literature on observational learning remains equivocal on its proposed position as a general and distinct psychological process (e.g., Galef, 1988; Heyes, Dawson, & Nokes, 1992). Why should this be so? The answer lies in the gap that exists between the conceptual problem and its operationalization.

The measurement frequently used to investigate observational learning is the *savings approach* ("profit through observation," Davis, 1973) or the "non-exposed control" method (e.g., Biederman & Vanayan, 1988). If observers demonstrate an accelerated rate of acquisition compared to controls who had no benefit of model, or compared to animals operantly trained in the task, they are said to have demonstrated observational learning. The approach is contradictory to conceptual premises in that is essentially positions social facilitation effects—social shaping—as equivalent to observational learning, even within experiments that attempt to guard against social facilitation effects. Social facilitation is not theoretically equivalent to "seeing into" a task observationally; yet, when a savings in time to criterion is demonstrated after exposure to a model, authors frequently claim that "observational learning" has occurred. In 1937, Spence observed that such methods *necessarily* permit no distinction between purposeful and incidental behavior by observers. The continued popularity of the approach is perhaps understandable on an intuitive level. One would expect that observational learning, like insight, would occur quickly, as opposed to operant learning in which a graduated learning curve bearing a relationship to reinforcement schedule is expected. (To help ensure that the behavior is not likely to occur by operant means in observational studies a novel behavior is used, one that has a near-zero likelihood of occurring without instigation.) However, the performance/competence distinction insures that speed is a questionable measure of observational effect in any case (see Hall, 1963).

Some recent attempts have been made to demonstrate that understanding of a novel action-consequence pairing occurs by true observation rather than by local enhancement. With humans, symbolic encoding enhances performance, implicating a cognitive involvement (Carroll & Bandura, 1990). Among animals, it has been shown that rats are influenced by a response pattern in a conspecific demonstrator when permitted alternative ways to approach a stimulus (Heyes, Jadlow, Dawson, & Nokes, 1994). As the evidence and the methodology now stands, however, results across species necessarily favor the enhancement or operant point of view. If learning by observation is the ability to grasp a cause/effect relationship *while* watching a task performed, then the bulk of the literature, constrained by the above-described methodological assumptions, demonstrates not *observational learning* but only *observational (socially facilitated) effects.* Our knowledge of the generality of observational learning capabilities across species remains uncertain, as does our grasp of the variables affecting such learning.

The Question of Process

An additional issue in the procedures outlined above is a reliance on aggregate data. In attempting to wash out individual differences in hopes of confirming or disconfirming a general principle, traditional methodologies also wash out the one aspect of observational learning that must be revealed in order to begin to resolve the theoretical dilemmas, namely, the *process* by which observation leads to learning. The argument, after all, is an argument about process, about the mechanisms involved with performance change under observational conditions. Here the behaviorists would most likely agree: single-subject designs are conceded to be the only way to fully understand the process leading to behavioral change. *Average* change has no meaning when fundamental processes are at issue (the question of whether it has validity for other uses remains for another discussion).

A few beginning attempts to analyze the substance of the observational learning process were made early on. In these cases, the authors considered *what* behaviors the observers exhibited relative to the model. For example, Warden, Fjeld, and Koch (1940) looked at what they called *degrees of imitativeness* in rhesus monkeys. *Immediate imitation* was correct performance of the task within the first 60-second test period. *Partial imitation* was defined as topographical imitation without sufficient force to operate the mechanism (for example, a rope pull or a latch), similar but not complete imitation of the model's actions, or approaching the mechanism without contacting it. Individual variation was considerable, but 76.4 percent immediate imitation was found when data was considered over 24 tests per animal. There was 22.9 percent partial imitation, mostly of the first type. The findings suggest individual differences in capability, though the roots of variation are not clear. In a second study, Herbert and Harsh (1944) found that in cats, local enhancement effects preceded learning, but that observers were more focused from the outset than operant learners. The authors used *activity paths* to plot the different behavior patterns of each subject; the observers showed less rambling activity than did models who were operantly trained. A third example is Dawson and Foss's 1965 study of budgerigars. The birds were required to remove the lid from a pot of seeds. Regardless of success, the observers in all cases approached the task in the same manner as had the model, either edging or lifting the lid or using either the feet or the beak. Additional, anecdotal analyses can be found with ape studies (for example, Goodall, 1986; Hall, 1963; Hayes & Hayes, 1952; Koehler, 1925; Sevick & Savage-Rumbaugh, 1994; Watson, 1908). The studies are interesting but inconclusive as to differences and similarities between observational and operant learning and the intentional/unintentional dichotomy.

Other studies seem to point to the existence of two fundamentally different processes. Corson (1967) and Powell (1968), for example, compared the relative effectiveness (based on speed of learning) of observing a model versus shaping by extrinsic reinforcement. The studies produced conflicting results: Corson found that observation leads to faster skill acquisition, while Powell, using a larger sample, found that successive approximations was the faster method. The data reveal, in both cases, a much greater individual variation among observers than among the operantly trained rats. All of the operant trainees learned the task in two to eight sessions, with the average around 4.5. Observer rats either learned the task in 1 to 6 (with an average of 2.7) or in 10 to 25 sessions (with an average of 14.8). In other words, the observer rats tended to be bimodally distributed. Speed aside, extrinsic reinforcement by successive approximations produced far more uniform results across subjects. On the other hand, four of the 23 observer rats learned the task in the first session, compared with none of the operantly trained rats.

Similar results were found in a study by Powell, Saunders, and Thompson (1968), which compared shaping, autoshaping, and observational learning for a bar press task. Observers learned the task in five to 14 sessions (range = 9); operantly trained rats learned in two to six sessions (range = 4). The range for observer animals was twice that of operantly trained animals. A study by Del Russo (1971) with hooded rats shows that in a group of six rats, two could be said to have learned the response by observation, since they performed correctly at the first opportunity. The other four showed what might be called social facilitation effects: they nosed the lever, tried to bite it, pushed it upward, and so on. The actual correct response seemed to be learned by trial and error. A study by John et al. (1968) reveals a similar phenomenon. Two of six cats observing an avoidance response learned immediately; the other four did not. In a discriminated lever-press task, one of six observer cats performed at a 100 percent level immediately, another on the second day, and the other four reached 90 percent on the third day. The authors concluded that overall the observer cats demonstrated fewer errors than trained cats. They observed that "some of these animals behaved as if they 'knew' what they were doing" (p. 149) from their first test trial, and some did not. An earlier study with cats by Adler (1955) also showed great individual variation in performance, as do reports on observational learning in monkeys (Warden & Jackson, 1935; Warden et al., 1940) and chimpanzees (see Hall, 1963).

The weight of the evidence overall seems to point to two differences between observers and operant learners. First, the process of shaping by extrinsic reinforcement tends to evoke less variation among subjects than does learning by observation. In this sense, operant conditioning may be described as a more reliable method. Second, operant learning *on average* proceeds more quickly than does observational learning but, in any individual case, observational learning may occur faster than operant learning. Since there is little qualitative analysis of factors leading to individual differences, the mechanisms responsible remain unknown, though the difference in distributions on surface appears to support the argument for two fundamentally different processes. The description of observational learning as primarily a cognitive event suggests a much greater complexity of influences than are ascribed to operant conditioning. Warden and Jackson (1935) looked to intelligence as a possible mediating factor. They compared the performances of observers in the Jenkins Problem Box but found no relationship between problem solution and observational learning. They concluded that the tasks employed tapped different types of capabilities. To restate the issue, *intelligence* in terms of successful performance in observational learning studies with animals has not yet been analyzed in terms of the critical variables defining it.

Bandura continues to provide the most detailed proposal of variables affecting observational learning outcomes. In his 1986 reworking of his social cognitive theory, he again presents his criteria for observational learning to occur: attention, motivation, memory, and the physical ability to perform the task modeled (the task must also be of a level of complexity amenable to being learned observationally). Lack of attention is the most obvious reason for learning to fail to occur, and it provides a default explanation for individual differences. However, many animal investigators have not attempted to determine the amount of individual orientation toward a model, nor what the model is doing at the time of the observer's orientation. Simple presence in the training chamber is regarded as "observational opportunity" (e.g., Powell, 1968; Del Russo, 1971). Still more complex implications of attention—that which occurs beyond the level of simple orientation—are also not generally considered. Bandura touches on this when he acknowledges the complications of selective attention:

> The process of attention is not simply a matter of absorbing sensory information that happens to impinge upon a person. Rather, it involves self-directed exploration of the environment and construction of meaningful perceptions from ongoing modeled events. (Bandura, 1986, p. 53)

The statement makes clear the need for careful examination of how the observational task environment is constructed by individuals in order to begin to assess the learning processes involved.

In sum, qualitative, descriptive accounts at the individual subject level of the process by which learning occurs in operant and observational learning situations are lacking, despite their potential to provide insights into longstanding theoretical problems. In particular, a sequential analysis of the process by which an animal moves to first correct response in each paradigm would seem to be critical information. According to operant theory, the causes of first response are beside the point in demonstrating the control of behavior by contingency. However, it seems clear that insight into the observational/operant distinction can only be obtained by analyzing the pathways by which learning organisms move from nonresponse to first response and then subsequently to stable, informed performance. Some investigators (e.g., Denny, Clos, & Bell, 1988; Heyes, Dawson, & Nokes, 1992) have accordingly begun to emphasize first response behaviors in their analyses.

A PROCESS APPROACH

To examine this question further, a new study was designed to take an in-depth look at the construction of the learning process by individual subjects in operant and observational learning situations. Since the central challenge was to attempt to infer the state of mind of the learners, the approach taken was based on the Tolman-Krechevsky (Tolman, 1932; Krechevsky, 1932) notion that behaviors can be analyzed as to the mental hypotheses they reflect. In order to compare similarities and differences between observational and operant processes the same cognitive terminology was employed in both cases. The term *interpretive plateau* was used to mean the hypothesis suggested by observable behaviors at each point in the learning process. To gauge the effects of observation, the extent and content of each orientation toward the model was recorded along with the immediate and delayed responses to those observations.

The study incorporated factors of natural ecology and group dynamics (in this case the social structure of a captive primate group) that would normally be operable in operant and observational learning experiences. This was accomplished in three ways:

• social permissions and relationships within the group were permitted to exert natural influence
• model-present/response-possible conditions were used
• animals were generally permitted to come and go from the test apparatus as they chose

Two groups of red ruffed lemurs (*Varecia variegata variegata rubra;* order Prosimian) at the Duke University Primate Center (DUPC) were used as subjects. The animals at DUPC are typically housed in small nuclear units. Group 1 was a nuclear family consisting of the mating pair Himalia (7-year-old female) and Jove (5-year-old male), and 1-year-old triplets (two males, Crater and Sculptor; one female, Mimosa). The juvenile Crater was operantly trained as model for this group, and Jove, Sculptor, and Mimosa served as observers. Himalia was pregnant, and was not used as a subject. Group 2 constituted a nuclear family consisting of the mother, Columba (3-year-old female), who was trained as model, and 1-year-old triplets (two females, Pasiphae and Miaplacidus, and one male, Lynx) who served as observers.

In two studies of observational learning in lemurs (Anderson, Fornasieri, Ludes, & Roeder, 1992; Feldman & Klopfer, 1972), both with *Lemur fulvus*, observational effects were suggested. Issues of social relationships within the group were found to be key factors in lemur performance. The author is not aware of any observational studies with *Varecia*. The capacity for operant learning of the task to be modeled had, however, been demonstrated for *Varecia* (Goodyear, Lightfoot, & Crane, 1988). The task was to pull a specific rope and cross to a dish to receive a raisin reward. The behavior qualified as novel in Bandura's sense in that the connection between rope contact and food is not a normal part of the lemurs' ecological repertoire. Lemurs in captivity do suspend from ropes when the ropes are available (Pereira, Seeligson, & Macedonia, 1988), and they are used to receiving food from dishes in captivity. The novel behavior to be learned observationally was the rope–food relationship. Since the rope and food dish were at opposite ends of the chamber, there was near-zero probability that a lemur would pull a rope at one end and immediately cross to inspect the dish at the other end without some extrinsic instigation.

The training apparatus (Figure 4.1) was similar in principle to the duplicate-

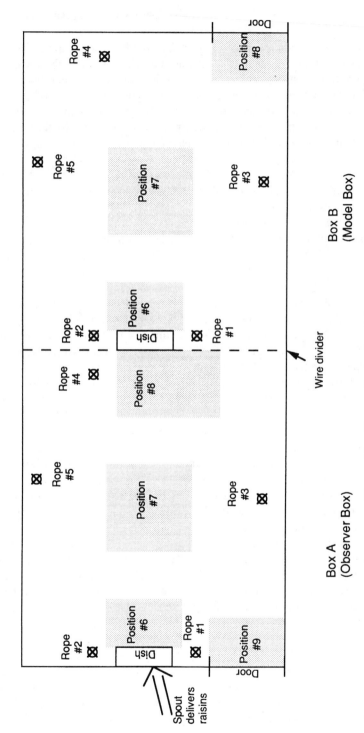

Figure 4.1. Observation and training apparatus.

118

cage apparatus used by Warden and Jackson (1935) with rhesus monkeys. Since it permits immediate, model-present response, the procedure lost favor when observational learning issues centered on the attempt to distinguish between intentional performance and social facilitation effects by permitting only delayed response. The two chambers were separated by a wall made of chicken wire, permitting excellent visibility. Five ropes were hung in each chamber in the positions shown, numbered accordingly. Rope #5 was chosen as the target rope for Group 1; rope #3 was chosen as the target rope for Group 2. The salient positions within each chamber are numbered in Figure 4.1. Position #8 in Chamber A (the observer box) was the best vantage point from which to observe the model in Chamber B.

Reinforcement was manually delivered to each box through a plastic spout leading to each dish. Feeders operated from behind a screen so as not to draw the lemurs' attention. The dish in the model's chamber was made of metal and gave a resounding thunk when raisins dropped. This was to assist in operantly training the models and could also serve as evidence to observers that models were receiving food rewards. Reinforcements were delivered to models when they were in the vicinity of the target rope, when they contacted the rope(s) with any part of the body, or simply to shape their attention back toward the apparatus when distracted. The model in Group 1 (Crater, 1-year-old male) was first trained to pull any rope to receive reinforcement, then the focus was narrowed to rope #5. The model in Group 2 (Columba, 3-year-old mother) was trained directly to the target rope (#3).

Once the performance of the models had reached criterion (90 percent of the ropes contacted were the target rope), the observer chamber was opened. Occasional "welcome raisins" were provided on the floor of the chamber to ensure repeated return and to convey the message that raisins could be obtained in the observation chamber as well as in the model's chamber. Unlike the shaping procedure used with models, observers were reinforced only *after* they had pulled the target rope *and crossed* to the dish. Reinforcement was delivered only for pulling on the rope with the hands, which was the behavior demonstrated by the model; nosing and biting the rope were not rewarded. No arbitrary observation period was imposed; rather, the observers were generally permitted to enter and leave the apparatus at will.

All sessions were videotaped for detailed analysis. The amount of time subjects spent oriented toward the model was recorded, along with the model's specific activity at that moment. These important features were not left to videotape analysis alone; rather the experimenter was positioned in such a way as to observe at close hand the orientation of the observer and kept up a detailed commentary on videotape. At the same time, an assistant kept a running commentary (recorded on the same videotape) as to the exact position and activities of the model. Sessions were conducted once a day, at times when the lemurs were generally most active (early morning or dusk) and at least 8 hours from last feeding. Twelve sessions of approximately 45 minutes each were conducted with Group 1, and 17 sessions of approximately 40 minutes each with Group 2. Length of session was primarily dictated by the lemurs' willingness to continue approaching the apparatus.

Global Results

Table 4.1 provides summary data of the performances of all subjects. Only one observer out of six learned the task (Miaplacidus, Group 2). As can be seen in Figure 4.2, performance began to stabilize on Day 5 and reached criterion on Day 6. Both of the operantly trained models learned the task, and learned it more quickly. The operant trainees each required approximately 9–10 successful reinforced performances before reaching reliable behavior. The observer required 24 task presentations before reaching reliable behavior. As shown in the figure, Columba performed correctly more than 50 percent of the time on the first day and performed reliably by Day 3. Crater, who was first permitted to select his own target rope, initially preferred rope #2 located alongside the dish (the low point of the curve at Day 4 indicates a 65 percent preference for rope #2 at this juncture). When reinforcement was withheld for all but rope #5, he was trained to the new circumstance in one session. The curves for Days 1–3 for Columba and Days 1–4 or 7–8 for Crater may be compared with the learning curve for the observer, Miaplacidus. Miaplacidus reached 50% performance after 5 days of observation and criterion after 6 days. On this quantitative level, the data seem to support the notion of two separate processes: operant trainees learned faster and more reliably than observers (100% versus 17%). The difference between Miaplacidus's learning curve and the hypothetical perfect curve for

Table 4.1. Performance Characteristics

Subject	Sex	Age	Role	Learned?	# Reinf Perform	# of Task Observs.	# of Orients	
Group 1:								
Crater	M	1yr	Model	Yes	10*	—	—	
Sculptor	M	1yr	Obser	No	1	2	8	
Mimosa	F	1yr	Obser	No	2	3	17	
Jove	M	5yr	Obser	No	4	11	41	
Group 2:								
Columba	F	3yr	Model	Yes	9	—	—	
Miaplacidus	F	1yr	Obser	Yes	1	24	114	
Pasiphae	F	1yr	Obser	No	1	76	215	(mom)
							241	(sib)
Lynx	M	1yr	Obser	No	0	18	84	(mom)
							16	(sib)

*Statistics for preferred rope (#2)

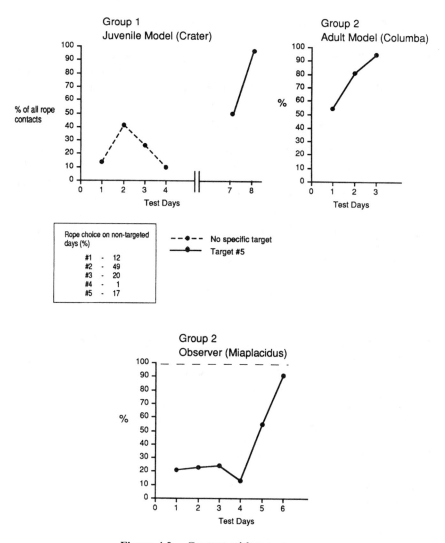

Figure 4.2. Contact with target ropes.

observational learning is also important to note. The perfect curve is represented by the dotted line in the graph for Miaplacidus and depicts what might be called an immediate grasping of the cause–effect relationship in the task simply by seeing it performed. As can be seen, the performance of the observer who learned the task was significantly different from this expectation; "instant learning" was not seen in the six observers used in this study. It is crucial to note, however, that the curves for the operant models also depart from the hypothetical possibility. If it is reasonable to ask why observers do not learn from a single observation, it is also reasonable to ask (as it often has been) why operantly trained subjects do not learn from one reinforcement experience. Automatic assumption of different processes based on speed of learning may be erroneous. Stepwise analysis of the processes by which learning occurred in operant models and observers is necessary to gain further insight into the question.

The Behavior of Operantly Trained Models

The key elements in Crater's performance are presented sequentially in Figure 4.3. The general process by which learning occurred can be described as follows: initially, the loud sound of raisins falling into the metal dish drew the subject to the dish from other parts of the apparatus whenever rope contact was made. Raisins were frequently received. This pattern continued haphazardly into Day 3. On Day 3, however, an important behavioral change occurred. Crater began to *look toward the dish while* pulling various ropes. He then crossed to the dish and was reinforced (see a,b,c,d in Figure 4.3). On one occasion, he looked into the dish, found no raisins, and immediately pulled rope #2 while continuing to monitor the dish. On another occasion, when reinforcement was slow, he continued to hold on to rope #2 and to look into the dish until raisins arrived. It was on Days 3 and 4 that his preference for rope #2 also stabilized. These were the first indications that a new interpretive plateau had been reached: the idea that ropes may somehow be related to the appearance of raisins had been suggested. Crater had moved from a questionless state to one in which a question had been raised.

That learning had taken place (i.e., confirmation of the tentative hypothesis) was demonstrated on Day 4. Rope pulling behavior was consistent and reliable (90% of behavior), extraneous behavior fell away, and overall orientation toward the dish predominated. Pulling became more vigorous and deliberate. Crater continued the pattern of holding on to the rope and looking into the dish until reinforcement arrived; he also responded to slow reinforcement by changing hands or holding the rope at an emphatic, exaggerated angle.

The learning process for the adult model, Columba, in Group 2, is shown in Figure 4.4. On the very first day, Columba gave evidence that a possible rope/raisin relationship had been suggested. Two events aided the process: On one occasion, the experimenter became momentarily visible as Columba pulled rope #3; she appeared to monitor the feeder's hand moving to the top of the spout to deliver raisins, then crossed to the dish and received reinforcement (a, Figure 4.4). Later, she accidentally hit rope #3 with her tail and started it swinging. She looked at it and nudged it with her nose. Raisins fell noisily; she looked toward the dish and slowly crossed (b).

The first occasion of looking toward the dish *while* contacting a rope occurred in connection with rope #5 (c) on Day 1. No reinforcement resulted. She next accidentally struck rope #3, heard raisins fall, and looked toward the

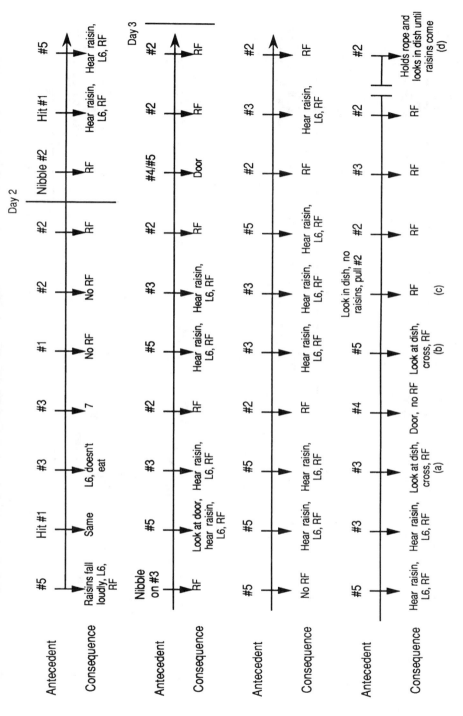

Figure 4.3. Sequential description of operant learning process Crater (juvenile).

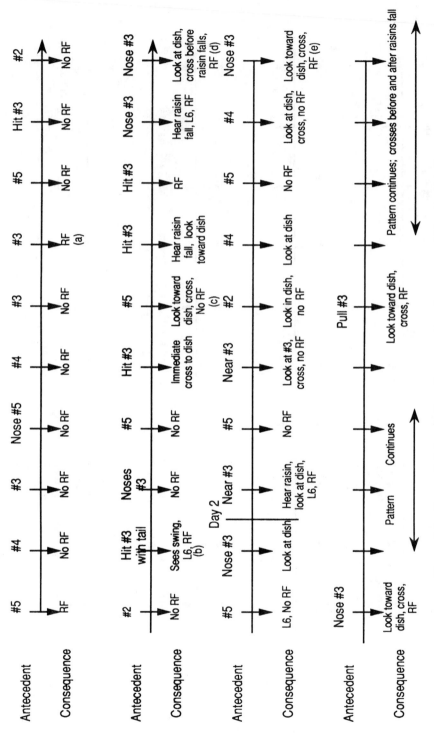

Figure 4.4. Sequential description of operant learning process Columba (adult).

124

dish. The frequency of looking toward the dish while contacting different ropes continued to increase thereafter during the Day 1 session, with emphasis on rope #3. On Day 2, the first clear pulling of rope #3 using the hands occurred; by the end of the session, a pattern of pulling rope #3, looking at the dish and crossing was established (no contact with other ropes). Crossing occurred both after and before raisins fell. Day 3 performance was at criterion.

As indicated by the sequential description of her rope-related performance, Columba looked toward the dish *without the sound* of falling raisins or actually inspected the dish in connection with different ropes prior to settling on rope #3. The behaviors suggest the formation of a general question or hypothesis— namely, that a rope/raisin relationship might exist—*prior* to confirmation of the correct relationship (that pulling rope #3 leads to raisins). Confirmation—or perhaps increasing confidence in the hypothesis is the better way to characterize it—occurred by means of correct performance juxtapositioned with incorrect performance; therefore, confirmation seemed to occur by means of trial and error testing of a general concept or notion.

The Behavior of Observers: Group 1

None of the four observers in this group learned the task. Three contributing factors could be identified: sporadic modeling, little tendency to orient toward the juvenile model, and social competition and territoriality on the part of the model.

Sporadic modeling. The 1-year-old model displayed an ambivalent relationship to task performance. He showed great anxiety in the training apparatus and his modeling was therefore intermittent. A recurrent behavior pattern was "look out the door–pull the rope–go to the dish–look out the door"; in general, a great deal of attention was focused on the door. The distractibility contributed to a collective total of only 16 task presentations over the course of the study (12 sessions).

Orientation tendency. The low status of the juvenile male model seems to have impacted heavily on the failure to learn in this group. Put simply, Crater was frequently ignored. *Varecia* is a female-dominant species; in general, females enjoy higher status than males (Jolly, 1966). Mimosa, the only female observer in Group 2, in particular paid very little attention to her brother's modeling. Most attentive was the adult male, Jove, who logged 41 orientations but saw only 11 task presentations over the entire study period. The number of orientations by siblings was remarkably low; they observed only two and three task presentations over the entire 12 days.

Social competition. Social dynamics in Group 1 impacted on the young male's performance and effectiveness as a model. When Himalia, the mother and dominant female in the group, was near the apparatus, none of the siblings could approach without being overtly threatened, including Crater. Subsequently,

Himalia was sequestered prior to each session. This had the effect, however, of increasing the status of the other female in the group, the 1-year-old Mimosa. She in turn would intimidate Crater periodically. The inconsistent nature of the intimidation, and the fact that during the course of the study each of the sibs had displaced and been displaced by one of the others more than once, suggests that among these 1-year-olds a linear hierarchy may not be rigidly determined. However, a general environment of potential confrontation subsequently existed for each of the triplets, and more so for the two young males. This was best demonstrated by Sculptor's performance; his general preference for approaching the apparatus when it was vacant contributed to nearly four times as much time in the box without benefit of model as when the model was present.

The adverse effect of social tension and competition on the observational learning experience was most clearly seen on Days 8–12. Over the first seven days of testing, observers frequently tried to enter the model's chamber. On Day 8 they were permitted to do so; it was thought that observers might equate performance with chamber B rather than A. The result of the sudden invasion of Crater's domain was threefold:

- Crater's performance level when alone in the box and the proportion of time spent in the box dramatically increased.
- There was suddenly a great deal of interindividual attention among siblings; not by observers toward the model but by the model toward the observers.
- A level of competitiveness was set for the group as a whole which established behavior patterns for Days 9–12 which were not conducive to observational learning.

Figure 4.5 provides a sample of the competitive behavior seen in the model's chamber on Day 8. Crater's behavior when others were in the chamber was defensive and evasive. When alone in the apparatus, he performed the task with a fervor that stood in marked contrast to his performance on previous days. This within-group territoriality by *Varecia* demonstrated a variable not generally visible in laboratory controlled experiments: that is, an attempt by the model not to model. Crater staunchly defended his recently acquired raisin treasure despite social hazard: he entered immediately after other members entered, combatively defended the apparatus, and repeatedly checked the door to monitor the position of others. Predictably, Crater's behavior changed depending on who was present. With Sculptor, he displayed a primary concern for preventing his brother's contact with the target rope; on two occasions he literally took the rope out of his hand; at other times, he simply chased him away. The methods are appropriate to a juvenile-peer relationship. With Himalia, such a procedure could have been potentially hazardous. Crater usually refrained from any aggravating behavior with his mother, including crossing to the dish to obtain raisins if

Episode	Observer	Model (Crater)
1	S.enter box	enter box, perform task
	S.nose rope	pull rope, cross to dish
	S.swipe at rope	cross to rope, pull
	S.reach for rope	cuff S., cross to dish
	S.pull rope	chase S. from box
2	S.enter box	chase S. from box
3	S.sit in doorway	cuff S.
4	S.enter box	pull rope, cross to dish
	S.chew on rope	cross to rope, take it from S.
	S. leave box	
5	J.look in dish	pull rope, cross while J. not looking
	J.move near rope	move near rope, do not pull
	J.move away	pull rope, cross while J. not looking
	Sequence repeats	
6	S.enter box	enter box
	S.look out door	perform task
	S.hold onto rope	cross to rope, take it from S., cross to dish
	S. hold onto rope	cross to rope, take it from S.
	S.leave box	
7	S.enter, hold rope	try to take rope away
		scuffle ensues
	S.leave box	
8	M.look out door	pull rope, cross to dish
	M.enter box	move to rope and hang onto it until M. leaves
	M.enter box	stand at center, do not perform
	M.leaves box	check door, return to task
9	H. enter box	pull rope, do not cross to dish
	H. leaves	return to task

Figure 4.5.   Competition factor in observational learning.

Himalia was in his path. Because of this, he eliminated Himalia's opportunity to observe the task performed. With Jove, Crater demonstrated the rudiments of a behavior pattern which was later seen in Group 2: He appeared to perform only when Jove was not watching. There were similar suggestions of this with Mimosa; Crater simply stood still or hung from rope #5 while Mimosa was present. When she left, he checked the door behind her and then returned to the task. In the many interactions occurring in this session there was only one instance of an observer witnessing the full task performed.

The general level of competition and group tension set by multiple access to one box on Day 8 was seen for the remainder of the study. By Days 11 and 12, a dominant pattern of single occupancy had developed in which each member left shortly after another entered. The potential for observational learning accordingly eroded.

The Behavior of Observers: Group 2

In Group 2, one of the three juvenile observers learned the task. Miaplacidus reached criterion after having observed 24 performances of the task by her mother, Columba.

What was the process by which this successful lemur came to learn? Figures 4.6 through 4.10 presents the sequential analysis for Miaplacidus. The top line in the figure describes what the model was doing while the observer was watching. The bottom line describes the observer's behavior after the orientation.

Day 1. (Figure 4.6): Miaplacidus's first response to observing Columba pull rope #3 was to move to her own dish (a in Figure 4.6). The sequence occurred twice. Since Miaplacidus had not yet seen the task performed at all, the best explanation for the response is that she was able to see and hear raisins fall into Columba's dish (see Figure 4.1). The first time Miaplacidus saw the task performed (pull #3, receive raisins in the dish, cross to the dish), she responded by pulling rope #4, the rope beside her (b, in Figure 4.6). As can be seen, her responses from this point were primarily rope oriented. The second time she witnessed the task she pulled ropes #5 and #4 and returned to watching. The third time she responded with task performance: she pulled rope #3, *looked at her own dish* and immediately crossed to her dish where she received reinforcement. She then immediately pulled rope #5 (the spatial opposite of #3), again looked at her own dish and crossed (no reinforcement occurred; e, in Figure 4.6). The dish-orienting behavior suggests that the subject had moved from simple curiosity about the box and an interest in the raisins found in its vicinity to the first suggestion that a rope/raisin relationship might exist. In this case, observation of the model rather than reinforcement provided the impetus. Miaplacidus's response also suggests some appreciation of the parallel structure of the two chambers. The subsequent sequence with rope #5 indicates that the importance of rope #3 per se was not apparent at this point.

Miaplacidus's selective attention toward the rope-pulling component of the task (rather than the alternative possibilities of simple movement, a focus on raisins per se or simple dish-crossing behavior) was a key factor in the learning process, as was her predominant use of the hands to pull ropes (rather than nosing or mouthing the rope as lemurs frequently do, which would not have resulted in reinforcement). This perhaps is linked to the chance circumstance that her first three observations of the model were all at the moment that Columba was pulling rope #3.

Day 2. (Figure 4.7): Miaplacidus entered the box, pulled rope #5, and immediately crossed to her dish (a). The rapidity of the behavior suggested a carryover from Day 1 of a general rope/raisin relationship as well as a lack of knowledge of the correct rope–raisin link. When she next saw Columba eating raisins at her dish, Miaplacidus again pulled rope #5 (b). After the first task performance of the day, Miaplacidus moved near her own rope #3 and then crossed to her dish (c). She did not pull the rope. The second observation of the task

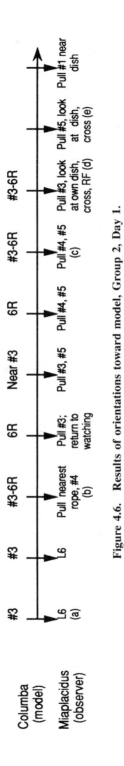

Figure 4.6. Results of orientations toward model, Group 2, Day 1.

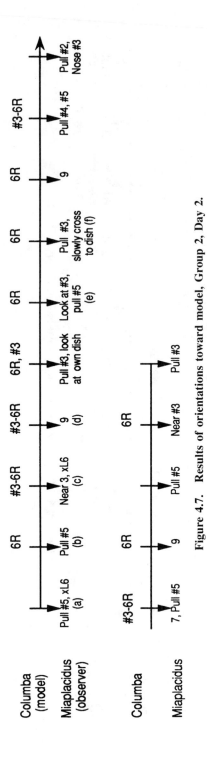

Figure 4.7. Results of orientations toward model, Group 2, Day 2.

had no significant performance reaction; the lemurs were often distracted or startled by events going on outside the boxes (including frequent eruptions of the *Varecia* alarm call) and frequently darted to the door of the box (d). These normal occurrences were factors which could impact on observational learning under natural circumstances.

After the third task performance, Miaplacidus *looked at rope #3 and then pulled rope #5.* The behavior suggests that the spatial relationship of the two ropes was a factor, and that the correct one of the two was not immediately apparent. When Miaplacidus next saw Columba eating raisins at her dish, she responded by looking at rope #3 and then pulling it. She moved to the dish but raisin delivery was slow; by the time the raisin arrived, Miaplacidus had moved away from the dish and did not see it. (On other occasions, even when raisin delivery was not slow, observers darted to and away from the dish so quickly they did not see the raisin. For both reasons, reinforcement results were not always immediate and reliable; in this sense, the reinforcement experience could be said to more closely parallel real-world contingencies than rigidly controlled laboratory procedures.) As can be seen in Figure 4.7, Miaplacidus's general response orientation continued to focus most heavily on ropes.

Days 3 and 4. (Figures 4.8 and 4.9): Miaplacidus continued to demonstrate the suggestion of a rope–raisin link with rope contacts and dish inspection. In one instance she pulled rope #3, looked at her own dish, then crossed back to position #8 and reoriented towards Columba (a). In another instance, she watched her mother pull #3, immediately looked at her own rope #4, and pulled it (b).

Day 5. (Figure 4.10): On this day, Miaplacidus demonstrated movement to a new interpretive plateau; by the end of the session, she had demonstrated knowledge that rope #3 was the key to obtaining raisins. Her first response to seeing the task performed was to pull rope #4 (a, in Figure 4.10); she then immediately pulled #3, looked at her own dish, and crossed. She was successfully reinforced. She performed the task three times, interspersed with other activities, including moments when Columba was not present in the model's box. When Columba left the apparatus for the second time, Miaplacidus performed the task interspersed with contacts with other ropes; in general, she looked toward the dish while pulling rope #3, but not while pulling ropes #1, 2, 4, and 5. Finally, she performed the task successfully 23 times.

Of special interest was Miaplacidus's behavior after this successful run. She again began to pull other ropes (see e, in Figure 4.10) and to look toward the dish, frequently crossing to inspect the dish after doing so. Correct task performance was interspersed with these other attempts. The pattern suggests that the result of pulling rope #3 and crossing to the dish was being compared to the results of pulling other ropes and crossing to the dish.

On Day 8, Miaplacidus was permitted to enter the model's chamber alone in order to determine whether the learned task would transfer. Her performance,

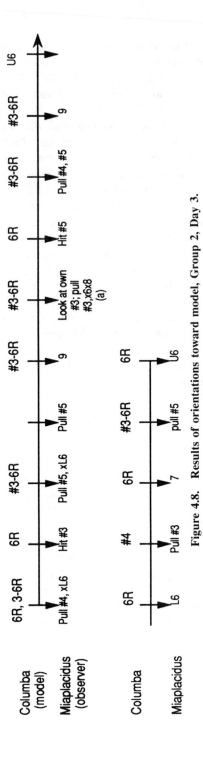

Figure 4.8. Results of orientations toward model, Group 2, Day 3.

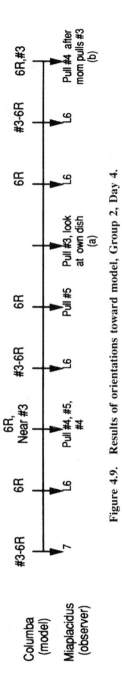

Figure 4.9. Results of orientations toward model, Group 2, Day 4.

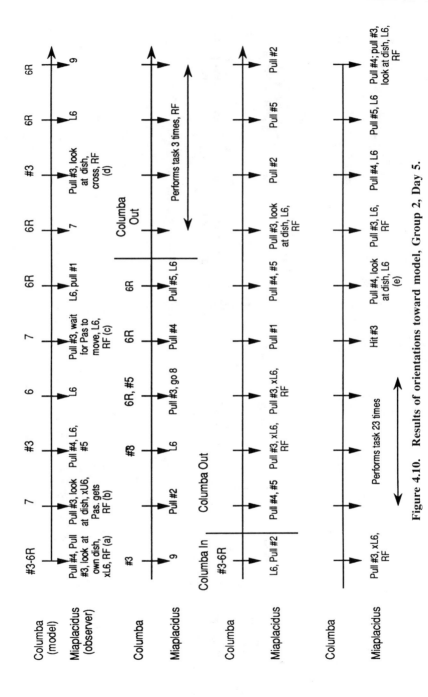

Figure 4.10. Results of orientations toward model, Group 2, Day 5.

134

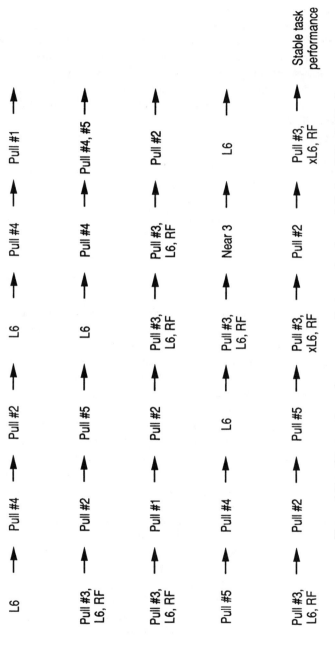

Figure 4.11.   Observer's performance on first occasion in model's box (Miaplacidus).

outlined in Figure 4.11, supports the contention that a general concept had been imparted. In rapid-fire fashion, she pulled one rope after another, intermittently inspecting the dish and interposing task performance, before settling down to reliable behavior with the correct rope. On subsequent entries to the model's box, this pattern was not repeated. Clearly, Miaplacidus was initially attempting to determine which rope(s) worked in *this* chamber.

On Day 6, Miaplacidus reached criterion performance of the task. With no model present, 91% of all rope contacts were with rope #3 and the pull/cross pattern was reliable and consistent.

The other two observers in Group 2, Pasiphae (female) and Lynx (male), did not learn the task. The key factor in Lynx's failure to learn was that he was seldom permitted safe access to the apparatus. For Pasiphae, the key feature was her selective attention to the food dishes rather than the rope-pulling component of the task. In a nutshell, Pasiphae engaged in scrounging behavior (Fragaszy & Visalberghi, 1989; Giraldeau & LeFebvre, 1987), which resulted in her obtaining raisins without learning to pull ropes.

DISCUSSION

The study demonstrates that observing a conspecific model perform a particular task can impact on the behavior of the red ruffed lemur. Also demonstrated are social effects predicted by general theory to impact heavily on the ability of an organism to learn by watching, including social permissions and opportunity to observe the task. In particular, the strong territoriality demonstrated by the lemurs, even within nuclear groups, indicates that active attempts by the models *not to demonstrate the task* is a factor which must be added to the list of variables impacting on observational learning in natural contexts.

In terms of the question of chief interest in the current discussion—namely, the operant–cognitive comparison—the results seem to support the role of observation as primarily a shaping device (by earlier definition, an observational effect) rather than as the sole factor in skill acquisition (true observational learning). As the sequential analyses demonstrate, the observer who learned the task did not appear to fully grasp the specific cause/effect relationship embodied in the task simply by watching it performed. (Obviously this was also the case for the other observers whose sequential performances were not presented in detail here, those who did not learn the task at all.) Rather, the behavior of observers indicated that a general suggestion of a possible rope/raisin relationship was raised by observation and that this suggestion was intermittently tested until some level of confidence was attained by consequences. In the case of Miaplacidus, selective attention to the rope-pulling component of the task eventually led to confirmation of a general hypothesis by means of reinforcement experience.

The labeling of the role of observation as a shaping device, however, achieves some clarification in the present study. In traditional R-S-R terms, shaping by extrinsic reinforcement increases the probability of a behavior occurring by means of stimulus enhancement; shaping by observation traditionally is seen to instigate uninformed copying behavior, and reinforcement consequences actually transfer the behavior of interest to a new operant class. However, behavior patterns observed in the present study suggest that a *cognitive shaping* is what actually occurred, *both in the operant and observational cases*. This was not merely an artifact of a cognitive-based analysis. Rather it is the most parsimonious (and possibly the only) explanation for the prelearning, visual orientation behavior of the subjects. In the operant case, models looked toward the dish expectantly while pulling ropes, prior to confident, criterion performance. Incorrect performance continued even after a number of reinforcements for correct performance had been received. Reinforcement alone is therefore an inadequate explanation of the cause of correct behavior in any automatic sense. Something else—cognitive participation—mediates the transition from behavior to learning. Reinforcement served to raise the initial question or hypothesis, but it could play a confirmatory role—that is, it could result in learning—only after a question had been asked. In the observational case, it was modeling that seemed to impart the new idea that a rope–raisin relationship might exist. The observer's behavior of visually orienting toward the dish prior to having received any reinforcement for the behavior strongly suggests that this *general possibility* of a potentially meaningful link between rope and raisin had been established *observationally*. Other behaviors also support this notion: for example, sequences in which the subject simply orients toward ropes in its own chamber after watching the model, or those in which the subject looks at ropes #3 and #5, and then pulls #5 and crosses to the dish, or those in which a subject, watching another pull or hang on a rope, crosses to its own dish. Subjects who behaved in this manner appeared to have derived a general question from the model's performance (and seeing their raisin rewards) and then had to discover the answer experientally. Learning was still accomplished by means of feedback from the environment; however, the role of observation as a "shaper" of behavior was not limited to simple arousal, mindless copying, or stimulus enhancement. What the model imparted was a suggestion or hypothesis, a motivation to perform a response. Consequences confirmed or disconfirmed the hypothesis.

The difficult question of why in cases of observational learning some observers learn quickly, some slowly, and others not at all, even when social permissions and other variables are relatively equal, becomes less puzzling if one concedes that organisms will vary naturally in their cognitive and affective predispositions. These differences result in different construction of the learning situation by individuals, including differences in selective attention and strategies or interpretations (for example the case of the lemur for whom a scrounging strategy prevailed). If cognitive participation is seen to underly both forms of learning, it then becomes predictable that operant training would be a more "reliable" method. It may be argued that in cases of deliberate operant training—as in this study, the laboratory, the classroom, the family—ideas are more intrusively manipulated by the trainer. There is perhaps less latitude for differences in predispositions and ideas to function. Indeed, deliberate shaping procedures, when skillfully handled, are *designed* to diminish selective options and to bypass or overcome individual inclination (not always successfully). The reverse might also be predicted: less skillfully handled or less deliberate operant training—that is, the kind of learning by contingency that tends to characterize much of development in natural contexts—may be expected to allow more interpretive activity to come into play, leading to greater difficulty in predicting specific outcomes.

Such is the case in observational learning. In observational circumstances, attention and interpretation are not as intrusively manipulated by the model simply because the organism by itself must *first* turn the occurrence of witnessing into a behavior which can then produce confirmatory feedback from the environment. For the operant learner the question arises post hoc, after the behavior and feedback has occurred. In any learning situation, an organism may have an idea immediately or after a while or not at all. Operant procedures succeed by hedging the bet, by increasing the *probability* that a particular idea will occur. This is equivalent to saying that the key difference between observational and operant learning is not that one is cognitive and the other is not, but that operant learning does not require cognitive participation *prior to* first response. The observer must have some motivation to cross to a rope and pull it; the operant learner has already happened to pull the rope and has experienced the result.

The *interpretive plateaus* (task structure) suggested by the performances of operant and observational learners are presented in Figure 4.12. As seen, the structure of each process was similar. Subjects in both cases were first drawn to the apparatus by curiosity and by the presence of raisins in the vicinity. No questions, no hypotheses, no goal orientations, or any awareness that one's own behavior could impact on raisin delivery is present at the outset.

In the operant case, subjects initally contacted ropes (target ropes and others) in the normal process of moving around the apparatus. Indeed, first response occurred accidentally. These contacts produced an immediate result, *regardless of the subject's orientation at the time,* in that the very loud thunk of the raisins drew the lemurs' attention from wherever they happened to be. In this sense, their cognitive state was strongly manipulated by the experimenter. There was no requirement that the full task to be learned by observers—pull rope, cross to dish—be performed prior to obtaining feedback.

By means of accidental rope contact and immediate reinforcement, the models grasped the idea that a rope/raisin relationship existed; however, a number of reinforcement experiences were required prior to reaching this second interpretive plateau. It was not until Day 3 that Crater began to look toward the dish

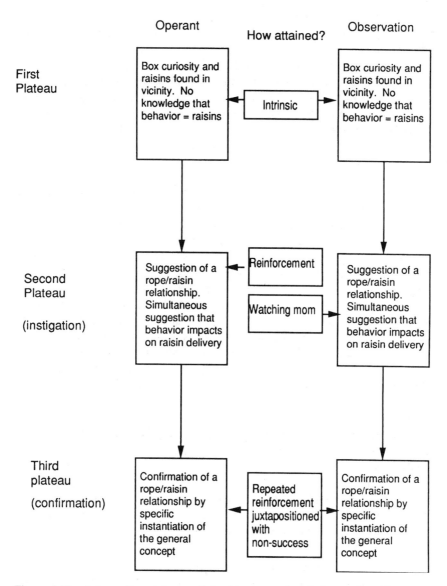

Figure 4.12.   Interpretive plateaus attained by operant and observational learners.

while pulling ropes, prior to the dropping of the raisin. Once his hypothesis was sufficiently confirmed by experience he gave clear indications of expectation, such as holding the rope at a more emphatic angle. The adult, Columba, grasped the concept more quickly than the juvenile. As early as Day 1, she began to look at the dish while pulling various ropes; by the end of the session she was emphasizing her expectations by crossing to the dish before as well as after raisins fell.

The third interpretive plateau in the operant case was reached with the discovery of *which* rope worked. The transition was aided by discovering which ropes did *not* work as well as which of them did. The hypothesis had been confirmed and instantiated by experience. In cognitive terms, the role of reinforcement for the operantly trained models can be described as first *instigative* of an idea and then *confirmatory*. The learners' expectant orientation behavior leads to this conclusion.

Unlike the models, observers had to correctly perform the task prior to receiving reinforcement. Instigation for pull/cross behavior was observation rather than feedback produced by accidental encounter. Miaplacidus looked toward the dish prior to crossing on her very first performance of the task, after having seen it modeled three times. In that the initial question or suggestion of a rope/raisin relationship was raised for Miaplacidus by observation of a model, it can be said that observation provided the same instigative role that reinforcement served for the models. However, reinforcement played a confirmatory role in both cases. As seen in Figure 4.12, the sequences of interpretive plateaus are indistinguishable for both operant and observational learning. The central difference between the two processes is in the initial impetus for transition to the general concept that a rope/raisin relationship might exist.

In summary, a study of the processes by which operant and observational learning are attained leads to the following conclusions:

- Observation may be instigatory, not confirmatory
- Observational learning requires cognitive participation prior to first response and is therefore more subject to the effects of differences in cognitive predispositions
- In both processes, cognitive mediation is operative. In observational learning, modeling seems to impart a question or suggestion that must then be confirmed, and in the operant case, direct experience raises a suggestion that must then be confirmed before learning occurs.

In this line of argument, learning is implicitly defined as a degree of certainty. In a sense, behavioral psychology has always implicitly defined learning in this manner. The concept of criterion performance is little more than an intuitive attempt to select a moment at which we may all agree that some certainty, behaviorally demonstrated, seems to exist on the part of the learner. The transition from the prelearning state (a state of questioning) to certainty (a state of knowledge) may be said to require insight almost by definition; that is, a sudden reorganization of a preexisting situation in some new way. If this were not the case, a single observation or a single reinforcement could be expected to result in criterion behavior, bypassing inconsistent, prelearning instances of correct performance.

The distinction between a state of questioning and a state of knowledge may further clarify why the many attempts to demonstrate a "humanlike" observational learning capability among nonhuman species have been less than successful. Careful analysis of the process by which observational learning occurs in humans may reveal a similar movement from question to certainty, rather than the instantaneous knowing traditionally associated with "true observational learning." By studying the process rather than the product of the learning experience, many of the longstanding issues of relating to the psychological generality of observational learning may be clarified.

REFERENCES

Adler, H.E. (1955). Some factors of observational learning in cats. *Journal of Genetic Psychology, 86,* 159–177.

Anderson, J.R., Fornasieri, I., Ludes, E., & Roeder, J.J. (1992). Social processes and innovative behavior in changing groups of *Lemur fulvus. Behavioural Processes, 27*(2), 101–112.

Baldwin, J.M. (1902). *Social and ethical interpretations in mental development: A study in social psychology,* (3rd ed.). New York: Macmillan. (Original work published 1897)

Bandura, A. (1986). *Social foundations of thought and action: A social cognitive theory.* Euglewood Cliffs, NJ Prentice-Hall.

Biederman, G.B., & Vanayan, M. (1988). Observational learning in pigeons: The function of quality of observed performance in simultaneous discrimination. *Learning and Motivation, 19,* 31–43.

Carroll, W.R., & Bandura, A. (1987). Representational guidance of action production in observational learning: A causal analysis. *Journal of Motor Behavior, 22*(1), 85–97.

Corson, J.A. (1967). Observational learning of a lever pressing response. *Psychonomic Science, 7,* 197–198.

Davis, J.M. (1973). Imitation: a review and critique. In P.P.G. Bateson & P.H. Klopfer (Eds.), *Perspectives in ethology* (pp. 43–72). New York: Plenum Press.

Dawson, B.V., & Foss, B.M. (1965). Observational learning in budgerigars. *Animal Behavior, 13,* 470–474.

Del Russo, J. (1971). Observational learning in hooded rats. *Psychonomic Science, 24* (1), 37–38.

Denny, M.R., Clos C.F., & Bell, R.C. (1988). Learning in the rat of a choice response by observation of S-S contingencies. In T.R. Zentall & B.G. Galef (Eds.), *Social learning: Psychological and biological perspectives* (pp. 207–223). Hillsdale, NJ: Erlbaum.

Feldman, D.W., & Klopfer, P.H. (1972). A study of observational learning in lemurs. *Zeitschrifte fur Tierpsychologie, 30,* 297–304.

Fragaszy, D.M., & Visalberghi, E. (1989). Social influences on the acquisition of tool-using behaviors in tufted capuchin monkeys (*Cebus apella*). *Journal of Comparative Psychology, 103* (2), 159–170.

Galef, B.G. (1988). Imitation in animals: Histroy, definition and interpretation of data from the psychological laboratory. In T.R. Zentall & B.G. Galef (Eds.), *Social Learning: Psychological and biological perspectives* (pp. 3–28), Hillsdale, NJ: Erlbaum.

Giraldeau, L.A., & LeFebvre, L. (1987). Scrounging prevents cultural transmission of food-finding behavior in pigeons. *Animal Behavior, 35,* 387–394.

Goodall, J.V.L. (1986). *The chimpanzees of Gombe.* Cambridge MA: Harvard University Press.

Goodyear, T., Lightfoot, C., & Crane, D. (1988). *Operant learning in Varecia variegata variegata.* Unpublished manuscript.

Hall, K.R.L. (1963). Observational learning in monkeys and apes. British *Journal of Psychology, 54,* 201–226.

Hayes, K.J., & Hayes, C. (1952). Imitation in a home-raised chimpanzee. *Journal of Comparative and Physiological Psychology, 45,* 450–459.

Herbert, M.J., & Harsh, C.M. (1944). Observational learning in cats. *Journal of Comparative and Physiological Psychology, 37,* 81–95.

Heyes, C.M., Jaldow, E., Dawson, G.R., & Nokes, T. (1994). Imitation in rats (Rattus norvegicus): The role of demonstrator action. *Behavioural Processes, 32*(2), 173–182.

Heyes, C.M., Dawson, G.R., & Nokes, T. (1992). Imitation in rats: Initial responding and transfer evidence. *The Quarterly Journal of Experimental Psychology, 45B*(3), 229–240.

Hilgard, E.R., & Bower, G.H. (1966). *Theories of learning* (3rd ed.). New York: Appleton-Century-Crofts.

Jolly, A. (1966). *Lemur behavior.* Chicago: University of Chicago Press.

John, E.R., Chesler, P., Bartlett, F., & Victor, I. (1968). Observation learning in cats. *Science, 159,* 1489–1491.

Koehler, W. (1925). *The mentality of apes* (E. Winter, Trans.). New York: Harcourt Brace and World.

Krechevsky, I. (1932). The genesis of "hypothesis" in rats. *University of California Publications in Psychology, 6(4),* 45–64.

Pereira, M.E., Seeligson, M.L., & Macedonia, J.M. (1988). The behavioral repertoire of the black-and-white ruffed lemur *Varecia variegata variegata* (Primates: Lemuridae). *Folia Primatologica, 51,* 1–32.

Powell, R.W. (1968). Observational learning vs. shaping: a replication. *Psychonomic Science, 13,* 167–168.

Powell, R.W., Saunders, D., & Thompson, W. (1968). Shaping, autoshaping and observational learning with rats. *Psychonomic Science, 13,* 167–168.

Sevick, R.A., & Savage-Rumbaugh, E.S. (1994). Language comprehension and use by great apes. *Language and Communication, 14*(1), 37–58.

Spence, K.W. (1937). Experimental studies of learning and the higher mental processes of infra-human primates. *Psychological Bulletin, 34,* 806–850.

Thorpe, W.H. (1963). *Learning and instinct in animals* (3rd ed.). London: Methuen.

Tolman, E.C. (1932). *Purposive behavior in animals and men.* New York: Appleton-Century.

Warden, C.J., Fjeld, H.A. & Koch, A.M. (1940). Imitative behavior in Cebus and Rhesus monkeys. *Journal of Genetic Psychology, 56,* 311–322.

Warden, C.J., & Jackson, T.A. (1935). Imitative behavior in the rhesus monkey. *Pedagogical Seminary, 46,* 103–125.

Washburn, M.F. (1908). *The animal mind.* New York: Macmillan.

Watson, J.B. (1908). Imitation in monkeys. *Psychological Bulletin, 5*(6), 169–178.

Zajonc, R. (1965). Social facilitation. *Science, 149,* 269–274.

CHAPTER 5

Computer Systems as Learning Environments

Siegfried Greif

University of Osnabrück, Germany

Computer systems have been brought in nearly everywhere. We have them in our offices, where we use them for writing, information seeking and administration, calculation, preparation of presentations, or planning our work. On manufacturing jobs we apply them to program and control computer-based machines or robots, computer-aided design, or to run components and even whole departments of firms by computer-integrated manufacture. Also on our way to the job or back home we are invisibly supported or stirred by computer systems that guide the traffic. We also may mention the ticket machines at the bus or railway station, and so on. In some households people use video information systems, and of course our children play with computers.

This broad diffusion of computer systems into nearly every sphere of life has alarmed many people. Scenarios of the dangers of universal control of human life by computer systems get a great deal of public attention (Weizenbaum, 1976). Indeed work has been changed since the computer revolution. If we empirically evaluate the observable changes in such places as the workplace, they seem to be much less dramatic than expected (Kühlmann, 1988).

Our real problems with computer systems are mundane and concrete. A typical problem is that computer-based systems often do not do what we want them to do. Ticket machines may be taken as an example. In many towns they are different. We need special expertise to use them. I remember well a situation example where I and other computer experts were nearly helpless standing at the ticket machine of a lonely underground station of a German city. I will also never forget the strange behavior of people in the modern underground of Washington, D.C., lining up at the ticket machines trying to feed dollar bills into the slots. Some were experts, had a lot of bills, or knew how to even the bills. Many tourists had to give up (and take a taxi). Obviously, people have to develop special knowledge and motor skills to manage such systems.

At work computer tools also seldom are as easy to manage as they have been sold to be by the software firms. Even if systems are designed to be simple, extremely complex and straining error situations may occur. The firms try to sell new hard- and software. Therefore, every two or three years we have to adapt to new and—as our experience shows—more complex systems. Even experts are not prepared for the unexpected chaos when they buy a new computer, printer, or software system. We may complain about these problems if we try to make computer systems do what we want them to. If we interpret these problems as challenges for permanent human learning, we may develop positive attitudes.

Through failure and success, we learn how to cope with these problems. Therefore, from a learning perspective, we can state that the rapid diffusion of computer-based tools has spread new learning demands to nearly every sphere of human life. It is probable that no other technical or artificial system ever has stimulated more problem-solving or learning activities in so many different spheres of everyday life.

It is a challenge for psychology to test the applicability of different theories of learning and principles for the design of learning tasks and environments to new learning demands in human–computer interaction. In the following sections, a summary of traditional and new theoretical approaches that have been applied to this growing field of learning will be presented. We will concentrate on the field of training office software systems and give a review of our work.

Classical learning theories and their application to computer-based instruction will be described in the next section. After this, in the next section I will summarize and discuss basic approaches of cognitive science and action theory in the human–computer interaction field. Exploration theory, principles of different approaches of self-organized learning, and exploratory learning by errors and their practical application will then be described, followed by a review of experimental evaluation studies. Perspectives of an integration of connectionistic and other theoretical approaches are given in the last section.

TRADITIONAL LEARNING THEORIES AND COMPUTER-BASED INSTRUCTION

Learning Theory and Computer-based Tutorials

Skinner's (1954) principles of operant conditioning had a strong influence on computer-based-instruction (CBI) during the 1950s. Crowder's (1962) branching concept soon became more popular because it could be applied to adaptive and efficient sequencing in learning (cf. Shlechter, 1991).

The military, schools, and universities are the most important institutions where CBI programs for different teaching purposes (for example, courses in basic electronics and programming, mathematical skills, the use of basic military equipment, and medical training) were developed. More recently, there have been efforts to design tutorials for standard software systems. Examples are tutorials for word processors and complex multifunctional software packages. Today, all professional software systems are delivered with tutorial systems. Instead of the early promises of CBI, there is only limited evidence for a short-term reduction of training costs (McCombs, 1991). The success of tutorials applied without additional active support of teachers for the training of novices seems to be very limited. In professional industrial training, they have not displaced traditional teaching courses.

Our results and observations, given in an evaluation study (Greif & Janikowski, 1987) of a typical tutorial for a classical word processor (WORD-STAR), may help to describe the difficulties of classical programmed instruction in the training of novices. The tutorial we evaluated covered personalized instruction, information prompts, or performance tasks using a simulated WORDSTAR (branching was only partly possible). The learners always received immediate acoustic and verbal feedback to their responses (beeps signalling the use of wrong keys, and verbal reinforcement or encouragements to try again to find the correct solution).

We instructed the learners to repeat all parts of the tutorial, and they practiced the tutorial exercises at least two times. Teachers were present, but they were instructed to help only if the tutorial did not work as expected. After successfully finishing the whole training in about 16 hours (four hours per day), the learners' scores on a multiple choice knowledge test were comparatively high. Practical performance tests with the real word processor system, however, showed that nearly all subjects behaved very helplessly.

A majority of subjects were not able to perform such simple practical tasks as loading, correcting and printing a file if they were not trained repeatedly before. In the test situation, the anxiety level of the subjects (self-report scales) rose significantly. Additional observations showed that most subjects were unable to cope with typical problems resulting from their own input errors. The subjects tried to manage the problems using the online help information system (the tutorial included a special learning session for its use). As individual observations applying a thinking-aloud technique showed, the help information was not at all helpful. The subjects could not find the relevant information or interpret it correctly.

These and other experiences convinced us that learning by tutorials without instruction and concrete help from teachers is not very meaningful. Typical tutorials merely simulate the real software environments, and immediate performance feedback does not support novices' development of competencies coping with normal input errors. Supplementary training sessions with the software system are necessary. Since this is time-consuming and confusing, professional trainers prefer to use the real system from the beginning.

Of course, computer experts are able to learn by tutorials. They also seem to prefer to learn by exploring the real system or to read relevant parts of the handbook instead of learning by the often tedious instructions and dialogues interacting with the tutorial system.

A future direction of research and application that could solve these problems is called *Intelligent Tutoring Systems* (ITS) (Mandl & Lesgold, 1988). In principle, it should be possible to develop systems able to interpret different inputs of the learner when interacting with the standard system in a meaningful way. Since responses of learners using standard software may be extremely divergent and complex, successful expert systems solutions have not yet been developed in applied fields of office software training.

Derry and Hawkes (1991) describe an interesting prototype ITS for the training of elementary arithmetic problem-solving skills being currently developed by them. It includes different subsystems for the recognition of feasible plans and strategies for given problems, a problem-generation system, problem-solving tools for the student, a lesson planner, a record system for storing knowledge models, and a "coaching expert" that interprets moves, errors, and even indicators of motivational breakdowns.

Learning Theory and Instructional Behavior of Human Trainers

The difficulties in developing efficient tutorial systems demonstrate that tutoring refers to a complex competence. We therefore should not prematurely dispense with human trainers who seem to be able to react flexibly and to interprete the individual learning behavior. Our next question is, therefore, whether human instructional behavior derived from principles of learning theory can successfully be applied to the teaching of office software. Lohmann and Mangel (1988) tested the effects of trainer instruction and trainer feedback based on reinforcement principles in a small group learning setting for a standard word processor (WORD). They carefully designed the learning tasks, handbooks, and instruction behavior. Trainers were instructed not to help subjects (for example, by pressing keys) but to tell the subjects how to perform correctly, and to reinforce their behavior with verbal feedback. Therefore, subjects were stopped if they started to explore the system on their own. When subjects got into complex error situations that could not be solved by verbal instruction, they were told to restart the task from the beginning.

According to basic principles of learning, verbal reinforcement and repetition of correct behavior should be an effective learning device. This expectation is supported by the results of the study. After training, the learners are able to perform simple and complex tasks in a test (similar to the tasks in the learning situation). Trainer reinforcement of adequate behavior is therefore recommended as a simple and effective didactic principle for learning to perform given tasks of standard software systems. In the same study most subjects reacted helplessly and failed when they were directed to perform new tasks that could be solved by another experimental group being allowed to explore the system (see below). Several subjects in the reinforcement group spontaneously complained about the lack of opportunities for self-determined exploration of the system. Results like this, as well as our field observations, should not be misinterpreted. We are not able to test the validity of basic assumptions and principles of traditional learning theories by our study. It shows that the application of these principles in the field of teaching complex software systems by typical tutorials and instructional behavior may result in plausible practical consequences. From such experience we may derive the hypothesis that the transfer of learning from old to new tasks is an unsolved practical problem of the reinforcement approach of instruction and similar applications of learning principles.

COGNITIVE SCIENCE, MOTOR LEARNING, AND KNOWLEDGE ACQUISITION

Elementary Learning Models of Cognitive Science

The assumption that human information processing can be described by computer models of cognitive systems is basic for cognitive science (Stillings et al., 1987). Card, Moran, and Newell (1983), in their well-known theoretical approach, developed a model for the human processor composed of a long-term memory, different working memories (visual and auditory image store), and processors (perceptual, motor, and cognitive). Deriving functions and parameters from experimental psychological research, they tried to simulate and predict human interaction behavior with computer systems.

For a description of both cognitive and motor learning processes, they referred to the classic power law of practice (Card et al., 1983, pp. 57 ff.). According to this simple model, task repetition results in shorter task time and the task time is a power function of the number of trials. Bösser (1987, pp. 34 ff.) discussed the general model and concluded that "learning is not adequately represented" since the model cannot handle changes of tasks and problem spaces during task execution. A model of human learning should represent flexible human reprogramming of sequences or dynamic optimization. In early learning theories (cf. Thorndike, 1914), the influence of repetition on learning has been treated much more precisely in relation to individual differences, distribution of practice-associated emotions, new learning, overlearning, fatigue, inhibition, and extinction.

Kieras and Polson (1985) somewhat refined the basic model of Card et al. (1983) in their Cognitive Complexity Theory (CCT). They described the complexity of technical systems in terms of the goals of the user (or task representations), decomposition into subgoals, and the number of procedures necessary to perform these tasks. For a given computer program the complexity of tasks is defined by both the subtasks and the number of system functions (for example, menu functions or commands) invoked by the user in order to perform the procedures. Kieras and Polson (1985) showed that, as predicted, learning time of simple tasks in terms of CCT is lower than learning time of complex tasks. As Bösser (1987, p. 39) argued, one weakness of CCT refers to its basic assumption of constant learning time for different functions. At least for applied context conditions its validity is questionable.

In their learning history users will produce large differences in the frequency with which they apply functions, depending on the duration of prior practice tasks and individual preferences, that may result in differences of learning times of system functions. We also may ask whether the task and the system complexity can be assumed to be a constant overall attribute of goals and systems. One may observe that complexity may change dynamically and radically depending on the individual input operations of the user. After an error (such as an unnoticed push of a wrong function key) the complexity of a simple task can become extremely high for an unexperienced user.

A basic implicit demand of CCT is to save learning time. This can be accomplished by a design of systems that for task performance are as simple as possible. Below we will show that from other theories we should be careful not to generalize this design rule prematurely over all subjects and learning stages.

Motor Skills Learning

Cognitive models of motor skills acquisition (Anett, 1983) are related to cognitive theories of learning (Anderson, 1982). As research shows for motor skills learning, immediate reinforcement and overlearning are important principles. It seems to be even more promising, however, to combine "learning by doing" with "mental training" (Ulich, 1967; Volpert, 1983b), where the learners are trained to imagine the task, cues, and motor movements in a correct manner. Mental training techniques have been widely used for learning complex control operations. Particularly in the field of sports the application of mental training has received much public attention. Practical examples can also be found in the application of cognitive models of movement learning to robot programming (Albracht, Scherff, & Spijkers, 1992).

Stages of Learning and Anderson's ACT* Theory

Rummelhart and Norman (1978) distinguished three stages of learning:

1. accretion (assimilation and gradual accumulation or encoding of new information).
2. tuning (evolution of schema), and
3. restructuring (schema creation).

This model shifted scientific attention from the stage of accretion to the later phases of learning and their simulation, using higher programming languages (production systems). Anderson (1982, 1983) developed a well-known complex computer simulation model of human information processing and knowledge acquisition, the ACT* (Adaptive Control of Thought) theory.

In his multiple stages model he postulated interactive processes between declarative knowledge (through a semantic net that controls for the long-term storage and retrieval processes) and procedural knowledge (or know-how) that regulates performance. The working memory, with its limited capacity, transmits and integrates information derived from both subsystems.

After the early declarative stage, knowledge acquisition is interpreted as an analogy to the production and compilation of computer program procedures and their integration into larger programs. Learning is seen as a process of modification of task-specific procedural knowledge. Following classical theory of learning in this model, tuning can be simulated by discrimination generalization and the strengthening of task procedures. The network model has been proven to work successfully for simulating behavior in the field of arithmetics, geometry, and concept learning (cf. Anderson, Boyle, & Yost, 1985; Reiser, Anderson, & Farrell, 1985). The strength of Anderson's theory lies in the simulation of learning processes. Even if modern Intelligent Tutorial Systems (ITS) relate to the ACT* model, its practical implications for the design of tutorial systems or learning environments is still questionable (cf. Kunz & Schott, 1987). Perhaps one concrete design rule that follows from ACT* theory should be mentioned here. Learning tasks ought to be similar (in terms of task procedures being necessary) to performance tasks in order to maximize transfer of knowledge. This rule is of course a well-known insight of practitioners and refers to a classical principle of psychological learning theory (cf. Thorndike & Woodworth, 1901).

Similarity and the strenghtening of responses by repeated actions are also basic principles of modeling learning in other theories of neuronal networks. Modern neurocomputer systems try to use such principles. Nevertheless, the basic theoretical models and computer systems differ from conventional hierarchical information-processing systems in both structure and behavioral outcomes. They postulate parallel information processing and structures that are loosely connected. According to neuronal network theory our human brain can be described in terms of a network of self-organized neuronal connections that process patterns of stimuli by restructuring the connections in the network. These "connectionistic" models have stimulated research on pattern recognition and network learning (cf. McClelland & Rummelhart, 1988) and their simulation by parallel processing computers or associative memory software systems.

Systems like these are efficient in "learning by doing" even if information is incomplete or inaccurate. In cases where complexity of the network architecture is not too high, the probability of correct responses is of a reasonable magnitude. At least for some combinations of patterns and connected elements, weighting functions, the proportion of correct answers mediated by these systems can be raised substantially.

Depending on the number of connections and the number of different input patterns, the number of necessary trials in the learning phase is very large. Until now, it is an open question whether and which domains outside pattern recognition can be simulated by neuronal systems. Because we are still in the beginning phase of connectionism and we do not know which systems and efficient learning rules will be constructed, it is too early to evaluate the future practical implications for the design of human learning tasks and environments of instruction techniques for discrimination and pattern learning. Interesting perspectives refer to approaches that are aimed at studying metalearning procedures using neurocomputers for teaching other neurocomputers.

Action Theory and Operative Mental Models

More than 30 years ago, Miller, Galanter, and Pribram (1960) started to analyze goal oriented human planning behavior in terms of traditional serial information processing computer systems. If we watched the behavior of other humans, we would observe sequences of operations. These sequences are only the observable part of complex goal-oriented actions autonomously regulated by structures that, according to Miller et al., are determined by the goal and its decomposition into a hierarchy of subgoals. The basic element of this hierarchy is a cybernetic cycle, the TOTE unit (Test–Operate–Test–Exit). According to Miller et al., TOTE units function in analogy to if–then loops or the subroutines of serial computer programs. Following their model, acting humans always test the starting state, compare it to the goal state, eventually operate to change the state, and exit if they reach the desired goal state.

In German psychology, Miller et al.'s (1960) book has become very influential and it has stimulated the development of refined cybernetic models of self-regulation processes of human performance, especially in the field of work psychology, and particularly the action theory of Hacker (1986) and Volpert (1983a). In the field of learning, action theory assumes the existence of adequate mental models, "self-initiated" (Hacker & Skell, 1993) and self-regulated learning processes. Learning by goal-oriented, self-regulated actions, mental training and practice, according to this approach, aims at "active acquisition" (the German term *Aneignung* is not fully translatable) of the objects of learning by efficient and flexible regulatory structures and operation processes handling them. For example, heuristic schemata have been successfully applied to support the development of mental models and of generalizable problem-solving strategies in different fields of industrial education (Hacker & Skell, 1993; Semmer & Pfäfflin, 1978; Sonntag, 1989).

This approach has stimulated the designing of important techniques that may be of special value in the the field of computer training, because it is difficult

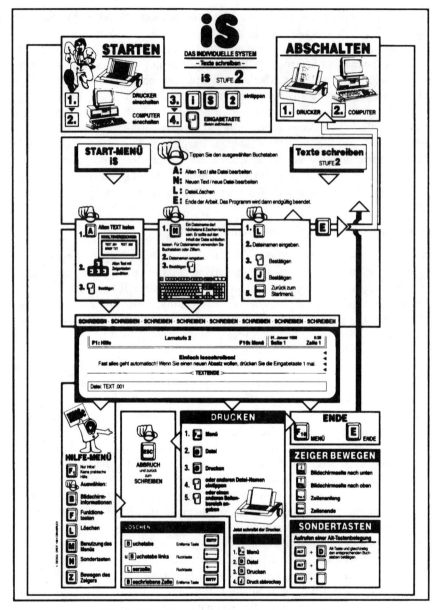

Figure 5.1.   Example of an orientation poster.

for novices and even experts to develop adequate mental models and heuristic guides and find their way through the computer labyrinths. Following action theory, we designed pictographic "orientation posters" for several standard word processor and other office programs. The orientation poster can be compared to maps that represent different ways a given location (for example, a hotel) can be reached. The poster (see Figure 5.1) is very complex. Each area of the poster is explained separately in the handbook, and users learn it step by step. The areas have different colors and represent different tasks (like "starting the computer" or "printing a text"). A short verbal label of the task ("printing") and a graphic (an icon of a print) are shown at the head of the area. Below the heading, a list of input operations necessary for performance (in the form of icons and/or short labels) and their sequence is presented.

In an experimental study, Blachetta (1990) evaluated the performance of people trained in the use of a word processing program by orientation posters and handbooks, and compared those results to the performance of users trained only on handbooks with no pictographic support. The results demonstrate that if adequately introduced in the training seminar, the orientation posters are useful "external memories" even for professional users. No help system that involves pressing help keys or using the mouse before getting the right information can be quicker than eye movements looking for help information on an orientation poster.

EXPLORATORY AND SELF-ORGANIZED LEARNING

Learning and Exploration Theory

Exploration of new or complex computer and software environments may be interpreted in terms of coping responses to cognitive conflicts and information deficits. Exploration activities regulate the relationship between individual and environment (Voss & Keller, 1983). Developing knowledge by exploration means building knowledge structures by repetition and variation. This view is similar to the understanding of learning in action theory and in connectionistic models. Modern exploration theory not only concentrates on cognitive schema development by cyclic repetition of learning by doing, discrimination, and generalization schedules, but it also embraces processes of activation and anxiety resulting from the novelty and complexity of the environment. According to theories of exploration, successful acquisition of new knowledge depends on a balance between novelty and complexity in comparison to the background knowledge of the individual, his or her curiosity, tolerance of ambiguity, and self-confidence (Berlyne, 1960; Schneider, Moch, Sandfort, Auerwald, & Walther-Wichkman, 1983; Schölmerich, 1990; Voss, 1984; Voss & Keller, 1983, 1986). Greif and Keller (1990) tried to transfer basic concepts of exploration theory to the design of learning environments in human–computer interaction.

Principles of Self-Organization in Learning

Like exploratory learning concepts, connectionistic models of learning assume the existence of elementary processes of active self-organization of knowledge acquisition and physiological activation. Connectionism accentuates the importance of pattern similarity for discrimination and transfer of learning, and especially for the number and distribution of repeated successful trials. The expected optimal schedules derived from connectionistic technology should be considered as being different from reinforcement schedules of classical learning theory and the technology of individualized learning by programmed instruction according to Skinner (1986).

In adult education, one can find approaches of self-controlled or self-determined learning that have even less in common with classical learning theory. Central to different approaches of self-controlled learning applied to diverse industrial domains ranging from basic occupational education programs in metal and chemical industry, to management training, action or project management learning, and group development or "quality circle" approaches to learning (cf. Greif & Kurtz, 1989) is their assumption that the individual learner or the learning group can control their own learning process. They should be allowed to control not only the learning speed but also the type of feedback, and in some approaches even the learning method and task.

Approaches like this have become very popular in German industry. The German Institute of Occupational Education in Berlin (cf. Wagner, 1989) developed an approach for traditional apprenticeship based on a self-controlled learning. This interesting concept, called *Leittextmethode* ("guided-by-text method"), has already been applied to apprenticeship programs (especially in the German metal industry), to training by projects or training on-the-job, and to computer training in several large occupational fields. The basic idea is that learners should actively prepare, plan, organize, and recheck their learning tasks completely by themselves. Starting a new task, the learner has to answer guiding questions, look for necessary information, make a rough draft, and talk over problems, outlines, and results with his or her instructor. The whole sequence of the learning process is guided systematically by questions, rules, information, and counseling.

Similar approaches have also been applied to open learning centers for computer and software systems. Funded by the European Community, a large model project called SELECT (self-controlled learning with computers) embraced the design of training rooms, hardware and software selection, learning tasks and tools, instruction behavior, and supportive organizational networks (cf. de Boer & Herzog, 1989).

The theoretical starting points of self-controlled learning approaches such as the Leittextmethode can be found in psychological Gestalt theory, concepts of learning by doing, and action theory (cf. Skell, 1980; Hacker & Skell, 1993). There are also similarities to active exploratory learning or discovery learning. The common roots of the different concepts can be traced back to humanistic educational ideals (for a review, see Deitering, 1995).

In *self-determined* learning, the learners are never completely free in that they are not allowed to do what they want. They have to respect the informal behavioral rules of the group, the learning setting cannot be changed at will, and the ultimate learning tasks are often predetermined by external demands or standards (for example, an examination at the end of a course). Such terms as self-determined or self-controlled learning, therefore, are somewhat misleading. It would be a paradox if we always demand self-determination in learning, even if some learners (sometimes) want to be told what and how they have to learn. Therefore, we would rather use the term self-organized learning, which merely means that the learner actively influences, plans or coordinates, and performs the learning process by himself or herself. The degree of self-organization may be defined by the degree by which the learner influences:

1.   the learning tools and methods,
2.   the learning tasks and steps,
3.   the task times and trials,
4.   the type of feedback and expert help, and
5.   the social support wanted by his or her colleagues.

The concept of self-organized learning implies a change in role expectancies, shifting from the role of a teacher to a designer of stimulating learning environments and counselor or coach of individuals and groups in open learning encounters. The learners also have to be prepared carefully to accept these changes. Before the beginning of the learning encounter and in its course, the learning counselor should explain the basic idea, his or her contribution to the design and preparation of different learning resources, and the nature of the approach, contrasted with typical classroom teaching behavior.

The learners by themselves must organize their learning tasks, tools, and other resources according to their individual preferences. The learning councils and other course members can always be asked for concrete help or advice. Since adults always have different background experiences, knowledge, and preferences, they should be stimulated by self-observation and self-reflection to find out which learning resources and methods can be most helpful for them.

Where carefully designed and implemented, such concepts of self-organized learning seem to be successful and motivating for learners. A successful implementation is nevertheless a very critical phase. It is a sometimes insurmountable problem to convince traditional instructors, and even where they seem to be cooperative it is difficult for them to change their instruction styles and roles. Some learners cannot cope with the demands of self-activity and planning in advance. Simons (1989) discussed practical advantages and problems of the Leittextmethode. He concluded that many people seem to hate thinking and planning in advance and would prefer to start learning right away, without preparing activities (Simons, 1989, p. 163). He therefore recommended simple methods of learning by doing, at least for the starting phases, and special training for the development of planning compentencies with respect to tasks, where planning would be really necessary.

Action theory accentuates rational planning and self-regulation of actions. From an energy-saving perspective, people often seem to avoid the effort of planning and self-monitoring in learning. Theories of self-organized learning, which can also be applied for describing and explaining spontaneous learning activities without conscious planning and reasoning, are therefore necessary. Exploration theory and the design of exploratory learning environments described in the following section may be considered to represent such complementary approaches.

The Design of Exploratory Learning Environments

Protocols of exploratory learning activities. An important methodological advantage in the study of learning in human–computer interaction refers to the saving of protocols of all keystrokes as well as of other input movements, including duration (*logfiles*). Researchers have stressed the fact that it is difficult to interpret the meaning of precisely recorded behavioral data.

Even with simple standard tasks, people differ greatly behavior, and in the field of human–computer interaction authors have concluded that nothing is as constant as the differences between people. Ackermann and Ulich (1987) therefore have stressed the necessity of designing computer and software systems that have the potential to be adapted to individual differences.

Carroll and Mack (1983) were among the first to analyze keystroke protocols of novices learning the use of a word processor. The protocols gave an impression of seemingly chaotic trial and error behavior (see also Voss, this volume). For a better understanding of the interaction process Carroll and Mack prompted the learners to think aloud and to report their inferences, strategies, and plans. The authors concluded that people

> see many things going on, but they do not know which of these occurrences are relevant to their immediate concerns. Indeed, they do not know if their current concerns are the appropriate concerns for them to have. The learners read something in the manual, see something on the display unit and must try to connect the two—to integrate, to interpret. . . . Yet people do act. Indeed, perhaps the most pervasive tendency we have observed is that people simply strike out into the unknown. (Carroll & Mack, 1983, p. 262).

Interactions are interpreted in terms of active learning processes exploring the hardware and software environments.

Handbooks and minimal manuals. Empirical evaluation studies (Carroll, 1985; Peters & Bichler, 1989) have shown that computer handbooks, even if they have been designed very carefully, are often inadequate for the training of novices. In order to be of real help when actual difficulties arise, manuals often present too much information and thereby prevent learners from pursuing active exploratory activities. Carroll (1985), therefore preferred to design learning tasks and minimal manuals that provided short descriptive statements and space for people to write their own notes.

Minimal manuals have been produced and evaluated for a broad variety of standard software systems (cf. Carroll, 1991; Gediga, Janikowski, Lemm, Monecke, & Pezalla, 1989; Lohmann, Monecke, & Greif, 1989; Greif & Janikowski, 1987; Lohmann & Mangel, 1988). The design of task descriptions and minimal manuals is an important part of applied work and is also relevant in the train-the-trainer courses that have been developed in our laboratory.

Design of Learning Environments with Reduced Complexity

Training wheels. Most standard software systems are capable of executing a large number of functions. For beginners, too many functions are difficult to manage, and there is the risk that they might mask errors that add to the complexity of the problem. Carroll (1985) developed a software design concept called *training wheels* to avoid these problems. He recommended that some functions of the full system be disabled or closed off. A novice trying to use the disabled function is provided with a system message saying "this function is not available in the training wheels system." As an example Carroll designed a training wheels word processor—that is, a menu system where the novice can only select, create, edit, or print a document. Other specialized menu functions are disabled to "protect" the novice "from the consequences of reckless exploration" (Carroll, 1985, p. 42). Typical error states are "unreachable." He assumed that this reduction of complexity supports positive transfer of learning, since all functions of the full system are visible and can be reached by the novice.

Carroll calls the training wheels system a "real exploratory environment" for learning because it is "responsive to users (in virtue of its many disablement messages), forgiving errors (by blocking them), and encouraging active learning strategies. And it can as well be a real step toward mastering the full function of an office application system" (Carroll, 1985, p. 44).

Carroll's training wheels system is an interesting design solution to the problem of complexity. However, the following problems remain:

1. It may be frustrating for at least some users if they try a function and get the standard message that it cannot be used and has been (virtually) blocked.
2. If the full system is complex the user gets much unnecessary information on the screen. He or she may be reinforced to ignore relevant information.
3. Users with different working tasks do not need the same complete set of functions. Some users merely have to learn elementary word processor tasks.

Genetic growing systems. In order to solve these problems, we designed a prototype system where the user is given only the functions that are necessary for his or her working tasks. No function visible on the screen is blocked, but he or she can choose between different complexity levels of the system. At each level it is possible to perform complete tasks, such as writing, correcting, saving, and printing a text. On the higher levels both the complexity and the number of functions for special tasks increase, and the users have the choice between different interaction styles—for example menu, commands, or alt-key macros.

The Level 1 word processor we designed is a very simple system with a short menu and a minimal number of basic functions ("new text," "load old text," "print text," and "end"). Since saving and other standard routines are done automatically, this level is easy to learn by exploratory activities. If the user needs more functions he or she has to call the second level. On the last "professional" level he or she has access to the full range of all function of the system. He or she can also apply or define short cut commands or redefine the menu labels and structure, depending on the individual task demands and preferences. The word processor is merely a part of the full multifunctional system with a large number of additional functions for file and disk management, database, or a calculation and combined tasks. For each module the user may also choose between different levels of complexity.

A basic principle of our design concept derived from exploration theory and the concept of individual self-regulation of the complexity of learning tasks (Greif & Keller, 1990) is to enhance the knowledge, exploratory skills, motivation, and competence to cope with complex software systems. Our approach to software design embodies this goal through the design of a natural step-by-step development from concrete thinking and direct manipulation toward actions that also integrate higher order abstract thinking levels and flexible operations (cf. Piaget, 1936). Palme (1983) designed a database system encouraging the "growth of the user" by beginning with a simple menu and then including command language level, step by step. We call such systems, which support the natural process of developing knowledge and competence, *genetic growing systems* (Greif, 1989). Since our system can also be adapted individually to tasks, habits, and preferences, we called our prototype office system *individual System* (iS). (The system design and program has been developed by Günter Gediga in a project granted by the German Minister of Research and Technology.[1])

---

[1] The project "Multifunctional Office Software and Qualification" (MBQ) was funded between 1987 and 1990 by the "Humanization of Working Life" (now called the "Work and Technology" program. On request we offer to send the prototype software system together with procedures for menu design and automatic logfile protocols. The system can be run on all standard personal computers operated by DOS 3.1 and higher.

Training wheels and genetic growing systems represent different design solutions to the complexity problem. In the training wheels solution the user will explore a standard system and always will be aware of the full system. Risks resulting from complexity are reduced by blocking the performance of functions. In contrast, the genetic growing system offers different environments for different users or tasks. Users can choose the complexity or risk level by themselves. If they wants to lower the risks, they may choose a lower level system with a smaller set of functions. As in the training wheels solution, the user has no access to risky functions. How can learners cope with the different environments of genetic growing systems? Contrary to some expectations, namely that a choice of different levels might be disturbing and disorienting, our observations reveal that these systems are easy to learn. At the lowest level, the learners are confronted with a very simple system that shows the basic structure of the system. Therefore, the users are able to acquire the basic system structure and its operation more easily. Since the structure of the general system, the menus, and commands over the complexity levels of the system (even across different modules of the integrated multifunctional system) remain stable, transfer of earning to other levels and to complex software systems is high. In other words, the users seem to be able to develop a mental model of the basic structure of standard programs.

Exploratory learning by errors. The development of coping strategies for predictable and unpredictable, simple and complex error situations is an intellectual as well as an emotional challenge. Psychological training procedures are needed, which in addition to knowledge acquisition support the development of self-confidence and persistence to cope with annoying or straining problem situations. The sequence of learning tasks, and an encouraging feedback by the trainer, therefore should guarantee experiences of success and efficacy and a steady habituation to typical workload situations confronted with computer or software problems. It is of high importance for novices to develop realistic expectancies about difficulties and risks in the practical use of modern software and computer systems, self-confidence, and the persistence to cope with unpredictable problems. Anxious novices should not always fall back upon trainer or expert support if they get into a minor problem that they can manage by themselves. If the problem is too complex, or if the consequences of errors cannot be eliminated, novices should be cautious and ask for personal help. Social support is also a potential factor for reducing stress reactions. Like Carroll and Mack (1983) we tried to support self-organized exploratory behavior in the learning process. Since we concentrated especially on the exploration of error situations we call our learning concept exploratory learning by errors (Greif, 1986, 1989; Greif & Janikowski, 1987; for an alternative error training approach cf. Frese, Brodbeck, Heinbokel, Mooser, Schleiffenbaum, & Thiemann, 1991).

"Make errors! You can learn from your errors!" is our message at the beginning of a training session. By this we try to encourage our subjects to develop a more relaxed problem solving attitude in error situations and to learn from exploring these situations and the errors of their colleagues. How the trainer reacts to the first requests for help may be very important. The learner should develop the impression that his or her errors are interesting and thus represent important learning opportunities.

It is very impressive to observe how radically the attitudes towards errors change in a course where the trainer reacts with sensitivity to errors, shows interest, comments on the problem solving strategies, and sometimes even draws the attention of the other participants to an interesting error situation.

The learners who made an "interesting" error sometime even seem to be proud of it, openly discuss the problem, and without signs of stress test different solutions. This can be supported by a systematic instruction aimed at applying heuristic schemata for error diagnosis and problem solving steps.

As written rules of thumb we incorporated schemata like those in our "minimal manuals" (see above) for the system. The trainer is instructed not to help by giving direct information on the solution of problems but to refer to these rules.

The basic goal refers to reducing stress and psychological blocking in unavoidable error situations by developing coping competencies. Principles of stress inoculation training (Meichenbaum, 1974) allow for a useful model that may be utilized for gradual psychological immunization and for reducing strain in error situations. Instead of relying solely on the online help systems provided by the manufacturers of the program or "hotline" telephone help, we try to facilitate mutual personal social support in the training courses and to develop personal help networks provided by colleagues.

Learning Tools and Design of Resources

For practical use the design of exploratory learning environments that are optimal for different learners is rather difficult. Our solution is to combine exploratory and self-organized learning concepts, where the individual can choose among learning environments (learning tasks, learning tools and resources, or environments of varying complexity). According to theory (Greif & Keller, 1990), self-determination of novelty and complexity in exploration should facilitate the development of competence, positive self-evaluation, and self-efficacy. This might stimulate further exploratory learning, creativity, and role innovation (Farr & Ford, 1990).

A careful design and application of exploratory learning environments is important, starting with the design of the first informational letter to the participants, short comprehensible instructions at the beginning of the course, briefings, learning tasks, and resources, and ending with the design of an encouraging epilogue. The trainer may use a checklist for these design tasks and the preparation of the course.

Following the idea of self-organization, the learners may rearrange the tables, as well as time schedules, rest pauses, and social encounters. In the beginning, and by short talks in later phases, the trainer demonstrates how to use the different resources. Differing from the *Leittextmethode* mentioned above and other concepts that demand written advance planning, we are trying to stimulate the learner to spontaneously explore the learning environments and learning resources and to develop intuitive (associative) knowledge and response patterns.

For real computer novices, the successful completion of the first meaningful tasks (such as correcting and printing a letter with a simple word processor) are expected to pioneer the ways for elementary associative task performance patterns and the immediate impression of self-efficacy. With respect to novices, a careful design that starts with very easy exploratory tasks, a clear structure, and an environment of reduced complexity (and a high probability of success) is therefore very important. After the initial phase of easy exploratory tasks we recommend to stimulate exploring different learning resources. (A problem here is that most subjects are more inclined to try to solve the next problem or change the complexity level of the software tool.) If the learner has a problem or is in an error situation, we instruct and help him or her to apply a heuristic schema (error diagnosis or problem solving schema) presenting general rules or guiding questions to find a solution. (The idea is derived from the action theory approach of Skell, 1980, and it is similar to the Leittextmethode mentioned above.) From time to time, trainers may also wander around and encourage questions or even give short summary talks to instruct the whole group. Short summary instructions may help to structure the learning situation and may also provide a compensation for decentralized and sometimes chaotic learning processes. They also may present information on special contents or the use of resources. The trainer should use such talks to stimulate discussions on special problems or error situations.

Experimental Evaluation Studies

The exploratory learning by errors and self-organized learning approach was evaluated by six experimental studies. These were training courses for novices—learning different word processor software systems and multifunctional office packages. With the exception of the second study, they all were conducted with regional typists (found through newspaper advertisements) who had no previous experiences with computer systems. In the last three studies we used professional trainers for training the control groups. In all studies experimental research designs included two or three groups and chance or matched pair selection of subjects. Since the costs for trainers, staff, material, and technical equipment were high, relatively small experimental groups (6–8 subjects) were formed. In the following summary, only major results ($p < 0.05$) are given.

In the first study (Greif & Janikowski, 1987) we compared knowledge and task performance of two groups (each N = 6) of novices who learned the classic word processor WORDSTAR. One group was trained by our exploratory learning-by-errors concept. The other one was trained by a standard tutorial (see above). Results revealed no significant differences in a multiple choice computer knowledge test but remarkable differences in simple and complex performance tasks. Most subjects in the exploratory learning-by-errors group were able to solve practical performance tests. There was evidence in test performance and thinking aloud protocols that in the tutorial group most subjects reacted with complete helplessness.

In the second experiment, Lohmann and Mangel (1988) developed training handbooks and an orientation poster for the standard word processor WORD. Subjects here were assigned to two groups according to different trainer instruction behavior (N = 31). In the first group the trainers instructed the subjects how to perform the training tasks correctly and reinforced correct behavior by verbal feedback. (Subjects who tried to start to explore the system on their own were not allowed to do so.) In the second group, the exploratory learning-by-errors approach was applied. Results demonstrate that both groups reached good mean performance on standard tests that had been learned before. However, the exploratory learning groups did much better on complex new tasks.

According to exploration theory, activation and knowledge are expected to be optimal if novelty and complexity of the learning tasks are neither too high nor too low depending on the individual knowledge level. In our third study, Müller (1989) tested our prototype individual System with different complexity levels for the first time (see above). All subjects were trained according to the exploratory learning approach, using minimal manuals. One group (N = 14) learned our word processor version in a setting with a step-by-step enlargement of five complexity levels (and five minimal manuals). The second group (N = 16) had the same learning tasks, but got the complete, highest level version of the word processor and a minimal manual from the beginning. Differing from the other studies so far, Müller tested the first version of our genetic growing system version. Since in this study the subjects (students with different computer knowledge) were not allowed to choose the complexity level of the system and learning tasks by themselves, there were gains in the test performances in the first group only for special exploration tasks. (The subjects had to explore a new function, which had not been learned before. They had to find out as many different ways as possible to perform the task.) No significant differences could be found in other tasks. A comparison of subgroups allowed for the interpretation that the experts with computer knowledge made more errors and—especially in the second group with the complex tool—had more opportunities for exploring and learning. In the first group inducing a step-by-step growing complexity, several subjects of the expert group complained that they were becoming bored by the simple levels of the word processor. (In this study subjects were not allowed to pass to a higher level when they wanted to, but had to wait until all learners ended the learning tasks at each level.) Results demonstrate that large individual differences can be found in responses to complexity. A system may be both too complex for some learners and optimal for other subjects.

In Experiment IV, Gediga, Lohmann, Monecke, and Greif (1989) for the first time studied the advantages of self-control of complexity by applying our complete concept in comparison to a professional trainer. All subjects were novices (mostly typists from the region) who wanted to learn to use a word processor. The experimental group (N = 8) was learning by the exploratory training approach and was allowed to choose the complexity of system and learning tasks using our prototype genetic growing system, minimal manuals, and orientation posters. The control group (N = 7) was trained by a highly recommended professional trainer who used a comparable complex word processor subsystem of a multifunctional system (OPEN ACCESS) which at that time, according to a survey study, was the multifunctional system being used by most regional firms. Results were very impressive. The groups did not show any differences in elementary menu performance (for example, centering a line). Large differences could be found in complete standard tasks such as starting the computer for loading a file, writing, and printing a text. At the end of the two-day course, only 29 percent were able to perform this task without external help in the control group, whereas in the experimental group 88 percent were successful at the end of the second day and 100 percent at the end of the third day. In a follow-up six weeks after, these differences became even more pronounced. All subjects of the experimental group and none in the control group were able to perform the standard task.

Gediga, Janikowski, Lemm, Monecke, and Pezalla (1989) and Sauvageod (1990), in our fifth study, designed and evaluated our complete multifunctional individual System (a nine-level version, Gediga, 1989) and developed a self-organized training concept (minimal manuals and orientation posters for all levels) for our system. For OPEN ACCESS, too, they developed a set of minimal manuals and orientation posters with growing complexity and learning sessions following the exploratory error training approach. (Here we could not change the complexity of the software system. The learners had to use the complex system from the beginning.) Our control group again was trained by a professional trainer, who worked with the normal OPEN ACCESS system, and instructions were as usual. All subjects were real novices from the region. The courses lasted one week (like typical professional courses on complex multifunctional systems). Results demonstrate that the genetic growing systems group (N = 7) again reached nearly 100% success in the standard system start, line writing, and printing tests and did also better in some other tasks, especially in the database tasks. In the control group (N = 6) there were significantly lower values in these tasks except several elementary menu processing and the spreadsheet calculation tasks. The results of the OPEN ACCESS group (N = 6) being trained according to our exploratory learning concept were in between the other two groups. We concluded that the design of our spreadsheet subsystem and learning tasks in this part were not optimal. In contrast our database system and training concept seemed to represent a better design solution than that of the other two groups.

The sixth study (Lohmann, 1994) was meant to repeat study five and to test a more advanced design of our training for the somewhat abstract spreadsheet calculation module. At the end of the training sessions, subjects in the experimental group (N = 7) had reached the same good test performance in the word processor tasks as in the previous study. This time the control group (N = 8) also became better in the standard system start, line writing, and printing task, since the trainer concentrated on those areas (and neglected some others). As desired, the performance of the group on the calculation tasks was better (but not significantly different from that of the control group). As expected, the experimental group had the best performance in the database tests ($p < 0.05$). The results of the OPEN ACCESS group trained using our concept (N = 8) were about the same as in the first study.

A special event that challenged our experimental group and changed the whole situation has to be mentioned. On the second day, a woman who had not told us before about her illness fell to the floor suffering from a fit of epilepsy. The course had to be interrupted and she was brought to her doctor. Of course, the whole group was strained and talked about the dramatic event. On the next day, the epileptic woman rejoined the class (and her doctor recommended it), and she did quite well in the remaining sessions. We expected that after this event the results of the experimental group would show a permanent breakdown, and in fact the reaction of the whole group can be seen clearly in the learning curves. The word processor data that were covered that day revealed a strong decline. It was not before the fourth day that the values rose to high performance results again. This whole situation was comparable to a critical test of all subjects and the learning counselor in the experimental group (see Lohmann, 1994) and also of our learning approach.

As the six studies show, with some very plausible exceptions, exploratory learning-by-errors combined with the genetic growing systems design of software seems to lead to predictable and long-term stable performance results. This supports our theoretical expectations. We have to be cautious, nevertheless, with premature generalizations. We should not assume that our approach is the best way to high learning performance on whatever task we may apply for testing. Learners can of course get the same and even better performance levels with other training methods. Which method is adequate will depend on the experiences and basic knowledge of the learners, the learning tasks, the design of learning resources and environment, and the time available for learning and practice. Our approach has advantages for real novices or for the starting phase of learning complex systems and in successful long-term memorizing. Intensive training and permanent practice can of course in the long run have the same benefits. As some data on tests where experimental subjects show a lower performance may indicate, the learners of the self-organization group who make a decision on what to learn and how often to repeat the exercises seem to avoid the effort for exercising intriguing tasks (which are simple but involve many annoying substeps). Here, the teacher who demands from the subjects that they have to learn and to repeat such tasks may be more effective and prevent normal avoidance behavior.

The most interesting overall results of our studies from the perspective of psychological practice might be that an approach derived from exploration theory, even under hard test conditions, resulted in stable and high performance test values, where professional tutorials, and even recommended professional trainers, obviously have difficulties in reliably reaching satisfying learning results on holistic tasks.

PERSPECTIVES OF A TASK-ACTION THEORY OF SELF-ORGANIZED LEARNING

So far in this chapter I have given a summary of different theoretical and applied concepts in the field of learning in human—computer interaction, especially in complex office software systems. There are many obvious similarities among different theoretical approaches. That learning by doing and repetition of task–action contingencies is often useful is a simple principle that is applied in nearly every approach. Principles of transfer of knowledge by discrimination and generalization of common elements or schemata also are integrated in several models. Examples refer to the ACT* theory and the knowledge acquisition process in exploration theory, or the connectionistic model of pattern recognition and learning.

Some theories contribute to special issues. Exploration theory may be used for a treatment of complexity in order to find a proper balance in the learning process between individual knowledge and novelty or complexity of the learning environment. Both motor learning theories and action theory have stimulated an integrated view of mental regulatory processes (mental training) parallel to learning by skill training and feedback. Action theory specializes in planning and in an application of heuristic rules to the learning process, while exploration theory can do better when spontaneous and intuitive learning activities are to be stimulated.

The accentuation of rational planning processes and skills may be both a strength and a weakness of action theory. Planning depends on volitional effort, which is often avoided in learning. This can be inferred from experience in training approaches with special planning tasks (cf. experiences with the *Leittextmethode* mentioned above) and also from observations in laboratory experiments. We have applied intensive task analysis methods in order to understand the processes regulating problem solving tasks and error situations. Subjects typically react by intuitive and associative action patterns even if the problems are complex and if planning would be useful. The spontaneous and seemingly chaotic but always flexible and reactive coping processes that have been so vividly described by Carroll and Mack (1983) characterize not only novice but also expert behavior. Where the novices make more knowledge and reasoning errors interacting with typical office software, a higher number of permanent motor "action slips" and habitual errors is typical of experts (Zapf, Brodbeck, Frese, Peters, & Prümper, 1992). Therefore, we may doubt the validity of the serial computer model of hierarchic–sequential mental regulation processes and the assumption that efficent human performance is always determined and initiated by conscious higher order goals, regulated by a hierarchical network of feedback loops and a comparison of the results of an action with the goals. If expertise, following action theory, depends on highly routinized and automatic reaction patterns and motor subroutines, it has to be explained why experts typically make errors that show that they did not develop automatic and reliable action patterns. Their oscillating interaction process with the computer system may be better interpreted as resulting from low attention and low volitional self-control before responding to task patterns. I would, therefore, like to express some doubt about the validity of the *closed feedback loop cycles* or TOTE-units of Miller et al. (1960) as being the basic unit of human action.

One has to assume either that the permanent self-control system of experts is unreliable, or that they seem to react quickly and spontaneously and *then* control and correct for their responses, if they detect an error. The resulting *open loop sequence* is: task–spontaneous reaction–error detection–correction. Modern results of error research in human–computer interaction demonstrate that human errors are very frequent and that it seems to be more realistic to train error management than to try to prevent errors (Frese, 1991; Frese et al., 1991; Prümper, Zapf, Brodbeck & Frese, 1992; Zapf et al., 1992). The efficiency of experts interacting with complex computer systems is not high because they are less disturbed by motor routines and habitual problems. They are more efficient than novices because they make fewer knowledge and reasoning errors and because they are able to correct their permanent motor and habitual errors by flexible and quick response patterns (Hamborg, 1994).

If we question the general validity of the closed loop and serial hierarchical regulation model of action theory, we may explain the interaction and learning process analogous to neuronal network theory by heterarchic and partly autonomous self-organized adaptive and parallel information processes. When observing elementary reaction patterns and learning processes, we may describe them by learned associations between attribute patterns of task and tool states, and by complex open loop reaction patterns of spontaneously responding (and not permanently self-controlling and rational-planning) individuals.

A basic assumption is that the repetition of successful reaction patterns (for example, the parallel movements of the mouse and the pointer on the screen) will strengthen the connection between task and tool state and movement patterns in an adequate learning setting. We need not assume, however, that in order to learn to use the mouse to reach a point on the screen, the observed performance patterns must continuously be elicited and controlled by conscious higher order goals or subgoals and closed loop control cycles. It seems to be a more efficient self-organization structure if we postulate that merely the recognition of different task and tool states ("The pointer of the mouse is down in the right corner of the screen; what now?") directly activates a (low-level) intuitive self-organized motor pattern in a network of associated inner reaction patterns. We may call such elementary associations *open loop task–action connections*.

As an example, observe a boy who by permanent learning-by-doing can professionally practice a so-called adventure game with a computer system and a joystick. The task and tool he sees on the screen refer to the display of a picture of a hall with an elevator and some furniture. Then the state attributes change. A figure of a boy comes in through the opening door of the elevator. Suddenly another strange figure appears and walks towards the boy.

The child playing the game now very quickly recognizes any critical task pattern and associates the pattern of the running strange figure with an attacking enemy. He merely elicits the reaction pattern of turning the joystick to move the boy virtually in the direction of the enemy and with a contingent move presses a key at the joystick and shoots the enemy. Only if he makes a wrong movement will he try to correct it (also by spontaneous movement patterns). There are some situations where he knows from his failures that anticipatory movements are necessary (after entering a special room, for example, he must begin to shoot before he sees the enemy, who appears very quickly). Such anticipatory reaction patterns might be interpreted as elementary planning activities.

Observing the responses of our professional children in computer games, we may notice that they are responding extremely quickly and with an impressive virtuosity. The expert players masterfully hit the enemies and move the figures with the joystick in the two-dimensional space of the screen. The high-speed responses are not as precise as programmed movements could be, but show very flexible reaction patterns, quick adaptions of pacing and timing, and avoidance of dangerous areas. The responses also become smoother as a function of experience. (The figures in a typical computer game have several lives. Therefore, the game does not stop when the figure is killed. I assume that this inbuilt error compensation is essential. It would be difficult to learn to play such games without this function.)

The playing child may have started the game with the definite goal of reaching a certain number of points (the points for killing enemies are continuously visible on the screen). We need not assume that this goal or derived subgoals (to kill enemy x or y) permanently activates and controls each impulse of the micromovement processes. Literally speaking, the game is too quick and the player has no time to derive and imagine a hierarchy of goal and subgoal states and closed loop control cycles, comparing results with a desired goal. It is possible to give a simple and plausible explanation in connectionistic terms (cf. also the associative networks and production systems or Anderson's ACT* theory). What the child has learned during long hours of practice may be quick connections of complex task–action patterns (schemata, mental models or attributes of rooms, enemies, and situations of the figure). Parallel processing in associative networks produces adequate reactions even if the pattern information is incomplete or even partly wrong. According to the tendency to complete the pattern, and since there are always associative connections that may be elicited, the observable spontaneously changing (and sometimes wrong) reactions can be explained. The playing child, being fully absorbed when eliciting the necessary high-speed reactions, in a holistic way concentrates all his or her senses on the rapid identification of task and tool-state patterns. If the child begins to reason and bothers about eventually missing an enemy or anxiously looks too long at an enemy, he or she will lose points. Therefore, the professional playing child has learned to concentrate and to avoid bothering. The rewarding points are proudly registered *at the end* of the game (and the name of the winner can often be entered into a list of highest scores).

We may summarize that in human high-speed precision movements, pattern recognition processes of tasks and tool attributes seem to elicit the associated response patterns. In analogy to the assumption of multiple autonomous physiological regulatory processes (for multiple arousal models, cf. Boucsein, 1991) we may assume that parallel self-regulating task–action connections normally are not controlled by central cortical processes. The elementary model stimulates many obvious problems and questions.

The first question concerns the similarity to the model of S-O-R contingencies. Hebb (1949) developed his neuronal model of learning and integrated basic assumptions of learning theory. Diverging somewhat from classical contingency theories, we may assume more active and holistic self-organization processes of exploratory learning, embracing both concrete and abstract mental problem-solving schemata, phases of volitional self-control and higher order flexible heuristic metastrategies, lower order movement patterns, sensations, and emotions. Depending on individual experiences and the type of the task, different connections become dominant and active in a given moment.

Human memorizing and thinking may be described by spontaneous and mental explorations of inner associative networks, comparable to a wandering around in these networks (the free-association procedure is an example). Through self-exploration and self-monitoring, metacognition schemata and metacompetencies can be consciously be developed. Such conscious self-reflection processes (perhaps only their volitional control) are often seen as a special attribute of the human species. From a connectionstic viewpoint, they may be described as higher order self-monitoring schemata that can be intentionally activated for tuning, changing, or repressing response patterns elicited in networks of task–action connections. According to a neuronal network model—in contrast to three- to five-level models of action theory—only two levels would be sufficient for a description of effective self-regulation processes. (Low-level structures are more efficient performance systems than higher order hierarchic systems with many levels.) Depending on the task and on previous learning, an individual may also develop multiple or even meta-metaschemata. Since it may be efficient for tuning, self-monitoring schemata are assumed to be highly task specific. Their generalization to new and different tasks will become possible by means of transferred learning experiences and conscious exploration of our association networks, and also by means of intentionally "thinking" new paths "into" the networks. For example, merely by thinking the child is able to compare task patterns of the computer game with other tasks—for example, when he or she is in school. Such comparison processes may be evoked by chance connections or "fantasies" but also can be stimulated by a sensible teacher who convincingly can try to explain the similarity of the tasks. (Nevertheless, suppressing the completely different emotional associations of game and school context will be a difficult problem.)

Our associationistic interpretion of these examples remains very speculative. Connectivistic analogies of neuronal computer systems should never be taken in a naive way as literal, valid, or complete models. We may use them merely as metaphoric analogies. Emerging connectionism has opened our scientific minds for speculating about the seemingly chaotic, associative mental processes. Both exploratory learning by doing and repeating task–action associations that have been performed successfully can be interpreted according to connectionistic models. We have to add that inner sensations, emotions, and passions can be associated with task–action patterns (sensations of body movements, feelings of pleasure, frustration, anger reactions, and different states of self-consciousness). Passions and emotions that have a strong connection with task–action patterns perhaps are much more important than goals and plans.

Going back to the roots of modern psychology one can find elaborated associationistic theories which, together with a vivid description of typical phenomena and experiences, still contribute to our understanding of the complex and dynamic inner processes and functions of humanbeings. In psychologys past the role of human drive, passion, emotion, and volitional control have been important theoretical issues. Therefore at the end of this section on theoretical perspectives I would like to refer to a statement made by William James (1905), where he speculates with deep psychological insight about the relations between passion, emotion, volition, thinking, and action:

> What constitutes the difficulty for a man laboring under an unwise passion of acting as if the passion were wise? Certainly there is no physical difficulty. It is as easy physically to avoid a fight as to begin one, to pocket one's money as to

squander it on one's cupidities, to walk away from as towards a coquette's door. The difficulty is mental: it is that of getting the idea of the wise action to stay before our mind at all. When any strong emotional state whatever is upon us, the tendency is for no images but such as are congruous with it to come up. If others by chance offer themselves, they are instantly smothered and crowded out. If we be joyous, we cannot keep thinking of those uncertainties and risks failure which abound upon our path; if lugubrious, we cannot think of new triumphs, travels, loves, and joys; nor if vengeful, of our oppressor's community of nature with ourselves. The cooling advice which we get from others when the feverfit is on us is the most jarring and exasperating thing in life. Reply we cannot, so we get angry; for by a sort of self-preserving instinct which our passion has, it feels that these objects, if they once but gain a lodgment, will work and work until they have frozen the very vital spark from out of all our mood and brought our airy castles in ruin to the ground.... "Let me not think of that!" "Don't speak to me of that!" This is the sudden cry of all those who in a passion perceive some sobering considerations about to check them in mid-career. (James, 1905, p. 451)

REFERENCES

Ackermann, D., & Ulich, E. (1987). The chances of individualization in human-computer interaction and its consequences. In M. Frese, E. Ulich, & W. Dzida (Eds.), *Psychological issues of human-computer interaction in the work place*. Amsterdam: North-Holland, 131–146.

Albracht, H.K., Scherff, B., & Spijkers, W.A.C. (1992). Motorisches Gedächtnis beim Programmieren von Industrierobotern. *Zeitschrift für Arbeits- und Organisationspsychologie, 36* (1), 30–36.

Anderson, J.R. (1982). Acquisition of cognitive skill. *Psychological Review, 89,* 369–406.

Anderson, J.R. (1983). *The architecture of cognition*. Cambridge, MA.: Harvard University Press.

Anderson, J.R., Boyle, C.F., & Yost, G. (1985). The geometry tutor. In *Proceeding of the Ninth International Joint Conference on Artificial Intelligence* (pp. 1–7). Los Altos, CA: Morgan Kaufmann.

Anett, J. (1983). Motor learning: A cognitive psychological viewpoint. In H. Rieder, K. Bös, H. Mechling, & K. Reischke (Hrsg.), *Motorik und Bewegungsforschung* (S. 220–230). Schondorf: Verlag Karl Hofmann.

Berlyne, D. (1960). *Conflict, arousal, and curiosity*. New York: McGraw-Hill.

Blachetta, D. (1990). *Softwaregestaltung und Computertraining: Piktogramme und Orienntierungsplakate im Computertraining*. Unpublished Thesis (Diplomarbeit), Department of Psychology, University of Osnabrück.

Boer, B. de, & Herzog, A. (Hrsg.) (1989). *Lernchanche Computer*. Berlin: Walter Friedländer Bildungswerk.

Bösser, T. (1987). *Learning in man-computer interaction*. New York: Springer.

Boucsein, W. (1991). Arbeitspsychologische Beanspruchungsforschung heute—eine Herausforderung an die Psychophysiologie. *Psychologische Rundschau, 42* (3) 129–174.

Card, S.K., Moran, T.P., & Newell, A. (1983). *The psychology of human-computer interaction.* Hillsdale, NJ: Erlbaum.

Carroll, J. (1985). Minimals design for the active user. In B. Shackle (Ed.), *INTER-ACT'84.* Amsterdam: North-Holland, pp. 39–44.

Carroll, J.M. (Ed.). (1991). *Psychological theory in human-computer interaction.* New York: Cambridge University Press.

Carroll, J.N., & Mack, R.L. (1983). Active learning to use a word processor. In W.E. Cooper (Ed.), *Cognitive Aspects of Skilled Typewriting.* Berlin: Springer, pp. 259–282.

Crowder, N.A. (1962). Intrinsic and extrinsic programming. In J.E. Coulson (Ed.), *Programmed learning and computer-based instruction.* New York: Wiley, pp. 58–66.

Deitering, F. (1995). *Selbstgesteuertes Lernen.* Göttingen: Verlag für Angewandte Psychologie.

Derry, S.J., & Hawkes, L.W. (1991). Future directions for ICAB. In T.M. Shlechter (Ed.), *Problems and promises of computer-based training.* Norwood, NJ: Ablex, pp. 151–174.

Farr, J., & Ford, C.M. (1990). Individual innovation. In M. West & J Farr (Eds.), *Innovation and creativity at Work: Psychological approaches.* New York: Wiley, pp. 63–80.

Frese, M. (1991). Error management or error prevention: Two strategies to deal with errors in software design. In H.J. Bullinger (Ed.), *Human aspects in computing: Design and use of interactive systems and work with terminals* (pp. 776–782). Amsterdam: Elsevier.

Frese, M., Brodbeck, F., Heinbokel, T., Mooser, C., Schleiffenbaum, E., & Thiemann, P. (1991). Errors in training computer skills: On the positive function of errors. *Human-Computer Interaction, 6, 77–93.*

Gediga, G. (1989). Das Funktionshandbuch zum System IS (5.05). *Schriftenreihe Ergebnisse des Projektes MBQ,* Heft Nr. 15.

Gediga, G., Janikowski, A., Lemm, H-D., Monecke, U., & Pezalla, C. (1989). Ein Seminar- und Testkonzept zum Bereich integrierte Software-Systeme. *Schriftenreihe des Projekts MBQ* Heft Nr. 13.

Gediga, G., Lohmann, D., Monecke, U., & Greif, S. (1989). Exploratorisches Lernen in einer Seminarumgebung: Erste empirische Ergebnisse. *Schriftenreihe des Projekts MBQ* Heft Nr. 14.

Greif, S. (1986): Neue Kommunikationstechnologien—Entlastung oder mehr Stress? Beschreibung eines Computer-Trainings zur "Stress-Immunisierung". In K.H. Pullig, U. Schäkel, & J. Scholz (Eds.), *Stress. Reihe Betriebliche Weiterbildung, 8.* Hamburg: Windmühle.

Greif, S. (1989). Exploratorisches Lernen durch Fehler und qualifikationsorientiertes Software-Design. In S. Maaß & H. Oberquelle (Hrsg.), *Software-Ergonomie '89. Aufgabenorientierte Systemgestaltung und Funktionalität (S. 204–212).* Gemeinsame Fachtagung des German Chapter der ACM und der Gesellschaft für Information in Hamburg. Stuttgart: Teubner.

Greif, S., & Janikowski, A. (1987). Aktives Lernen durch systematische Fehlerexploration oder programmiertes Lernen durch Tutorials? *Zeitschr. f. Arbeits- u. Organisationspsychologie, 31*(3), 94–99.

Greif, S., & Keller, H. (1990). Exploratory behavior in human-computer interaction. In M. West & J. Farr (Eds.), *Innovation and Creativity at work: Psychological approaches* (pp. 231–250). New York: Wiley.

Greif, S., & Kurtz, H.J. (1989). Ausbildung, Training und Qualifizierung. In S. Greif, N. Nicholson, & H. Holling (Hrsg.). *Arbeits- und Organisationspsychologie. Internatiobnales Handbuch in Schlüsselbegriffen* (pp. 149–164). München: Psychologie Verlags Union.

Hacker, W. (1986). *Arbeitspsychologie.* Bern: Huber.

Hacker, W., & Skell, W. (1993). *Lernen in der Arbeit.* Bonn: Bundesinstitut für Berufsbildung.

Hamborg, K.-C. (1994). Zum Einfluß der Interaktion von Nutzer-, Aufgaben- und Systemmerkmalen auf die Benutzbarkeit von Softwaresystemen. University of Osnabrück, Dep. of Psychology: *Forschungsberichte* No. 101.

Hebb, D.O. (1949). *The organization of behavior.* New York: Wiley.

James, W. (1905). *Psychology.* London: Macmillan.

Keller, H., & Voss, H.-G. (1976). *Neugier und Exploration.* Beltz: Weinheim.

Kieras, D., & Polson, P.G. (1985). An approach to the formal analysis of user complexity. *International Journal of Man-Machine Studies, 22,* 201–213.

Kreuzig, H. (1981). Über den Zugang zu komplexem Problemlösen mittels prozeßorientierter kognitiver Persönlichkeitsmerkmale. *Zeitschrift für experimentelle und angewandte Psychologie, 28* (2), 294–308.

Kühlmann, T.M. (1988). *Technische und organisatorische Neuerungen im Erleben betroffener Arbeitnehmer.* Stuttgart: Enke.

Kunz, G.C., & Schott, F. (1987). *Intelligente Zutorielle Systeme.* Göttingen: Hogrefe.

Lohmann, D. (1994). Vergleich unterschiedlicher Trainingskonzepte zur integrierten Software. University of Osnabrück: Dep. of Psychology (unpubl. Dissertation).

Lohmann, D., & Mangel, I. (1988): *Alternative Trainingsmethoden für ein Textverarbeitungsprogramm.* Unpublished Thesis (Diplomarbeit), Department of Psychology, University of Osnabrück: Dep. of Psychology (unpubl. Dissertation). Vergleich untersdiendlicher Trainingskonzepte Zue integrierten Software.

Mandl, H., & Lesgold, A. (Eds.) (1988). *Learning issues for intelligent tutoring systems.* New York: Springer.

McClelland, J.L., & Rummelhart, D.E. (1988). Explorations in parallel distributed processing. Cambridge, MA: Bradford Books, MIT Press.

McCombs, B.L. (1991). CBT: Its current and future state. In T.M. Shlechter (Ed.), *Problems and promises of Computer-Based Training* (pp. 291–308). Norwood, NJ: Ablex.

Meichenbaum, D. (1974). *Cognitive behavior modification.* Morristown, NJ: General Learning Corporation.

Miller, G.A., Galanter, E., & Pribram, K.H. (1960). *Plans and the structure of behavior.* New York: McGraw Hill.

Müller, M. (1989). *Softwaregestaltung und Computertraining: Entwicklung und Evaluation eines mitwachsenden Softwaresystems auf der Basis eines explorationsfördernden Trainings.* Unpublished Thesis (Diplomarbeit), Department of Psychology, University of Osnabrück.

Nilshon, I. (1989). Computer in der Ausbildung benachteilligter Jugendlicher. In B. de Boer & A. Herzog (Hrsg.), *Lernchanche Computer* (p. 13–44). Berlin: Walter Friedländer Bildungswerk.

Palme, J. (1983): A human-computer interface encouraging user growth. In M.E. Sieme & M.J. Coombs (Eds.), *Designing for human-computer communication.* London: Academic Press, 139–156.

Peters, H., & Bichler, S. (1989). Benutzerfehler und Nutzungsprobleme bei der Arbeit mit Software: Welchen Beitrag leisten die Handbücher? In S. Maaß & H. Oberquelle (Hrsg.), *Software-Ergonomie '89. Aufgabenorientierte Systemgestaltung und Funktionalität (S. 233–243).* Gemeinsame Fachtagung des German Chapter der ACM und der Gesellschaft für Information in Hamburg. Stuttgart: Teubner.

Piaget, J. (1936). *La naissance de l'intelligence chez l'enfant.* Neuchâtel: Delachaux & Niestlé.

Prümper, J., Zapf, D., Brodbeck, F.C., & Frese, M. (1992). *Errors of novices and experts: Some surprising differences from computerized office work.* Behaviour and Information Technology.

Reiser, B., Anderson, J.R., & Farrell, R.G. (1985). Dynamic student modelling in an intelligent tutor for LISP programming. In *Proceedings of the Ninth Joint Conference on Artificial Intelligence* (pp. 8–14). Los Altos, CA: Morgan Kaufmann.

Rummelhart, D.E., & Norman, D.A. (1978). Accretion, tuning, and restructuring: Three modes of learning. In J.W. Cotton, & R. Klatzky (Eds.), *Semantic factors in cognition* (pp. 37–60). Hilldale, NJ: Erlbaum.

Sauvageod, F. (1990). *Explorationsfördernde Maßnahmen im Computertraining.* Unpublished thesis (Diplomarbeit), University of Osnabrück.

Schneider, K., Moch, M., Sandfort, R., Auerwald, M., and Walther-Wichkman, K. (1983). Exploring a novel object by preschool children: A sequential analysis of perceptual, manipulating and verbal exploration. *International Journal of Behavioural Development, 6,* 477–496.

Schölmerich, A. (1990). *Der Erwerb neuer Informationen im Verlauf des Explorationsprozesses: Eine sequentielle Analyse von Handlungsketten.* Osnabrück: Fachbereich Psychologie der Universität Osnabrück (unpubl. Diss.).

Semmer, N., & Pfäfflin, M. (1978). *Interaktionstraining.* Weinheim: Beltz.

Shlechter, T.M. (Ed.) (1991). *Problems and promises of computer-based training.* Norwood, NJ: Ablex.

Simons, P.R.J. (1989). Selbstreguliertes Lernen durch Computer—selbständiges Arbeiten mit Computern. In B. de Boer & A. Herzog (Hrsg.), *Lernchanche Computer* (p. 149–180). Berlin: Walter Friedländer Bildungswerk.

Skell, W. (1980). Erfahrungen mit Selbstinstruktionstraining beim Erwerb kognitiver Regulationsgrundlagen. In W. Volpert (Hrsg.), *Beiträge zur Handlungstheorie* (p. 50–70). Bern: Huber.

Skinner, B.F. (1954). The science of learning and the art of teaching. *Harvard Educational Review, 24,* 86–97.

Skinner, B.F. (1986). *The technology of teaching.* New York: Appleton Century Crofts.

Sonntag, K. (1989). *Trainingsforschung in der Arbeitspsychologie.* Bern: Huber.

Stillings, N.A., Feinstein, M.H., Garfield, J.L., Risslland, E.L., Rosenbaum, D.A., Weisler, S.E., & Baker-Ward, L. (Eds.) (1987). *Cognitive Science. An Introduction.* Cambridge, MA.: MIT Press.

Thorndike, E.L. (1914). *The psychology of learning.* New York: Teachers College.

Thorndike, E.L., & Woodworth, R.S. (1901). The influence of improvement in one mental formation upon efficiency of other functions. *Psychological Review, 8,* 247–267, 384–395, 553–564.

Ulich, E. (1967). Some experiments on the function of mental training in the acquisition of motor skills. *Ergonomics, 10,* 411–419.

Volpert, W. (1983a). *Handlungsstrukturanalyse.* Köln: Pahl-Rugenstein (4. Aufl.).

Volpert, W. (1983b). *Sensumotorisches Lernen. Zur Theorie des Trainings in Industrie und Sport.* Frankfurt/M.: Fachbuchhandlung für Psychologie (4. Aufl.).

Voss, H.G. (1984). Curiosity, exploration and anxiety. In H.M. van der Ploeg, R. Schwarzer, and C.D. Spielberger (Eds.), *Advances in Anxiety Research, Vol. 3.* Hilldale, NJ: Erlbaum.

Voss, H.G., & Keller, H. (1983). *Curiosity and exploration. Theories and results.* New York: Academic Press.

Voss, H.G., & Keller, H. (1986). Curiosity and exploration. A program of investigation. *German Journal of Psychology, 10*(4), 327–337.

Wagner, K. (1989). Informations- und Kommunikationstechnologien als eine zentrale Aufgabe in der Jugendberufshilfe. In B. de Boer & A. Herzog (Hrsg.), *Lernchanche Computer* (p. 9–12). Berlin: Walter Friedländer Bildungswerk.

Weizenbaum, J. (1976). *Computer power and human reason.* San Francisco: Freeman.

Zapf, D., Brodbeck, F.C., Frese, M., Peters, H., & Prümper, J. (1992). Errors in working with computers: a first validation of a taxonomy for observed errors in a field setting. *International Journal of Human-Computer Interaction, 4,* in press.

PART III

Discourse and the Structure of Learning: The Processes of Co-Construction in Human Development

CHAPTER 6

Understanding the Co-Constructive Nature of Human Development: Role Coordination in Early Peer Interaction*

Zilma Moraes Ramos
de Oliveira

Maria Clotilde Rossetti-
Ferreira

Brazilian Investigation Center on Early Child Development
and Education (CINDEDI)
University of São Paulo at Ribeirão Preto, Brazil

INTRODUCTION

A theoretical-methodological approach based on sociointeractionist postulates and using the concept of *role* is proposed to analyze some interactional episodes in two groups of toddlers in a day care context. In a first moment, a microgenetic examination of some data is discussed as revealing the children's interactions as co-constructions in which they negotiate meanings for their actions. Secondly, some short interactional episodes are presented to show the evolution of role coordination in the period extending from 21 to 57 months of age. Finally, a discussion is offered about the functions of early peer interactions in human development.

A SOCIOINTERACTIONIST PERSPECTIVE

A sociointeractionist perspective of human development, based on G.H. Mead (1934), Vygotsky (1978, 1986) and Wallon (1942), states that mind, knowledge,

* The authors acknowledge grants from FAPESP, CNPq and CAPES, which helped to develop this research project, and are thankful to the fruitful discussions with our colleagues Drs. Claudia Lemos, Ana Maria Almeida, Ana Luiza B. Smolka, Maria Cecília Goes, Heloysa Dantas, and Claudia Davis, who helped to improve this text.

language, and self are constructed through the interactions the individual establishes, from birth, with other individuals in social settings, especially in those
organized by adults according to their conceptions about child development and
the way to promote it. Thus, intersubjective functioning in cultural activities
constitutes a necessary condition for intrapsychological processes.

This developmental path originates from the long dependence and immatu-
rity of the human infant, which requires that his or her basic needs be provided for by another competent member of the species in order to guarantee his or
her survival. Moreover, the adult–child dyad is inserted in sociohistorical matri-
ces created in complex economical and political systems that continuously
structure their development, allowing varied paths of behavior for the human
species. The symbolic nature of human behavior results thus from the appro-
priation and modification of cultural historical meanings by each individual.
Human development, therefore, is a joint construction in which both the child
and his or her partners are constituted in the interactions they get involved in.

The environment in this perspective is conceived as the social space of experience as well as the condition/instrument of development. At each moment, the
individual structures his or her action and constructs his or her personality and
thought through his or her conflicts with the environment. As the environment
and the individual–environment relationships are dialectically and simultaneously transformed, aspects of the environment that are important for the construction of certain abilities or cluster of meanings by the child at a certain age
give way, at another moment, to other aspects of the environment as privileged
sources for development. The dynamic individual–environment interactions in
socially meaningful practical activities bring into being new psychological tools
for the individuals contingent upon the productive material conditions of that
given society. Most influential among those are the systems of signs developed
by the preceding generations in that particular culture. Thus, the exclusive characteristic of the human species is the mediation of behavior by culturally elaborated and transmitted systems of signs.

This mediation involves representations and values constructed in the social
interaction. Gestures directed to the partner are taken as the initial basis of symbolic activity. Later, some new mediators, such as images and words, integrate
and transform the construction of representations, as the child constructs symbolic substitutes and functional equivalents of his or her actions. This allows the transition from act to thought, giving way for the construction of discursive thought.

THE VALUE OF EARLY PEER INTERACTION
IN CHILD DEVELOPMENT

Most studies using a sociointeractionist perspective have focused on the
adult–child joint action, the adult being seen as the more experienced partner
(Bruner, 1975; Cole, 1985; De Lemos, 1981; Hickman & Wertsch, 1978;
Valsiner, 1987; Wertsch & Stone, 1980).

In the early moments of the mother[1]–infant dyad the asymmetry of competence between partners is most obvious. For the mother, the infant is full of meanings that have emerged from sociocultural representations obtained through her own previous experiences, while for the newborn, the mother is an empirical object. Nevertheless, she is not perceived as any other object. The baby has been shown to present some innate perceptual bias and response organization that favor an arousal and readiness to perceive and respond to some characteristics, such as facial features and rhythms as well as human and particularly female voices (Kaye, 1982; Schaffer, 1977, 1984; Trevarthen, 1989). More acquainted than the infant with the symbolic sphere of the world, the mother has interpretational resources for attributing certain meanings to the baby's diffuse movements, based on representations constructed during her own personal life in a specific sociocultural context. The baby's movements are taken by her as communication cues that suggest some joint course of action. On doing so, the mother provides some specific meanings for the situation in which she and her baby are involved. Consequently, the dyad sets out from a state of no-differentiation (Lyra & Rossetti-Ferreira, 1991).

The emphasis on adult–child interaction, however, hinders the opportunity to discuss the value of early peer interaction in child development. As Mueller and Cooper (1986) have pointed out, the question about the functions of early peer interaction in child development has still to be answered, and the investigations proposed in this area demonstrate a lack of theoretical coherence. In his 1984 review, Schaffer states that until recently, children under three years of age were considered to be unable to establish complex and lasting interactions with same-age peers, although interest in other children's behavior has been recognized as occurring even early in infancy.

Child–child interaction research, however, has been receiving increasingly more attention (Hartup, 1983). It corresponds to a transformation that has occurred in the ecological-cultural developmental setting for many young children during the last decades. Instead of large families with many children of various ages, typical of the extensive family model, the pattern of nuclear families with one or two children is becoming more prevalent. However, an increasing use of day care facilities for very young children is occurring all over the world. This context differs from the usual family environment, where few adults are responsible for caring for and educating a large number of young children. In the day care situation, same-age children are usually the partners most available for interaction, as proposed by Camaioni (1980) and Rossetti-Ferreira, Secaf, Rubiano, and Oliveira (1985).

To enhance our understanding of the main postulates of the sociointeractionist perspective, child–child interactions in a sociocultural context should be analyzed in an attempt to understand the joint construction of their actions. This

---

[1] Although we refer to mother, the same considerations apply to other experienced members of the culture who interact with the child.

task implies apprehending how the young partners negotiate the meanings they attribute to their action, and thus relating the partners' interactions to the individuals' later performance, as a means of obtaining some indication about the mediational and internalization processes.

That enterprise, however, faces a serious methodological difficulty, due to the lack of true interactional categories capable of capturing the ongoing interactional process, in order to understand its dynamic, as pointed out by Schaffer (1984). Many studies on early peer interaction try to correlate interactional modalities and individual characteristics (Hartup, 1983). They usually focus on each individual involved in the situation as an independent agent who establishes some kind of relationship with partners. The result is an individualistic view of the interactional process, more concerned with successive chains of observed actions than with a transactional view of human interactions, in which the partners are always being constituted by their reciprocal actions with their shared meanings in a specific situation.

According to Light (1988, p. 74), a clear understanding of the relationship between quality of social interaction and cognitive outcome should need a generalizable but sensitive coding scheme for such interactions.

To face Schaffer's and Light's challenge, a theoretical-methodological perspective for studying human interactions based on the concept of *role* will be presented.

HUMAN INTERACTION AS COORDINATION OF ROLES

G.H. Mead (1934) extended J.M. Baldwin's concept of role as indicating the process of taking the partner's attitudes through imitation and directing them to oneself. Considering human behavior as responses to interpreted stimuli in a specific sociocultural frame, Mead pointed out that human cooperation involves responding to the intended behavior of others. Human interaction is proposed by him as a "dialogue of gestures" where each participant has to take the gesture—that is, the attitude of the others—in order to respond to them. This interpersonal experience in a certain culture from birth leads the children to develop some abilities to respond not only to the gestures of their partners, taking their role in the situation, but also to their own gestures, seeing themselves as objects.

In a first stage of the developmental process, according to Mead, imitation on the part of the infant is frequent and young children customarily put themselves in the position of others and act like them. In a second stage, children get involved in play and games. By enacting various roles (of mother, baby, driver, and so on), although in an disorganized fashion, they see themselves as being made up of a number of separate and discrete objects, based on the roles they perform towards themselves. In a third stage, children build a generalized role or standpoint from which they view themselves and their behaviors by abstracting a composite role out of the concrete roles that particular persons assume when they interact with them. In doing so, children develop their own selves and have the opportunity of making indications to themselves, which constitute their minds.

The conception of the role relationship in the dialectic perspective brought by Vygotsky and Wallon emphasizes the social historical practices as locus of role construction, according to the needs imposed by the situations. Approaching human action as deeply inserted in cultural and individual psychological processes, it invites us to apprehend it in the intersection of motives present in the task, activity, or event culturally defined structure, that is, in the roles assumed by the subjects.

For Vygotsky (1986), all higher psychological functions are semiotically mediated and originate from the internalization of social relationships involving the child and more experienced members of their culture. In this conception, adults interact with infants trying to incorporate them, from birth, in the symbolic sphere of culture, in its historically constructed meanings and ways of behaving and of operating with information. That is done through indicative gestures and structuring questions in joint tasks, in which adult ways of dealing with knowledge interact with the child's spontaneous reasoning, promoting his or her development.

As the child imitates the adult's process of simplifying the matter and solving the problem in the adult–child functional system of participation, he or she is able to analyze the joint experience and differentiate the roles involved in the task solution. With this, he or she can make indications to himself or herself.

Wallon's great contribution for the understanding of human development was to explain the organic basis of thought linked to the paradoxical character of emotions lived out in interpersonal situations, especially with the mother or main caretaker, who constitutes the first environment for human babies and their first condition for development (Wallon, 1942).

According to Wallon (1949), before oral language, meaning construction and consciousness formation occur by subtle and dynamic affective postural channels that involve the infant and his or her mother or other caregivers, his or her dialectic antagonists and constitutive partners. This affective frame arises at the same time as practical actions shape the baby's movements, transforming them into gestures. Being organized by the environment's influence, the emotions, by their expressive function, create a fusion of sensitivity between the child and his or her partners that helps the child to take certain *roles* that express certain dispositions in his or her own sensitivity.

The ontogenesis of representation for Wallon occurs jointly with the self–other differentiation. Completely immersed in the social world, the infant is unable to distinguish between his or her own motives and those of the other. Starting from a close experience with another person, he or she cannot, at first, differentiate his or her own from the partner's perspective. Only gradually, as the infant learns to take the other's role, he or she becomes aware of social relationships and forms his or her own idea of his or her *self*. This occurs especially through imitation, when the child, by imitating the partner's gestures, expressions, and intonations, makes comparisons between his or her own actions and those of the model he or she imitates. Thus, the child explores the movements he or she imitates and the affective-postural meanings linked to them. In that way children build up a duplication of the real, that is, an equivalent made up of images, symbols, and ideas, in a sensitive and concrete plan. On doing so, they differentiate aspects of themselves from those of the model. A representation is thus being achieved (Wallon, 1942).

In the sociointeractionist perspective, thus, gestures and actions with their sociocultural meanings framed by privileged partners constitute the roles that the developing individual assumes and modifies throughout life experience in new settings, involving new goals proposed by new desires and motives.

The idea of interaction derived from the sociointeractionist perspective differs from that of social guidance, which can be found as a facilitating device held by autonomous individuals in other theoretical perspectives such as social learning theory (Bandura, 1969) and in the neo-piagetian notion of sociocognitive conflict (Perret-Clermont, 1980; Doise & Mugny, 1984). Its starting point is the idea that the reciprocal constitution of individual and environment, as discussed before, gives way to always new and singular situations, which are constructed by the partners' interactions. Hence, in the human interactional process, meanings are settled by the individuals through their actions in a here-and-now context, through the roles that the participants continuously enact and confront.

As human actions have their meanings negotiated and defined in sociocultural experiences with others, framed behaviors constitute roles associated with counter-roles played in fact or as a possibility by each individual partner. An example can better elucidate this point: to extend an object towards the partner means "to give it" if the partner takes the object and thus accepts the implicit offer. The same gesture can mean "to exchange objects" if the partner, while taking the extended object, proffers another one. It may also mean "an invitation for a symbolic game" if the partner falls to the floor pretending to have been killed by an imaginary gun.

Thus, in human interaction roles are enacted, confronted, and coordinated by the participants, who simultaneously have to negotiate the cultural frame taken to the situation by their actions (in a strict sense, their social roles) and the positions they adopt in it, one in relation to the other (their role attitudes).

As roles emerge in the interpersonal experience, their main characteristic is an intersubjective polarity and even when alone the individuals' behavior presupposes a partner. For that reason, the actions of each partner in a dyad, triad, and so on constitute role/counter-role pairs confronted with the roles (and its implicit counter-roles) assumed by the partner(s). This role-playing process creates tensions and resolutions that continuously resignify the context, the objects, the roles to be enacted, and the participants themselves. Human interactions can thus be conceived as a process of confrontation and coordination of the roles played by the participants.

The interpsychological field created by the role-playing process mediates psychological development, acting as a "zone of proximal development" as proposed by Vygotsky (1978), and allows the construction of objectivity and subjectivity. This occurs by the internalization of social relationships, that is, by the mastery of the role/counter-role dynamic mechanism of coordination.

CHILDREN'S ROLE CONSTRUCTION: AN EMPIRICAL STUDY

In our perspective, human beings play roles since birth and throughout life. However, although the role-playing process cannot be reduced to symbolic play or make-believe play, the study of children's symbolic play constitutes an important source for understanding the internalization processes and for the discussion of the function of early peer interaction in child development.

Some questions may be raised to help this discussion: How do children coordinate the roles they play in their interactions? How does this role coordination develop with age and experience?

For that purpose we will present data from a short-term longitudinal study on young peer interaction in a Brazilian day care center (Oliveira, 1988). These data were obtained from video recordings of 15-min free play sessions of two groups of children from low-income families in a public day care center located at the poor outskirts of the city of São Paulo. Most of the children's families live in slums or in other poor housing. The parents work in unskilled jobs, and the mothers usually work as domestic helpers. Over 50 percent are single mothers living alone with the children and occasionally with another partner who frequently is not the subject's father.

Group A included two boys and four girls, aged 21 to 25 months old at the beginning of data collection. Group B included six boys and two girls, aged 33 to 46 months old at the same period. Seventeen sessions were obtained for group A and 14 sessions for group B, spread over 12 months.

The children attended the day care center from 7 a.m. to 6 p.m., in groups of 18 children with one caretaker for each six-hour period. The caretakers were all females, with no specific training for developing educational activities with the children. They spent most of their time in physical assistance, helping with food, bath, or toilet, and on supervision of the children's free play activity. During that period, they just watched the children, occasionally stimulating them to play or comforting a whimpering child. Some story telling and doing jigsaw puzzles were observed, but the caretakers were seldom seen taking part in the children's symbolic games or establishing a lasting dialogue with them. Similar conditions and situations have been described in an extensive study by Silveria, Fiorini-Piccolo, Perrone Delphino, Mortari-Faria, and Rossetti-Ferreira (1987) at nine Brazilian day care centers located in the region of Ribeirão Preto, State of São Paulo.

The observations were made in the groups' playroom, a sparsely structured open area of about 25 m², with some pillows, small mattresses, chairs, and, occasionally, a small table or sofa. A small variety of objects and toys were usually left on the table or were available in boxes or on shelves. Sometimes the investigator brought some other objects such as stuffed animals, dolls, items of clothing, toy cars, large white plastic blocks, some play cutlery, dishes, and pots. Those objects were sometimes available for the children in their day care environment.

The video records were made by the first author, who, for a period of three months before data collection, made weekly visits to the day care center, in order to allow the children to get to know her. As the focus of the investigation was the children's interactions with no direct mediation of the caretaker, the first author invited the children of the two groups in succession to play for a while in their playroom, while the other children remained in the playground with the caregiver. This invitation was always happily complied with by the children. During the session, the investigator limited her interference as far as possible, responding only when approached or questioned by the children, or occasionally comforting a distressed child or cautioning a child about some possible danger. It should, therefore, be emphasized that the situation contained mostly elements that were familiar to the children—the other children, the observer, and the playroom, with its usual furniture and objects.

A microanalytical transcription of the continuous behavioral flow of the participants in each episode was made for all the sessions recorded, with a detailed report about the situations and the objects involved. For the exhaustive transcription of each observational session describing the temporal sequence of the children's activities, the tapes were reviewed as many times as necessary. Postures, gestures, vocalizations, and body and facial expressions were recorded in succession at 15-sec intervals in order to apprehend the ongoing interactions. Each tape was independently transcribed by two trained observers, who then discussed their disagreements while reviewing each specific scene.

Some episodes were selected from the transcribed sessions for further analysis. A processual view of young children's interaction, able to capture their flux, was adopted, as it enhances the opportunities for illuminating how roles emerge and how they are coordinated. Thus, in the synchronic and diachronic analysis of the linkages between successive interactions, the whole situation in which the children, the researcher, the physical space, the objects and the institution's routine were intermingled was taken into consideration. Consequently, the behaviors of a child or of a dyad or group were not considered independently of the overall situation which gave them meaning by characterizing them as roles (see Interactional Episode 1).

Interactional Episode 1 (Group A)

Situation: Vania (21 mo) and Telma (23 mo) are seated side by side. Another boy, João (23 mo), is sitting on a rocking chair in another part of the playroom.

As the children enact parts of the Brazilian birthday singing ritual in this episode, we will describe it with some detail. It usually involves a sequence of the happy birthday song, when everybody claps hands, followed by an excited ritual dialogue in which a person elicits from the others greetings and all good wishes ("tudo") for the birthday person. The relevant part of this dialogue is presented below.

leader: - Para ele/ela nada [For him/her nothing?]
others: - Tudo! [Everything!]
leader + others: - E então como é que é? [So, what will it be?]
everybody: - ÉÉÉ! [Yea!] (with the same final sound of the previous
　　　　　phrase)

Vania	Telma
1. Takes some wooden blocks from the floor and holds them piled in her hands.	-Picks up some blocks and throws them into a large container.

Vania	Telma
2. Makes a movement to take another block. (The blocks she is holding falls down, making a noise). She puts her hands together, rests them on her lap, looks at the blocks on the floor, raises her head and claps her hands, shouting excitedly "ééé!" ("Yes!"), while she looks at Telma.	-Stands up and looks at the floor around her. She picks up a block and manipulates it. She crouches beside the container and manipulates the block. -Stands up, takes the blocks fallen on the floor and piles them in front of Vania.

(continued)

185

Vania	Telma
3. She half rises from the floor, while clapping her hands and shouting "tuto! tuto!" (childish way of saying "tudo" - Everything), looks at the block that Telma is holding.	-Looks at Vania, stands up, walks and picks up a block. She holds the block and looks at Vania.
4. Repeats "tuto!tuto!", clapping her hands and looking at Telma.	-Turns towards Vania and offers her the block.
5. Takes the offered block and places it on the floor in front of her.	-Watches Vania, attentively.
6. Picks up the block again, lets it drop down and shouts: "abidi!" (modified reproduction of the final part of the birthday ritual previously described), clapping her hands.	-Watches Vania.

Vania	Telma
7-Shouts "aidité" (same as "abidi") clapping her hands, shaking her legs, smiling and looking at the block on the floor.	-Watches Vania.
8-Claps her hands, exclaiming, in a singing voice "tuto! tuto!", looking at Telma.	-Shows Vania another block and lets it fall to the floor.
9-Picks up the block Telma has dropped.	-Makes a pile in front of her with several other blocks.
10-Offers Telma her block.	-Receives Vania's block and places it on the top of the pile.
11-Watches Telma.	-Claps her right hand rhythmically on the top of the pile, while looking around and sings "paara . . ." (happy . . .) with the intonation of "parabéns) [happy birthday].
12-Takes a block, extends it towards Telma and looks at her.	-Takes the block from Vania's hand, places it on the top of the pile, claps her hands looking at Vania, shouting something.
13-Looks at Telma for a while, then begins to clap her hands, smiling and looking at the researcher (videotaping).	-Watches Vania.
14-Claps her hands saying "béééém" (with the tone of "happy birthday"), and "tuto," looking ahead.	-Observes Vania, looks at the blocks and takes one of them.
15-Looks at Telma with a serious expression	-Arranges the pile of blocks built on the floor in front of her.
16-Watches Telma.	-Raises her upper body and claps her hands, turning towards Vania to look at her hands. (Vania is not holding anything).
17-Looks around.	-Claps her hands, looking at Vania.
18-Claps hands once, with a distant gaze.	-Claps her hands, looking at Vania.
19-Smiles and claps her hands, looking ahead of her.	-Claps her hands, looking at Vania.

(continued)

Vania	Telma
20-Looks and smiles at Telma. 21-Watches Telma.	-Looks at Vania. -Opens and closes her arms dramatically, shouting "ééé!", while looking at Vania.

22-Claps her hands, looking around. 23-Looks at Telma.	-Repeats the gesture of opening and closing her arms and sings "a-ben-a" (with the intonation of happy birthday), looking at Vania. -Claps hands and shouts "ééé."

The noise of Vania's blocks falling to the floor acts as a cue for her to clap hands and shout, "Ehhh!" smiling, observed by Telma. These gestures and expressions constitute part of a well-known adult–child game in our and other cultures, in which the adult helps the child to pile up some blocks and the child knocks them down, both of them clapping hands, smiling and shouting, repetitively. Vania's actions are followed by Telma's, who stands up, takes the fallen blocks, and piles them up in front of Vania, who begins to clap hands and to

Vania	Telma
24-Claps her hands.	-Watches Vania.
25-Watches Telma and claps her hands.	-Looks around and claps her hands, singing "tei."

(The episode lasted 1 min. 32 sec.)

shout the final part of the birthday greeting. We can say that the pile of wooden block built up by Telma in front of Vania was interpreted by Vania as a new theme for a common symbolic game. The pile provided the children with a cue for interpretation of each other actions as it is taken by them as a substitute for another object (a cake?). Instead of continuing the pile up and knock down game, Vania changes it by acting in an imaginary birthday party situation. The role she plays at that moment, being part of a well-known script, helps Telma to take up the same role. In this case, the birthday scene appears as role imitation. The two girls stimulate each other to play a common game by looking and smiling at the partner, while making a conspicuous gesture, until the other imitates them and enacts the other part of the birthday script.

The analysis of how the roles are enacted by the children in this episode indicates that, in this initial period, expressive gestures and an attitude of attending to the partner's actions are the children's main mode of action in this episode. There is a salience of expressive over instrumental acts, denoting the dynamogenic effect of the others' presence, in Wallonian terms. Expressive gestures, brought by the children into the situation, affect the partners and impregnate their behavior in a process that cannot, however, be reduced to a simple emotional contagion. It approaches true imitation, which, for Wallon (1942), is a delayed process. This expressivity, revealed in the child's tonus and gestures, functions as hints for his or her symbolic behaviours.

Discussing the episode from our sociointeractionist point of view, we may say that, in a period when self-other differentiation is at its beginnings and when the dialogical structure of the interaction with its coordination of different parts is being mastered by the children, the role coordination occurs mainly through reciprocal imitation (Nadel, 1986; Wallon, 1942). The children reenact previously experienced rites, expressing joy and pleasure at attaining a common goal.

Another possibility of role coordination at this age can be seen in Interactional Episode 2, taken from the same session.

Interactional Episode 2 (Group A)

Situation: Immediately after the "birthday" episode described above, Vania and Telma begin to play with a cylindrical container, repetitively throwing blocks into it and then taking them out again.

Vania	Telma
1. Sitting on the floor, lifts her hand holding a block, looks around, turns towards Telma and quickly strokes Telma's hair with the block, as if it were a comb.	-Offers a block to Vania saying "tó" ("here, take it!").
2. Looks at Telma, holding the block.	-Looks at the block Vania has used as if to comb her hair.
3. Rubs the block on Telma's hair and smiles.	-Lifts up her left arm, in such a way as to push Vania away, and keeps it there.

(Both girls stare at each other's face very closely)

Vania	Telma
4. Smiles, showing her teeth and repeats the hair combing gesture, while saying "ai!" ("ouch!")	-Looks at Vania's face and takes her head away.
5. Rubs the block on Telma's hair three more times. At the first, says "repi" (word with no meaning known to the observer) and, at the last two, doesn't say anything.	-Watches Vania.
6. Leans back on the mattresses heaped up behind her and handles the block.	-Watches Vania.
7. Holding the block, takes another one out of the container, knocks one against the other rhythmically, saying "ui" ("ouch").	- Looks into the container, turns towards Vania and watches her.
8. Throws one of the blocks to the floor and rubs the other on Telma's hair a few times.	-Watches Vania.

Vania	Telma
9. Bends down near Telma, looks closely at Telma and asks "ta' bom? hum?" ("Is that alright?"), while nodding her head.	-Watches Vania.

(The two girls stare at each other for two seconds)

Vania	Telma
10. Rubs the block again on Telma's hair.	-Shakes her head vigorously from side to side, and turns to look at Vania.
11. Sitting, keeps her hand raised, holding the block.	-Watches Vania.

(another period of mutual observation)

Vania	Telma
12. Watches Telma, while holding the block.	-Opens her mouth, putting it near the block Vania is holding.

(continued)

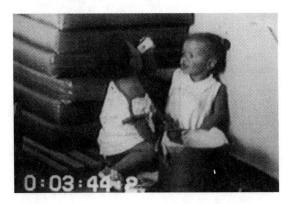

Vania	**Telma**
13. Moves the block towards Telma's mouth.	-Keeps her mouth open in front of Vania's block.
14. Making faces, touches Telma's mouth with the block and smiles, first without fully opening her lips and then showing her teeth.	-Watches Vania, close her mouth, turning her head sideways.
15. Watches Telma.	-Looks at Vania, looks at the block and says "ah!".
16. Turns towards the container and takes out another block.	-Watches Vania.
17. Rubs one block against the other, looks at Telma and says "Hum . . . heim?", nodding her head.	-Watches Vania.
18. Drops one of the blocks, holding the other out towards Telma.	-Watches Vania, puts her head forward, opens her mouth and approaches it towards Vania's block as if to bite it saying "aum!" (onomatopoeic eating sound)
19. Pulls the block back and places it on her lap, and rests her head on her right shoulder.	-Watches Vania.
20. Looks at Telma next to her, opens and closes her mouth showing her teeth.	-Watches Vania.
21. Takes another block from the container. Looks at the blocks while fiddling with them.	-Watches Vania.
22. Holds the blocks, watching Telma.	-Watches Vania.

Vania	Telma
23. Throws one of the blocks into the container, smiles showing her teeth and touches Telma's face with the other block.	-Turns her face to the left and lifts her hand towards her own face.
24. Draws back the block, smiling.	-Keeps her hand over her mouth.

(Both girls watch each other closely)

Vania	Telma
25. Touches Telma's face with the block.	-Watches Vania, still covering her mouth with her hand.

(Both girls stare at each other)

Vania	Telma
26. Looks at Telma, draws the block away from her face and shouts "não!" ("no!"), in a reproaching adult tone.	-Keeps her hand over her mouth.
27. Quickly lifts up the block, touches it on Telma's hair and pulls it back, moving backwards a bit and watching Telma.	-Head tilted back, looks at Vania with her mouth wide open.
28. Gets up in front of Telma, looks at her, keeping the block up in front of her and opens her mouth.	-Watches Vania, mouth wide open.
29. Draws back her arm, touches the block on her body, closes her mouth, looks at Telma, frowns eyebrows and forehead, closes her lips firmly and, making a grave face, shouts "não!" ("no!")	-Watches Vania and closes her mouth.

(Both girls stare at each other — See Photo 10)

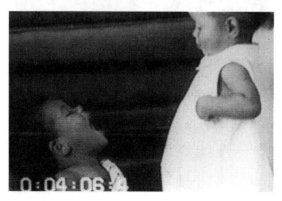

(continued)

Vania	Telma
30. Shouts "ba!" (word with no meaning said in an annoyed intonation).	-Watches Vania.
31. Standing up, lifts her hands and places them on her waist still holding a block in one of them, stands still and, with a serious face, stares at Telma.	-Watches Vania.
32. Puts the block near Telma's face.	-Seated, bends towards Vania, moves her open mouth towards the block Vania is holding out to her.
33. Watches Telma.	-Moves her head abruptly closing her mouth quickly.
34. Lowers the hand which holds the block, watching Telma.	-Watches Vania.
35. Holds Telma's head with one hand, while rubbing block on it with the other.	-Bends down, tries to put her head between her knees, pushing Vania away.

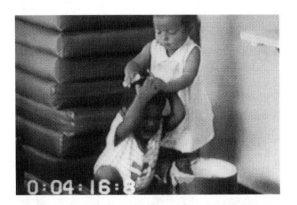

Vania	Telma
36. Releases Telma's head, puts her hands together and says "no."	-Pushes Vania away.
37. Rubs the block on Telma's hair, lowers her hands, looks forward and shouts "no!".	-Stops pushing Vania still bending down, looks at the researcher.
38. Rubs the block on Telma's hair.	-Puts her arms above her head, looks at the researcher and whines ("tia! tia!" ("auntie! auntie!": common way of calling the caretaker).
39. Rubs the block on Telma's hair.	-Still whining, lifts up her left arm and pushes Vania away.

Vania	Telma
40. Draws back, clapping her hands and says "ai meu Deus!" ("oh my God") looking at the researcher and smiling.	-Looks at the researcher as if she is going to cry.

(Both girls go back to play with the blocks)

Vania	Telma
41. Looks at the container and handles some blocks from it.	-Looks at the pile of blocks she has made in front of her, lifts up her hands, claps them and, looking at Vania, sings "a . . . vo" (syllables sung as part of the birthday song).
42. Looks into the container, takes two blocks out of it, sits next to Telma, knocks one of the blocks down.	-Arranges the pile of blocks.
43. Gets up, looks at Telma's head, lifts up her right hand and rubs the block on Telma's hair.	-Claps her hands and sings the birthday song.

(This episode lasted 1 min. 2 sec.)

Various "strategies" are used by Vania, trying to involve Telma in her game. Vania acts as an adult and, by her actions, attributes to Telma the role of a baby-to-be-taken-care-of. In Vania's acts one can perceive how the caregiver role is presented, showing its complexity in terms of attitudes involving postures and verbalizations (affection, as in turn 9, or authority, as in turns 26 and 29, etc.). Telma, on the other hand, reacts by trying to escape from the script proposed by Vania. The two girls have to adjust their actions through a dynamic meaning negotiation that involves both opposition and imitation. Telma initially remains more passive, while Vania rubs the block on her hair. Then she confronts Vania with a new script by attempting to bite the object that Vania is using to "comb"/wash her hair (turns 27 to 29 and 32 to 33). Vania appears to comply but, a second later, assumes an authoritarian postural attitude (turns 29 to 37), refusing Telma's script, and repeats her action related to the combing/shampooing script.

Differently from the first episode, when the girls enacted the same role, in episode 2 they try to articulate their roles. The two episodes, which occurred in a sequence in the same observational session, involve a specific way of role coordination. Both show the same characteristics: an unstable role/counter-role differentiation, more evident in episode 2. For example, while "combing" Telma, Vania shouts "no!" as if experiencing the discomfort of being "combed." In this case, however, one cannot exclude the possibility that on shouting, Vania is not taking Telma's role, but stressing the authoritarian adult's role she herself is playing. If that is the case, she is being able to distinguish hers from the partner's role.

The scene is created by the expressivity of the children's movements and by the postures and mimics they adopt. In it, the roles are articulated through an alternation between observing the partner and imitating her, coordinated with a modification of the script being constructed by the incorporation of new elements of the situation (a sound, an object, eventually an external noise) to the roles being played. This gives the syncretic and global character of role coordination at this first period when the role articulation is mainly controlled by expressivity.

The use of objects in episodes 1 and 2 can also be discussed from the developmental perspective presented above. This use indicates certain dettachment of the canonical use of the object and its integration with the sphere of the imaginary which is being constructed. It constitutes already a symbolic, substitute use that is at the same time autonomous and subordinated to the emotions. It differs from the use of objects by the younger child, which is basically determined by the concrete characteristics of the object.

THE EVOLUTION OBSERVED IN ROLE COORDINATION

Discussing the transformations observed in the children's role coordination process, we can say that, initially, around 21 months of age, the child is frequently observed playing simultaneously both a role and its counter-role, when interacting with a peer. These characteristics can be noticed in episode 2, when Vania, stretching her hand out towards an object held by Telma asking, "Give it to me?" nods her head affirmatively. Besides that, there is a frequent confrontation of different scripts with their associated roles proposed by each child's action. At another moment, while Telma, seated in front of a pile of wooden blocks, claps her hands, singing the birthday tune, Vania, standing up near her, makes gestures of combing/shampooing Telma's hair with a little wooden block.

A role/counter-role fusion is thus frequent at that early age, as the situations representation and the roles involved in it are still very rudimentary, being syncretic and context bound. To coordinate their actions by assuming complementary roles, the children should be able to assume the other's point of view. In order to do it, they have to observe the situation in detail and to apprehend the partner's gestures, an ability that is still being developed.

This syncretic, global apprehension of the situation and the difficulty of planning in advance a detailed script for a joint game contribute to the fact that children's joint game is first constructed as a kind of collage of fragments of well-known routines daily experienced in their own homes or in the day-care center. These routines are often prompted by objects, songs, gestures, and rhythms.

A coordination of roles can be also attained, at that early period, either by synchronization of rhythms (see Interactional Episode 3), or by imitation of gestures and/or postures, as in Interactional Episode 4 and 5.

Interactional Episodes 3, 4 and 5

Episode 3:

João (23 mo) approaches the metal cylinder containing wooden building blocks which is being moved up and down rhythmically by Vivi (21 mo) and leans on it with one hand. Standing up and without moving away, João lowers and raises his trunk while flexing his knees, accompanying the rhythm with which Vivi is moving the cylinder. He then takes his hand off the cylinder and moves his arms up and down in the same rhythm, without swaying his body.

Episode 4:

João (23 mo), standing still, observes Vivi (23 mo) who walks around the room holding a toy car under her right arm. He places the stuffed toy dog he is holding under his right arm and walks around the room.

Episode 5:

João (28 mo) and Vivi (26 mo) standing up side by side holding wooden hammers, jump up and down with a joyful expression repeatedly shouting "Ei!" (he after her) and hit the same wooden toy with their hammers.

In Episode 3 the synchronization of movements for a very short period of time constitutes a primitive way of role coordination, in which the apprehension of the meaning of the gestures imitated is not the most important issue. In Episode 4 there is a gesture of object holding, which is imitated, although the objects held are different. The reproduction of basic aspects of the partner's behavior is again seen, with some elements being modified. In Episode 5, the same objects, gestures, and shouts are simultaneously and repetitively presented by the children. The similarity is complete and also involves facial expressions of joy. The children's pleasure in the situation seems to be due to the achievement of that shared synchronized activity.

Another important way of coordinating their participation in the interaction occurs through the use of verbal expressions which focus the others' attention on an object (Episode 6) or mark an alternation of turns (Episode 7).

Interactional Episodes 6 and 7

Episode 6:

Telma (25 mo) holds out an object in the direction of Vivi (23 mo) who is manipulating attentively an object, saying: "Olha Vivi!" (Look, Vivi!).

Episode 7:

Fabio (45 mo) and Fernando (45 mo) are holding little wooden trunks. Fabio tells Fernando: "Agora eu!" (Now me!) and starts hitting the lid of his trunk. When Fabio stops, Fernando says: "Now me!" and hits the lid of his trunk. Fabio then says "Now me!" and hits the lid of his trunk. Fernando says "Now me!" and does the same.

The incipient function of verbal language can already be seen, helping the children in their new way of coordinating roles through the alternation of turns. The verbal expressions used to call the partners' attention constitute an important condition for a more coordinated role playing. By providing the opportunity for role reversal, they help the children to observe the partner while they wait for their turn to play that same role. The initially affective language now follows the action and will eventually guide it. Thus, gradually language becomes a fundamental regulator of the children's interactions. The intonation, the rhythm of the speech and the linguistic content, become basic elements in role playing, as can be observed in Interactional Episodes 8 and 9.

Interactional Episodes 8 and 9

Episode 8:

Fabio (46 mo), pretends to pour out an empty plastic bottle over his head, telling Davi (42 mo) "põe na cabeça. assim!" (Put it on your head! Like this!) and cups his hands, placing the empty bottle on the floor.

Episode 9:

Fabio (47 mo) places a large styrofoam bar next to some others, saying to Fernando (47 mo) "É uma passagem" (It's a passage!)

A better organization of common activities can be observed in children's interaction, as verbal language becomes more functional in mediating their role coordination. When he or she states how to use an object or what is the meaning of a gesture or object used, the child acts both as an actor and as a director of the created scene, assigning those elements that define the roles being constructed in the situation. Their greater linguistic mastery allows older children not only to suggest activities (as in Episode 8) or to organize the scenery (Episode 9) but also to check their role ("Eu sou a mãe, não sou"?—I'm the mother, isn't that right? Vania, 40 mo, group B), to propose a theme ("É de mamãe que quero brincar": I want to play mummy; Vania, 46 mo, group B), to attribute roles to himself or herself or to the partner ("Sou a polícia de chapéu": I'm a policeman with a hat; Fábio, 49 mo, group B; "Sou a mãe, você é a filha": I'm the mother and you are the daughter; Maristela, 47 mo, group B).

YOUNG CHILDREN'S ROLE PLAYING AND THE FUNCTION OF EARLY PEER INTERACTIONS IN HUMAN DEVELOPMENT

To enlighten some points about the internalization of social relationships, postulated by the sociointeractionist tradition as giving way to discursive thought and to the construction of self, the concept of *role* has been proposed as a focus for a dialogical analysis of early peer interaction episodes. We have investigated how 2- to 4-year-old children coordinate the roles they play in the situations they create together, with a microgenetic approach that takes gestures and postures, besides conversations, as indices of transformation and meaning construction by the children. In that way, we were able to capture the fluid nature of early peer interaction and its evolution with age.

Changing the perspective traditionally used in developmental psychology and focusing on long sequences of actions to capture its constructive process, it was possible to reinterpret data which has often been taken as an evidence of young peers' incompetence for lasting interactions. At 2 years of age, or even earlier, children can handle situations in which their privileged partners are other children and not adults, confronting meanings with them and constructing themselves as subjects.

Young children's symbolic play is jointly constructed through the roles they assume when attributing some meanings to the ongoing situation. Fragments of scripts already constructed, which prescribe certain roles to be enacted, are weaved together by each child's action, who tries to involve the partner in his/her own script, negotiating shared meanings for their symbolic role playing through imitation/opposition. These roles constitute ways that the children use to confront themselves with others, in order to attain their own goals which emerge at each moment. They can be assumed by more than one child and are available in the group's repertoire to be taken up by the participants. In that sense, the fact of being in daily contact with each other at the day care center might help such young children to build up shared-play sequences.

Some mechanisms of role coordination have been sequentially observed in use: observation of the partner, synchronization of gestures, taking up a role incited by a rite or a rhythm, immediate reciprocal imitation, alternation of turns, taking up a role incited by an object and delayed imitation. Verbal sharing of meanings and verbal attribution of roles emerged later. The observed evolution of role coordination thus indicates that the younger children coordinate their roles by enacting fragments of well-known scripts, making a kind of syncretic picture brought up by starters present in the situation, such as objects, songs, gestures, rhythms, in a process that is expressive rather than goal directed. Their actions are more linked to the present moment and to the situation than in the older group. As verbal language more effectively intermediates role coordination, older children present a better planned script, in which some representations are more clearly being negotiated. This verbal process of role attribution illuminates the internalization of social relationships by the children who still need to make their role regulations more explicit.

The transformations observed in the way children play certain roles while coordinating them with the roles played by others provide some cues for the discussion about the integrated process of self–other differentiation and the ontogenesis of representation. Children's role playing allows them to differentiate certain roles available in their milieu and constructed by their previous and present interactions. This process involves a confrontation of gestures, postures, sounds, and, consequently, meanings and propositions. The differentiation between pairs of complementary roles that is being settled down by them through their role conflicts in the situations is reflected in the evolution of children's interactions. This evolution promotes and, at the same time, depends on the greater ability for role reversal and language functional use. Simultaneously, the control over the children's actions, initially dominated by the affective sphere, is gradually relinquished to the cognitive domain.

A comparison between adult–child and child–child interaction might help to elucidate this issue. As previously stated, in the early moments of life, the roles and their counter-roles are so intermingled for the baby, his or her interpersonal experience with the caregiver is so integrated, that only an active work on it, provided by new experiences that promote conflict and its overcoming, will help the infant to apprehend his or her own part in that whole and to differentiate the other's characteristics from his or her own. Adult–child interaction, by its asymmetrical character, is supposed to allow more role complementarity, as the adult frequently tries to be sensitive even to the infant's subtle cues in order to appropriately respond to them. The attachment studies (Bowlby, 1969; Ainsworth, Blehar, Waters, & Wall, 1978) have stressed that syntony and have attributed great relevance to harmonic interactions in the development of the child. From that perspective, same-age peer interactions are probably seen as less harmonic and thus less beneficial for the development of young children.

In his early writings, Piaget recognizes the value of peer interaction in psychological development. For him, child–child interactions promote cognitive development, since arguments created in the discussion among equals are necessary for logical reasoning, conceived as an internal reproduction of a real argument (Piaget, 1928). This conception, so similar to the sociointeractionist idea of discursive thought as an internalized dialogue, was put away by Piaget in his later work, as he became more involved to prove the biological and intraindividual roots of cognitive development (Piaget, 1967). On the other hand, the Piagetian idea of egocentrism (Piaget, 1932), which postulates young children's inability to take the other's perspective, contributed to bring child–child interaction under suspicion. As pointed by Camaioni (1980), many studies have discussed that idea, equivocally taken to inspire the view of young children's incompetence for interacting together. Recent studies stemming from a Piagetian tradition, nevertheless, have reinterpreted some data on child–child interaction. Doise and Mugny's (1984) and Perret-Clermont's (1980) studies, chiefly, have emphasized the value of peer sociocognitive conflicts on promoting development.

For Camaioni (1980), as the type and quantity of social interactions influence the overcoming of egocentrism, peer interactions provide more opportunity than adult–child interaction for role taking and for the differentiation of the self and the other's points of view. By studying two groups of children of 2 and 4 years old with and without their caretaker, this author states that the adult usually acts by complementing the child's action, while same-age children act more in a reciprocal way.

Our data allow us to agree with Wallon (1942) that "egocentrism" has to be understood as a primary and necessary developmental tendency for fusion with the environment and not as an "autistic" manifestation. We have tried to investigate this point by using an interpersonal conception of searching for differentiation, while coordinating roles also through imitation.

In our opinion, we should discuss adult–child and child–child interactions as integrated processes. The comparison between these two types of interaction makes more evident the tutorial role of the adult as an experienced and privileged partner than any passive or incompetent trait one might attribute to the young child. In the make-believe atmosphere characteristic of their play, children have the opportunity to reenact and examine situations with their plans and arrangements, including role expectations ritualized in a certain culture. These situations, especially for young children, usually involve adult–child relationships, For examining them, children have to assume the adult's role in two ways: first, by playing some adult social roles in the "as if" situation, especially those of child care, in which they often take part as the child being cared for; secondly, by assuming attitudes of tutoring or supporting their own peers, attitudes that are frequently taken by the adult as a more experienced member of the culture. As soon as some role/counter-role relationships are controlled by the children, they gradually learn to master them, exploring their characteristics, by taking the other's role while, by their actions, they attribute their own role to someone else. This alternation of roles can be seen in mother–child daily interactive routines, as suggested by Bruner (1975), but is much more evident in children's symbolic role playing, as observed in our data.

In their development, children not only construct more flexible ways of role coordination, but, on doing so, they form and improve their representations, by creating in their minds discursive structures which allow them to apprehend various perspectives. In their symbolic role playing, by assuming the adult's role while stimulating or comforting another child, asking if he or she wants to eat or to be combed and so on, the child explores, appropriates himself or herself of, and transforms the role/counter-role dialogical structure defined in his or her experience in a certain culture. This process reveals the children's cognitive and linguistic competencies as well as their feelings and emotions in dealing with all those features. In this process, the children also elaborate a representation of the act with its meanings, including the relationships between its elements. This representation consequently emerges from their social experiences.

Our perspective goes in the direction pointed out by Cole (1985), who proposes Leontiev's concept of activity as a starting point for the investigation of the relation between socially organized experiences and cognitive development. For Cole, the best unit of analysis of cultural and individual processes is the activity, the task, or the event with its structure and its interrelationships. We also agree that scripts and schematas structure the situations, by prescribing some roles for the participants and by guiding their routine encounters. However, the process of meaning negotiation and of acquiring and recreating scripts in the here-and-now context of the situations in our view are more encompassing than suggested by Nelson (1981). The interdependence of individual consciousness and subjectivity with its social context, though, cannot be understood as an one way determinant which models human development. On the contrary, the idea stressed here is that the dialectic character of compliance–transformation of cultural rules and roles is a basic characteristic of our species.

Using the concept of role for interpreting human actions, we recognize with Harré (1979) the symbolic nature of human behavior, which is present even in the newborn's interactions with his or her mother. Our approach emphasizes human action as a drama continuously created by gestures and words expressing feelings and representations. Thus, self is built up as people assume roles, creating the **persona** in the Greek sense, the various cultural masks modelling human sensitivity and being transformed by human interactions.

REFERENCES

Ainsworth, M.D.S., Blehar, M.C., Waters, B., & Wall, S. (1978). *Patterns of attachment: a psychological study of the strange situation.* Hillsdale, NJ: Erlbaum.

Bandura, A. (1969). Social-learning theory of identificatory process. In D.A. Goslin (Ed.), *Handbook of socialization theory and research.* Chicago: Rand Mc Nally.

Bowlby, J. (1969). *Attachment and loss* (Vol. 1). New York, Hogarth.

Bruner, J. (1975). From communication to language: a psychological perspective. *Cognition, 3,* 255–287.

Camaioni, L. (1980). *L'Interazione tra Bambini.* Roma: Editora Armando.

Cole, M. (1985). The zone of proximal development: Where culture and cognition create each other. In J.V. Wertsch (Ed.), *Culture, communication and cognition: Vygotokian perspectives* (pp. 146–161). Cambridge, UK: Cambridge University Press.

De Lemos, C.T.G. (1981). Interactional process and the child's construction of language. In W. Deutsch (Ed.), *The child's construction of language.* London: Academic Press.

Doise, W., & Mugny, G. (1984) *The social development of the intellect.* Exeter, UK: A. Wheaton.

Harré, R. (1979) *Social being.* Oxford: Basil Blackwell.

Hartup, W.W. (1983) Peer relations. In P.H. Mussen (Ed.), *Handbook of child psychology* (Vol. IV). New York: John Wiley & Sons.

Hickman, M., & Wertsch, J.V. (1978) Adult-child discourse in problem solving situations. *Papers from the Fourteen Regional Meeting of the Chicago Linguistic Society.* Chicago: Chicago Linguistic Society.

Kaye, K. (1982). *The mental and social life of babies.* Sussex, UK: Harvest Press.

Light, P. (1988). Social interaction and cognitive development: A review of post-piagetian research. In S. Meadows (Ed.), *Developing thinking: approaches to children's cognitive development* (pp. 67–88). New York: Methuen.

Lyra, M.C., & Rossetti-Ferreira, M.C. (1991). Transformation and construction in social interaction: A new perspective of analysis of mother-infant dyad. In J. Valsiner (Ed.), *Child development within culturally structured environments III.* Norwood, NJ: Ablex Publishing Corp.

Mead, G.H. (1934). *Mind, self and society.* Chicago: University of Chicago Press.

Mueller, E.C., & Cooper, C.R. (Ed.). (1986). *Process and outcome in peer relationships.* Orlando, FL: Academic Press.

Nadel, J. (1986) *Imitation et communication entre jeunes enfants.* Paris: PUF.

Nelson, K. (1981). Social cognition in a script framework. In J.H. Flavell & L. Ross (Ed.), *Social cognitive development* (pp. 97–118). Cambridge, UK: Cambridge University Press.

Oliveira, Z.M.R. (1988). *Jogos de papéis: uma perspectiva para análise do desenvolvimento humano.* São Paulo: Universidade de São Paulo (tese de doutorado).

Perret-Clermont, A.N. (1980). *Social interaction and cognitive development in children.* London: Academic Press.

Piaget, J. (1928) *The child's conception of the world.* New York: Harcourt, Brace.

Piaget, J. (1932). *Le jugement moral chez l'enfant.* Paris: Librarie F. Alcan.

Piaget. J. (1967). *Biologie et connaissance.* Bussière, France: Gallimard.

Rossetti-Ferreira, M.C., Secaf, R.E., Rubiano, M.R.B., Oliveira, Z.M.R. (1985) Day care as substitute mother care or as a diverse socialization context? *Cahiers de psychologie cognitive* 5(3/4):282.

Schaffer, H.F. (1977). *Studies in mother–infant interaction.* London: Academic Press.

Schaffer, H.F. (1984). *The child's entry into a social world.* London: Academic Press.

Silveira, R.E.S., Fiorini-Piccolo, T., Perrone Delphino, V.R., Mortari-Faria, L., & Rossetti-Ferreira, M.C. (1987). Oportunidades de contato entre o adulto e a criança em creche. *Revista Brasileira de Estudos Pedagógicos, 158,* 130–163.

Trevarthen, C. (1989) Origins and directions for the concept by infant intersubjetivity. In B. Rogoff (Ed.), *Newsletter for the Society for Research in Child Development.* Salt Lake City, UT: University of Utah.

Valsiner, J. (1987) *Culture and development of children's action: a cultural historical theory of developmental psychology.* New York: John Wiley and Sons.

Vygotsky, L.S. (1978). *Mind in society.* Cambridge, MA: Harvard University Press.

Vygotsky, L.S. (1986). *Thought and language* (2nd ed.). Cambridge, MA: MIT Press.

Wallon, H. (1942). *De l'acte a la penseé: essai de psychologie comparée.* Paris: Flammarion.

Wallon, H. (1949). *Les origines du caractère chez l'enfant.* Paris: Presse Universitaire de France.

Wallon, H. (1959). Le rôle de "l'autre" dans la conscience du "moi." *Enfance* (3–4), 279–285.

Wertsch, J.V., & Stone, A.C. (1980) The adult–child dyad as a problem solving system. *Child Development, 51,* 1215–1221.

CHAPTER 7

The Dynamics of School Learning

Bert van Oers

Free University of Amsterdam, The Netherlands

STRUCTURING THE LEARNING PROCESS

Reflections on the structure of human learning processes sooner or later must lead to the question of the origin of structure. Is the structure of learning generated by a cause or by some agency? Many different answers have been given to this question. Most of these answers tend to take structural features of the learning situation and characteristics of the learner as structuring forces for learning processes.

The kind of factors, as well as the kind of interaction between factors, that must be accounted for in the organization of learning processes somehow or other depend on a view of learning and development. Theories of learning and development indicate more or less precisely what should be accounted for in the organization of learning, and how this learning should be promoted in practice. They define what ought to be done in order to produce learning and, consequently, what from a theoretical point of view may be counted as good instruction. Theories of learning and development have been described in this respect many times (see, among others, Bruner, 1967; Dillon & Sternberg, 1986; Reigeluth, 1983).

Following Foucault, we might say that theories always set up a *regime of meaning and truth* defining what legitimately can be said or done, and what is to be taken as true in a certain context. Regimes of meaning tend to regulate and normalize human activity in an obligatory way by organizing the material environment (according to culturally developed rules and habits—see, for example, Valsiner, 1987), and by introducing moral constraints on human activities (rules of conduct, conventions about methods, expectations about results, etc.).

School learning is a kind of institutionalized learning that is deliberately promoted within a context so organized as to produce intended learning results in pupils. Basically, the structure of the school learning process is the result of the dynamic interplay of different meaning regimes, brought into play by teacher and pupils. We can recognize such regimes in:

- norms and values (relating to views on man, knowledge, society, the future);
- contents of the school subjects (roughly spoken: scientific disciplines);
- psychological theories (layperson's or scientific) on learning, development, and personality.

In the historical development of views on learning, the meaning regime set up by learning theories has also changed gradually with time. Traditionally the pupil is seen as a potential force of labor that has to be mastered and shaped into a productive factor, as required by societal needs. More recently, however, it has been recognized that pupils are agents as well, trying to make personal sense of the cultural heritage that is offered to them (see Davydov, 1983). The view of learning itself has essentially been altered in connection with this change: learning is now conceived of as a process of meaningful production of knowledge, and as acquiring proficiency in applying this knowledge for personal ends (see, for example, Fichtner, 1985; Forman, Minick, & Stone, 1993; Rogoff, 1990). I take as a basic assumption that activity psychology (see, for example, Leont'ev, 1975; Van Oers, 1990; Van Parreren, 1954, 1978) presents a strong theoretical view to explain the psychological phenomena involved.

From this starting point I will analyze the structure of school learning as a result of the dynamic interplay of two different meaning regimes:

1. the aims of education
2. a theory of learning and development

The actual dynamics of classroom learning can be understood as depending on such meaning regimes. They are embodied in the curricula employed and in the strategies of teaching and learning. In my reconstruction of the school learning process, I will take the activity psychological view of learning and development as my starting point.

THE EDUCATIONAL AIMS OF SCHOOLING

All education implies canalization. As educative institutions, schools are historically invented selective organizations that are meant to contribute to the continuation and improvement of mankind and society. As such, schools are development-canalizing systems in which a selection of culture is taught in one particular way (rather than another). In order to legitimize the system's selectivity, it is generally assumed by educationalists that the contents and strategies chosen may be defended as the best for the pupils and for society as a whole. I cannot discuss this thorny issue here in depth, but I will return to it later on.

It is obvious that education always and essentially implies aims (see White, 1982). From the perspective of specified aims some actions will be declared reasonable, while other actions are prohibited. Aims of education are to be considered as strong normalizing forces in the context of schooling. The first questions that now arise are: how to identify suitable aims, and how can they be legitimized?

Often it has been tried to define aims as a series of objectives that can be derived objectively from psychological theories of learning and development. However, this is deceptive. It can be shown that there is always some general normative aim involved based on the hidden suppositions of the theory (see White, 1982). Psychological theories cannot convincingly lead to the specification of educational goals. In fact, psychological theories of learning first of all should be capable of interpreting and explaining all kinds of learning as it occurs, be it meaningless drill-and-practice, unconscious learning, systematically induced learning, or whatever form learning may take. A psychological theory of learning, then, can never prescribe exclusively from its own tenets the ideal structure of learning, because learning can take so many forms. For practical purposes, learning theory always has to be combined with a value system (concept of education) suggesting what ought to be taught at school, as well as what is morally acceptable in the intercourse with pupils. Of course, this doesn't mean that learning theory itself is value free. It is only denied that the values strictly pertaining to the general learning theory have enough directing force to found an education system on it. Rather, a learning theory should always be combined with an explicit concept of education that starts from compatible anthropological and epistemological tenets.

A Normative Conception of School Learning

Activity psychology starts from an image of a human being as a sense-seeking and sense-making creature, striving to be an agent in cultural activities. Sometimes he or she succeeds and gets the feeling of becoming a master of his or her inner and outer world. Often he or she also fails, and must try again and change his or her mind. Somehow or other, the agent's personality is involved in all human pursuits. Basically, activity psychology studies the psychological processes involved in these laborious endeavors. From this starting point, I assume that, in the preferred education system, the personality factor is also a central value. With White (1982) I would like to say that the ultimate aim of education ought to be that pupils become morally autonomous persons. Personality development, then, becomes an essential aim of education. It implies a form of school learning as a transactional process in which the child is trying to figure out the personal relevance of the cultural meanings as passed to him or her by significant others (Bruner, 1986). Teachers cannot force pupils to adopt culture, but they should help pupils to reconstruct culturally developed insights in a personally meaningful and critical way. The process of teaching is, then, to be conceived as a transformative process in which the learner can develop his or her own personality, as well as acquire culture at the same time (see also Jackson, 1986). Schools, consequently, should not be institutes for the learning of culturally developed answers to predetermined questions, but they should be working-places for finding culturally acceptable answers to the pupils' own questions. Trying to find questions, as well as answers and methods of evaluating the answers, in cooperation with the teacher should be, then, the core of the education system.

Clearly, we cannot give a complete curriculum design here. For the sake of brevity I will only point out some basic starting points that will provide a general reference frame for the discussions that follow:

- the highest aim of schooling must be personality development, in which cognitive, motivational, and emotional dimensions of humanity are integrated in one person (in this I follow Vygotsky; see Yaroshevsky, 1989; Petrovskij, 1985, pp. 211 ff.);
- transmission of culture should only take place as an attempt to make culture available for pupils and to let pupils re-create actively the aimed-at cultural elements;
- the selection of culture to be transmitted should not only comprise a body of knowledge (i.e., results of learning of former generations), but also methods of learning;
- the highest developed form of learning is the method of scientific thinking; or rather: the method of productive learning activity in which a pupil can try to produce his or her own knowledge as a solution to explicit problems in cooperation with other pupils and the teacher; it follows from this that schools must instill *learning activities* in children (like mathematizing, reading activity, historical thinking, music making, etc.), and not confine themselves to the transmission of the results of former human activities;
- schooling takes place in a social context in which many voices are being sounded, trying to get authority over matters of public concern; teaching, then, is the systematic attempt of bringing this 'polyphonous universe' (Bakhtin) under the pupils' personal control. Learning activity is essentially a discursive activity—or, as Davydov (1988) would say, a *polylogue*—in which historical and contemporary others play a role. In this respect Carpay and Van Oers (1990) suggest that education and school learning should develop 'thoughtfulness' in pupils (instead of downright cleverness or intelligence). Here we can return to the earlier referred to issue of selectivity in the education system. Educating pupils for the management of this diversity of meanings, and learning them to deal with the inevitable necessity of

selecting and self-canalization, might turn out to be the only valid legit-imization of the selective character of the school curriculum.

• meaningful learning takes place within a context of sociocultural activities in which—as a rule—the necessary resources (knowledge, abilities) are dis-tributed among participants (Salomon, 1993). At first the learner plays a peripheral role in the activity, but gradually his or her position can change signifying a growth of relative autonomy in the performance of that activi-ty (see Lave & Wenger, 1991).

In the following section I will present an outline of a theory that can account for the psychological aspects of these educational aims.

AN ACTIVITY-PSYCHOLOGICAL VIEW ON LEARNING AND DEVELOPMENT

A Psychological Action—Event Theory.[1]

According to Leont'ev (1975), human behavior must be characterized as an attempt to change a material or mental object from a given form into some other (more desirable) form, or as an attempt to prevent an object from chang-ing into an undesirable form. When we tie a shoelace, we change the form of this lace from a situation with two loose ends into a form with a knot. So we perform an action. But we also perform an action when we transform an equa-tion $2 + x = 7$ into: $x = 5$, or make a plan of an article to write, transforming a vague idea into a structured scheme.

In relation to such descriptions, Leont'ev would argue that behavior can be analyzed at different levels. At the most general level the stream of human behavior is analyzed as *motivated activity,* in which the *human need,* the intend-ed *object,* and the *general idea* of how to act in this situation are the essential elements of description. Activities are historically developed cultural registers that can be acted out in various ways, but not in any way. As such, activities also can be conceived of as a source of possible actions. Imagine mathematical activity, playing football, or shopping. These activities consist in different ways of doing that will easily be recognized as such in a particular community. How-ever, within one such activity, not everything is allowed. Culture places limits on the actions that legitimately can be considered a proper part of an activity. Activities are often put under social control, but they can be innovated as well. Characterizing human behavior as 'mathematizing' in our culture obviously

---

[1] Not to be confused with Davidson's conceptions of actions and events (see Davidson, 1982). I described and defended the action–event theory of psychological functioning in detail in my dis-sertation (Van Oers, 1987).

gives a meaningful description of that behavior, assuming some need, object, and general idea (rules of conduct, etc.).

However, describing human behavior as a special activity gives no information about what the person actually is doing at a given moment in time. Characterizing human activity by describing what exactly a person is doing within the context of a given activity is an analysis at the level of *actions*. In these descriptions information is given about the special goal a person is trying to reach, what in particular he or she is doing, with which instruments, according to which rules, and what aberrations occur in his or her actions, etc.

The Relevance of Meaning

Psychologically it is often not enough merely to describe an action in detail. It is also very important to know which personal *meaning* (sense) someone attaches to his or her goals and actions in the context of that activity. In the psychological analysis of actions, one must try to find out *why* someone is doing something. A man running on the street, fleeing from the police, is performing an action that is different from that of a jogger, or from a person who is trying to catch the last train. Besides such personal meaning actions often also have a metapersonal (cultural) meaning. These actions have been worked out in history and have been put on the cultural record as meaningful knowledge, as successful or even necessary instruments in the context of some activity. In the context of mathematical activity, for instance, the action of measuring has been connected with the action of defining the unit of measurement and (mostly, but not always) applying it very precisely, according to definite rules. These actions are obligatory for measuring. We are not allowed to change the rules or actions according to our own personal mood. In this case cultural meaning dominates personal meaning. Compliance with these cultural meanings is often sanctioned with punishment. Here we see how an activity constitutes a meaning regime for the individual.[2]

Actions and Psychological Events

The distinction between activity and actions, and the distinction between cultural meaning and personal meaning, are very important in the psychological analysis of human behavior. However, human activity as here depicted turns out to be a complexity that will not be very easy to deal with. The actor constantly has to make so many decisions. It is not surprising, then, that human activity during cultural history has tended to 'automation' of the routine parts of its register. Close inspection of human activity, sure enough, shows that many

---

[2] This is exactly the reason why a theory (as a general idea of activity) constitutes a 'meaning regime' for individual actions in a real practice (as described in the opening section of this chapter).

decisions and processes are not performed consciously. These processes seem to run off autonomously as mechanisms, mainly determined by the starting conditions and the contextual features. These automatized processes (operations) have the character of *events,* because they proceed without apparent cognitive effort, as if mechanically, mainly controlled by situative features. These mental events turn out to be indispensable elements of all complex psychological functioning.

It is impossible to get a valid description of human psychological functioning on the basis of the concept of action alone. Instead we need an *action–event theory* of human psychological functioning (see van Oers, 1987). The psychological difference between actions and events should not be overlooked. Both are related to human intentions, but the kind of this relationship is different in both cases. Actions are intrinsically related to intentions: In the case of actions, some goal is formed and the action is identical with trying to reach this goal and, consequently, with *trying to realize* the intention. This 'tentativity' is essential in the concept of action. In the case of operations, on the other hand, the main intended goal lies outside the operation's range of possible results. The operation is only instrumental; it does not require an explicit moment of goal formation, but it runs off automatically, as if triggered by some cue in the context of the action. The operation is a straightforward process without any tentativity. It occurs or doesn't occur, and when it does, it proceeds in an automatic and uniform way. At best the operation is monitored and—if necessary—stopped or adjusted. We often even don't have any experience of its process (as in perception or association). The relation of operations and intention is therefore extrinsic. This makes operations psychologically different from actions.

Psychological events can be clearly demonstrated at the level of perceptual activity. Usually we see things without even realizing that we are performing perceptual operations. We only become aware of our perceptual activity when we have to identify an unknown object, following explicit identification rules. After a while, however, it can be observed that this conscious perceptual identificatory action also has turned into an operation. It now has become a mental event. Psychological events obviously bring along many benefits for human activity, because they reduce the efforts of cognitive functioning. As a result, a person can spend his or her efforts for the sake of problem solving, creation of ideas, evaluation, etc.

Some of the psychological events seem to be built on man's constitution (like reflexes), but other events can be built up by learning during life (see section below). This possibility of "event formation" explains why machine models of human cognition may be successful to a certain extent in the prediction of cognitive functioning. Some parts of human cognition have become machinelike indeed. In essence this fact is also the basis for the existence and the success of the computer. Psychological events evidently can be simulated in physical events, and human operations can be exteriorized into the physical configurations of hardware and software. This very fact might be considered a definitive argument for the event nature of some parts of cognitive functioning. However, as my previous argument tried to show, events are only a part of the psychological world. No machine model of the human mind can account for all the facts of human psychological functioning.

Many examples of the abovementioned culturally determined mental events can be given, not only in the domain of perceptual activity, but also in relation to memory, speech activity, and thinking (see, for example, Podolskij, 1987). I will refrain from doing so. Instead I will turn now to the phenomenon of learning from the perspective of action–event theory.

Learning: Microgenesis and Learning Activity

Learning can now be defined as a process of qualitative development of activity. In general we can distinguish two types of learning within the context of a particular activity (see also van Oers, 1990, pp. 60–61):

1. *Improvement of individual actions* (microgenesis):
   In this case, the proficiency in the execution of an action is raised as a result of changes in the action. Actions may become mastered on a mental level, automatized, or abbreviated. The process of abbreviation has been shown to be an important qualitative improvement of actions (see Gal'perin, 1969; Haenen, 1995; Van Parreren, 1978). In this case the action can be executed in a fast and automatic way. It has become an operation that can be triggered by some short instruction or sign. Therefore we don't have to count five times six when we see 5×6. Instead we can't help seeing '30' in it. To give another example: We don't read separate letters, but we immediately see whole words or even sentences. As Sabel'nikov (1982) and Podol'skij (1987) have shown experimentally, all kind of actions can be improved by instruction into such an automatized form. It turned out that *anticipation* of future decisions to be made in the execution of an action program is a favorable condition in the microgenesis of actions into operations. Automatization of, for instance, 5×6 is favored when the pupil learns to see this as $5 + 5 + 5 + 5 + 5 + 5$, and when he can group this series as $(5 + 5) + (5 + 5) + (5 + 5)$. Learning to anticipate the result of $(5 + 5)$, i.e., 10, in the learning process turns out to be a strong favorable condition for the final development of the multiplication action into an operation. These are examples of the aforementioned culturally determined psychological events. It goes without saying that these events are most important for human cultural activity. Representational processes creating mental objects by converting epistemic procedures into immediate interpretations of situations are also often eventlike. Such interpretations, endowing our mental processes with a substantial mental reality (aptly named *ontic dumping* by Feldman, 1987) are generally the starting points of problem solving processes.

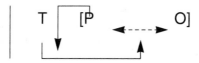

Figure 7.1.   Basic structure of school learning. (T = teacher; P = pupil; O = object)

Clearly, the qualitative improvement by instruction of all kinds of actions (microgenesis) into eventlike operations in the context of cultural activities is an important issue.

2. *Deliberate extension of an activity:*

In this case the repertoire of available actions related to an activity is extended by the deliberate addition of new actions. The pupil now learns new ways of performing an activity. We use to speak of productive learning activity when this learning takes the form of conscious and systematic production of new action possibilities by reflection on the activity, its means, methods, and goals (see Davydov, 1988, 1990; Lompscher, 1985). I will dwell on it a little longer in a later section.

Both kinds of learning basically are attempts of learning how to handle (mental) objects. In both kinds of learning the interaction between cultural meaning and personal meaning (regarding the handling of an object) is an important issue. In both of them the interaction between teacher and pupils is essential. Both kinds of learning embody the same basic structure for school learning processes.

We can see in Figure 7.1 that learning is related to dealing with (material of mental) objects in interaction with another person (mainly a teacher, or a parent) who tries to regulate the actions (i.e., the way of dealing with the object) of the pupil. It shows that teaching and learning are intrinsically related. The teaching–learning process is a transactional process, in which the pupil is not only an object of teaching, but also a subject answering, correcting, and sometimes even resisting the attempts of the teacher to control the activity. Although actual school practices often reduce the realization of this basic structure (for example, by restricting the pupil's responses to the teacher's instructions), it is plausible to insist on the fundamental meaning of this structure for the school learning process from an activity-psychological point of view. This structure is to be taken as the key scheme of school learning. As such, it is the theoretical basis of the interpretation of the dynamics of the school learning process.

DEVELOPMENTAL TEACHING

The lines of reasoning in the sections above must be put together to find an appropriate design for the school learning process that fits our assumptions. As suggested before, following Vygotsky, I want to emphasize the developmental relevance of schooling. In fact, good instruction must contribute to the personal development of pupils. Teachers who do take responsibility for the quality and pace of pupils' development are involved in what we may call *developmental teaching*.

What, then, are the characteristic features of educational institutions in which developmental teaching in principle will be possible? Considering what has been said in the foregoing sections, we can identify the following as basic conditions for the organization of developmental teaching:

Setting High Quality Aims

Schools in our society aim at developing pupils into independent cultural agents within cultural activities, and towards morally autonomous persons. This implies the following general qualities to be aimed at in schools (compare Wardekker, 1990):

- *emancipation:* pupils should learn to take a share in cultural activities as critical and independent agents in a social community;
- *development of theoretical thinking:* pupils should learn to reflect on the relation between objects and their representation in models, as well as learn to deal with objects on the basis of available theoretical models;
- *mastery of modern scientific insights* as results of theoretical thinking; this amounts to saying that pupils should learn to use—in an emancipated way— scientific concepts in daily life and in problem solving, as well as the scientific method of learning as a product of history (see Davydov, 1988, 1990; Engeström & Hedegaard, 1985).

Teaching in the Zone of Proximal Development

Developmental teaching should try to foster development, as Vygotsky (1982) argued, by starting instruction within the zone of proximal development. This highly significant but still puzzling concept needs to be elaborated carefully. Vygotsky relates the zone of proximal development to *imitation* (see Vygotsky, 1982, p. 250). He declares that learning by imitation is the real content of the zone of proximal development. Imitation is to be interpreted here in a broad sense, and in his essay *'Problema Vozrasta'* (The problem of age) he clarifies the idea of imitation by adding that it does not refer to simply copying the behaviors of others (Vygotsky, 1984, p. 263).[3] Imitation, he argues, refers to the process of accomplishing an *activity* in cooperation with another person (*sovmestnaja*

---

[3] According to Valsiner (1988), Vygotsky's concept of imitation is largely congruent with Baldwin's notion of *persistent imitation*. For Baldwin (1902) the child is not merely copying the adult's actions: the child's activity generally transcends the characteristics of the model that is imitated.

dejatel'nost'). By being inserted in a sociocultural activity, the child sure enough imitates an activity that already existed and that is exhibited by other cultured people. But obviously the child cannot accomplish this activity on its own. Some parts of this activity must be taken care of by others (parents, teachers, older children) until later on, when the child has interiorized these functions. Then he or she can do on his or her own what he or she previously only could do with help (see also Cole & Engeström, 1993; Lave & Wenger, 1991).

In this interpretation, the zone of proximal development is related to the level of sociocultural *activities*. Basically, it is an indication of the sociocultural activities in which the child *wants* to be involved and in which he or she *can* take a meaningful part. Evidently the specific actions within this activity are not (necessarily) rigidly programmed, although teachers and parents will often try to promote certain actions rather than others. The child in principle obtains a certain degree of freedom to choose the actions that seem meaningful to him or her and that turn out (by negotiation on the meaning of the actions) to be acceptable for the other participants in the activity at hand. As an example, look at the way children learn to play games or other cultural activities. Children do not learn to play football by isolated preliminary training on techniques or studying the rules. They learn the game most of the time by participating in the game with older children. At first they only run across the field, accidentally hitting the ball. After a while they will learn step by step the rules, the techniques, strategies, etc., by being told by other children. Analogously children learn shopping: at first by accompanying their parents or older siblings and being allowed to push the trolley or to take the shop goods from the shelf. To mention another example, picture how children learn to read. At first they are involved in a social activity of making sense out of a story read to them by a parent or teacher. At first the parent/teacher thus fulfills the function of deciphering the written words—a function that the children themselves evidently cannot perform. The children participate in that activity by remembering the names, building the plot for themselves etc. A nice example of this process is also given by Ramirez et al. (this volume). Depending on both the reader's cognitive reference system and the text to be read, the teacher might have to assist students differently, considering the functions the students already can and cannot yet accomplish for themselves.

These examples demonstrate how children learn to accomplish an activity by being inserted in a social practice. Social practice constitutes a scaffold (Bruner, 1986) by which children can learn to master cultural activities. These examples show how learning within the zone of proximal development occurs. As a rule, this approach can be generalized to all kinds of sociocultural practice (see also Rogoff, 1990; Walkerdine, 1988).

The zone of proximal development, then, is the result of the shared activity of both the child and the adult (Wertsch, 1985, p. 67–76). It should be noticed that this interpretation fits perfectly well in the key figure of learning activity I sketched in Figure 7.1. This interpretation is clearly at variance with many Western interpretations of the zone of proximal development in which an individualistic view is advocated, relating this concept to the concept of action (instead of activity). See, as an example of this view, Brown and Ferrara (1985). As alluded to elsewhere, Valsiner (1987) also seems to have fallen into this pitfall (Van Oers, 1988).

According to my view teaching in the zone of proximal development implies that pupils be inserted in sociocultural practices in which they can learn the desired objectives. Above all the pupils must be involved in the sociocultural processes of making sense within a learning class-community in which the cultural impact is warranted by the teacher. We agree with Bruner (1986) that, if education is to prepare the child for the life as lived, the teacher and the learner must engage in a negotiation of shared meaning. In a like manner Edwards and Mercer (1989) conclude, in their study of the development of common knowledge in the classroom:

> It appears to be a major issue for research and theorizing about Vygotsky's 'zone of proximal development' that there occurs within pedagogic activities a tension between the demands of, on the one hand, inducting children into an established, ready-made culture and, on the other hand, developing creative and autonomous participants in a culture which is not ready made but continually in the making. (pp. 163–164)

A further elaboration of this idea for the context of schooling will be given in the next section.

Designing a Developmental Curriculum

Aims refer to the desired end state, while the zone of proximal development refers to the actual educative interactions between teacher and learner. The question now is how such sessions ought to be sequenced in time in order to pave the road to the aims. Curriculum theory traditionally tends to advocate the view of a scientifically founded series of learning contents, in which the learner (and the teacher, too) must follow the route that has been set out as optimal for them. The curriculum, then, is a canalizing device in which the pupil has little or no authority. He or she usually has to consume the learning contents that are said to be selected for his or her good, and he or she has to follow the sequence of lessons as prescribed, regardless of his or her interests at that moment. The curriculum looks like an assembly line adding new elements to passing pupils.

A developmental curriculum, on the contrary, doesn't take the curriculum as a fixed route but as a common concern for both teacher and pupils to elaborate the developmental course of the pupils. Pupils are stimulated, not only to learn the selected cultural elements, but also to *learn to select cultural elements* in interaction with other participants of their culture. A developmental curriculum refers to two different, but strongly related construction principles:

1. The curriculum should be conceived of as an educational endeavor that is aimed at transforming an activity into a higher developmental state. As such the curriculum document should contain the following issues specifying the essential aspects of the school learning process:
    a. a *description of the activity* concerned, indicating the functions to be performed in order to accomplish a genuine imitation of that activity within the class community. We notice again that it is the teacher's responsibility to guarantee the nature of the activity by taking care of the functions that the pupils still c̄annot perform by themselves. In general this also implies what Cole and Engeström (1993, p. 23) have called "bringing the endpoint 'forward' to the beginning" in order to get a realistic reconstruction of the cultural activity involved.
    b. a *developmental plan* that guides the genesis of the activity concerned in the individual pupils. With the help of this plan the teacher must be able to decide for a given group of pupils which new actions are to be promoted and how, and which actions are to be transformed into operations.
    Taking these two facets together we can construe the following scheme of the developmental process of the curriculum-in-statu-nascendi (see Figure 7.2).
2. The curriculum aims at developing pupils toward agents capable of participating independently in a sociocultural activity. However, taking the curriculum as a learning route for the pupils does not mean that only the pupil should be allowed to choose learning contents (as was frequently advocated in child centered pedagogy). The teacher retains his or her own educational responsibilities, but he or she should take the pupils seriously as participating subjects in the learning process. It is the teacher's responsibility to pose the cultural constraints by bringing a part of the cultural heritage (as school subjects) into negotiation with his or her pupils. The advance-

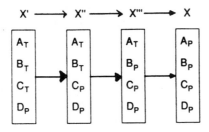

Figure 7.2. **Development of an activity (T = function/task executed by teacher, P = function/task executed by pupil.**

ment of the curriculum, then, is planned within the classroom analogously to a scientific research program: every step must be related to the body of common knowledge already shared by the class community (including both pupils and the teacher). In this imitation of the scientific learning activity every new step is publicly defended and legitimized as a contribution to the body of shared knowledge. It is assumed that pupils will gradually become independent agents in this cultural activity of learning by being involved in this process of negotiation of meaning, reflection on concurrent problem solutions, and valuation of possible questions and answers. It is important, however, to keep in mind that the pupils in the beginning cannot accomplish all the functions required in this process. As in every zone of proximal development, the teacher must take care of many essential functions in this process, such as planning systematically, finding additional information, testing critically, reflecting, and concluding (see Ramirez et al., this volume). Through teacher-supported interiorization, however, pupils gradually learn to plan and regulate their learning activity, and—as a consequence—their own curriculum (although it might take years to acquire this expert quality).

Some beginning research on this issue has been done by Thyssen (1985). He explored the possibilities of a similar curriculum concept with pupils from the lower grades of elementary school in the domain of mother-tongue teaching. He succeeded in engaging the pupils in this process of common curriculum planning. Admittedly, there is still a lot of conceptual and empirical work to be done concerning this aspect of developmental teaching.

THE DEVELOPMENT OF LEARNING ACTIVITY IN SCHOOL

Bringing together the different lines of reasoning suggests a picture of the school learning process of which learning activity constitutes the core. High-quality aims, simulation of the culture's most developed way of learning in the classroom, and adoption of a developmental stance, all of them taken together, converge into the issue of development of learning activity in pupils.

Learning as Discursive Activity

The concept of learning activity needs to be elaborated a little further. According to the above-described idea of learning activity, the genuine aim of this learning is that the pupils become constructors of knowledge. In a learning activity they must try to find out what legitimately can be said in relation to some object of knowing, considering the available (historical) norms and evidence. They must do this by experimentation and by debate. The result of this learning should be a better *conception* of the activity to be accomplished. To put it another way: personally meaningful concept formation is the ultimate goal of all learning activity. This goal determines to a great extent how the learning activity is to be established in the classroom.

First of all, this leads to the question of the nature of concepts. Without reviewing the abundant literature on concept formation, I will sum up the essential features of the kind of high-quality concepts that must be developed by instruction in schools. In this respect I will follow Vygotsky and Davydov to some extent in their argument for the development of scientific concepts in pupils (see Davydov, 1972, 1988, 1990; Vygotsky, 1982). In school pupils must be assisted to appropriate the intellectual instruments that have been built during cultural history as the best available ways of handling and interpreting objects.

As Vygotsky has stressed, this is made possible by *sign formation:* acquiring the meaning of signs implies that one learns the mental or practical actions that are embodied by the sign concerned. By systematizing and generalizing these actions, the related repertoire of meaning is transformed into a concept. As Davydov and his colleagues have shown convincingly, the use of models (as structuring signs) is indispensable in this process (see Davydov, 1990; Engeström & Hedegaard, 1985). The development or improvement of models (as theoretical representations of objects) in fact is the principal intended outcome of learning activity. Quite rightly, Davydov puts strong emphasis on reflectivity in this learning process. Reflection on the activity, and on the actions (including speech acts, such as propositions) that are allowed in the context given, is an essential element in this model forming process.

In my opinion, however, Davydov lays too much emphasis on the acceptability of the end product for the scientific community as a criterion in the valuation of the pupils' learning activity. The formation of scientific concepts for Davydov, then, amounts to the acquisition of the scientific models. In his view the scientific model appears to be the model to be learned. This model (and the cultural meaning conveyed by it) functions as a *goal* in the learning activity. As a consequence, pupils in a Davydovian curriculum seriously run the risk of being overruled by science and the scientific language. They successfully can learn to speak the scientific language formally, but they are not systematically put in the position of attaching personal meaning to it and to the choices that have been made during the learning process.

Contrary to Davydov, I conceive of the scientific model (to be introduced by the teacher) as a cultural model to be used as a starting point for the pupils' active construction of understanding. As such, the teacher's model is primarily only a *means* (not necessarily an end) in the learning activity. In my definition of learning activity it is *the dynamic process of meaning production* that defines the scientific character of that activity and its results. The core of learning activity, then, is *the sociosemiotic process of making meaning* with the help of historically developed methods and insights.

As an example I can give a short description of a cooperative teaching–learning process that we have observed in one of our own research projects (reported by Liem, 1985). In a lesson series (eight lessons of 80 minutes each) on the subject of 'shelter' in the life of animals and men, the discussions in the classroom at a certain moment focused on the topic of heat and insulation. In the classroom discussion on the phenomenon of heat insulation the teacher introduced the notion of *heat transportation*. The pupils then were invited to put forward their views on how heat could be transported, or to give examples of heat transportation. This conversation resulted in examples (given by the pupils) such as:

- "Warm water flows from one place to another in the bathtub."
- "A spoon in a hot cup of tea becomes hot after a while."
- "A room can be warmed up by a radiator at the wall, but it'll take some time."

By analyzing and comparing such assertions the teacher and the pupils together drew up a classification system of kinds of heat transportation (flow, radiation, conduction). This discussion was strongly guided by the teacher, but he never merely transmitted categories or concepts onto the pupils. The resulting classification system was a cooperative product of pupils and the teacher together. Besides discussions on heat transportation the teacher also suggested new methods of gaining further understanding in insulation by:

1. experimentation
2. model making.

The pupils experimented, for instance, with glasses of hot water, observing and registrating the rate of cooling down under different insulation conditions (glass insulated with a piece of cotton, with absorbent cotton, or with tin foil). During this process of discussion and experimentation the teacher and his pupils gradually built up a scheme of heat insulation. One of them was the following: the scheme given is a specimen of intermediate complexity; more complex schemes were also built up (see Figure 7.3).

This classroom illustration is meant to emphasize that learning activity (including concept formation) is in essence a *discursive activity,* in which the participants try to figure out what legitimately might be said about a particular object in the light of available evidence, and considering logical consistency. As such, learning activity can also be conceived of as a social practice of *text making.* As all learners initially probably will have their own personal 'text' (story) concerning the subject at hand, different texts come together and are compared and related in the learning activity. This *intertextuality* makes the learning activity essentially into a rhetorical endeavor (Carpay & Van Oers, in press). In this

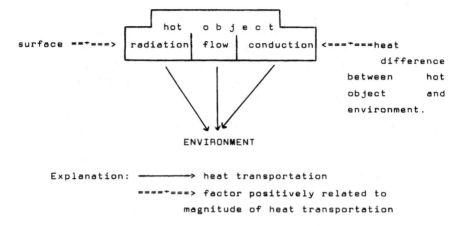

Figure 7.3. Heat insulation scheme.

we agree with Bruner (1986) and with Edwards and Mercer (1989), who believe that "all education is essentially about the development of some shared understanding" (p. 1). In their interesting study Edwards and Mercer (1989) showed that building understanding is a social process of joint activity in which propositions about the world are exchanged and negotiated. Presenting, receiving, understanding, distorting, misunderstanding, generalizing, sometimes even pretending knowledge are real elements in this negotiation process of making meaningful knowledge. This is the genuine embodiment of the language game between teacher and pupils, in which they attempt to regulate the others' way of talking and thinking about a problem and its solution. Characteristically, the nature of this conversation tends to comply with strict conversational rules (e.g., requiring relevance and non-ambiguity from the participants) that make this negotiation of meaning different from everyday conversation (see, for example, Forman, 1992).

Many studies can be cited to support the claim of the fruitfulness of this approach to school learning. In a large-scale Dutch curriculum development project (called *Rekenwerk*) for the domain of mathematics for elementary school, pupils learn to solve mathematical problems in the context of meaningful problem situations. This problem solving is, furthermore, systematically combined with discussion of possible problem solutions. This curriculum attempts to develop mathematics as a discursive activity of pupils. It turns out (Nelissen, 1987, 1988) that these pupils in the end learn to perform arithmetical operations with the same proficiency as pupils from a more traditional drill-and-practice curriculum. Moreover, the pupils from this new curriculum show more insight and ability in solving unusual mathematical problems, and they show more reflection in their problem-solving actions.

In several small studies we have explored details of this discursive learning process in school situations. In one study one of our students investigated the development of a concept of child labor in 11–12-year-old pupils (Fijma, 1987). As a teacher he allowed pupils to work cooperatively (groups consisting of three or four members) on some problems relating to child labor and supported the groups in the task of text formation. He supported the actions of writing the results of their discussions down in a text, generalizing, and systematizing their outcomes (by relating child labor to economic, geographic, and historical factors). A control group followed the same course on child labor. These pupils worked with the same enthusiasm and interest on the project, but they didn't receive instructions for text formation and they had less support in problem solving, systematization, generalization of results. After a project of five lessons the teacher asked all pupils to write individually their own text on child labor. The results show that the concept of child labor in the experimental group is of higher quality (more generalized, and more systematic assertions on the subject) than in the control group. The control group, for example, tended to restrict their assertions on child labor to the example given in the lesson (child labour in the 19th century in one part of Holland); the experimental group tended to generalize their assertions, for example, by stating that child labor was still going on somewhere on the world, or maybe even in Holland.

Starting from the assumption that the teacher must perform or support those functions in the learning activity that the pupils don't yet master, Van Velzen (1990) showed that the teacher might have to act differently in different groups (considering the background of the group). Studying the development of the concept of homeostasis by discursive learning activity in two small groups of 15-year-old high school students (in which the investigator participated as a teacher/researcher/group member), it turned out that in one group she had to function as a tester of possible solutions to a problem of homeostasis. The pupils could handle the problem without much help. In the other group, however, she had to invest considerably in the clarification and translation of the problem, too. It is important to notice that both groups reached an acceptable result, but they needed different kinds of support by the teacher (Van Velzen, 1990).

Soviet studies regarding the realization of learning activity in elementary school practice showed similar results. Ul'enkova (1989) showed that it is possible to insert pupils (about 6 years old) meaningfully into a learning activity within a social context. But if the teacher doesn't succeed in supporting these pupils properly in those functions of learning activity that they don't yet master, then it is likely that he or she will obtain disappointing results. Ul'enkova's research showed, for example, that most of the pupils were interested in the particular learning activity; they even could describe the general goal of that activity. Nevertheless, at the intermediate level of functioning, pupils showed difficulties in executing the learning activity independently; in general they could not verbalize the rules of their actions, and they showed a low level of self-control.

I now must take my argument concerning the dynamics of school learning one little step further. In most of the research (including our own) relating to discursive learning activity, attention is mainly given to the negotiation on solutions to shared problems. However, as the idea of developmental teaching requires, the negotiation should not exclusively be directed to *solutions* of shared problems, but to *the problems as well*. Pupils must also learn to decide what problems/questions adhere to their acquired knowledge, which problems/questions appear to be fruitful as to yield better insight, how these problems/questions should be defined and tackled reasonably. The development of an attitude towards learning as an unending quest is essential in developmental education. This very quality is the basis for making curriculum development a part of the pupils' own responsibility (see also Roegholt, 1993).

What qualities must be fostered in pupils at what developmental moment so as to provide them with a steadily growing independence in taking a meaningful role in discursive learning activity and curriculum development?

The Development of Discursive Learning Activity

In another study of one of our students (Van Rekum, 1986) it was found that cooperative learning groups (12-year-olds) performing seemingly the same learning activity, still differed in the quality of their learning results. Qualitative analysis of the respective activities revealed that the basis of the engagement of the pupils was different. Some pupils were activated by a social motive (reporting: "it is nice to work with your friends in a group"), other pupils demonstrated a cognitive kind of motivation (reporting: "by cooperation I can learn more"). The cognitively motivated pupils made the learning content more actively into an object of study, while pupils with a social motivation only did what was minimally required by the task, for the rest being engaged in social activities. Some pupils seem to have developed a cognitive motive, necessary for the participation in discursive learning activity, while others did not. As a group, these pupils must be supported more by the teacher with this respect to cognitive interest. It seems reasonable to believe that one of the developmental outcomes of early learning must be the development of a cognitive learning motive. Research studies suggest that the mastery of methods of learning might contribute to the development of this cognitive motivation (Markova, 1986). In addition, it is suggested that play activity of nursery school children is the appropriate context for the development of this learning motive. By communicating with young children on problems during play, and by giving them opportunities for experimentation, the development of the learning motive can be stimulated (see among others Hakkarainen, 1985).

Another essential element for the meaningful participation in discursive learning activity is the ability to make models (Davydov) and to figure out the meaning of these models in the context of problem solving, experimentation, and discourse. Several studies of Soviet psychologists proved that the development of this semiotic activity can already be started in nursery school by supporting young children in the production of schemes that might contribute to their play activities (see Venger, 1986; Podd'jakov & Michailenko, 1987; Salmina, 1988), as well as supporting them to develop an interest in another person's plan of action (Lisina & Kapčel'ja, 1987). It appeared to be possible and favorable to get young children involved in social activities of making sense of schematic representations of all kinds, and let them reflect on the relation between an object and its representation. We found similar results in our own investigations with young children (Van Oers, 1994). According to the results of Soviet studies with 4–7-year-old children the development of the semiotic function (making meaning and reflecting on it) can be stimulated within the context of child play, without affecting negatively the character of play. Some proficiency in *semiotic functioning* turned out to be a highly favorable developmental condition for the successful participation in discursive learning activity (Podd'jakov & Michailenko, 1987).

The studies mentioned here concerning nursery school strongly suggest that the roots of discursive learning activity lie in the play activities of the young child (see also Elbers, 1988). Play is the context in which the pursuit of searching for meaning and negotiation of meanings can be started. As being intrinsically meaningful to the child, play is also the context in which the child can experiment with the regulation of social practices and with role taking and role change (El'konin, 1978; Walkerdine, 1988). Semiotic activity, as the prototype of discursive learning, can already be realized in nursery school. Taken up adequately we can use this *learning in play* (learning of semiotic functioning, development of cognitive interest, learning of social positioning) to foster the development of *learning as play,* that is to say, the playing of language games, as employed in the context of discursive learning activity. The decision of which particular actions should be developed microgenetically into mental events should be made within this context of learning (Van Oers, 1995).

CONCLUSION

The dynamics of school learning depend on an interplay between different meaning regimes: the aims of education, and a psychological theory of learning and development. The basic aim of education is to make pupils independent cultural agents and morally autonomous persons.

The psychological concept of discursive learning activity is proposed here as the basic educational idea that brings together the normative and psychological meaning regimes. Within the context of schooling, learning activity should foster the development of insightful actions and proficient (eventlike) operations, but only so if this can be accomplished in a personally meaningful and critical way. It is argued here that discursive learning activity based on the negotiation of meanings can manage the theoretical (domain specific) and normative aspect of school learning within the class-community of pupils and teacher. On the basis of recent research outcomes, it is reasonable to assume that purposeful promotion and improvement of semiotic activity in early education will be a favorable condition for the formation of discursive learning activity.

This concept of discursive learning activity establishes a heuristic means for the identification of developmental requirements, for the strategy of cooperative selection of curriculum content in the classroom, and for the determination of meaningful microgenetic learning. The dynamics of school learning ultimately depend on the elaboration of this concept at a theoretical and practical level in the minds of the participants in the learning process.[4]

REFERENCES

Baldwin, J.M. (1902). *Social and ethical interpretations in mental development.* New York: Macmillan.

Brown, A.L., & Ferrara, R.A. (1985). Diagnosing zones of proximal development. In: J.V. Wertsch (Ed.), *Culture, communication, and cognition.* (pp. 273–306). Cambridge, UK: Cambridge University Press.

Bruner, J.S. (1967). *Towards a theory of instruction.* Cambridge, MA.: Harvard University Press.

Bruner, J. (1986). *Actual minds. possible worlds.* Cambridge, MA: Harvard University Press.

Carpay, J.A.M., & Oers, B. van. (1990). Onderwijspsychologie [Educational Psychology]. In P.J. van Strien & J.F.H. van Rappard (Red.), *Grondvragen van de psychologie* (pp. 196–208). Assen: van Gorcum.

Carpay, J.A.M., & Oers, B. van. (in press). Didactic models and the problem of intertextuality and polyphony. In Y. Engeström, R. Mietinen, & R-R. Punamäki (Eds.), *Research on activity theory.* Cambridge: Cambridge University Press.

Cole, M., & Engeström, Y. (1993). A cultural–historical approach to distributed cognition. In G. Salomon (Ed.), *Distributed cognition. Psychological and educational considerations* (pp. 1–46). Cambridge: Cambridge University Press.

Davidson, D. (1982). *Essays on actions and events.* Oxford: Clarendon.

Davydov, V.V. (1972). *Vidy obobščenija v obučenie. Logikopsichologičeskie problemy postroenija učebnich predmetov* [Kinds of generalization in school. Logical-psychological problems of the construction of subject matter]. Moscow: Pedagogika.

Davydov, V.V. (1983). Istoričeskie predposylki učebnoj deja-tel'nosti [Historical constraints of learning activity]. In V.V. Davydov (Ed.), *Razvitie psichiki škol'nikov v processe učebnoj dejatel'nosti* (pp. 5–22). Moscow: A.P.N.

---

[4] I thank my colleagues Jacques Carpay, Wim Wardekker, and Sietske Roegholt for their support and critical advice in the writing of this article.

Davydov, V.V. (1986). *Problemy razvivajuščgo obučenija* [Problems of developmental teaching]. Moscow: Pedagogika.

Davydov, V.V. (1988). Problems of developmental teaching. *Soviet Education, XXX,* 8,9,10. (Translation of Davydov, 1986).

Davydov, V.V. (1990). *Psichičeskoe razvitie mladšich škol'nikov* [Psychological development of elementary school pupils]. Moscow: Pedagogika.

Dillon, R.F., & Sternberg, R.J. (Eds.). (1986). *Cognition and instruction.* Orlando/San Diego/New York: Academic Press.

Elbers, E. (1988). *Social context and the child's construction of knowledge.* Unpublished dissertation, University of Utrecht.

Edwards, D., & Mercer, N. (1989). *Common knowledge. The development of understanding in the classroom.* London/New York: Routledge.

El'konin, D.B. (1978). *Psichologija igra* [The psychology of play]. Moscow: Pedagogika.

Engeström, Y., & Hedegaard, M. (1985). Teaching theoretical thinking in elementary school: The use of models in history/biology. In E. Bol, J.P.P. Haenen, & M.A. Wolters (Eds.), *Education for cognitive development. Proceedings of the Third International Symposium on Activity Theory* (pp. 170–193). Den Haag: SVO.

Feldman, C. (1987). Thought from language: the linguistic construction of cognitive representations. In J. Bruner & H. Haste (Eds.), *Making Sense. The child's construction of the world* (pp. 131–147). London/New York: Methuen.

Fichtner, B. (1985). Learning and learning activity. In E. Bol, J.P.P. Haenen, & M.A. Wolters (Eds.), *Education for cognitive development. Proceedings of the Third International Symposium on Activity Theory* (pp. 47–63). Den Haag: SVO.

Fijma, N.C. (1987). *Internal report* (Concept Formation and social science). Amsterdam: Free University/ Dept. of Education and Didactics.

Forman, E.A. (1992). Discourse, intersubjectivity and the development of peer collaboration: A Vygotskian approach. In L.T. Winegar & J. Valsinger (Eds.), *Children's development within social contexts: Metatheoretical, theoretical and methodological issues* (Vol. 1, pp. 143–159). Hillsdale, NJ: Erlbaum.

Forman, E.A., Minick, N., & Stone, C.A. (Eds.). (1993). *Contexts for learning: Sociocultural dynamics in children's development.* New York: Oxford University Press.

Gal'perin, P.Ja. (1969). Stages in the development of mental acts. In M. Cole & I. Maltzman (Eds.), *A handbook of contemporary Soviet psychology* (pp. 249–273). New York: Basic Books.

Haenen, J. (1995). *Piotr Gal'perin: A lifetime of searching for the context of psychology.* Commack: Nova.

Hakkarainen, P. (1985). Learning motivation and instructional intervention. In E. Bol, J.P.P. Haenen, & M.A. Wolters (Eds.), *Education for cognitive development Proceedings of the Third International Symposium on Activity Theory* (pp. 136–151). Den Haag: SVO.

Jackson, P.W. (1986). *The practice of teaching.* New York/London: The Teachers College Press, Columbia University.

Lave, J., & Wenger, E. (1991). *Situated learning: Legitimate peripheral participation.* Cambridge: Cambridge University Press.

Leont'ev, A.N. (1975). *Dejatel'nost', livnost', soznanie* [Activity, personality, consciousness]. Moscow: Izd-vo Politiveskoj Literatury.

Liem, D. (1985). *Internal report*. (The relation between cooperative learning activity and reflection). Amsterdam: Free University/ Dept. of Education and Didactics.

Lisina, M.I., & Kapčel'ja, G.I. (1987). *Obščenie so vzroslymi i psichologiceskaja podgotovka detej v skole* [Communication with adults and the psychological preparation of children to school]. Kisinev: Stiinca.

Lompscher, J. (1985). The formation of learning activity—a fundamental condition of cognitive development through instruction. In E. Bol, J. Haenen, & A.M. Wolters (eds.), *Education for cognitive development* (pp. 21–38). Den Haag: SVO.

Markova, A.K. (ed.). (1986). *Formirovanie interessa k učeniju y škol'nikov.* [The formation of learning interest in pupils]. Moscow: Pedagogika.

Nelissen, J.M.C. (1987). *Kinderen leren wiskunde.* Een studie over constructie en reflectie in het basisonderwijs. [Children learn mathematics. A study of construction and reflection in elementary school.] Gorinchem: De Ruiter.

Nelissen, J.M.C. (1988). Reflecteren in systematische samen-spraak [Reflecting in a dialogical context]. *Tijdschrift voor onderwijsresearch, 13,* (5), 245–270.

Oers, B. van. (1987). *Activiteit en begrip. Proeve van een handelingspsychologische didactiek.* [Activity and concept. A trial of action-psychological didactics.] Amsterdam: VU-Publ.

Oers, B. van. (1988). Activity, semiotics and the development of children. *Comenius, 8* (4), 398–406.

Oers, B. van. (1990). The development of mathematical thinking in school: a comparison of the action-psychological and information-processing approaches. In *International Journal of Educational Research, 14* (1), 51–66.

Oers, B. van. (1994). Semiotic activity of young children in play: The construction and use of schematic representations. *European Early Childhood Education Journal,* 2(1), 19–33.

Oers, B. van. (1995). *Teaching opportunities in play.* Paper presented at the Third International Conference on Activity Theory. Moscow, June 26–30.

Parreren, C.F. van. (1954). A viewpoint in theory and experimentation on human learning and thinking. *Acta Psychologica, 10,* 351–380.

Parreren, C.F. van. (1978). A building block model of cognitive learning. In: A.M. Lesgold, J.W. Pellegrino, S.D. Fokkema & R. Glaser (Eds.), *Cognitive psychology and instruction.* New York: Plenum.

Petrovskij, A.V. (1985). *Studies in psychology.* Moscow: Progress.

Podd'jakov, N.N., & Michailenko, N.Ja. (Eds.). (1987). *Problemy doškol'noj igri: psichologo-pedagogičeskij aspekt* [Problems of young children's play: psychological-pedagogical aspects.] Moscow: Pedagogika.

Podolskij, A.I. (1987). *Stanovlenie poznavatel'nogo dejstvija: naučnaja abstrakcija i real'nost'* [The development of cognitive actions: scientific abstraction and reality.] Moskou: Izd-vo Moskovskogo Universiteta.

Reigeluth, Ch.M. (Ed.). (1983). *Instructional-design theories and models: An overview of their current status.* Hillsdale NJ: Erlbaum.

Rekum, C. van. (1986). *Internal report* (The personal sense of cooperative learning). Amsterdam: Free University/ Dept. of Education and Didactics.

Roegholt, S. (1993). Towards a concept of multiperspective education. *Journal of Curriculum Studies, 25*(2), 153–167.

Rogoff, B. (1990). *Apprenticeship in thinking. Cognitive development in social context.* New York/Oxford: Oxford University Press.

Sabel'nikov, V.K. (1982). *Formirovanie bystroj mysli* [The formation of fast thinking]. Alma Ata: Mektep.

Salmina, N.G. (1988). *Znak i simvol v obučenii* [Sign and symbol in education]. Moscow: Izd-vo Moskovskogo Universiteta.

Salomon, G. (Ed.). (1993). *Distributed congition: Psychological and educational considerations.* Cambridge: Cambridge University Press.

Thyssen, S. (1985). Motivation and activity in early school age. In: E. Bol, J.P.P. Haenen, & M.A. Wolters (Eds.), *Education for cognitive development. Proceedings of the Third International Symposium on Activity Theory* (pp. 127–136). Den Haag: SVO.

Ul'enkova, U. (1989). Formirovanie obščej sposobnosti k učeniju u šesti letnich detej [The formation of general learning abilities in six year old children]. *Doškolnoe Vospitanie, 3,* 53–57.

Valsiner, J. (1987). *Culture and the development of children's action. A cultural-historical theory of developmental psychology.* New York: John Wiley.

Valsiner, J. (1988). A constraints-based theory and its interpretations: a reply. *Comenius, 32,* 427–441.

Velzen, C. van. (1990). *Internal Report* (An investigation on discursive learning activity). Amsterdam: Free University/ Dept. of Education and Didactics.

Venger, L.A. (Red.). (1986). *Razvitie poznavatel'nych sposobnostej v processe doskol'nogo vospitanija* [The development of cognitive abilities in nursery.]. Moscow: Pedagogika.

Vygotsky, L.S. (1982). Myvlenie i reč [Thinking and speech]. In *Sobranie Sočinenij. T.2.* [Collected Works, Vol 2]. Moscow: Pedagogika.

Vygotsky, L.S. (1984). Problema vozrasta [The problem of age]. In *Sobranie sočinenij, T.4.* [Collected works, Vol. 4]. Moscow: Pedagogika.

Walkerdine, V. (1988). *The mastery of reason. Cognitive development and the production of rationality.* London/New York: Routledge.

Wardekker, W. (1990, May). *Decontextualization and multiperspectivity in education.* Paper presented at the International Congress on 'activity theory', Lahti (Finland).

Wertsch, J.V. (1985). *Vygotsky and the social formation of mind.* Cambridge, MA: Harvard University Press.

White, J. (1982). *The aims of education restated.* London/New York: Routledge & Kegan Paul.

Yaroshevsky, M. (1989). *Lev Vygotsky.* Moscow: Progress.

CHAPTER 8

Making Literacy: A Dialogical Perspective on Discourse in Adult Education

Juan D. Ramirez Garrido   Jose A. Sanchez Medina
Andrès Santamaria Santigosa

University of Sevilla, Spain

ON LITERACY: AN INTRODUCTION

It is obvious that there does not exist a single point of view about what literacy is. Depending on the notion of the learning process we have, we will understand the process of literacy in one sense or in another one. In this chapter, we are going to assume a notion of learning that is not only referred to the mere acquisition of specific concepts or contents, but also to the internalization of discursive and interactive patterns that are generated in the cultural setting where the learning process is developed.

In this context, to find a definition of literacy that completely satisfies educational experts has become a difficult task. This problem is worse when we try to create a definition that equally gives answers to childhood education, adult education, those responsible in education in countries of different levels of development (First, Second, and Third World countries), researchers centered on individual processes (e.g., psychologists, linguistics), or those who analyze sociocultural processes (sociologists, ethnographers, anthropologists). In past years, studies of literacy have been centered around two perspectives, neither complementary. Some researchers have concentrated on the analysis of psycholinguistic and cognitive processes implicated in literary conduct, paying special attention to acquiring individual skills. Others, meanwhile, have used ethnographic analysis in the study of the conditions that facilitate the development of literacy (Cook-Gumperz, 1986; Heath, 1983, 1989, 1990). A new focus has emerged in recent years which pretends to unify both perspectives, with the object in mind of furnishing a global vision of the changes produced by learn-

229

ing literacy (Snow & Dickinson, 1991). And yet the investigation in the world of adult education has just begun. The high level of illiteracy today is a world-wide concern. Not only does it affect Second and Third World countries, but due to immigration in the last decades even the more industrialized countries are being affected. The importance of this problem does not correspond to the scant number of studies developed in this field, reflected by the fact that a major part of the literature refers to childhood education. Nevertheless, a study that tackles this complex problem should consider the specifications and shy away from the generalizations to all the educative fields. They will have to take into consideration a series of questions that differentiate the learning of literacy in children from the learning of literacy in adults. While the child must adapt to the new educative context with linguistic forms and different manners of expression to what he or she is normally used to using at home and in other activities outside of school, the adult, besides all this, has to confront a world that is, in some cases, completely alien to him or her and, in other cases, contradictory to his or her own world viewpoints. In our judgment, the conflict is greater for the adult, and, therefore, the necessity to investigate that conflict is profound.

In this chapter, we will center our attention on the perspective that defends the idea that literacy implies much more than the mere acquisition of reading-writing skills, but also the acquisition of social and discourse skills that permit an adult to develop activities in diverse contexts. In this manner, we would be in a condition to surpass the usual unidimensional focus of the problem, as other researchers have suggested (Cook-Gumperz, 1986; Goody, 1978, 1986; Snow & Dickinson, 1991).

The Context of our Investigation

The program of learning literacy that is now taking place in Andalusia (Southern Spain) supposes a natural laboratory where it is possible to study the process of learning literacy as well as the changes of the sociocognitive skills related to it. The P.E.A. (Programa de Educación de Adultos de Andalucía—Adult Education Program in Andalusia) is inspired directly on Paolo Freire's pedagogic ideas (Freire, 1970), in that all educative practices try to adapt themselves to the best of their ability to the social and cultural reality of the student, reflecting the problems of the community, and at the same time, giving him or her an active role in the teaching–learning process. The P.E.A. is essentially directed to adults who have not had previous schooling experience, or, if they have had it, it has been brief and discontinuous. A proportionally minor number of students, who for different reasons were not able to graduate and get their primary education diploma, see the need to go back to school to finish. The majority of the students who attend literacy courses are women whose age varies between 30 and 60 years old, putting the average mean at 40 and 45 years old. All the students belong to the working class, with a low income level and a high unemployment rate in the family ambience.

The data we are presenting in this chapter were obtained in two centers ascribed in the P.E.A.. One of them is located in a small town (Valencina), close to a big city (Seville), and has all the socioeconomical and cultural characteristics of a rural population. The other is located in a suburban area of Seville. Although later studies[1] may demonstrate differences between both of them, up to this point we have found a great similarity between the two groups (rural and urban). This may be due to the fact that the majority of the students that attend the urban school center emigrated to the city during the growing economic and industrial period that developed in the sixties.

A PERSPECTIVE OF ANALYSIS

The defining feature of adult literacy is characterized by the confluence of different forms of communication, culture, and views of the world based on the institutionalized setting of the adult center. A methodology centered on the individual skills of the student is limited in the analysis of subjects and an institution where sociocultural factors meet, as mentioned above. A focus that approaches the complexity of the process should not limit itself to analyze solely the interactions of the students with their teacher in the school setting. The relations of the students among themselves, with the teacher, and all of them with the texts refer to a cultural context that goes beyond the immediate scholastic situation, in the *here* and *now,* where these interactions develop.

A Sociocultural Approach

The development of a sociocultural approach is vital in the study of such a complicated fact. This approach was developed in the past by Vygotsky and the Soviet School (Leontiev, 1978, 1982; Luria, 1976; Vygotsky, 1962, 1978). It is now reaching a high level of development in and out of the former Soviet Union by way of different researchers (Cole & Scribner, 1974; Davidov & Zinchenko, 1985; Scribner & Cole, 1981; Valsiner, 1988; Wertsch, 1985a, b, 1991). We must add other authors who come from different fields of social science whose integration in the School is aiding its ample development. The more relevant figure is the philosopher of language and semiologist, M.M. Bakhtin, the author who inspired a large part of this chapter. His influence on the theorists of the sociocultural approach has come by way of James V. Wertsch, who has known how to demonstrate the parallelism between the ideas of Bakhtin and Vygotsky (Wertsch, 1980, 1985c, 1987, 1991). His notions on voices, polyphony, genres, social languages, and heteroglossia represent an ensemble of

---

[1]At this moment we are developing two researches that can provide us data about the possible influence of the environment (rural or urban) on the adult center activities and on the way these activities are performed.

fundamental ideas to develop our focus and adapt it to the realm of study that we are interested in, adult literacy. The dialogic perspective that articulates these ideas broadens its field, and we can study complex situations where different cultures, means of communication, and world viewpoints meet.

In order to observe these notions in all their explicative power, this study is based on a series of interactive episodes during the development of literacy activities in the school centers that we mentioned earlier. We are going to observe the way in which a student confronts a text and the way in which the teacher mediates this relation. We will use episodes that register the interaction between the voices of the student, the author of the text, and the teacher in situations where they can be included in the forms of writing and oral literacy.

Reading and understanding a text is an activity that goes beyond the simple decoding of the signs present in the text. It is a dialogic process where contact is established between two individual consciousness, the author of the text and the reader, where he or she paraphrases the text, answers it, or comments on it. Likewise, he or she evaluates its contents or connects with the text says. Voloshinov consider that understanding is, at all times, of a dialogic nature. In his own words: "Understanding is to utterance as one line of a dialogue is to the next. Understanding strives to match speakers' words with a *counter word*" (Voloshinov, 1986, p. 102).

Understanding on the part of the subject who reads begins when the utterance ends. The process implies the necessary encounter of two words or utterances, which are in the text and in the reader's answer. When we talk about the answer, we do not mean only an audible verbal answer but an utterance that can be generated exclusively through the inner speech of the reader. In conversation as in reading, the subject actively responds to each and every one of the utterances heard or read, maintaining a *responsive attitude* throughout both forms of exchange. This attitude gets him or her to answer each utterance with one of his or her own, be it external or confined in the realm of the private (Bakhtin, 1987; Voloshinov, 1986).

In the act of reading as well as in any other form of dialogue, two speaking personalities, two individual consciousnesses, two voices that reflect their own perspectives, establish contact. Contrary to a conversation, this contact does not have to be explicit. Among the respective points of view that the voices reflect in that dialogue, in which only the author is publicly expressed while the reader does it in the private plane, lie hidden different views of the world (Bakhtin, 1981). The perspectives can be clearly differentiated in the case that concerns us, literacy students and the texts they can read. Any school text (geography, history, natural science, etc.) through the knowledge that it transmits reflects a certain view of the world that the student must learn. Nevertheless, the acquisition of this knowledge is only possible when the student learns to manage the language and the view of the world expressed in. Bakhtin, in some of his papers, defended the existence of different forms of language that are expressed with and in a national language. The history of a speaking community is characterized by being simultaneously submitted to two forces, the centripetal force that heads towards the maximum unification of one language and the centrifugal force that tends to create different *social speech types* (Wertsch, 1987). For Bakhtin, social language is the media in which a determined view of the world is expressed, and it serves a concrete part of the members of that community. Jurists, religious personnel, men of science, each professional or scientific group, etc., tend to develop a type of social language according to the viewpoint of the world they defend and develop (Bakhtin, 1981). From our point of view, school language, more than a specific social language, should be understood as a *language of languages,* that is, a form of social speech types that teaches the student how to use decontextualized means of communication that are the key to penetrating into future genres of speech and social language.

How can the Bakhtinian notions contribute to the analysis of adult literacy? To answer this question we have to remember, primarily, the encounter of diverse voices, languages, and cultures that the adult center produces. The students who come to the center possess their own culture that enters into contact with a different one whose basic means of expression is written language. The center compiles a good demonstration of what Bakhtin denominates *heteroglossia,* the point where diverse voices, genres, and social languages meet (Bakhtin, 1981). How can the student accede to other means of expression and their corresponding viewpoints of the world? The acquisition of the basic mechanisms of literacy alone does not give access to the knowledge of school texts and, inevitably, the presence of a third voice capable of putting scholastic discourse and the voice of the student in contact. When the teacher explains a text difficult for the student to understand, his or her main mission is to create a new text, a paraphrase of the first one, susceptible of being understood by the student. As Bakhtin would say with regard to this subject, the teacher *interanimates* the utterances that the voice of the author and the voice of the student expresses. This interanimation of voices is possible because the teacher's utterances put the two voices in contact with the same utterance. What is the process where the teacher creates that intermediating voice? The process where a voice speaks through another's lets us understand the mediating role that the teacher's utterances carry out. The Bakhtinian concept of *ventriloquization* describes the manner in which the two voices emerge together:

> The word in language is half someone else's. It becomes "one's own" only when the speaker populates it with his own intention, his own accent, when he appropriates the word, adapting it to his own semantic and expressive intention. Prior to this moment of appropriation, the word does not exist in a neutral and impersonal language (it is not, after all, out of a dictionary that the speaker gets his words!), but rather it exists in other people's mouths, in other people's context, serving other people's intentions: it is from there that one must take the word, and make it one's own. (Bakhtin, 1981, pp. 293–294)

The process of ventriloquizing allows us to see the teacher as a two-way bridge through which other voices travel. The teacher's voice is put to the service of other authors and, above all, to the service of scholastic discourse. As we will have the occasion to see, without the teacher's mediating function, the learning of literacy would be just the acquisition of a group of very basic mechanisms of decoding incapable of creating the necessary dialogue between the text and the reader.

READING, DIALOGUE, AND VOICES

How can we observe these dialogic processes in the literacy activities at the adult school center? The center, due to its nature, is characterized by diverse situations where these processes take place.

In order to illustrate the dynamics of these processes, we have chosen two different reading tasks, where the dialogic dimension of reading comprehension is demonstrated. The first is based on the reading of a text taken from a school newspaper. The texts included in this newspaper were written by the students themselves with the teacher's help or with their classmates' help, which makes them especially interesting. Despite the low level in reading and writing skills, the students can write a text expressing what they want to say. Guided by the teacher, they formulated different statements in such a way that they can be written syntactically correctly and without losing the meaning of the text. Throughout this process, other classmates intervene to contribute an idea or thought on the subject the author of the text is trying to describe. In relation to the students' performance in writing skills, the teacher may give a final syntactic form of the text that the student will copy later. In this case, the elaboration of the contents of the text and part of the structure is due to the student as the main author, with the teacher in the role of co-author whose basic mission is the final syntactic articulation of the text. This process of discursive elaboration will not be analyzed here. We hope to develop it in a later study. The complexity and richness of this process demands a detailed study that is not the objective of this chapter. What is important to point out is that this type of text is frequently used as reading material by the classmates and even by those students who will attend the center in further years. In the second reading task, the student must read a passage taken from a school text book. The interest in studying both texts lies in observing the role the different voices (reader, author, and teacher) can play in their reading and understanding. We can also observe in comparing the reading of both texts, the role the different social speech types play in each of the texts written.

The following episode shows the reading of a text from a school newspaper. The student, Pq., a woman in her mid-forties, attends the center in Valencina (rural area). Her reading skills allow her to go slowly even though she has surpassed the reading syllable-by-syllable phase. She reads out loud in the teacher's presence. The teacher periodically interrupts the reading asking Pq. to repeat what she has read.

EPISODE I[2]

Text:

La Seguridad Social Ayer hice tres horas de cola en la Seguridad Social. El médico sin mirarme me dió una receta. Hoy he ido a una clínica privada donde me han atendido muy bien, pero me han cobrado mucho dinero. Sólo van a enriquecerse. La solución sería que la Seguridad Social tuviera más médicos, y que se dieran cuenta que están cobrando de nuestros impuestos.	(National Health Service Yesterday I was in line for three hours at the National Health Clinic. The doctor gave me a prescription without looking at me. Today I went to a private clinic where I was well looked after but they charged me a lot of money. They only want to get rich. The answer would be if the National health clinic had more doctors and that they realized they were being paid with our taxes.)

T. -Teacher
Pq. -Paquita, the student.

1 Pq. La seguridad social (lee el título). Ayer hice tres.. tres ho:ras de ca.. de cola, *tres horas de cola* (repite lo que ha leido) en la seguridad social. El me:dico sin.. sin mirarme di:ó una receta. Hoy he . . ., *no* he..do, *no?,* *espérate!*	(National Health Clinic (she reads the title). Yesterday, I was in.. in li:ne for three ha.. for three hours, *for three* *hours* (repeating what she has read) in the National Health clinic. The doc:tor gave.. ga:ve me a prescription without looking at me. Today I . . . ,*right?* today I want, *right? Wait!*)

---

[2]TRANSCRIPT NOTATION

1. (..) indicates a silent interval.

2. (:) indicates a elongation of the syllable.

3. *Italic* words or sentences (*espérate—wait*) are indicative of a comment or question in relation to the reading.

4. (xxx) represents a word that is whispered or uttered in a low volume of voice and is impossible to transcribe.

5. A letter or a word in brackets indicates a letter or a word omitted by the speaker and included by the transcriber to make the understanding of the text easier.

2 T. ido
(went)

3 Pq. *ah que no la veía* (exclama
refiriéndose a la letra d)
xxx
.ido a una clín:ica privada
donde me ho.. han atendido
bien, pero me han cobrado
mucho dinero.
Claro!, es lo normal
Sólo va a escri.. a en..
enri:quecerse.

(I didn't see it (she
refers to the letter d.)
xxx
(went to a private clin:ic
where I was well looked
after, but they charged me
a lot of money.)
(Sure! That's normal.)
(They only want to go.. to
get ri:ch.)

4 T. Esperate, cuentame
Wait a minute, tell me
about it.)

5 Pq. Que fue al médico de
cabecera y el médico de
cabecera le recetó una
medicina sin mirar, porque
eso lo tenemos aquí en
Valencina. Tú vas al
médico, como el otro día
fuí yo al grano en el ojo y
como me dijeron que no
estaba Don Manuel. Porque
el ojo se está poniendo un
poquillo:. Y digo voy a ir,
pero no fuí, porque (se
ríe) porque sabía que me
iba a mandar una cosa y no
lo iba a ver, ni (a) Don
Manuel ni (a)l otro, digo
pues no voy. Y entonces
cogió el camino y se fue al
médico de cabecera (se
equivoca) de: pago.

La ha llevado un ojo de la
cara, la ha llevado un ojo
de la cara, que es el mío
(se ríe).

(She went to the general
practioner and the general
practioner prescribed some
medicine without looking,
because that's what we have
here in Valencina. You go
to the doctor, just like I
did the other day for a
pimple in my eye and they
told me Don Manuel wasn't
there. Because my eye's
becoming a little:. And I
says I was going to go, but
I didn't, because, (she
laughs) because I knew
they'd give me something
and I wasn't going to see
D. Manuel or the other one,
I says I won't go. And then
she went of and went to the
National health doctor (she
makes a mistake) paying doctor.
It cost her an eye and a
tooth, it cost her an eye
and a tooth, mine (she
laughs).)

6 T. que la mira(d)o bien
(she was well looked after)

7 Pq. si, la ha mirado bien pero:
..xxx (continúa con la
lectura)
(yes, she was well looked
after but: ... xxx (she
continues to read)

8 Pq. la solu:ción sería que la Segu:ridad, no? (pregunta a T) Segu:ridad Social tu:viera más mé:dicos y que se dieran cuenta que están cobrando de nuestros impue:stos.	(The solu:tion would be if Na:tional, right? Na:tional Health Ha:d more doc:tors and that they realized they are being paid by our tax:es.)
9 T. Cuentame.	(Tell me.)
10 Pq. Que el médico de cabecera se debería de dar cuenta que tenían que poner más médicos porque no puede xxx siempre sóla, eso hay que reconocerlo, pero vamos que tambien cobra el igual y nos lo quitan a nosotros de nuestra paga, no?	(The National health General Practioner should realize that they need to have more doctors because they can't always xxx alone, we can see that, but we.., they also get paid the same and they take that from our paycheck, right?

All through this episode we can observe a series of comments, some spontaneous and others provoked by the teacher's question which manifests a *responsive attitude* towards what is read and a strong disposition to evaluate the content of the text. This is manifested in the utterance that Pq. spontaneously emits when the reference is made to the elevated cost of private medical care (3Pq .... *Claro, es normal.—Sure, that's normal.*). The rest of the comments that Pq. introduces through the teacher's repetition (5Pq.) reflect her attitude towards the contents of the reading. This student immediately synthesizes what she has read by introducing comments on the text from her own experience with the medical service where she lives. If we look carefully at 5Pq. we can verify that she completely reproduces what she has read but she adds comments that refer to the little attention the local doctor pays to the patient. A complete understanding of the text is granted even down to the most minute detail. All we need to do is remember how Pq., in the last part, uses the expression "*quitar de la paga—take away from our paycheck*" (10Pq.) to refer to the more sophisticated term "*impuesto—tax*" used by the author of the text (8Pq.). This occurred before when she substituted "*clinica privada—private clinic*" (3Pq.) for the colloquial term "paying doctor" (5Pq.).

All the answers, whether spontaneous or induced by the teacher, are clear reflections of the process of understanding according to the description by Voloshinov (1986): "The understanding of a sign is, after all, an act of reference between the sign apprehended and other, already known signs; in other words understanding is a response to a sign with signs" (p. 11).

The student creates a perfect paraphrase of the text read, introducing commentaries, evaluating the contents, and substituting words and expressions from the text for others that mean the same and that she is more familiar with (e.g., private medicine for paying doctor; tax for take away from our paycheck). What is the reason for this sophisticated elaboration of the meaning of the text? From our point of view, the answer to this question lies in the entire identification of the perspective that both voices reflect. The theme developed by the author expresses an experience shared equally by the reader and by the members of the community that both belong to. As it is easy to infer from Pq.'s answers (repetition, commentaries, and evaluation), the teacher's role as regulator of the reading activity is limited to asking for the repetition of each announcement, with the object of checking if the text has been understood. Her function as mediator between the implicated voices (author and reader) is rare, as both share the same perspective concerning the problem that affects them.

Up until now we have approached the process of understanding from the individual voices implicated in the dialogue in an activity of learning to be literate. The heteroglossia that characterizes the school situation is translated at times into a noticeable difference as far as the social speech types in which the voices are expressed. While the distance broadens between the means of expression of the voices, the mediating voice of the teacher changes substantially, as we will see in the following episode.

The episode we now present is an extract of a passage on geography from a school textbook. The student is a woman in her mid-forties with reading skills similar to those of the student in the previous episode. The teacher also guides this student in her task asking her to read the text outloud.

EPISODE II

En Madrid viven los miembros del gobierno de la nación, el presidente y los ministros.

(Members of government of the nation, the president and the ministers, live in Madrid)

T. -Teacher.
A. -Antonia, the student.

1.T. Vamos a leer. (Let's read.)

2.A. En Madrid viven los miembros del gobierno de la nación. El pre..presidente y los ministros.
(Members of government of the nation live in Madrid. The pre- president and the ministers.)

3.T. ¿Qué pasa en Madrid? (What happens in Madrid?)

4.A. Pues que vive el gobierno, el *principal* que somos el gobierno, ¿no? y los que están *al lado* de él.
(Well, they live the government, the *main body* of our government, right? and the people that are *next to* it.)

5.T. Los que están *al lado* del presidente, ¿cómo se llaman?	(The people *next to* the president, what is their name?)
6.A. Pues se llaman los *concejales,* ¿no?	(They're called *town councilors,* right?)
7.T. ¿Los concejales?, o ministros.	(Town councilors or ministers?)
8.A. Los ministros.	(The ministers.)
9.T. Los concejales son los que están a *la vera* del alcalde.	(The town councilors are the people *side by side* the mayor.)
10.A. Los ministros. Allí se encuentra el congreso de los diputados y el senad:o.	(The ministers.) Representatives and the Sena:te can be found there.)
11.T. Párate un poquito. Hay un punto, párate.	(Wait a minute. There's a period there, wait.)
12.A. En ellos, se reúnen los representates de los pueblos españoles.	(There they assemble, the representatives of the Spanish people.)

The most relevant fact we can observe here has to do with the types of speech as well as the views of the world that come together in the reading. The text represents a typical case of scholastic discourse. As we previously pointed out, this is a type of social language that prepares the students for the further advancement of more sophisticated social languages. The student's voice acts through everyday discourse, manifesting the existing differences between both means of expression. Nevertheless, this is not the only conflict that arises in this episode. The means of expression are refections of different views of the world, or *axiologic systems of beliefs* (Bakhtin, 1981; Wertsch, 1985a, 1991). While the text refers to the political system of a country, the student refers to the type of local political organization she is familiar with. While the text deals with concepts like *government, president, minister,* or *nation,* the student evokes the terminology town councilor. We cannot say that A. does not know the more general system, but her representation of it is construed of the political power she knows best (townhall). In the previous case (see Episode I) comprehension is produced with little intervention from the teacher, given the contact between the voices of the author and the reader. In this episode, the discrepancies between both means of expression and their corresponding views of the world demand a more active role. The teacher, in her mediating role, includes terminology from both means of expression. Let's analyze in detail the utterance 5T.: "*Los que están* al lado del *presidente, ¿cómo se llaman?—The ones* next to *the president, what's their* name?" This utterance is made up of terminology taken from previous turns in the dialogue, including a colloquial expression and terminology that belongs to the text itself. *"Los que están al lado de . . . —The ones next to . . ."* is an expression included by A. (4A.) when trying to paraphrase the text after being asked to do so by the teacher. The term *president* is taken from the reading by the teacher. After being asked the last question, A.'s answer is given using her own view of the political organization she knows best. That is when she uses the term *town councilor.* Due to the discrepancy between the representation of the student and the representation reflected in the text, the teacher tries to connect them through a means of expression that interlaces political terminology with words taken from the local dialect (9T.: *Los concejales son los que están* a la vera[3] *del alcalde.— The town councilors are the people* side by side *with the mayor.*) How can we interpret the teacher's intervention in the light of the Bakhtinian perspective? From our point of view, she is interanimating both the author's voice and the reader's voice and, therefore, the means of expression, the social language of the school text, and the usage of local dialects in everyday discourse. The interanimation of the voices and means of expression lets one establish a clear analogy between both political organizations. (The ministers are to the president, what the town councilors are to the mayor.) The teacher plays with this analogy with the object of facilitating a better understanding on the part of the student.

THE INTERANIMATION OF VOICES AND ORAL LITERACY

The dialogism observed in the reading process equally presides many other literacy activities in the school setting, including those which at first seemed to be essentially monological. A conference or a lecture explained to the whole class forms a part of the literacy activity with as much rights as reading has. A conference has a text that must be transmitted to an audience. Throughout this chapter we can find a form of dialogue that goes beyond the mere taking turns between interlocutors in a conversation. If the contact of voices in a conversation is direct, it is produced through the interlocutors; in a conference we find a speaker who mediates between the text and the diversity of the audience. This would present, according to Bakhtin, a form of dialogue that transcends turn taking. The notion of dialogue extends to phenomena as diverse as the exchange between two individuals linked in a conversation, the relation between the author and his character in the novelistic discourse or the debate between the conflictive positions in the intrapsychological functioning (Wertsch, 1985).

Now we will present a series of episodes that can be found in the activities of oral literacy. The situation shows an activity developed in an adult education center in Seville (an urban center). This consists of a conference and a debate

---

[3]The expression *a la vera de* has the same meaning as *besides*, but it is a dialectical form used only in some very traditional settings.

on a subject matter that was chosen by the students of the center, drug abuse. It is important to point out that this center is located in a neighborhood where there is a high level of drug addiction. The conference was directed to a group of students of different educational levels (total illiterates, functional illiterates, elementary education students) living in the same neighborhood where the center is located. All the episodes we are going to analyze correspond to the first part of the activity where the speaker expounds the subject.

EPISODE III

". . . lo mejor es prevenir el consumo. Por lo menos nosotros desde el centro, dado que no tenemos nada que ver con la policía, lo que tenemos que hacer es intentar que aquella gente que está en situación de poder consumir en un momento determinado, pues que no consuman, con lo cual evitamos que entren drogadictos. // Y ¿esto porqué es tan importante? Porque a mí no me sirve de nada quitar a un chaval de la droga si luego por otro lado se me están metiendo cinco. ¿Emm? Bien por el chaval que ha salido pero mal por los cinco que han entrado."

". . . and the best (thing to do) is to prevent consumption. At least, we from the center, since we don't have anything to do with the police, what we have to do is try to get the people that are in a situation where they could consume (drugs) at any time, that they don't, that way can avoid their becoming drug addicts. //And, why is this so important? Because it doesn't make any sense to me to get one kid off drugs if over on the other side five are getting hooked. Umm? Good for the kid who gets out but bad for the five that get in."

We can observe, as we analyze this episode, the way the speaker describes the objective he and other professionals consider to be the key in the fight against drugs. By using the expressions that come from his social language, that is to say the professional discourse, such as "*prevenir el consumo—prevent consumption*" and "*situación de poder consumir—situation where they could consume*". All these expressions are situated in a decontextualized plane, even though they are understood by the dialogue between different professional groups (police, doctors, judges, psychologists, etc.). Nevertheless, the speaker knows his audience is heterogeneous and some of them could have difficulties in understanding these means of expression. We find ourselves with the professional perspective of a speaker who uses another person's words with the voices of their interlocutors, housewives worried about the possible repercussions of drug abuse in their families. How does the speaker overcome the distance between the two voices? The answer is clear: by dialogizing the discourse. The speaker elicits the question that would have been formulated by a member of the audience in a daily conversation, "... *¿Y ésto porqué es importante?—And why is this important?*" Later, he answers it, going away from the professional means of expression used at first, by using his professional perspective through the means of expression of the audience (... *quitar de la droga ..., meterse en la droga ..., chaval—get off drugs ..., get hooked ..., kid*). In other words, the speaker repeats his arguments expressed in the first part of his discourse in a colloquial manner that lets him sympathize with the group of women who are listening to him. We can observe how the speaker interanimates the voices of the author and the audience in trying to obtain a better comprehension of the text, similar to what occurred in Episode II. But this rhetorical mechanism can become even more sophisticated by making this contact between voices more subtle as we will see in the next episode.

EPISODE IV

"Lo que llamamos la prevención inespecífica, es decir cómo conseguir sin hablar tanto de drogas, conseguir que nuestros hijos no tomen drogas. Y la verdad, es enseñarles, nosotros por lo menos es lo que hacemos, enseñarles hábitos sanos de la vida, ...
//es decir, que haya, que hay otras alternativas, qu:e hay un modo determinado que es estar con el hijo, que hay que decirle: "mira, hay otras cosas que hacer, hay otras cosas". ..., de tal forma que cuando llegue el momento, que va a llegar, que le ofrezcan droga, porque le va a llegar, pues que diga que no.

"What we call unspecific prevention, that is to say how to get our children to not take drugs by not talking about drugs so much. And the truth is to teach them, at least that's what we do, teach them healthy habits about life, ...
//that is, that there are other alternatives,... that there's a specific way to be with your child, you have to tell him or her: "Look, there are other things you can do, there are other things". ..., so that when the time comes, and it will come, they'll offer him drugs, because it will come, well he'll say no.

The interanimation of voices, in this case, gets the speaker to separate the arguments through the different enouncements that elapse, from the purist professional discourse (*unspecific prevention*) that represents the most decontextualized level to the usage of reported speech in direct style (... *Hay que decir-*

le: "mira, hay otras cosas que hacer . . ."—*You have to tell him or her: "Look, there are other things you can do . . ."*) or indirect style (*. . . Pues que diga que no.*—*. . . well he'll say* no").

Looking at the episode carefully, we can verify the consecutive steps in the development of the notion of *unspecific prevention* that the speaker is trying to explain. A progressive contextualization of discourse is produced which is developed through the following steps: at first, the speaker tries to obtain understanding and transmit his own perspective, by speaking to an audience in first person (*. . . pero cómo conseguir, sin hablar tanto de drogas que nuestros hijos no tomen drogas.*— *. . . by getting, without talking about drugs so much, that* our children *don't take drugs*). By using the adjective our he tries to transfer his professional perspective in a collective perspective assumed by the audience. The road towards the contextualization of discourse does not end here. In order to reach a deeper understanding on the part of those that listen to him, the speaker incorporates an individual voice to his own discourse. He uses what, according to Bakhtin, is one of the most important semiotic instruments to ventriloquize the speech of another. We are referring to reported speech (Bakhtin, 1981; Voloshinov, 1986) in any of the forms speakers use to express it (direct or indirect style). In the last part of the episode we can see that the speaker ventriloquizes the voice of an imaginary parent in the situation of talking to his son about searching for an alternative to drugs (*Mira hay otras cosas que hacer. . .*—*. . . look, there are other things to do. . .*). Through this utterance, the speaker manages to make an example of the most abstract notion of unspecific prevention with which he opened that part of the conference.

In the two episodes we have commented on, we have observed the property that characterizes the acquisition of literacy. And that is the relation existing between the text and its mediated addressee through a third voice, capable of interanimating the voices, which express the text and the audience.

SOME REFLECTIONS REGARDING THE NATURE OF LITERACY

Making literacy means developing a process of great complexity that cannot be dealt with from just a single perspective. All efforts directed to the analysis of the learning of literacy, especially in the field of adult education, should contemplate the problem as a whole, surpassing the views concentrating on the development of individual skills. The sociocultural approach allows us to go beyond the solipsistic views of learning, to consider simultaneously the subject that learns and the sociocultural reality he or she moves in. This approach becomes richer by a dialogic perspective that lets us develop the adequate instruments of analysis in the study of communication in the sociocultural setting. The dialogic perspective initiated by Bakhtin, and continued by such authors as Holquist, Emerson, Wertsch, and others, lets us study literacy when the activity is eminently dialogic.

The main characteristic of literacy activities is the profound heteroglossia that impregnates them. The production of a text, as well as its understanding, are characterized by the meeting of voices, genres, social languages and cultures. The learning how to read and write consists of moving between the voices and the means of expression that come together in the text. In the first episode we could observe how it is not necessary to have a high level in reading skills in order to reach the understanding of a text, when the voices that interact reflect similar perspectives. And yet, when the student reads a text expressed in a social language he or she does not understand or is unfamiliar with, a third voice (e.g., the teacher's) is necessary to interanimate the voices of the author and the reader. This fact can also be seen in oral literacy activities. As in writing literacy, we showed in the episodes we commented on how the speaker mediates between the text he or she is trying to transmit and the voices that comprise his or her audience. The mediating function consists of transmitting his or her own perspective by ventriloquizing the means of expression of his audience.

Dialogue and literacy go hand in hand. The teaching of how to read and write, especially in adult education, needs to pay attention to the dialogic aspects of the text, to the joining of the views of the world that are inevitably produced in any literacy activity. The dialogic perspective improves the capacity of analysis of the sociocultural approach in the study of communication in general, and in literacy in particular.

REFERENCES

Bakhtin, M.M. (1981). *The dialogic imagination.* Austin: University of Texas Press.
Bakhtin, M. M. (1987). The problem of speech genres. In M. M. Bakhtin, C. Emerson, & M. Holquist (Eds.), *Speech genres & other late essays* (pp. 60–102). Austin: The University of Texas Press.
Cole, M., & Scribner, S. (1974). *Culture and thought: A psychological introduction.* New York: Wiley.
Cook-Gumperz, J. (1986). *The social construction of literacy.* Cambridge, MA: Cambridge University Press.
Davidov, V.D., & Zinchenko, V.P. (1988). Vygotsky's contribution to the development of psychology. *Soviet Psychology, 11,* 22–36.
Freire, P. (1970). *Pedagogy of the oppressed.* Seabury, NY: Continuum.
Goody, J. (1978). *Literacy in traditional societies.* Cambridge, MA: Cambridge University Press.
Goody, J. (1986). *The logic of writing and the organization of society.* Cambridge, MA: Cambridge University Press.
Heath, S.B. (1983). *Way with words: Language, life and work in communities and classrooms.* Cambridge, MA: Cambridge University Press.
Heath, S.B. (1989). The learner as cultural member. In M.L. Rice & R.L. Schiefelbusch (Eds.), *The teachability of language* (pp. 333–350). Baltimore: Paul H. Brooks.

Heath, S.B. (1990). The children of Trackton's children. Spoken and written language in social change. In J.W. Stigler, R.A. Shweder, & G. Herdt (Eds.), *Cultural psychology. Essays on comparative human development* (pp. 496–519). Cambridge, MA: Cambridge University Press.

Leontiev, A.N. (1978). *Activity, consciousness, and personality.* Englewood Cliffs, NJ: Prentice Hall.

Leontiev, A.N. (1982). *Problems in the development of mind.* Moscow: Progress Publishers.

Luria, A.R. (1976). *Cognitive development: Its cultural and social foundation.* Cambridge, MA: Harvard University Press.

Scribner, S., & Cole, M. (1981). *The psychological consequences of literacy.* Cambridge, MA: Harvard University Press.

Snow, C., & Dickinson, D. (1991). Skills that aren't in a new conception of literacy. In A. Purvis & T. Jennings (Eds.), *Literate systems and individual lives* (pp. 179–191). Cambridge, MA: Harvara University Press.

Valsiner, J. (1988). *Developmental psychology in the Soviet Union.* Brighton, UK: The Harvester Press.

Voloshinov, V.N. (1986). *Marxism and the philosophy of language.* Cambridge, MA: Harvard University Press.

Vygotsky, L.S. (1962). *Thought and language.* Cambridge, MA: MIT Press.

Vygotsky, L.S. (1978). *Mind in society: The development of higher psychological processes.* Cambridge, MA: Harvard University Press.

Wertsch, J.V. (1980). The significance of dialogue in Vygotsky's account of social, egocentric and inner speech. *Contemporary Educational Psychology, 5,* 150–162.

Wertsch, J.V. (1985a). *Vygotsky and social formation of mind.* Cambridge, MA: Harvard University Press.

Wertsch, J.V. (Ed.). (1985b). *Culture, communication and cognition: Vygotskian perspectives.* Cambridge, UK: Cambridge University Press.

Wertsch, J.V. (1985c). The Semiotic Mediation of Mental Life: L.S. Vygotsky and M.M. Bakhtin. In E. Mertz & R.J. Parmentier (Eds.), *Semiotic mediation* (pp. 49–71). Orlando, FL: Academic Press.

Wertsch, J.V. (1987). *Voices of the mind.* Inaugural lecture delivered on the occasion of taking up the Belle van Zuylen Professorship at the University of Utrecht, October, 1987.

Wertsch, J.V. (1991). *Voices of the mind. A sociocultural approach to the mental action.* Cambridge, MA: Harvard University Press.

CHAPTER 9

Microgenesis of Relearning: A New View of the Process of Psychotherapy*

University of Bern, Switzerland

I will argue in this chapter for a reconsideration of some basic assumptions in traditional psychotherapy process research. In order to do this, I will adopt what might be called a nominalistic perspective of process variables for relearning in psychotherapy. I will claim that traditional process variables are not offering the firm empirical basis for process research we would wish for. With their decontextualized nature traditional process variables in fact qualify as metaphysical. Borrowing from linguistics, developmental, and perceptual research, alternative process variables based on commonsense language (CSL) and its proof structure, the grammar of language use (GLUE), are proposed. Alternative *conceptual variables* will be conceptual isolation, conceptual cues, accessibility of categories, and completion of process. Alternative *process variables* on a discursive level are differentiation (simple to complex), division of tasks into subtasks, and transfer of skills.

In order to describe process units, the useful theoretical concept *register* is introduced. *Registers* are the event units of actualized language use. Their change during the process of a therapy is determined by discourse analysis, specifically by the Interpersonal Process Recall, frequency counts, and other related methods. And finally, I will summarize one of our own experiments on concept formation and satisfaction. Results of this experiment indicate that accessibility of categories enhances satisfaction of task solution. Implications for therapy process will be discussed.

---

* Preparation of this chapter was financed by the Swiss National Science Foundation, Fellowship no. 8210-025979.

246

In order to start the argument, a more detailed look at recent literature on psychotherapy process research (e.g., Elliott & James, 1989; Fiedler & Rogge, 1989; Lambert, 1989; Orlinsky & Howard, 1986; Orlinsky, 1989; Wiener, Budney, Wood, & Russell, 1989) is necessary. This literature again shows the lack of any consensus and wealth of knowledge in the field. Despite of a few attempts to redirect process research (e.g., Russell, 1989; Stiles & Shapiro, 1989), most therapy process studies focus on variables like empathy, contracting, etc. Generally, process research in psychotherapy has constructed *its own variables* and its own, poorly corroborated, mechanisms of change, largely ignoring language and other related fields thereby. Moreover, most process research *is lacking a well-established theoretical frame* of its basic concepts. These two features of process research in psychotherapy have led to an almost infinite number of claims of effective variables in psychotherapy, and a rather uncoordinated research activity in the field.

It seems therefore imperative to reconsider and reformulate a few basic principles of process research again. Where are we starting from? What are process variables? What methodology should be adopted in process research? An attempt to answer these questions involves, first, a closer look at some traditional process variables. I will argue that the main problem with these variables is an inadequate treatment of the concept of time, perception, and development. A more adequate treatment of these concepts will necessarily lead to different research programs.

In the present chapter I will not deal with specific theoretical models predicting change. Further, although some empirical studies based on the present approach exist (Siegfried, in preparation b), future research will have to demonstrate the full empirical utility of this approach.

I will proceed in several steps. First I will summarize some fundamentals of present psychotherapeutic process research adopting a learning metaphor. I will then outline some problems faced by researchers of this tradition and will present views and consequences of a nominalistic perspective.

PROCESS RESEARCH BASED ON A LEARNING METAPHOR

One basic image of psychotherapy process research is related to learning and personal education (Orlinsky, 1989). Researchers operating with this perspective see *personality* as a set of learned responses, and *the environment* as a discrete number of specifiable and definable tasks confronting the individual. Accordingly, the learning or reeducation process in psychotherapy is structured in a task-specific manner. Five kinds of process variables are viewed as important under this perspective and linked together in a generic model (Orlinsky & Howard, 1987).

Process Variables

For the time being let me adopt the traditional definition of process variables of Orlinsky and Howard (1986). *Process variables* are viewed as discrete relevant units describing the interaction of the different systems involved. Process for them is everything that can be observed to occur between, and within, the main participants of an interaction during a specified event (Stiles & Shapiro, 1989).

The five kinds of process variables are

1. therapeutic contract,
2. therapeutic interventions,
3. therapeutic bond,
4. personal self-relatedness, and
5. therapeutic realization.

These variables have been specified by Orlinsky, Grawe, and Parles (1994).

Briefly, *contracting* refers to the implicit agreement between the parties regarding the conditions of their working alliance. *Therapeutic interventions* are the methods to be applied and include an evaluation of the patient before therapy. The personal qualities contributing to the success or failure of the therapeutic methods are summed up under the *therapeutic bond. Personal self-relatedness* refers to the degree of openness of the participants in relation to therapeutic interventions. The outcome of therapy constitutes the *therapeutic realization.*

These variables largely correspond to very familiar steps for solving problems in math and physics courses—what is given? what is asked? What is the algorithm leading to the solution of the problem?—and are adequate for problem solutions. Although a lot of research has been devoted to these process variables (e.g., Greenberg & Pinsof, 1986; Homans, 1961; Stein & Lambert, 1984; Truax et al., 1966) a number of questions specific to a psychotherapeutic process arise. How is the length of the process units determined? What is t_o, or the start of the activation of process variables, respectively? How do we determine what process variables are active at a given time t_1?

It is quite likely that common sense alone can provide "answers" to these questions. There is no readily available empirical method specifying process variables in the direction of these questions. Further, they have characteristics easily leading to their substitution by other variables.

Decontextualization

Another characteristic of traditional process variables is their relative independence both of context and prior and subsequent events. *Contextuality* I take to refer to an interdependence of all psychological terms to previous and subsequent states of affairs as well as to environmental characteristics (Siegfried, in preparation a). *Decontextualized process variables,* on the other hand, are supposed to work relatively independent of context and previous and subsequent states of affairs, and are supposed to act much like a drug (i.e., under any circumstance—Stiles & Shapiro, 1989).

Convincing critics, however, have pointed to the insurmountable problems intrinsic to the decontextualized approach. Valsiner (1987), for example, called for process variables in developmental psychology that take the interdependence of child and parents, together with their behavioral possibilities and sociocultural aims, into account. Stiles and Shapiro (1989) speak of an "excessive abstraction" (p. 528) in order to make therapy ingredients "pure," i.e., noncontextual and independent of prior and subsequent events. In summary, their basic argument comes down to the claim that psychology is dealing with open systems allowing for adaptation to the environment and the given circumstances at a specific time t_1. Affecting variables thus never meet the same state of an organism. Therefore, their context-free effect must be described as unspecific. However, in specific contexts they of course have an impact.

Metaphysics

Metaphysics is understood to be the study of how things are. A metaphysical process analysis thus reveals the real mechanisms at work and characteristically lacks an elaborate structure of valid empirical proof.

Today no serious scientist is committed to metaphysics anymore. Rather, metaphysical investigations are replaced by models linking the bits of empirical results together in a comprehensive theory (Harré & Secord, 1972). However, if empirical results are scarce, scientific theoretical models become mere metaphysical speculations prone to be over and again replaced by newer ones. Further, most of the concepts in the models are subject to a circularity in reasoning and third confounded variables (Smedslund, 1972) and thus are not empirically established with any validity. For example, Rogerian client-centered therapy is based on the assumption that therapeutic change is facilitated by therapeutic warmth, therapeutic genuineness, and patient's self-exploration. Therapeutic warmth or empathy thus is seen as an active ingredient in a process of therapeutic change. Empirical specifications of the meaning of empathy has led to the development of measuring systems, which in turn "prove" that empathy is an active variable in a therapeutic process. However, as the many different variables of change in other therapeutic schools have shown, a large number of competing variables may be confounded in the concept of empathy.

All process variables related to contracting, therapeutic interventions, therapeutic bond, self-relatedness, and therapeutic realizations in the same way are subject to circularity and alternative explanations and therefore are metaphysical in nature. The reason for this, as I will show, is that they are abstract concepts with only an empirical proof structure. They lack the complex proof structure of CSL for psychological concepts.

Summary

Although traditional process variables have stimulated process research to a large extent, they are subject to a number of problems that question their usefulness. Traditional process variables are insensitive to context, which actually is part of their intrinsic nature. There are no empirical methods available to determine the onset and termination of these process variables. The units of traditional process variables vary greatly and extend from a few minutes in therapy (e.g., empathy) to sessions (e.g., contracting) and even the whole therapy (e.g., the therapeutic bond). On top of that, they are subject to the methodological expressions of metaphysics, namely, circularity and confounding variables.

PSYCHOTHERAPEUTIC PROCESS RESEARCH RECONSIDERED

The features of traditional process variables outlined above call for a reconsideration of some basic concepts of process research. The development of a new research program entails first a specification of the research object and its related fields. I will now give the reasons why I think that CSL is a firm basis for relearning in psychotherapy. On this basis I will proceed to define the range of possible *ingredients* to a relearning process.

Commonsense Language and its Grammar

I take CSL to be the systems of socially established signs, historically developed and still developing for the purpose of communication. CSL refers to the socially established language and thus is understood by all competent users of the respective language. CSL does not refer to highly specialized or not-established language use. Note that CSL does not only refer to spoken and written signs, but includes nonverbal signs (such as traffic signs, gestures, or behavioral sequences) used for the purpose of communication.

CSL is governed by a system of rules referred to as the Grammar of Language Use (GLUE). This system is not equal to the various syntax grammars governing the spoken and written correct language use. Rather, it is a system governing social language use and specifies the proof structure of its various concepts. For example, GLUE specifies how certainty related to the presence of pain, emotion, thinking, etc. can be obtained, and how they can be *proved*. It enumerates the various conditions that are acceptable reasons in CSL for the assignment of categories. For example, a tree is there because I see it, because another person also sees it, because it has a certain shape, because it can be touched, etc. A different GLUE governs thinking. A person is thinking because somebody asked her something and she is silent at present, because she fixes her eyes at an uninteresting spot of the environment, because she stops moving, etc.

Traditionally the system of CSL and its proof structure (GLUE) have been rejected by scientists because of their imprecise nature. It is maintained that different conditions may explain the same thing, CSL is not general enough, different contexts require different descriptive categories. Science, on the other hand, has to be general, precise, and decontextualized. In order to fulfill these requirements, new and more precise concepts are freely invented to describe the respective processes.

No doubt this program has been successful in natural sciences. In social sciences and in psychotherapy process research, however, 30 years of controlled empirical research have led to contradictions, slow progress, and around 400 different theories (Kazdin, 1986; Grawe, Siegfried, Bernauer, Donati, & Louis, 1987) explaining largely similar phenomena. Further, a growing number of scientists from such different fields as theory of science (Harré, 1980), developmental psychology (Valsiner, 1987), social psychology (Billig, 1987; Shotter, 1987; Smedslund, 1986, 1988), linguistics (Bach, 1986), and psychotherapeutic process research (Russell, 1989) assert the nonfeasibility of decontextualized theories for social sciences. Their main argument runs something like this:

Language, development, and social interactions are basic to social sciences and are open systems dependent on contextual features of their occurrences. Any attempt to formulate precise decontextualized laws ends up in a circularity, in conceptual/historical or natural *necessities* or an inconsideration of some basic relevant variables. Organisms, unlike matter, adapt to the social and material environment and therefore are open systems. Human organisms further operate with culturally mediated social constructs determining them as well as the environment. In short, *in any piece of social science's research a much greater number of variables have to be considered than in natural sciences. Further, many of the relevant variables are hidden variables, which are not active all the time.*

Accepting this position is not without some rather unpleasant consequences, however. Apart from CSL there is no adequate descriptive system available in order to deal with such huge numbers of variables. Further, how are we going to control for some basic variables in a nonrandom fashion? What variables should be controlled for in research?

The methodological disorientation of what could be termed as *contextualists* becomes obvious by looking at the diversity of methods they propose. Some are advancing rhetorics as a promising new research tool (Billig, 1987; Shotter, 1987); others ethogeny, a system within which cultural behavior can be explained (Harré, 1980; Kroger, 1982); again, some are advancing a kind of a deductive developmental logic based on dialectics and materialism (Valsiner, 1987); and last but not least, some are trying to reformulate the aims of psychological research (as, e.g., the explication of common sense—Smedslund, 1986, 1988) all together.

It is probably fair to say that contextualists stress the importance of language and reasoning and try to find alternatives to the traditional experimental proof structure. However, CSL has not received even their full attention. Still, many of them operate with deontic technical terms and their exclusively empirical proof structure. However, a concept of CSL or of a specialized language is not only a designation of some aspect of the phenomenal world in language, but is related to a specific GLUE. Empirical process research specifies some proof structure. But it is important to note that it is an extremely limited proof structure in comparison to the proof structures of CSL. Further, as the many contradictions in psychotherapy research show, it is a vulnerable proof structure. CSL, despite all efforts to go beyond it, still offers a socially well-accepted, elaborate proof structure and generally allows for much better predictions than any specialized language related to psychotherapy processes research.

Working with CSL raises a number of questions specific to process research. For example, should we direct our attention to the meaning of language or to language use? Concentrating on the *meaning* of language instead of language use, and adopting a realist instead of nominalistic perspective of language—the perspective that each concept has something like an unanimously accepted core meaning—without considering context and situation leads to similar problems faced by traditional research methodology. For example, content analysis of therapeutic discourse operates with content but has not arrived at some more widely accepted conclusions. On the other hand, working with the surface structure and language use still leaves us with an enormous amount of transcripts of therapeutic discourse. Obviously, reduction for the purpose of generalization is required. This reduction can be achieved by a closer look of what process and therapeutic change is.

The Notion of Process and Development

Linguists tell us that a *process* is a bounded or unbounded temporal flow of events, subdividable or not subdividable into subunits of the same kind with the property of cumulative reference (Bach, 1986). The cumulative reference property refers to the fact that running + running = running. The following are CSL examples of processes involved:

1. He is running.
2. She is changing.

Searching for a model of an universal grammar, linguists were forced to distinguish between states, events, and process (for a comprehensive summary of the literature, see Bach, 1986). *Events* in CSL, roughly speaking, are bounded, countable, not subdividable temporal occurrences with no property of cumulative reference (to make a contract + to make a contract = two contracts). Events in general refer to something which is not yet over. Examples for events are;

3. The client complains about his relatives.
4. The therapist gives advice.

Both processes and events, with their common property of temporality, only happen in relation to something which is nonprocess/event, i.e., *states*. CSL examples of states are;

5. The client likes the therapist.
6. The therapist is directive.

These three linguistic distinctions expressed in examples (1)–(6) show several important aspects for a learning process in psychotherapy. As an example, let me take again the "process" variables referred to as *contracting*.

7. The therapist and the patient make a contract.
8. The therapist and the patient discuss a contract.
9. The patient and the therapist have a contract.

(7) is an example for an event, (8) an example for a process, (9) again an example for a state. One linguistic criterion to distinguish (8) from (7) and (9) is by way of possible inferences. (8) allows for the inference, "therefore they have discussed already something about the contract." (7) and (9) do not allow for this inference.

Events thus are temporal-spatial actualizations of the more unspecific process. Processes are to events like stuff to things (Bach, 1986). From the point of view of a CSL-perspective it is thus naive to assume a *specific* number of process variables relevant to a psychotherapeutic learning process. Moreover, as (7) to (9) show, whether a particular variable qualifies as a process variable depends on its specific form in CSL. *In fact, every activity related verb of a specific language may qualify as a process variable* (e.g., "the client and therapist are speaking" makes the speaking a process variable). Therefore, process research has to deal with all these process variables, unless a clear hypothesis based on empirical findings specifies the relevant features of a psychotherapeutic process. A relevant feature hypothesis in its turn is dependent on the client and therapist's perception at a given time t_1.

The *proof structure of processes* is closely linked to time and input/output. A process may take longer or shorter. Uncritical decontextualized language use assigns more complexity to longer processes and less complexity to shorter ones. Of course, the mere passing of time does not in any way reflect the complexity of processes. Subjects may also be bored, confused, or surprised by a specific tasks. Subjects are not machines trying their best all the time to solve problems. However, in order to categorize an event as a process, a certain time-span, from the point of view of the stable coordinates of the observer, has to elapse. Further, there must be some difference between input and output. *Input* is characterized by something unknown, not obvious or something yet to be understood. *Output* has to be some kind of response or behavioral change.

Development is a term closely related to learning, process, and therapy. Development in its turn is a bounded or unbounded temporal flow of events subdividable into subunits of different kinds, later subunits having the property of a specifiable addition to former ones by virtue of specific actions undertaken by the subject. There is no property of cumulative reference. *Learning* is task specific development. The following may serve as CSL examples of development and learning.

10.   He ate a lot, and his body developed very well.
11.   Her language development is very fast.
12.   They learned the conservation of liquid volume and to control their emotions.

Development and learning therefore are *processes with a direction*. Relevant questions related to the proof structure of development and learning are: what was the state prior to development/learning? and what changed during the development/learning?

In summary, the investigation in the language use of process, development, and learning should have clarified that traditional process variables in the learning or relearning metaphor of psychotherapy do not qualify per se as process variables. Whether they are process variables or not depends on their specific form in CSL. Therefore, I rather *prefer to speak of traditional process variables as conditional variables for change.*

Adopting the learning metaphor thus conceptually implies that psychotherapeutic processes are *task-related developments*. These developments find their expression in linguistic categories of a specific form. A psychotherapeutic process thus is not seen as a mystified process of reconditioning, a substitution of the id by the ego, or a self-actualization, but is viewed as a mastery of specific tasks related to the problem of the client.

The Interdependence of Events

In all process research *time* is one of the most crucial factors. Without the concept of time there is no learning, no development, or any other process happening. Time since Newton is considered as an absolute, basic ontological unit underlying the phenomenal world (Burtt, 1932). However, it was theory of relativity that later clarified that time is dependent upon an inertial frame and is a function unique to the choice of origin and unit. This definition is called the *Einstein time coordinate of the frame* (Torretti, 1986). For example, a learning process of social skills may be happening during t_1 and t_2. If an observer starts to observe the process at t_{11} and stops the observation at t_{21}, observations may be very different.

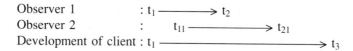

Observer 1 may have observed a considerable progress, whereas Observer 2, because of her later start, may have observed no improvement in self-assertiveness. Quite clearly, a process is dependent upon the time of observation. Recent trends to take events as basic units of process research are promising methods to tackle time (Elliott & James, 1989; Wiener et al., 1989).

Another interdependence of systems to be considered in process research is the dependence of previous and subsequent states of affairs. The regularity of behavior itself implies that the probability of a similar kind of event is higher at two time points close to each other than at two times quite apart. Bruner (1973), aware of this interdependence, has referred to it as *transitional probabilities*. Transitional probabilities are established in dealing with sequences of events and tell the organism in a learning process that certain classes of events are more likely to follow than others. A description of a therapeutic learning process therefore implies a state or event at a given time t_1 and t_2, a specification of all the process variables present during the respective interval, an empirical evaluation of the causal power of the process variables allowing for a difference between t_1 and t_2, and a formulation of a hypothesis with regard to the active process variables responsible for change during the interval. Tests and measurements related to psychological constructs like empathy capture but a few variables responsible for change. Through discourse and CSL analysis (Labov & Fanshel, 1977) as well as tape-assisted Interpersonal Process Recall (IPR—Elliott & James, 1989), on the other hand, it is possible to capture a much greater number of variables.

Subdivisions in Task-Related Processes

There are two related areas to a therapeutic learning process which mainly focus on task-related process descriptions; perception and developmental theories of psychology. These two fields offer a wealth of important variables to a therapeutic process.

Perceptual process. Briefly, Bruner (1973) has enumerated four mechanisms mediating perceptual readiness;

1. Grouping and integration
2. Access ordering
3. Match–mismatch
4. Gating process.

Bruner and associates view the *perceptual process as a constructive process that requires initial category formation and the development of elaborated categorical systems.* Accessibility is used to denote the ease or speed with which a given stimulus input is coded in terms of a given category. Stimulus input, in Bruner's view, has then to be matched to various specifications of the initially assumed category. However, because certainly not all stimuli in an environment can be considered to be relevant at a given time, a gating mechanism selects stimuli. Empirical grounds for the assumption of these four mechanisms are specific perceptual tasks as well as neurological assumptions.

Similarly, in the masses of process variables related to a marriage conflict, for example, clients first have to make a choice about which variables are relevant for their problem. They have to *isolate* some occurrences and relate them to a categorical system. CSL offers such a categorical system and often is enlarged by the therapists special vocabulary to describe conflict. Almost nothing is known in psychotherapy process research about the way clients form categories to describe their conflict. However, it is likely that category formation depends upon the verbal skills and social background (Cole & Bruner, 1971) of the client.

Again, the *relevant cues to describe an event* as a conflict, for example, are another important variable to be considered. Which are the relevant cues giving rise to the conflict–category assignment? Anybody who has worked with couples, for example, will know that conflict-assignment cues between individuals differ widely. What is a source of conflict for one person is not one for the other. However, again almost no literature exists in this domain.

We further hardly know anything about how cues are selected (Bruner's *selective gating*). Knowledge is lacking as well on the *accessibility of psychological categories.* Further, what Bruner calls the *completion of the process,* i.e., the conviction that the category matches with the preselected probable categories, is a further crucial step in the process of, e.g., conflict perception. Again, how man proceeds from *simple categories to the complex handling of CSL* in order to describe psychological states, events, or processes is another field of promising experimental research.

Although this is but a programmatic outline of future research, to do process research in psychotherapy on these lines seems more promising and less speculative than the attempts to formulate decontextualized metaphysical categories.

Process of development. Theories of perception have emphasized the process of categorization. Developmental theories, on the other hand, stress learning. For the present purpose it is not necessary to outline the different developmental theories, ranging from Piaget to Vygotski. Let me directly pro-

ceed to developmental variables relevant to learning and relearni..
chotherapeutic process.

First of all the literature on teaching skills to children has emphasizeu
process from *simple to complex and the division of tasks into subtasks*. It furthei
clarified the crucial role of language in a learning process. Research coming
again from Bruner (1973) and associates has indicated that improvement in language helps to solve problems. For example, if a therapist teaches the client a
new conceptual system such as a brand of psychoanalysis or behavior therapy,
in which way is this new "language" helping the client to solve the problem?

Further, much research has been committed to *transfer of skills* (Cox, Valsiner, & Ornstein, 1987). Again, how skills relevant to a therapeutic process are
transferred to other areas is much in the dark. Although problem-solving tasks
of experimental research give some hints of the possible functioning of this
process, it is only *therapeutic* tasks and their effects that lead to a better understanding of transfer of skills. As we will see below, a number of specific tasks
readily available for therapeutic processes will form the empirical basis for
these sort of research questions.

A last process variable to be mentioned for a relearning in a psychotherapeutic process is suggested by research coming from Valsiner. Valsiner (1987)
used *long term studies of behavioral frequencies* as indicators of development.[1]
This simple method again is readily applicable to therapeutic process research.

Towards More Adequate Process Variables

The first characteristic in a nominalistic perspective of an adequate process
variable for the study of psychotherapy processes therefore is that at the present state of the art it must be a CSL concept traceable in therapeutic discourse
fulfilling the linguistic qualifications of a process variable. A second characteristic is related to t_0 or the initial observation of the process variable. T_0 must
be the first moment of observation of the variable anywhere in the course of
therapy, i.e., the beginning of process sequence. The methods to follow up a
process variable and determine therapeutic development are nominalistic discourse analysis.

For example, talking or discussing may be nominalistic process variables to
be considered in a case of depression. *Depression* may be assigned to the client

---

[1] In one fruitful discussion, Valsiner argued that the behavioral frequencies are not indicators of
development but "merely a background summary for analysis of process at each age level." To me
the differentiation between background and real development raises more problems than it solves.
Is the more frequent correct articulation of the word *mother* during development, for example, a
background or "real" development? My nominalistic realism perspective just debates something
more real in development than increases and decreases of behavior frequencies (including language).

by himself or herself, or by the agents of his or her social environment. Depression is a meaningless label for process research and is broken down into meaningful process variables. It may mean that,

1. The client is hardly talking in therapy session.
2. His writing of letters is scarce.
3. He is restricting his activities.
4. He is drawing poorly if he wishes to do so.
5. His interaction with spouse and children are minimal.
6. His stereotyped movements are excessive, etc.

Note that it is not the therapist who gives an expert judgment of such deficits and obliges the client to remedy them. Rather, the therapist makes judgments as part of the social environment of the client, if the client wishes to change. Further, it is not the therapist who decides the direction of the process, but the client who makes the decisions. In this sense, the therapist is not the expert but should offer a favorable environment for change.

(1)–(6) are all *observer judgments* based on social expectations of the raters. These expectations reflect certain behavioral characteristics as well as short-term behavioral predictions of the patient's social environment. (1)–(6) are not only a relevant behavioral selection mediated by a particular language, but reflect the rater's expectations of future behavior of the client.

Minutely following the client's discourse in order to *determine how mutually acceptable target behaviors are taken up by the client,* and how frequency and nature of events change over time empirically determine the learning process of psychotherapy. Specifically for (1), the occurrence of process variables like talking, discussing, and speaking can empirically be determined by analyzing discourse.

The client's verbal and physical behavior thus is dependent upon the therapist's perception, upon the client's and therapist's structuring of the linguistic context (ability to form clusters, accessibility of concepts, matching judgments, and selective gating), the physical situation, and upon the therapist's and client's actual behavior. Thus, the client's development in psychotherapy from simple to complex or complex to simple, his or her transfer of skills, and his or her changes in specific behavior frequencies cannot be seen apart from the linguistic structuring of the situation and his or her language use (see Figure 9.1).

Borrowing from linguistics, we may call the interactive structures mediating the participants' behaviors *registers*. A register simply is an actualized language use of either therapist or client for the purpose of communication. The concept *register* does not describe psychic occult happenings, but describes actual language use. *Language use* in turn refers to the verbal and physical actions as far as they are related to communication. Note that not all nonverbal actions are communicative. Many psychologists have claimed the communicative function

Figure 9.1.   Interaction between client and therapist behavior, and mediating structures between them.

of almost all behavior (e.g., Scheflen, 1973). However, this seemingly profound insight in fact is nothing but a misuse of language. Only *some* nonverbal behaviors are communicative. My sitting in front of the computer, for example, ordinarily does not have a communicative function but is related to my work.

Registers may be elaborate or restricted, simple or complex, and structured or unstructured. Registers contain process, event, and state variables as well as concepts relevant to the respective context. For example, if a wife asserts that she has a marriage conflict because her husband is never at home, and if upon further questioning this reason is seen as the only one for the marriage conflict, then this is an example of a restricted register. On the other hand, if the conflict is described as being a result of many conditions and contributing factors from both sides, some factors being more important than others, then this is an example of a structured and complex register. Registers, obviously, also can be too complex. A schizophrenic man describing his stay at the ward as something determined by exterior forces, related to his astral body of former lives, influenced by extraterrestrial spacecrafts etc., is not only using too complex, but also socially unstructured, registers. If his learning task in a therapeutic interaction is defined as how to get out of clinic, he must learn to create the relevant conditions for the accomplishment of this task. He must get acquainted with the conditions relevant for release and detention, and must learn to use discourse in such a way that his intention is credible to observers.

What then are relevant research questions to a nominalistic approach of learning in a psychotherapeutic process? There are two groups of questions, the first being related to discourse with registers and tasks as event units; the second group is related to the conceptual level. On the *discourse level* relevant topics and questions are;

1.   Detailed explication of CSL and GLUE of task specific interactions, including nonverbal communicative events and rules of interaction.
2.   What regular contextual behaviors facilitate and prevent change? How can the client–context interaction be classified in relation to facilitating or preventing factors (e.g., persons who are eager to learn, who are humble and respectful, versus persons who are proud, convinced of their rights, easily angered in many contexts)?

3. What true process variables are particularly important in relation to thera- peutic change?
4. What parts of the therapeutic discourse increase/decrease satisfaction; are seen as particularly helpful in Interpersonal Process Recall?
5. How elaborate do registers have to be for change?
6. What are the subtasks to be achieved first? What steps are involved to con- trol anger, for example?
7. How can earlier achieved skills be used for different tasks?
8. How are the frequencies of process variables related to therapeutic change?

On the level of *individual concepts* relevant topics and questions are;

1. How are cues relevant to the assignment of psychological categories se- lected?
2. How are cues relevant to the structuring of the therapeutic process searched for? (e.g., by way of eye movement)
3. How is category accessibility related to therapeutic change? Which cate- gories have to be available for therapeutic change? Which categories have to be introduced for therapeutic change? Which categories do not facilitate change (e.g., does a new language of a therapeutic school unfamiliar to the client facilitate change)?
4. What moves in therapeutic speech under what conditions facilitate change? (i.e., giving new conceptual information, listening, praising, scolding)
5. What completes certainty of achievement? What is needed for conviction that the category is accurate?

Much research is still needed in most of these areas. How research can be done is illustrated by an example of conceptual research related to psychother- apy. Full details of the study will be reported in Siegfried (in preparation b).

Eighty-one undergraduate students were presented five descriptive tasks. A sailing boat, a clutch and a colored abstract figure were presented on slides, and subjects were asked to describe in 10 sentences what they had seen. Further, two 2-minute segments of films were presented, one with a schizophrenic patient and one with a relationship problem. After the first presentation the experimental group received information additional to the slides or the film segments. They received a drawing of a sailing boat and a clutch with the names of the differ- ent parts written on it. The names of the colors were simultaneously presented with the abstract figure. For the two segments of the films additional informa- tion was given for relationship problems and schizophrenia. Experimental sub- jects then were asked to describe what they have seen again in the presence of the additional information. Control subjects did not receive additional informa- tion. Both groups at both times of the description had to indicate on a scale from 1 to 7 how satisfied they were with each sentence of their description.

Briefly, results show that, with the exception of the additional information of the color names, satisfaction with description was higher when subjects used some additional information. The presence of a more elaborate conceptual system enhanced satisfaction of subjects with the specific tasks of description.

Although written descriptions of course are not usually part of a therapeutic process, the experiment nevertheless shows that additional conceptual information for tasks where the conceptual system of the client is clearly insufficient may have a positive effect on overall satisfaction. The experiment thus shows that the presence of a linguistic structure to conceptually capture a problem area enhances satisfaction.

A similar result was reported by Lenneberg and Roberts (1956) in developmental psychology. These authors showed that inappropriate linguistic encoding negatively influences task performances.

CONCLUSION

In this chapter I have outlined a new conceptual framework for process research adopting the metaphor of learning in psychotherapy. Current process variables used in research under the perspective of traditional process research are arbitrary, noncontextual and largely metaphysical. On the other hand, grounding process variables on CSL and GLUE not only eliminates contradictions between psychological and linguistic, developmental, and perceptual research, but further clarifies the proof structure of process variables. On the basis of this proof structure, empirical research on concept learning, concept assignment, concept accessibility, task structuring, and changes in registers can be performed. In short, both conceptual research similar to empirical research in perception and development, as well as task and discourse research, are needed in process research of psychotherapy. Labov and Fanshel (1977) and Russell (1989) have shown alternative valuable methods and thereby attempted to find a more integrative theoretical basis for process research. With the present chapter it is hoped that some contribution to the clarification of the fundamental theoretical problems in process research is achieved. It is also hoped that some solutions are offered and that more rapid progress in the field will be possible.

REFERENCES

Bach, E. (1986). Natural language metaphysics. In R.B. Marcus, G.J.W. Dorn, & P. Weingartner (Eds.), *Logic, methodology and philosophy of science VII* (pp. 573–596). Amsterdam: North-Holland.

Billig, M. (1987). *Arguing and thinking. A rhetorical approach to social psychology.* Cambridge UK: Cambridge University Press.

Bruner, J.S. (1973). *Beyond the information given.* New York: Norton.

Burtt, E.A. (1932). *The metaphysical foundations of modern physical science.* Garden City, NY: Doubleday.

Cole, M., & Bruner, J. (1971). Cultural differences and inferences about psychological processes. *American Psychologist, 26*(10), 867–876.

Cox, B.D., Valsiner, J., & Ornstein, P.A. (1987, April). *Children's generalization of strategies: An historical perspective on transfer.* Paper presented at the meetings of the society for Research in Child Development, Baltimore.

Elliott, R., & James, E. (1989). Varieties of client experience in psychotherapy: An analysis of the literature. *Clinical Psychology Review, 9,* 443–467.

Fiedler, P., & Rogge, K.E. (1989). Zur Prozessuntersuchung psychotherapeutischer Episoden (Process-research on psychotherapeutic episodes). *Zeitschrift für Klinische Psychologie, 18*(1), 45–54.

Grawe, K., Siegfried, J., Bernauer, F., Donati, R., & Louis, C. (1987). Qualitatsanalyse der Psychotherapieforschung. Eine empirische Untersuchung [Qualitative analysis of psychotherapy research. An empirical study]. *Schweizerische Zeitschrift für Psychologie, 46*(3/4), 259–266.

Greenberg, L.S., & Pinsof, W. (1986). *The psychotherapeutic process: A research handbook.* New York: Guilford Press.

Harré, R. (1980). *Social being: A theory for social psychology.* Savage, MD: Littlefield, Adams.

Harré, R., & Secord, P.F. (1972). *The explanation of social behaviour.* Oxford, UK: Basil Blackwell.

Homans, G.C. (1961). *Social behavior: Its elementary forms.* New York: Harcourt, Brace.

Kazdin, A.E. (1986). Research designs and methodology. In S.L. Garfield & A.E. Bergin (Eds.), *Handbook of psychotherapy and behavior change* (3rd ed., pp. 23–68). New York: Wiley.

Kroger, R. (1982). Explorations in ethogeny. *American Psychologist, 37*(7), 810–820.

Labov, W., & Fanshel, D. (1977). *Therapeutic discourse. Psychotherapy as conversation.* New York: Academic Press.

Lambert, M.J. (1989). The individual therapist's contribution to psychotherapy process and outcome. *Clinical Psychology Review, 9,* 469–485.

Lenneberg, E.H., & Roberts, J.M. (1956). The language of experience: a study in methodology. *International Journal of American Living, Suppl. 22* (memoir 13).

Orlinsky, D.E. (1989). Researcher's images of psychotherapy: Their origins and influence on research. *Clinical Psychology Review, 9,* 413–441.

Orlinsky, D.E., Grawe, K., & Parles, B.K. (1994). Process and outcome in psychotherapy—noch einmal. In A.E. Berjin & S.L. Garfield (Eds.), *Handbook of psychotherapy and behavior change* (pp. 270–376). New York: Wiley.

Orlinsky, D.E., & Howard, K.I. (1986). Process and outcome in psychotherapy. In S.L. Garfield & A.E. Bergin (Eds.), *Handbook of psychotherapy and behavior change* (3rd ed., pp. 311–381). New York: Wiley.

Orlinsky, D.E., & Howard, K.I. (1987). A generic model of psychotherapy. *Journal of Integrative and Eclectic Psychotherapy, 6*(1), 6–27.

Russell, R.L. (1989). Language and psychotherapy. *Clinical Psychology Review, 9,* 505–519.

Scheflen, A.E. (1973). *Communicational structure: Analysis of a psychotherapy transaction.* Bloomington: Indiana University Press.

Shotter, J. (1987, January). *Rhetoric as a model for psychology.* British Psychological Society Conference on the Future of Psychology: Session II: Alternative models for Psychology.

Siegfried, J. (in preparation a). *Traditional Indo-Tibetan psychology and its possible contribution to psychotherapy research.*

Siegfried, J. (in preparation b). *Basic issues on theory and treatment of emotional problems. An interdisciplinary and cross-cultural empirical study.*

Smedslund, J. (1972). *Becoming a psychologist.* Oslo: Universitetsforlaget.

Smedslund, J. (1986). the explication of psychological common sense: Implications for the science of psychology. In R.B. Marcus, G.J.W. Dorn, & P. Weingartner (Eds.), *Logic, methodology and philosophy of science VII* (pp. 481–494). Amsterdam: North-Holland.

Smedslund, J. (1988). *Psycho-logic.* New York: Springer.

Stein, D.M., & Lambert, M.J. (1984). On the relationship between therapist experience and psychotherapy outcome. *Clinical Psychology Review, 4,* 1–16.

Stiles, W.B., & Shapiro, D.A. (1989). Abuse of the drug metaphor in psychotherapy process-outcome research. *Clinical Psychology Review, 9,* 521–543.

Torretti, R. (1986). Conceptual reform in scientific revolutions. In R.B. Marcus, G.J.W. Dorn, & P. Weingartner (Eds.), *Logic, methodology and philosophy of science VII* (pp. 413–431). Amsterdam: North-Holland.

Truax, C.B., Wargo, D.G., Frank, J.D., Imber, S.D., Battle, C.C., Hoehn-Saric, R., Nash, E.H., & Stone, A.R. (1966). Therapist empathy, genuineness, and warmth and patient therapeutic outcome. *Journal of Consulting Psychology, 30,* 395–401.

Valsiner, J. (1987). *Culture and the development of children's action.* New York: John Wiley & Sons.

Wiener, M., Budney, S., Wood, L., & Russell, R.L. (1989). Nonverbal events in psychotherapy. *Clinical Psychology Review, 9,* 487–504.

PART IV

Prospective Conceptual Orientations

CHAPTER 10

Clever Hans Revisited: The Effects of Contextual Variability on Natural-Context Learning

Toni Goodyear

University of North Carolina at Chapel Hill

The famous case of Der Kluge Hans, the remarkable stallion whose performances convinced many turn-of-the-century Europeans that he could read, tell time, select colors, perform arithmetic, and answer questions on all manner of subjects, has occupied a unique berth in the history of psychological method and theory. Methodologically, the incident has been used to demonstrate the potency of subtle influences on a subject's behavior by the experimenter (Rosenthal, 1964). Theoretically, the case of Clever Hans has been claimed as strong evidence for the supremacy of S-R principles over alternative theories of animal cognition, problem solving, and intelligence (Pfungst, 1911). Initial inclinations to minimize the horse's amazing capabilities have over time given way to a legacy that essentially bears the form of a left-handed compliment: though Hans did not "think"—that is, he merely responded to subtle signals from his trainer—how marvelous indeed were his powers of observation!

As is frequently the case in science, the data *and* the prevailing interpretation, including the appended doff of the hat, stand as a complete package, a fait accompli. However, as is also frequently the case, a reanalysis of the data may suggest a theoretical framework somewhat at odds with the legend. The question arises: Does the Hans data really depict an animal providing rote response to his teacher's cues, or does it depict a highly active, adaptive organism led by the demands of learning in a natural context into behavior patterns reflective of higher order cognition? Obviously it is the purpose of this chapter to argue for the latter. Not only has evidence of the horse's considerable flexibility been underemphasized, but even more unfortunately the usefulness of the case as a clue to principles of learning under conditions of natural complexity has virtually gone unexplored.

In general, natural-context training situations (NCTS), such as the one constructed by Hans's dedicated and emotional trainer Wilhelm von Osten, have not found a firm niche in scientific psychology, though they constitute an immensely rich plain on which to study learning and cognition in real life. In that for humans, child development occurs within socially and culturally constrained "training situations," a study of the principles at work in semistructured environs can yield great theoretical reward (see Valsiner, 1987). What the case of Clever Hans and the case of a child being taught, for example, mealtime behaviors have in common is that they are both ecologically valid examples of the consistencies, changes, and challenges faced by an organism learning particular skills in natural settings over time. Both learn by social instruction embedded in a contextual complexity which, as many have noted (e.g., Galef, 1984; Timberlake, 1984) is a qualitatively different phenomenon from learning in the laboratory. In particular, the effect of instructional inconsistency in the NCTS on the developing organism is a critical question that requires accurate description in the field. Characterizing the relationship between consistency and inconsistency in natural contexts, and discovering the basic structure of learning within this framework, remains one of the great challenges for the study of learning.

THE NATURAL-CONTEXT TRAINING SITUATION (NCTS)

One of the immediately observable features of behavior in natural contexts is its flexibility. To be *flexible* in dictionary terminology is to be "adjustable to change; capable of modification", or, more metaphorically, "able to bend without breaking." It is this very characteristic of real-world behavior that initially spurred the flight to the laboratory, where, it was believed, basic principles could be discovered in less complicated circumstance. In terms of learning and the development of the mind, flexibility implies an ability to deal more effectively with new situations and problems, hence an increased ability to learn from the environment in active interaction with events. The core of Piaget's (1970, 1985) notions of assimilation and accommodation captures this flavor. Organisms give and take, bring to and distort, select and fail to select. In so doing, meaning is given to the term *experience*.

Behavioral flexibility has been studied in learning laboratories under the heading of *context effects*. The concept has been labeled *garbage can terminology* (Smith, Glenberg, & Bjork, 1978) for the variations in behavior obtained by altering any one of the many possible elements of context in which laboratory subjects may be placed. Though the findings demonstrate that changes in context affect behavior, the implication is that context exerts a controlling force on an organism still essentially seen as passively responding. Thus, the emphasis is on the inflexibility or helplessness of the organism, and *adaptability* is seen as a predetermined set of behavioral possibilities.

This view is fundamentally different from the concept of learning which emerges from studies that have focused on the developmental effects of complexity, diversity, and inconstancy per se. The classic enrichment paradigms, for example (Rosenzweig, Krech, Bennett, & Diamond, 1962), demonstrate that organisms are developmentally primed for maximum potential by contextual diversity and complexity. Rats provided with diverse and complex environs performed better in learning tasks, and had significant alterations in brain weight and chemistry, compared to rats who received less environmental opportunity. Fox (1975) likewise describes a program developed by the U.S. Army Veterinarian Corps to develop "super dogs" by providing "environmental enrichment coupled with liberal socialization with many different handlers" (p. 43). The emphasis in both cases was on maximizing individual potential by providing diversity. Other work, with brain-altered rats, has raised the possibility that different neurological networks may be primed by environmental consistency and inconsistency.

It is an easy move from such findings to the specific hypothesis that the mix of behavioral consistency/inconsistency seen in organisms in natural contexts is a developmental result of the natural consistency and inconsistency that characterize development in the real world. To begin to test the hypothesis, it is necessary to describe both the nature of inconsistency faced by the organism and the process by which the organism copes with this inconsistency. The present discussion focuses on the NCTS in the sense of taking a first step on this long road. Since the case of Clever Hans is perhaps the NCTS best known to psychology, his performance can serve as a framework in which to approach the question. What can be said about the structure of Hans's behavior, and of the experience leading to that behavior, that might shed light on the developmental forces at work in a natural-context training situation?

Clever Hans: Flexibility of Response

The story began in 1904 when Hans and his trainer, von Osten, a retired school teacher, created a stir with the horse's foot-tapping responses to complex arithmetical questioning. "How much is 2/5 plus 1/2?" brought two series of taps, first the numerator (9), then the denominator (10). Hans could select colors, read German, spell words, and indicate yes/no or particular directions; he knew the value of coins and carried the calendar in his head: "If the eighth day of the month comes on Tuesday, what is the date for the following Friday?" In order for Hans to spell, letters were translated to numerical values. Yes or no questions were answered by head movements, as were questions requiring Hans to indicate a particular direction. To select colors, Hans moved to a line of colored banners and physically removed the appropriate one. The horse was widely displayed and was credited with an intelligence equal to that of a 13–14-year-old human child.

Psychologist Oskar Pfungst's 1911 analysis of Han's abilities dispelled any such notions. For Pfungst, the horse merely performed rote responses to particular cues from its trainers and other examiners (the word *trainer* here is used loosely; Pfungst emphasizes that, since Hans learned something other than that which von Osten intended to teach, the word *training* is suspect). Hans did not "know" the correct answers to mathematical and other questions, Pfungst contended. He simply watched for a particular cue, often straining to view the questioner from a familiar angle, and provided a response that humans then interpreted as correct. Pfungst's report was taken as strong substantiation of the basic premise of binary association between stimulus and response. His myth-breaking conclusions are sufficiently well known to appear in many introductory psychology texts, frequently as a warning against the fallacy of cognitive interpretations of behavior. His in-depth writings on the case, however, are less widely discussed. The following is based on his original report.

When asked to investigate the Hans phenomenon, Pfungst first determined that some sort of experimenter cues were the cause of the horse's responses. When the questioner knew the answer to a question, Hans could get it right; when the questioner was without knowledge, so was Hans. Pfungst then determined that auditory cues were not significant. Hans made no distinguishable ear movements, and questions would be answered correctly even if the horse's ears were plugged. Moreover, questions could be asked "silently" and Hans would respond properly. That visual cues were critical was first determined by placing the questioner out of sight; Hans was then unable to answer correctly and would strain to see the questioner. By carefully observing von Osten, Pfungst determined that extremely minute involuntary movements were the cues to which Hans responded:

> As soon as the experimenter had given a problem to the horse, he involuntarily bent his head and trunk slightly forward and the horse would then put the right foot forward and begin to tap, without, however, returning it each time to its original position. As soon as the desired number of taps was given, the questioner would make a slight upward jerk of the head. Thereupon the horse would immediately swing his foot in a wide circle, bringing it back to its original position. (Pfungst, 1911, p. 47)

Upward movements in general were the signs to stop tapping. Raising the head was most effective, but so were raising an arm, an elbow, an object, and, most amazingly, a raising of the eyebrows or even a dilation of the nostrils.

Pfungst repeatedly emphasized the "extreme minuteness" of the movements, which were all the more difficult to read because of their inclusion in a busy complex of activity by the "vivacious" von Osten. He described the cues as "often quite imperceptible," saying, "All other persons who have seen me work with the horse, but who were not familiar with the nature of these movements, never perceived them, no matter how closely they observed me" (Pfungst, 1911, p. 50).

Though this contention has led some to question the validity of the findings (Sebeok & Rosenthal, 1981), the Hans phenomena has been taken as a demonstration that the chief process of animal learning is simple cue–response linkage. Pfungst emphasized that conclusion:

> The whole thing may be explained satisfactorily by means of a process of simple association established between the signs observed in the master and certain reactions on the part of the horse. (p. 185)
>
> Han's accomplishments are founded first upon a one-sided development of the power of perceiving the slightest movements of the questioner, secondly upon the intense and continued, but equally one-sided power of attention, and lastly upon a rather limited memory, by means of which the animal is able to associate perceptions of movement with a small number of movements of its own which have become thoroughly habituated. (p. 240)

In reality, Hans's performance was neither "thoroughly habituated" nor a matter of "simple association." The horse's responses were not only more complex than the author's conclusions imply, but his behavioral schemes were of his own devising. In the task of color selection, for example, Hans would start out for the line of colored banners. If he approached one that was incorrect, the trainer would yell "Look out" or "See there." In response to these cues, Hans would move on to other banners in a systematic way. First, he would continue moving along the line of banners as long as the vocalizations continued. Pfungst explains the rest of the process:

> If he was picking up, or about to pick up, a cloth when the exclamation was made, he would go on to the next; but if, at the time he was on his way to a certain cloth, he would change his direction in response to the call. If he stood before one of the pieces at the time, but had not lowered his head, he would pass on to the next. In all this he would adhere to a certain routine of procedure. If he was approaching a series from the right, then a call would cause him to turn to the left, if he was coming from the left, he would turn to the right. (p. 84)

In humans, such a scheme could reasonably be lauded as an intelligent problem-solving strategy, including the logical exclusion of alternatives.

The fallacy of rote response is primarily based in Pfungst's division of Hans's behavior into two categories: correct responses, and "errors." The "errors" are evidence of Hans's development of active, adaptive response strategies in a complex and varying context which Pfungst characterizes as a "chaos of visual impressions" and a "babel of word-sounds" (p. 219). A frequently seen "error" was Hans's "respond with repertoire" strategy. For yes/no questions or questions of direction, Hans would be required to nod or shake his head. Directional cues from the experimenter provided him with information as to which way to move his head: If the experimenter raised his head slightly, Hans would nod. He would stop when the head was lowered. If the questioner stood perfectly still and asked the question, Hans would "execute all sorts of head movements without rhyme or reason. . . . It was evident that he noted that a head movement of some kind was expected of him, but did not know the particular one that was wanted" (Pfungst, 1911, p. 75).

Thus the horse responded with a full "bag of tricks" in a manner more compatible with the notion of "hypothesis testing" (Krechevsky, 1932) than rote stimulus–response conditioning. In addition, he displayed, by Pfungst's admission, behavior that was better described by postulating knowledge of a general concept, e.g., head movement, into which various behaviors could fit.

The ability to respond-with-repertoire was evidenced in other instances that did not play a critical part in Pfungst's eventual conclusions. As mentioned, Hans was able to respond to questions asked "silently" (since only involuntary movements served as cues). On some occasions, however, the questioner failed to make the appropriate involuntary motions. Pfungst notes such an instance:

> The old gentleman (von Osten) commissioned Hans, presumably without uttering a word, to step backward to the left. Hans thereupon responded by giving his entire repertoire as follows: He moved his head to the right, then to the left. Then he leaped forward and repeated the same movement of the head. Hereupon he stepped backward and signified a "yes" by a movement of the head. He then lowered his head and made two leaps forward. After this performance, Mr. von Osten repeated the same command aloud and in every case Hans responded properly. Again the silent command was given and again the horse responded with the series of reactions described above. (pp. 96–97)

Pfungst uses the example to show that sometimes the muscle tensions required for Hans to read the cues could only be obtained during overt vocalization of command. But it also shows that Hans responded with habitual or reliable performance only if the task environment was itself stable—i.e., provided familiar information. If it was not, Hans *tried something else*. This particular coping strategy had apparently lent considerably to Hans's legendary status prior to Pfungst's arrival, for it was generally held that "whenever anyone asked a question without himself knowing the response, Hans would indulge in all sorts of sport at the questioner's expense" (p. 24).

Not only was cue delivery unreliable, but it was contextually diverse. At least 40 different people successfully questioned the horse. Body type and location relative to the horse would vary, as would the intensity of the critical signals. Moreover, Hans learned to cope with inconsistency in mannerisms, that is, the contextual package in which key movements occurred. Pfungst notes the extreme difficulty of cue detection, "not only on account of their extreme minuteness but also because that very vivacious gentleman (von Osten) made sundry accompanying movements and was constantly moving back and forth" (p. 48). Von Osten was explosive in his displeasure if Hans did not correctly respond, and was lavish in his praise and tidbits if correct response occurred. The combination of strongly motivating circumstances and contextual complexity led to Hans's construction of his own set of response rules. For example, when asked to calculate "10 + 2", Hans would begin tapping at the slight forward bend of the questioner's frame, and would cease tapping at the slight upward motion delivered when the correct number had been reached. When these cues were not clearly given or perceived, Hans would perform according to the following set of rules, noted by Pfungst:

• if the examiner is not totally upright or stoops forward a little once again, give an extra tap with the left foot
• if the examiner is still inclined forward, start tapping again
• if the examiner's head jerks upward, give a tap with the left foot, then go back to tapping with the right until the posture is erect
• if the examiner is standing to the left, tap exclusively with the left foot
• increase the rate of tapping according to the degree of forward inclination of the examiner's head or body
• if the examiner stands out of sight, manipulate your position until he is in view
• ignore head movements on a horizontal plane, or an upward jerks circuitous in form.

Han's ability to adjust his response on the basis of contextual configuration was both subtle and remarkable. Pfungst admitted that he was for some time "in a quandry" (p. 75) because the signals to stop nodding and to begin foot tapping were the same. Hans resolved the issue by combining elements of context:

> Further experiments showed that Hans responded with a nod of the head whenever the questioner, while bending forward, chanced to stand in front of, or to the side of the horse's head, but that he would begin to tap in response to the same signal as soon as the experimenter stood further back. (Pfungst, 1911, p. 75)

Signs for tapping were given after the question; signs for nodding were given while the question was being asked. Hand movements were not effective during questioning sessions yet, Hans responded to the slightest hand movements while running free around the courtyard or if engaged in the color selection task.

In summary, the Hans data suggest an organism capable of complex cognitive processing: hypothesis testing by repertorial response when confronted with an uncertain cue, the ability to combine various elements of context to infer the appropriate meaning of a cue, and the ability to derive a general concept. Hans utilized rules, strategies and systems of his own to cope with the chaotic contexts in which cues were embedded. Consistent response occurred with consistent context—*but inconsistency did not leave him helpless and unresponsive*. Instead, he responded with the ultimate behavior bestowed by evolution: thinking. How far this is from Pfungst's widely cited conclusion: "He was rather like a machine that must be started and kept going by a certain amount of fuel (in the form of bread and carrots)" (Pfungst, 1911, p. 202)

The Process of Learning in an NCTS

How did Hans come to his highly adaptive systems of response? Here Pfungst could only work backwards and surmise from Hans's current performance and from reports von Osten gave him of the training process. Von Osten had spent four years training the horse on a daily basis. Pfungst concluded that conditions were "unusually favorable" for learning these subtle cues, in that von Osten's movements were probably gross initially but became more subtle over time as his pupil demonstrated an ability for proper response. An example is the foot-tapping task. At first, von Osten would pronounce the number three and place three wooden pins on the ground in front of Hans. He would then physically take the horse's leg and move the foot up and down three times. This process would require that he bend forward while the foot movement occurred and then straighten up at its conclusion. Subsequently, the slightest bodily inclination became associated with action, and upward motion with the cessation of action.

What Pfungst did not ask, and therefore could not answer, is what could account for the cognitive sophistication in Hans's later performance? It is suggested here that the combination of consistency and diversity that characterizes an NCTS forces the successful organism to employ all of the cognitive forces witnessed in Hans. If this is correct, it should be possible to make visible the steps by which this occurs by examining the process of learning as it unfolds in a new natural-context training situation.

A NEW NCTS

The situation chosen was the home training of a domestic dog by a family of three—the father, G., a daughter, P., age 13, and a son, S., age 12. The occurrence of multiple owners is common in more than 90% of American dog–owner households. Consistent with behavioral theory, professional advice to dog owners emphasizes consistency as the prime requirement in training their animals.

The American Kennel Club (1985) offers the following advice: "The key words are confidence and consistency ... vacillation is the deadliest enemy of good training" (p. 728). The same general warning pervades manuals aimed at teaching children how to train their pets: "Most puppies have to be shown a new skill a number of times *in exactly the same way each time*" (Pinkwater & Pinkwater, 1977, p. 161; emphasis in original). "The most important part of training is to be consistent. That means to always do a thing the same way" (Wolters, 1978, p. 20).

Despite such advice it is inconsistency that is seen to best characterize pet training in American families. McIntire (1968), a behaviorist trained in the operant learning laboratory, expressed his despair over this reality:

> The most crucial characteristic that the psychologist must emphasize to the would-be trainer is the consistent use of the consequences described in these (operant) procedures .... Unfortunately, the precise control of the *trainer* in the uncontrolled learning situation of the American home has yet to be precisely developed. (pp. 830–831)

The subject in the current study was a registered tri-color, rough-haired Collie named Finnegan Star. Finnegan was purchased by the family from a local breeder and brought home at the age of 7 weeks. None of the family had exposure to formal dog-training techniques; however, Finnegan was their third dog, and predispositions about training derived from previous experience. The family's reported goal was to teach the dog certain behaviors that would make it liveable in the family structure, in particular to "sit", "stay," and "come."

Training sessions were held approximately weekly by each family member from the dog's homecoming at 7 weeks through 16 weeks of age, which incorporates the prime socialization period for the domestic dog (Scott & Fuller, 1965). Each training session was videotaped, and tapes were later subjected to frame-by-frame analysis. The trainers were prompted by the experimenter to begin a training session, but were left totally to their own devices as to how to accomplish their goals. The endpoint of a session was determined by the trainer. Each trainer worked with the dog privately.

By the end of the 9-week training period, the family regarded the dog as having been successfully trained to sit, stay, and come. Figures 10.1 and 10.2 show the learning curves for each task. All three tasks were taught concurrently, though "sit" was the logical starting point. All three trainers used the same global strategy: first have the dog sit, then back away while ordering the dog to "stay," then order the dog to "come."

Tapes were analyzed in an attempt to characterize (a) the extent of consistency/inconsistency of cues, assumptions, and strategies presented to the dog; and (b) the structure of the learning process as the dog advanced from untrained to trained state. The tape sample included approximately 200 instances each of

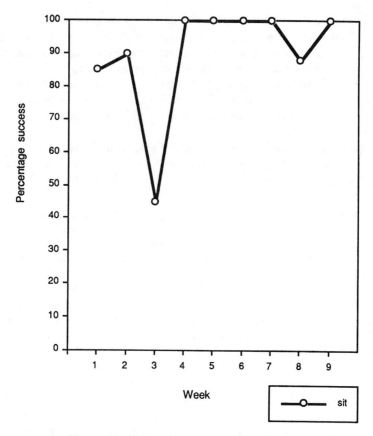

Figure 10.1.   Compliance with "sit" command.

"stay" and "come" commands, and more than 140 instances of "sit." Analysis focused on the four means of communication utilized by the trainers: physical manipulation, gestures, body postures, and vocalizations. Intonations were not analyzed, though it was noted that "come" commands were consistently higher pitched (more suggestive of invitation) than sit and stay commands, which tended to be firm, punctuated, and low pitched.

Characterizing Consistency and Inconsistency in the Task Environment

Strategies and assumptions of the trainers. The three trainers differed in their assumptions about their role and their strategies for obtaining compliance, and these differences were reflected in the structures of the sessions that confronted the dog across trainers.

For P., the task was to learn "what stands for what" in the dog's mind, and then to adjust her behavior accordingly. As she saw it, her job was to learn the

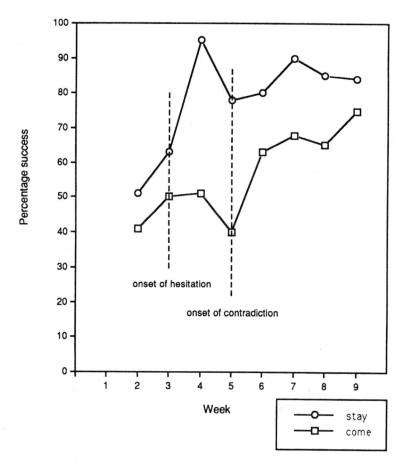

Figure 10.2. Performance in "stay" and "come" tasks.

dog's interpretations of her actions and then capitalize on them. This co-dependent structure of the learning process was apparent in numerous transactions in which P.'s next move was determined by the trainee rather than the trainer (discussed fully in a later section). Moreover, P's interest in knowing the dog's mind led to her deliberate use of contradictory cues to see if she could clearly isolate what he was selecting from her own complex set of cues. This decision by P. shed much light on the relationship between environmental demand and the development of cognitive tools.

For S., success in training was not seen to be critical. The youngest trainer, he felt it was more important to be kind than successful. S. therefore used coercion tactics to bring about compliance; for example, he would entice the dog to come by sending playful signals rather than orders. Training was comparatively disorganized.

The adult trainer, G., believed that immediate and absolute obedience was necessary for the well-being of both the family and the dog. Firmness, and a demonstration of superior physical strength, were felt to be critical during the learning period. G.'s philosophy significantly impacted on his training strategy. He used physical manipulation in the early stages (including light spanking) and deliberately moved to increasingly slight and subtle signals, forcing the dog to rivet attention on his actions. G. also kept the dog in a stay position prior to release for much longer than either of the youngsters, during which time the animal would remain tensely focused on the trainer. The progression parallels Pfungst's conjecture of how Hans came to appreciate minute signals, and will be discussed further below.

Diversity of cues. For training to succeed, trainers had to communicate two general concepts: (a) that a certain response was expected (i.e., compliance was necessary), and (b) that different responses were expected on different occasions (i.e., *when* one stays and when one comes must be distinguished). Tools for communicating these were the physical and vocal cues provided by the trainers. From Finnegan's point of view, the diversity of cues was considerable. Vocalizations and postural or gestural cues were issued in approximately 100 different combinations during the training period, with new combinations appearing even in the 9th week. The overwhelming majority of these "cue configurations" were unique to one trainer. Only eight combinations were used by all three trainers.

Five different gestures (ground slap, body slap, handclap, beckon, point down) represented the majority of gestural activity and eight different body postures were used (sit, stand, crouch, kneel, prone, waistbend, all fours, kneebend). Figure 10.3 shows the gestural/postural preferences across trainers.

When working with S., Finnegan was likely to encounter a sitting position with ground and body slap cues; with P., the dog frequently faced a trainer, who beckoned him from a crouching position; with G., the combination of waistbend and downward point of the finger was common. Figure 10.4 provides a visual display of the gestural world as seen from the animal's perspective over the 9 weeks of training. It attempts to characterize the complexity with which an organism learning in an NCTS must deal. No cue consistently dominates, nor is there great consistency across weeks. Table 10.1 takes another view: over the 9 weeks there is virtually no difference in the single gestures that result in the dog coming and not coming (staying). Rather, coming or staying resulted from elements of context in configuration rather than isolated components of the training situation.

Neither did the dog's response hinge on vocalizations; he would respond correctly to silent gestures and incorrectly to "correct" vocalizations in wrong contexts. Once contradictory cues began to be deliberately sent by P. in Week 5 of training, vocalizations seemed to increase in importance as more aspects of context had to be considered in order to resolve the communication dilemma (dis-

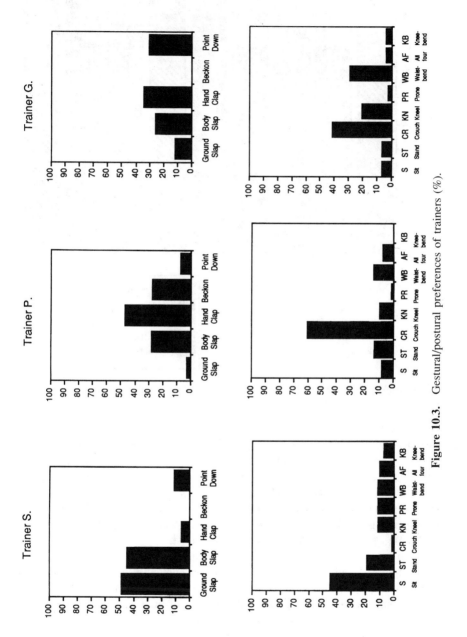

Figure 10.3. Gestural/postural preferences of trainers (%).

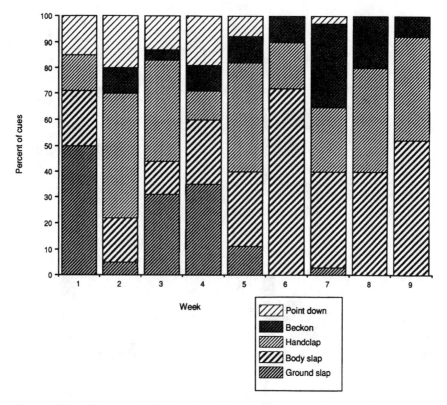

Figure 10.4. The gestural display from the animal's perspective over the course of training.

cussed later). Vocalizations in configuration—for example, the combination of crouch, handclap, and high-pitched "come here"—seemed to strengthen the dog's tendency to come. Indeed, the trainers resorted to these strong "exaggerated" cue combinations in difficult moments. If the dog's tendency was to respond to a noisy handclap, a crouching movement, or a high-pitched vocalization, using these in combination seemed to have the cumulative effect of increasing the likelihood that the dog would come.

In no case could cue combinations be identified that reliably distinguished between correct and incorrect response. Rather, context effects, as will be seen in the qualitative analysis of weekly responses, were vertical as well as horizontal: components were embedded in a context of both past sessions and past occurrences in the current session.

Diversity of consequences. All three trainers used praise and petting to express approval, albeit inconsistently. All three used shouting and a loud "no!" to express disapproval. Rump slaps were infrequent in all cases, but were used more often

**Table 10.1.   Overall Response
to Repeated Gestural Cues**

Component	Dog Comes (N)	Dog Stays (N)
Ground slap	16	17
Body slap	37	30
Hand clap	36	33
Beckon	16	17
Point down	11	10

by G. The primary negative response was to put the dog back in place to do the task again. The primary positive outcome was also to put the dog back in place to do the task again. The inconsistent nature of consequences from the dog's perspective resulted from the fact that praise and punishment were variable within and across training sessions. In general, three courses of action occurred:

- praise, then put the dog back in place
- no praise, then put the dog back in place
- verbal admonishment, then put the dog back

Use of the first two varied randomly in that they would occur when the dog had performed correctly and when he had performed incorrectly. In the case of praise, the dog may have come on the wrong cue but still be praised for coming per se. He would then be required to learn the proper cue, or unlearn the wrong one. Incorrect performance would sometimes result in verbal admonishment and sometimes in merely being returned to place with no praise (which, as stated, was also used then performance had been correct). Overall, no reliable relationship between consequence and subsequent response could be discovered.

In sum, variability in an NCTS may be characterized as a glass which is both half full and half empty. In the current case, the actual number of cues and consequences used during training could be said to be quite small compared to the number theoretically conceivable but large compared to the scenario of consistency implied by learning theories. Natural constraints of the task, perceptions of the subject's capabilities and basic assumptions about effective communication narrowed the field from the outset. But within that narrower world much variation occurs. How then does a learner in the real world learn? A qualitative analysis of the structure of Finnegan's learning process was undertaken to explore the question further.

The Learning Process

Analysis of the process by which Finnegan moved from untrained to trained state was accomplished by studying the interactive sequences of training activity in chronological order. The complete corpus of what occurred is presented in Tables 10.2 to 10.10, which provide the evidential record for the following discussion.

It will be remembered that the trainers chose the following training scenario: Get the dog into a sitting position and have him stay in that position until instructed to come. As described earlier, teaching the dog to sit on command was accomplished relatively easily with one or two consistent cues linked to physical manipulation. The "stay versus come" component of the training was the more sophisticated and complex task facing the dog, and the discussion after Week 1 focuses on this aspect.

WEEK 1: ESTABLISHING THE COMMUNICATIVE FRAME

Five major elements used in these early encounters served as building blocks for training throughout the nine weeks. In communicating with the dog, trainers adopted a position low to the ground or off-vertical (kneeling, crouching, sitting, etc.) when wanting to summon him; slapping was used (ground slap in teaching "sit"; body slap or handclap was used for "come"), as was a downward point of the index finger, and vocalizations ("come here" or "sit", "No!", the dog's name, a whistle). Week 1 focused primarily on establishing communication and secondarily on getting the dog to sit.

The behaviors selected by the trainers were clearly successful in engaging the dog in the communicative interaction, which is necessarily prerequisite to training. The question occurs: Why were these initial attempts successful at establishing communication at all? The choices of the trainers clearly exploited natural predispositions of the domestic dog. Slapping and clapping were effective in two ways: (a) The Collie exhibits a natural interest in hand movements; Finnegan repeatedly followed hand gestures visually and would come to the trainer for the purpose of playfully "attacking" the moving hand. The breed dis-

Table 10.2.   Sequence of Trainers' Behaviors and Their Outcomes: Week 1

Trainer (S.)	sit/ground slap/"come here" → dog doesn't come
Trainer (G.)	crouch/clap/"come here" → dog comes
	crouch/clap/"come here" → dog tries to come but stopped by stairs
	kneel/ground slap/"come here" → dog attends to hand
	kneel/slap ground/whistle/call → dog comes
	petting and praise
Trainer (S.)	sit/ground slap/"come here" → dog moves toward hand
	sit/ground slap/"come here" → dog orients to hand
	sit/ground slap/"come here" → dog ignores
	sit/ground slap/"come here" → dog lunges at hand
Trainer (P.)	sit/"come here" → dog orients but doesn't come
	sit/ground slap/"come here" → dog doesn't come
	sit/point down/"come here" → dog doesn't come

plays a considerable amount of natural paw usage, and this may have been a contributing factor. For instance, the raised paw is used in situations requiring help. In the first week, Finnegan attempted unsuccessfully to negotiate a deep step and found himself stranded between the two dangerous alternatives of trying to go up or trying to go down. He engaged the trainer in eye contact and raised his paw. (b) Noise attracts the dog's attention. In this sense, slaps and claps provided a compound stimulus. The low-to-ground position was also naturally attractive. The dog's own natural invitation to play is a crouch position, low to the ground, with front paws extended. Descent is thus an invitation.

Another critical factor in establishing communication was the natural social proclivities of the domestic dog. As Scott and Fuller (1965) have noted, social investigation of handlers, trainers, etc., including attempts to engage humans in play, peaks at about 7 weeks, the time of Finnegan's homecoming. The prime socialization period (7–16 weeks) is also a time for formation of dominance relationships. The current investigation was deliberately chosen to span these 9 weeks.

The selection of training behaviors in Week 1 clearly showed that predispositions on the part of the subject and the trainers worked together to constitute the first rung of the learning process. Efforts to train the sit task were brief in this first session and consisted of the trainers' selection of ways to convey the meaning of the word *sit*. G. placed an exclusive emphasis on physically manipulating the dog into a sitting position while repeating the word *sit,* a device he used through Week 4. The children adopted a downward-pointed finger held over the dog's head. The use of this device was initially puzzling, since the finger was held slightly out of the dog's visual field. Employing it in this fashion, however, led to the following sequence of events: in order to investigate the finger (consistent with the natural attention focused on hand movements), the dog was forced to look up; because of the trainers' positioning of the finger over the dog's head, Finnegan was automatically forced into a sitting position to see it. It seems fair to say that the critical factor in training here was the accommodation by the children to the realities presented by the dog.

WEEK 2: LEARNING THE BASIC OUTLINE OF THE GAME

In the first attempt to summon Finnegan from a sitting position, trainer P. began to descend to a crouch, preparatory to calling the dog. For Finnegan this was an invitation; he came on the descent. P. saw him coming and quickly issued her cue of choice—she clapped her hands, beckoned, and said, "Come here"—and then praised him for coming to her. Hence P. spontaneously began to shape the task by accommodating the dog's predispositions.

She then *returned him to a sitting position.* She moved away using the word *stay.* She descended to a crouch, beckoned and clapped, inviting him to come.

Table 10.3. Sequence of Trainers' Behaviors and Their Outcomes: Week 2

Trainer (P.)	a) descends/no words → dog comes on descent trainer accommodates/clap/"come here" petting and praise put back
	b) descends/beckon/clap → dog doesn't come clap/wide beckon/smile/lilting "come here" → dog comes petting and praise put back
	c) move back/stay/point at dog descends/"stay"/point → dog comes on descent "No!" put back
	d) descends/"stay"/point → dog comes on descent "stay!" put back
	e) move back/point descends/"stay"/point → dog comes on descent put back
	f) waistbend/clap/"come here" → dog comes petting and praise put back
	g) move back/"stay"/point waistbend/body slap/"come here" → dog comes petting and praise put back
	h) move back/"stay"/point waistbend/point down/"come here" → dog comes petting and praise
Trainer (G.) (outdoors)	i) crouch/"come here" → dog ignores crouch/clap/"come here" → dog ignores crouch/sharp call → dog comes rump slap for not attending put into sitting position close to trainer crouch/point down/"come here"
Trainer (P.)	j) waistbend/point down/"come here" → dog comes
Trainer (G.)	k) kneel (loom)/"stay"/point move back/"stay"/point standoff kneel/clap/"come here" → dog comes *as* hands move together for clap petting and praise
	l) move back/"stay"/point → dog twice tries to escape twice put back with "No!" move back/"stay"/point kneel/clap/"come here" → dog comes as hands come together for clap
Trainer (P.)	m) move back/"stay"/point → dog comes as she reaches 5–6 steps away put back same sequence occurs five times sixth time dog hesitates waistbend/clap/"come here" → dog comes

He did not respond; he sat and watched. Here we see the first instance of a problem central to operant learning: in a complex array of behavior, how does the organism determine which behavior is relevant? The process here suggests that the dog initially possesses an interpretation—a hypothesis—which is subsequently revised with experience. In this case, the dog interpreted the act of being put back to do the task again as meaning "stay there, don't come." This assumption was overcome by means of an *exaggerated* cue delivery: a wide beckoning motion, a big smile, a high lilting "come here," and a good solid clap. The combination is deliberately coercive; not only are activity and noise attractive, but, as Hirsh-Pasek and Treiman (1982) note, the spontaneous use of "doggerel" (the pet equivalent of "motherese") is naturally welcoming and attractive.

Given the exaggerated cue, the dog came to the trainer playfully and was lavishly praised for doing so. From the trainer's perspective, he was being praised for coming on cue rather than on the descent; from Finnegan's perspective, he had generated excitement and approval by *coming per se*. In the next three sequences he continued to come on the descent *despite his being put back* without praise after each occurrence.

The trainer then recognized that descent was the key. Since the dog found it naturally attractive, it detracted from her ability to train him to other cues. She thus *altered her behavior.* On the next three occasions she did not descend to a crouch; she simply bent from the waist (still off-vertical). The dog came again, but this time he was coming appropriately on cue from the trainer's viewpoint—on the clap, the body slap, the downward point. The dog could thus legitimately be praised. The interactive nature of the learning process in a social framework is clearly evidenced by such exchanges; training is in fact a mutual shaping, and it is Trainer P.'s particularly accommodating approach that highlights this in the early weeks of training. The dog's tendency to come on the descent was never "cured"; rather, the trainer simply stopped offering that cue.

With Trainer G., the dog encountered a rump slap for not attending properly, and physical looming linked to the word "stay." In general, Finnegan was repeatedly exposed to G.'s overriding purpose of displaying dominance and emphasizing obedience. G.'s sessions primarily focused on sending the dog the message that control belonged to the trainer. Once the dog was staying in place, G. enforced a period of "standoff" where he and Finnegan simply engaged one another in eye contact. The dog subsequently developed the habit of paying keen attention to the trainer's movements during this procedure, poised with a kind of tension that often resulted in his leaping forward when he felt a cue had been given. A similar mechanism could have led to Clever Hans's attention to the smallest details of a questioner's movements. In both cases motivation to attend was provided by the trainer's insistence on compliance in the form of negative and unpleasant consequences for error or inattention: in the case of G., a spanking or harshly shouted "No!"; in the case of von Osten, different demonstrations of his "explosive displeasure" (Pfungst, 1911).

Focusing on G.'s movements, Finnegan began to anticipate. His focus on hand movements had been reinforced by P.'s earlier use of the handclap. With G., Finnegan started in motion as soon as G. began to bring his hands together for the clap.

The dog's interpretation of the "game" to this point may best be explained as follows: "These humans are trying to get me to play this game in which first I sit and then I go." There is little indication that the question of *which cues* are appropriate has yet occurred. When Finnegan next works with P. he suddenly began to go to her as soon as she had backed a certain distance away from him (with him in a sit/stay position). He did this five times despite his being put back in place each time and repeatedly ordered to "stay" with a finger pointed in his direction. This bout of "mistakes" was never corrected; rather, the trainer waited for a fortuitous pause in his following response and then capitalized on it by bending from the waist, clapping and saying "come here." This particular behavior pattern—coming when the trainer achieves a certain distance—was not in evidence in the first part of this week's session. It was a new development, a new wrinkle of Finnegan's devising, consistent with a general sit/stay-then-go schema combined with a motivation to please. The fact that a *particular cue* was necessary was not yet understood to be critical but rather developed out of this first general understanding of the rules of the game.

WEEK 3: STARTING TO GENERATE RULES; CATEGORIES AND VERTICAL CONTEXT

In the third week of training, two notable events occurred. First, Finnegan showed the first improvement in performance from the trainers' perspective, indicating that a beginning idea that a particular cue was necessary had occurred. Second, the week was marked by the onset of overt *hesitation* on the dog's part. For the first time, Finnegan began to start and stop in place while riveting his gaze on the trainer's movements. The physical hesitation suggests the emergence of a new step in the process: the dog begins to perceive that his task is to figure out the trainer's desires as to *when* he should come or stay. Hesitation suggests that the dog has a sense that sometimes coming is "right" and sometimes it is "wrong." He does not, however, question that the fundamental structure of the game is the same. What can be said about how this change comes about?

At the start of the session, with the dog in a sitting position, P. moved some distance away and paired a descending motion with a handclap. Finnegan came and was praised. The trainer had forgotten her earlier attempts to sidestep the descent response and had used it as part of her cue. The dog was praised for coming and then put back to do it again. It will be remembered that the first instance of being put back in Week 2 was regarded by Finnegan as a signal to

Table 10.4.   Sequence of Trainers' Behaviors and Their Outcomes: Week 3

Trainer (P.)   a)   descends/clap → dog comes
                    petting and praise
                    put back
               b)   move back/"stay"/point
                    waistbend/point down/ "come here" → dog starts/stops
                    waistbend/clap/"come here" → dog starts/stops
                    descends/clap → dog comes
                    petting and praise
                    put back
               c)   move back/"stay"/point
                    waistbend/pint down/"come here" → dog comes
Trainer (S.)   d)   descends/"come here" → dog comes
                    petting and praise
                    sit/"come here" → dog comes
                    sit/body slap/"come here" → dog comes
                    petting and praise
                    slide backwards/no words → dog comes
                    trainer accepts it — petting and praise
                    "sit" → dog leaves — trainer laughs
                    descends/point/"stay" → dog comes
                    dog runs off
                    sit/"come here" (multiple) → dog ignores
                    sit/clap/"come here" (multiple) → dog comes, then runs away
                    sit/ground slap/"come here" (multiple) → no response
                    prone/ground slaps/"come here" → dog comes to play
                    sit/bang ground with bone/"come here" → dog comes
                    sit/ground slap/"come here" → dog doesn't come
                    all fours/"come here" → dog comes
                    sit/clap/"come here" (twice) → dog doesn't come
                    sit/come here gesture/"come here" → dog doesn't come
                    all fours/ground slap/"come here" → dog comes
Trainer (G.)   e)   all fours/ground slap/"come here" → dog attacks hand
                    "No!"
                    put back
               f)   move back on knees/"stay"/point → dog starts/stops then comes
                    "No!"
                    put back
               g)   move back/point/"stay" → dog starts as finger drops
                    "stay!" → dog stops in place
               h)   kneel/body slap/"come here" → dog stays
               i)   clap → dog hesitates
                    encouraged by trainer → dog comes
                    petting and praise
                    put back
               j)   move back/"stay"/point
                    kneel/clap → dog comes without hesitation
Trainer (S.)   k)   sit/random gesture → dog comes
                    put back
               l)   sit/ground slap/"come here" → dog attacks hand
                    put back
               m)   move back/"stay"
                    descends → dog starts/stops
                    sit/clap/"come here" → dog comes
                    petting and praise

stay put. Being put back carried more signaling weight in his case than did praise. In that instance the dog did not move at all, as if being put back indicated that his assumptions about the game itself were in error. This time hesitation occurred; he bobbed forward in place and then waited. Since he was more sure of the game itself, confusion arose. Twice he hesitated when beckoned by the trainer, until she used the strongest cue she knew—again pairing descent with a handclap. Despite the fact that his earlier response to this cue led to his being put back and to his subsequent confusion, Finnegan came without hesitation and was praised. After being put back again, he came without hesitation to the same gestures, the waistbend/point down/ "come here" which just a moment earlier had not worked. He had regained confidence in his own interpretation of the game and praise now overrode being put back; alternatively one could say that "praise and put back" was again seen as part of the game rather than an indication of wrongdoing. Specific cues were not yet an issue, but it is suggested here that this combination of increasing certainty about the general nature of the task forced an alternative explanation for actions that seem to indicate that coming was wrong (for example, being put back without praise, being told "No!" or "stay!" in a loud and harsh force). This was critical for achieving the next plateau—namely, that the real game is knowing *when* to come.

It is with Trainer G. that progress is made toward this end. First, G. said "no" to Finnegan's playful attack on his hand and put the dog back in place. Finnegan then started and stopped as G. moved away, saying, "Stay" and pointing a finger at the dog. He started to come as G.'s hand casually dropped downward from its pointing position and was stopped in place by a loud "stay!" He flatly declined to come to the next cue, but when confronted with the familiar handclap he again hesitated. This time he was encouraged by lilting verbal enticements and a series of small claps. He came and was praised. He next came on the clap without hesitation. Overall, his session with Trainer G. was a further lesson that there is a right time and a wrong time to come. Finnegan's behavior—coming on the pointed finger and G.'s casual hand movement, as well as to claps—suggests that a general category of "hand movements" constituted the dog's first hypothesis about *when* to come. It will be noted that the handclap had most often been used as a strong "reassurance" cue. It would be reasonable to expect Finnegan to begin coming on the handclap if a *particular* cue was now primary. This was not the case. His next interactions, with Trainer S., again revealed a focus on the general category of hand movements rather than a particular gesture. Finnegan came as S. gestured in conversation with the investigator; he playfully attacked S.'s hand when called to come with a ground slap. These were characteristic of his interactions with this trainer and could be thought of only as context-dependent behaviors in the sense that S. rewarded coming under any circumstances. That this explanation is insufficient was seen in the fact that, for the first time with any trainer, Finnegan hesitated on the trainer's *descent*. It was his first "reconsideration" of his original predisposition;

he had focused for the moment on the general category of hand movements as one way of distinguishing a right from wrong cue; this in turn resulted in a decision to stay through the trainer's descent (which was not a hand movement). Finnegan waited and watched S., and then came on the handclap.

The process here may be characterized as an emphasis on some *rule of the moment,* which is repeatedly revised during acquisition. Sometimes the rule is quite specific (e.g., handclap only), as will be seen; sometimes it is general, as in a category of response (e.g., hand movements). This is similar to the kind of categorical response Pfungst noted in connection with Hans' performance. In general, the rule cuts across trainers and is heavily impacted by what has recently proved successful. To this point a specific cue does not have power unilaterally; rather, cues are empowered by the recent *vertical* context (that is, the context of immediate past experience) of which they are a part.

WEEK 4: TOO MANY RULES; ATTENTION TO HORIZONTAL CONTEXT

The dog's compliance with the stay command reached 95% in Week 4. The ability to appropriately come on cue, however, did not significantly improve and hesitation continued. The "come" task, with its highly variable cue configurations, emerged as the most difficult cognitive challenge the dog had to face. As a result, it was the prime candidate for forcing utilization of more sophisticated cognitive skills.

With Trainer S., Finnegan's determination of what constitutes a release cue still focused on hand movements. In those instances of "come" in which the dog's attention had been won and he was in place, waiting for the release cue, there was 100% agreement between S.'s determination of the release cue (all hand movements) and Finnegan's. However, after being released Finnegan repeatedly chose to go somewhere other than to the trainer. This was the first indication that Finnegan was growing tired of the demands of training.

With P. the dog came on the waistbend/"come here" combination and on beckon/"come here" but did not come when "come here" was linked to an erect standing position. This not only suggests that the words alone had little meaning at this point, but that there were other instances when the dog failed to respond to a completely vertical position. All of the other postures typically used were off-vertical.

In this session, P. decided it was time for Finnegan to unlearn coming on descent. Unbeknownst to P., in the prior session with S., Finnegan had stayed in place through the descent motion. However, on P.'s first use of descent, Finnegan came to her. When he was told "no," he ran away. The episode suggests that, during the difficult and confusing learning process, the dog may alternately integrate and separate trainers in devising hypotheses for how to

Table 10.5.   Sequence of Trainers' Behaviors and Their Outcomes: Week 4

Trainer (S.)	a)	dog releases on: all fours/ground slap/"come here"
		sit/ground slap/"come here"
		sit/body slap/"come here"
		as hand moves toward ground for slap
		sit/point down/"come here"
		all fours/"come here"
		prone/ground slap/"come here"
		fails to release on: sit/ground slap/"come here"
		sit/clap/"come here"
		prone/ground slap/"come here"
		crawl/"come here"
		sit/point down/"come here"
		all fours/ground slap/"come here"
		stays on: move back
		descend/"stay"/point
Trainer (P.)	b)	move back/"stay"/point
		waistbend/"come here" → dog comes
	c)	move back/"stay"/point
		stand/"come here" → dog stays
		beckon/"come here" → dog comes
	d)	descend/"stay"/point → dog comes
		"No!"
		put back
	e)	descent/"stay"/point → dog hesitates (headbob)
		body slap/"come here" → dog comes
		petting and praise
	f)	descend/"stay" → dog stays without hesitation
		body slap/no words → dog comes
	g)	descend only/no words → dog hesitates
		beckon/"come here" → dog stays
		body slap/"come here" → dog comes
		put back
	h)	descend only/no words → dog stays
		clap/beckon → dog looks around uncomfortably
		ground slap/"come here" → dog hesitates
		body slap/no words → dog comes
	i)	descend only/no words → dog stays
		kneel/"come here" → dog stays
		kneel/body slap/no words → dog hesitates
		kneel/body slap/"come here" → dog leaps forward
Trainer (S.)	j)	descend/"stay"/point → dog stays
		body slap/no words → dog comes without hesitation
Trainer (G.)	k)	kneel/ground slap/"come here" → dog comes, then runs off and hides
		spanked and retrieved
		put back
		move back/"stay"/point → dog stays
		waistbend/point down/"come here" → dog comes

respond in each condition. Though the process requires sorting out, it ultimately fits well with traditional family dynamics in which the family is simultaneously seen as a single unit and as a collection of unique dyadic relationships.

Finnegan's decision to run away from a strong trainer lends support to the notion that he was very tired of trying to learn the game. When he was retrieved and put back, he hesitated on his next encounter with descent. He started in place but stayed. He came on the body slap/"come here" combination and was praised. On the next descent *he clearly stayed* without hesitation and came on the body slap. The progression was comes–hesitates–stays. In keeping with the proximal inferring of cues he now seemed focused specifically on the body slap. He stayed through two other cue combinations, including descent, and then came again on the body slap, the new rule of the moment.

One additional feature of this week's work was critical. In one instance, the dog clearly stayed on the familiar descent/"stay"/point combination and then hesitated on the unfamiliar descent only/no words. This suggests the beginning of discrimination on the basis of configuration. The descent/no words combination cue was new enough to cause doubt and familiar enough to cause doubt. Differential response to configurations containing similar elements requires an ability to interrelate features of *horizontal* context (within the event). Use of this skill, it is argued, is forced by the nature of natural-context learning in which cues are in some way same and in some way different. The next time P. descended with no words or pointing Finnegan *clearly stayed,* with the same progression seen earlier: he declined to come on the usually powerful handclap or the beckoning motion; he *hesitated* on the ground slap and came once again to the body slap.

WEEK 5: CHAOS AND THE SEARCH FOR SPECIFIC CUES

In this week P. decided to use intentional contradiction to both determine what the dog was responding to and to instruct him in proper cues. Her approach was to use postures/gestures/intonations which had previously been used to call the dog to come, but to use them in conjunction with the word "stay" instead. Finnegan's performance plummeted this week.

The trainer began with a spontaneous jump/foot-stomp intended to call the dog to her. Though this kind of vigorous activity would have been more than sufficient to attract the dog to her in earlier weeks, it now failed. Finnegan was now focused on *which* cue signals when to come, and he had never seen this movement before. P. induced him to come twice with the waistbend/clap/"come here" series. Attempts to call the dog from an erect position continued to fail.

The dog again saw the jump after several successful instances of "come" had intervened. The trainer wanted to use the same jumping cue to teach the dog to stay despite any bizarre activity in which she might be engaged. But this time Finnegan came! Again we see the attempt to vertically derive the meaning of a signal. P. put him back in position and launched into a flurry of activity: jumping in place, arm waving, finger snapping and clapping while jumping, all with the word "stay" barked simultaneously. The dog "played it safe"; he defaulted to staying. A familiar sequence occurred: when he was put back for coming on

Table 10.6.   Sequence of Trainers' Behaviors and Their Outcomes: Week 5

Trainer (P.)   a) jumps in place → dog stays
                    waistbend/clap/"come here" → dog comes
                    put back
                    waistbend/clap/"come here" → dog comes
                    put back

           b) move back
                    standoff
                    stand/"come here" (twice) → dog stays
                    waistbend/"come here" → dog comes
                    petting and praise

           c) descends/body slap/clap/"come here" → dog comes
                    put back

           d) move back
                    jump in place/no words → dog comes
                    put back
                    jump/snap/"stay" → dog stays
                    jump/clap/"stay" → dog stays
                    waistbend/beckon/"come here" → dog stays
                    waistbend/clap/"come here" → dog stays
                    descend/clap/beckon/"come here" → dog hesitates, then comes

(move outside) e) (dog spanked for failing to come when called; put in sitting position)
                    move back/"stay"/point
                    descends/"stay" → dog comes
                    rise/"stay" → dog stops in place
                    descends/"stay" → dog stays
                    crouch/clap → dog comes
                    petting and praise
                    put back

           f) move back/"stay"
                    descends/"stay" → dog comes
                    "stay!" → dog stops
                    put back

           g) move back/"stay"/point
                    descends/"stay" → dog hesitates
                    crouch/clap/"stay" → dog hesitates
                    crouch/clap/"come here"/beckon → dog comes
                    put back

           h) move back/"stay"/point
                    foot stomp → dog comes, then runs away
                    spanked and retrieved
                    put back

           i) move back/"stay"
                    foot stomp/"stay"/point → dog stays
                    descends/"stay" → dog stays
                    crouch/clap/"stay" → dog stays
                    crouch/clap → dog stays
                    crouch/clap/"come here" → dog stays
                    crouch/clap/"come here"/beckon → dog comes
                    petting and praise
                    put back

           j) move back/"stay"/point
                    stand/"stay" → dog starts to leave
                    "stay!" → dog stops and sits down

foot stomp/"stay" → dog stays
crouch/whistle → dog comes
petting and praise

k) descends/clap/"come here" → dog comes
put back
stand/foot stomp/"stay" → dog comes
"stay" → dog stops
foot stomp/"stay"/point → dog stays
descends → dog comes
"stay!"/point → dog stops
crouch/"stay" → dog stays
crouch/whistle → dog comes
petting and praise

Trainer (S.)   l) prone/ground slap/"come here" → dog comes to hand
put back

m) move back/"stay"/point
kneel/body slap/clap/"come here" → dog starts to come but distracted by itch
kneel/"come here" → dog stays
kneel/body slap/"come here" → dog stays
crawls toward dog, then backs up → dog comes on his backward movement
petting and praise
put back

n) move back/"stay"
all fours/ground slap/"come here" → dog comes
put back

c) move back/"stay"/point
descends/"stay" → dog stays
sit/ground slap/"come here" → dog comes
petting and praise
put back

p) move back/"stay"/point
descends/"stay"/point → dog stays
sit/body slap/"come here" → dog comes
petting and praise
put back

q) move back/"stay"/point
descends/"stay"/point → dog stays
sit/body slap/"come here" → dog comes
put back

r) move back/"stay"/point
descends/"stay"/point → dog stays
sit/clap/high "come here" → dog comes

(move outside) s) dog is disobedient and frisky: he is put into a sitting position)
move back/"stay"/point
stand/"come here" (twice) → dog stays
stand/point down/"come here" (twice) → dog stays
stand/body slap/"come here" (multiple) → dog stays
stand/body slap/"come here" → dog comes

t) stand/body slap/"come here" (multiple) → dog finally comes, playfully attacking trainer's leg

u) stand/body slap/"come here" → dog runs past trainer

Trainer (G.)   v) kneel/point down/"come here" → dog stays
waistbend/point down/"come here" → dog stays and is spanked
move back

293

Table 10.6. *(continued)*

<table>
<tbody>
<tr><td></td><td>waistbend/point down/"come here" (thrice) → dog comes after third command</td></tr>
<tr><td>w)</td><td>move back/point/"stay"</td></tr>
<tr><td></td><td>descends/point/"stay" → dog comes</td></tr>
<tr><td></td><td>trainer accepts it → petting and praise</td></tr>
<tr><td></td><td>put back</td></tr>
<tr><td>x)</td><td>move back/"stay"/point</td></tr>
<tr><td></td><td>descends/no words → dog comes</td></tr>
<tr><td></td><td>"No!"</td></tr>
<tr><td></td><td>put back</td></tr>
<tr><td></td><td>moves back/"stay"/point</td></tr>
<tr><td></td><td>descend/"stay"/point → dog comes</td></tr>
<tr><td></td><td>"stay!" → dog stops and sits</td></tr>
<tr><td></td><td>crouch/point down/"come here" → dog comes as hand moves downward</td></tr>
</tbody>
</table>

the jump he failed to come to familiar combinations, hesitated when more familiar cues were used in combination, and finally came to an exaggerated reassurance cue. Full transition had been made to the critical understanding that the real task was determining the meaning of the trainers' signals.

Overall, the week was awash with contradiction and confused signals. Descent was once again used to induce the dog to come, the very response that he was to unlearn in Week 4. Finnegan alternately came, hesitated, and stayed. Finally he ran away, was retrieved, and was given two taps on the rump by P. The upshot of the dog's confusion was alternating strategies: First he stayed through most cues until an exaggerated combination was used to call him; then he tried the opposite approach and came on most of the cues presented to him. Neither approach was very successful, but they show an attempt on the dog's part to cope with the problematic new situation he encountered.

With S. this week, cues were given in a comparatively straightforward and familiar manner, and Finnegan's performance was excellent. He made no move to come on the descent, and he stayed and came appropriately from the trainer's point of view.

Finnegan's behavior with Trainer G. was more similar to his behavior with P. than with S. The dog was given a rump slap for his disobedience at the start, for he was by this time quite inattentive. He then wrongly came on the descent three times in succession. A reasonable explanation for his earlier excellent performance with Trainer S. is that S. provided the most stress-free training context. Trainer P. evoked confusion; Trainer G. represented pressure for correct response. Playing it safe with G. entailed coming rather than staying.

WEEK 6: ATTENDING TO WORDS

The sample for this week was small but interesting. Finnegan responded inappropriately to the first contradiction he encountered (body slap/"stay"). Trainer

Table 10.7.   Sequence of Trainers' Behaviors and Their Outcomes: Week 6

Trainer (P.)	a)	move back/"stay"/point
		descends/"stay" → dog stays
		kneel/body slap/"stay" → dog comes
		trainer accepts it — petting and praise
		put back
	b)	move back/"stay"/point
		descends/"stay" → dog stays
		crouch/body slap/"stay" → dog stays
		crouch/clap → dog comes as hands move together
		petting and praise
		put back
	c)	move back/"stay"/point
		descends/"stay"/point → dog stays
		crouch/body slap/"stay" → dog in motion prior to "stay"
		put back
	d)	move back/"stay"/point
		descends/"stay"/point → dog stays
		crouch/body slap/"stay" → dog stays
		crouch/body slap → dog comes
		(trainer says she forgot to say "stay")
		put back
	e)	move back/"stay"/point
		descends/"stay" → dog stays
		crouch/body slap/"stay" → dog stays
		crouch/clap/lean forward/"come here" → dog leaps forward after clap, as trainer leans forward
		petting and praise
Trainer (S.)	f)	move back/"stay"/point
		waistbend/body slap/"come here" → dog comes
		petting and praise
		put back
	g)	move back/"stay"/point
		waistbend/body slap/"come here" → dog comes
		put back
	h)	move back/"stay"/point
		waistbend/body slap/"come here" → dog comes
		petting and praise
		put back
	i)	move back/"stay"/point
		kneebend/body slap/"come here" → dog comes

P. forgave his action and delivered petting and praise. The dog responded appropriately three times by staying in place on the body slap/"stay" combinations. Failure—i.e., coming on the body slap—occurred when the slap was not simultaneously paired with the word *stay*. When the dog's performance rating was adjusted to reflect this fact, his on-cue compliance was better than 90% overall in Week 6. With Trainer S. and his straightforward cues, Finnegan performed nearly flawlessly.

A parsimonious explanation for Finnegan's impressive performance on the contradictory tasks is that they tended to make vocalizations more critical cues than they previously had been. For example, Finnegan stayed on the crouch/body slap/"stay" combination and came on the crouch/body slap/no words combination, exactly as discrimination of vocalization would suggest. A precedent to this had been seen at the end of Week 4 (prior to the onset of contradiction), when Finnegan hesitated on the body slap but leapt forward on the body slap/"come here" combination. That in turn had a precedent, when Finnegan discriminated between descent/"stay" and descent/no words for the first time. Once the process of horizontal integration was part of the repertoire, it was possible for the contradictory tasks to sharpen the focus on the vocal component of combinations.

WEEK 7: BEGINNING TO STABILIZE

Finnegan's performance in this week continued to suggest (a) an ability to discriminate between the vocalizations "stay" and "come here," and (b) that the basic "come" task substantially had been learned.

With Trainer S. the dog responded clearly and appropriately, staying and coming on cue. Trainer P. continued her contradictory messages but Finnegan again performed well. He repeatedly stayed on "stay" vocalizations and came on "come here" vocalizations, while alternately (and usually appropriately) coming and staying on claps, body slaps, and so forth. The trainer concluded that vocal cues had gained a new importance. Her first conclusion was that the dog responded to a difference in intonation between "come here" and "stay." The recognized gross difference between the two intonations is that the "come here" command is generally delivered in higher pitch than the order to stay. In one episode, P. attempted to test Finnegan's response to the words "come here" delivered in a flat tone of voice (a mimicry of "stay" intonation). The dog stayed through four instances of the lower pitched "come here", then leapt forward to the higher pitched "come here." P. next attempted to use a high-pitched "stay" paired with various "come" gestures. However, the higher pitched "stay" was extremely odd in tone, not a good imitation of that normally used for "come here." The dog simply watched her during the high-toned "stay" and came on the lower pitched "come here" paired with the familiar clap and beckoning gesture. Nothing can be concluded from this incident except to say that the dog was not fooled by her scrambled intonations.

The session with G. in this week again suggested the process postulated by Pfungst (1911) in connection with Clever Hans. The trainer, feeling that the animal had mastered the basic task, began to slacken his movements. Cues became more subtle; a slight gesture of the wrist, a flick of the finger. Finnegan even came as G. started to take his hand out of his pocket. Vocalizations also became

Table 10.8. Sequence of Trainers' Behaviors and Their Outcomes: Week 7

Trainer (S.)   a)   move back/"stay"/point → dog stays
descends/"stay" → dog stays
sit/body slap → dog leaps forward

b)   move back/"stay"/point
descends/"stay" → dog stays
sit/body slap → dog comes
petting and praise

c)   "stay"/crawls off → dog follows
"stay" → dog stops
descends → dog stays
sit/body slap → dog comes
petting and praise

Trainer (P.)   d)   move back/"stay"/point
descends/"stay" → dog stays
crouch/clap/"stay" → dog stays
crouch/body slap/"stay" → dog stays
clap/beckon/"come here"/clap → dog hesitates, then comes
petting and praise

e)   move back/"stay"/point
descends/"stay" → dog stays
crouch/body slap/"stay" → dog stays
crouch/body slap → dog stays
crouch/body slap/"come here"/beckon → dog comes
petting and praise

f)   move back/no words
descends/"stay" → dog stays
crouch/body slap/"stay" → dog stays
crouch/clap/"stay" → dog comes *as* hands move together
"stay"/point → dog stops
crouch/clap/wide beckon/"come here" → dog leaps forward

g)   move back/"stay"
descends/"stay" → dog stays
crawl/ground slap/"stay" → dog stays
clap/"stay" → dog stays
beckon/"stay" → dog stays
body slap/"stay" → dog stays
crouch/clap/beckon/"come here" → dog comes

h)   move back/"stay"
descends/"stay" → dog stays
crouch/body slap/"stay" → dog stays
clap/"stay" → dog stays
beckon/"stay" → dog stays
"come here" (flat tone; four times) → dog stays
"come here" (high pitch) → dog leaps forward
put back

i)   body slap/"stay" (high pitch) → dog stays
clap/"stay" (high pitch) → dog stays
beckon/"stay" (high pitch) → dog stays
clap/beckon/"come here" (low pitch) → dog comes

Trainer (G.)   j)   move back/"stay"/point
waistbend → dog stays
body slap/"come here" → dog comes

Table 10.8.   *(continued)*

petting and praise
k) move back/"stay"/point
    descends/"stay"/point → dog stays
    crouch/standoff → dog stays
    removes hand from pocket → dog comes
    petting and praise
l) move back/"stay"/point
    descends/"stay"/point → dog stays
    crouch/standoff → dog stays
    flick of wrist/"come here" → dog comes
    petting and praise
m) descends → dog comes
    "stay"/point at dog → dog sits down
    descends/no words → dog stays
    stand/flick of wrist/"come here" → dog stays
    body slap → dog comes
    petting and praise

more quiet. As mentioned earlier, once in a sitting position Finnegan would rivet his gaze on the trainers, waiting for a release cue. This facilitated the movement to more subtle gestures. It is worth noting that only in confusing or contradictory moments are exaggerated cues necessary.

The trainers concluded that all three tasks were substantially learned by Week 7. Indeed, Weeks 8 and 9 added little that was new to the learning process.

CONCLUSION: BECOMING "CLEVER" LIKE HANS

The Finnegan data help explicate the process by which Pfungst's horse could have achieved his cognitive sophistication and flexibility of performance. As with Clever Hans, Finnegan gave evidence of categorical or concept learning, hypothesis formation, hypothesis testing and revision, and horizontal integration of contextual elements. Rather than passively and rotely responding to cues, Finnegan was required by the natural diversity of context to actively construct his learning experience.

The evidence suggests that, in an NCTS, learning proceeds as a function of both consistency and variation in context, each contributing its share to the development of an adaptive intelligence. The organism learns in a training context that includes different cues and consequences delivered in different ways, at different times, in different context of other cues, and in context of different trainer intentions. Cues are not static entities; they have a changing meaning and a changing importance dependent on context. The same must be said for the notion of learning by consequence; consequences are always determined from the subject's perspective and cannot simply be defined as that which follows the

Table 10.9. Sequence of Trainers' Behaviors and Their Outcomes: Week 8

Trainer (S.)
  a) move back/point
     descends → dog not attending
     kneel/body slap/"come here" → dog comes
     petting and praise
  b) move back/"stay"/point
     descends → dog not attending
     kneel/ground slap/"come here" → dog comes
     petting and praise
  c) move back/"stay"/point
     waistbend/kneebend/body slap → dog comes
     petting and praise
  d) stand/body slap/"come here" → dog stays
     waistbend/kneebend/body slap/"come here" → dog comes
  e) move back/"stay"/point
     flaps arms → dog stays
     waistbend/body slap/"come here" → dog comes
  f) move back/"stay"/point
     stand/body slap/"come here" → dog stays
     stand/body slap/kneebend/no words → dog comes

Trainer (P.)
  g) move back/"stay"
     descends/"stay" → dog stays
     crouch/whistle → dog comes
     "stay" → dog stops
     crouch/bounce in place → dog stays
     crouch/clap → dog comes
     (trainer says she forgot to say "stay")
     put back
     move back/"stay"/point
     descends/"stay" → dog stays
     crouch/clap/"stay" → dog stays
     crouch/snap/clap/"stay" → dog stays
     crouch/clap/beckon/"stay" → dog comes after clap
     "stay" → dog hesitates
     clap/beckon/"come here" → dog comes
     petting and praise
  h) move back/"stay"/point
     jump/"stay" → dog stays
     descends/"stay" → dog stays
     stand/descend again/"stay" → dog stays
     crouch/body slap/"stay" → dog stays
     crouch/clap/"stay" → dog stays
     clap harder/"stay" → dog comes
     "stay" → dog sits
     clap/"stay" → dog stays
     clap harder/wide beckon/high pitched "come here" → dog leaps forward
  i) move back/"stay"/point
     descends/"stay"
     crouch/body slap/"stay" → dog stays
     crouch/clap/beckon/"stay" → dog stays
     crouch/beckon/"come here" (flat tone) → dog leaps forward
     petting and praise
  j) crouch/clap/"stay, stay" → dog stays

299

Table 10.9. *(continued)*

		crouch/body slap/"stay, stay" → dog stays
		crouch/beckon/"stay, stay" → dog stays
		crouch/body slap/clap/"come here" → dog comes without hesitation
		petting and praise
	k)	same as j, but with high pitched "stay, stay" → dog stays
		crouch/beckon/"come here" (high pitch) → dog comes
Trainer (G.)	l)	move back/"stay"/point
		waistbend/takes hand from pocket → dog comes
		"stay"/point at dog → dog stops
		put back
		move back
		waistbend/body slap/"come here" → dog comes
		petting and praise
	m)	move back
		descends/"stay" → dog comes
		"stay" → dog stops
		descends/"stay"/point → dog comes
		"stay" → dog stops
		stands/descends again/point/"stay" → dog stays
		standoff → dog stays
		crouch/snap/point down/"come here" → dog comes
		petting and praise
	n)	move back/"stay"/point
		descends/"stay"/point → dog stays
		hands move together as if for clap → dog comes

organism's actions. Rather, an occurrence is empowered as a consequence, just as a cue is empowered as a cue, as the result of a more complex interaction of vertical and horizontal context effects and the progressive stage of the organism's learning, that is, what it makes of the "game" at any given point.

Overall, the blending of some degree of consistency and some degree of variation served perfectly to prepare the dog for the kind of flexible command scenario he would encounter in his everyday dealings with the family over time. One could speculate that, with a complete lack of consistency, nothing of the task could be learned; with a complete lack of variation, only a very specific stimulus–response relationship would develop. In an adaptive sense, such an animal may be less prepared to cope with environmental variation. In Finnegan's case, flexibility in his training environment led to his being able to cope with flexibility in the natural environment and to be "flexible" himself in the sense of not requiring specific cues delivered in a fixed way. After the completion of structured training he was (and remains) able to generalize commands to new contexts, different gestural and vocal cues, new social others, and so forth, for "stay" and "come." His ability to respond appropriately to a range of command cues could be described in behaviorist terms as stimulus generalization encouraged by the training context, or in cognitive terms as the possession of a general schema for the tasks.

Table 10.10. Sequence of Trainers' Behaviors and Their Outcomes: Week 9

Trainer (P.)
  a) move back/"stay"/point
      descends/"stay" → dog stays
      crouch/body slap/"stay" → dog stays
      clap/"stay" → dog comes
      put back

  b) move back
      descends/no words → dog stays
      crouch/body slap/"stay" → dog stays
      crouch/clap/"stay" → dog comes hesitantly
      dog runs off
      spanked and retrieved
      put back

  c) move back/"stay"
      descends → dog comes
      "stay" → dog sits
      move back/"stay"
      descends/"stay" → dog stays
      crouch/body slap/"stay" → dog stays
      crouch/clap/beckon/"come here" → dog leaps forward
      petting and praise

Trainer (S.)
  d) move back/"stay"/point
      descends to all fours → dog comes
      petting and praise

  e) move back/"stay"/point
      stand/body slap → comes hesitantly

Trainer (G.)
  f) move back
      waistbend/point down/"come here" → dog hesitates, then comes warily
      petting and praise
      put back

  g) move back
      waistbend/body slap/"come here" → dog comes
      petting and praise
      put back

  h) move back
      standoff → dog stays
      waistbend/body slap/"come here" → dog comes
      petting and praise

  i) move back
      waistbend/body slap/"come here" → dog comes
      petting and praise

In the tradition of Krechevsky (1932) and Tolman (1932), Figure 10.5 diagrams the hypothesis formation/testing process as it leads to the emergence of new cognitive functions. The animal's hypothesis about the task at any given point structures the task and directs his actions. Initial hypotheses are a result of predispositional elements and task constraints. Progress is made by learning the ways in which the initial hypothesis is adequate and/or inadequate. Inadequacy forces the revision of the hypothesis and the devising of some alterna-

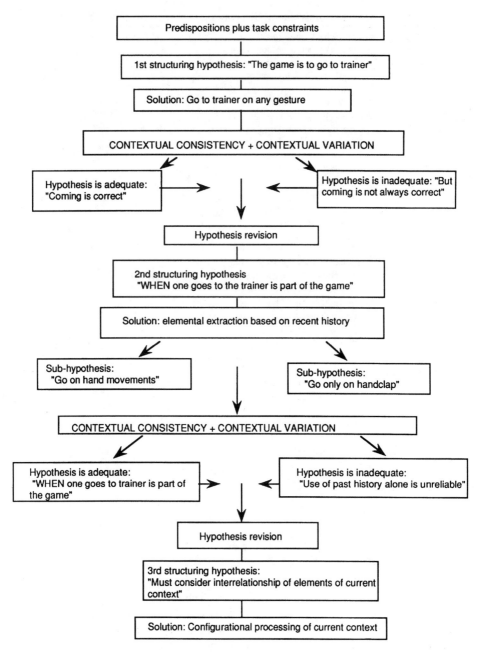

Figure 10.5. Structure of the learning process for the "come" task.

tive approach; at the same time, adequacy helps constrain the revision along certain limited lines. Hence, both variation and consistency are important to the structuring and restructuring of hypotheses. Only variation, however, is critical to forcing the act of hypothesis formation and testing in and of itself. Simply stated, variation forces the animal to think.

In terms of the specific task of learning to sit, stay, and come, the progression of hypotheses can be summarized as follows:

- first you stay, then you go
- when you go is crucial
- when you go depends on immediate past history (vertical context)
- immediate past history is insufficient; horizontal context must also be considered
- configural processing of current context must be combined with forming and testing new hypotheses per se when confronted with new or uncertain situations

Fundamental bases on which learning is built include the natural predispositions and biases of the dog and trainers and fundamental social/communications knowledge: spanking is bad, harsh tones are bad, doggerel is pleasing, play is good, approval is good, off-vertical means invitation, and so on. The owners accommodate to the dog as well as he to them. This two-way interaction grounded the process.

Increased experience with the general structure of the game in the form of a growing number of correct responses bolsters the "rightness" of the hypothesis. But at the same time some new accommodation must be made for those instances in which the dog receives indication that coming to the trainer was wrong. What could these mean, if the basic game hypothesis is correct? In Week 3 we see the result of this progression: the animal began to hesitate rather than exhibit the previous "go or no-go" mode of response. His increasing sureness of the general outline of the game, combined with suggestions of the trainer's displeasure with certain instances of coming, sets the stage for jumping the critical hurdle: namely, that *when* he comes to the trainer is the real issue. Once this point is attained the dog essentially faces a new task. As a result, new hypotheses are formed. The first is an attempt to infer proper behavior from context in a vertical sense, that is, attempting to determine the trainer's desires by a simple process of elemental extraction of cues linked to success in the immediate past. Hypotheses are alternately formed about general categories of behaviors (e.g., hand movements) or specific behaviors (e.g., a body slap). The impact of this attempt was seen in Week 3, when it resulted in the dog's reconsideration of a basic predisposition to come on the trainer's descent, because descent now did not fit with his prevailing hypotheses about hand movements.

This level of hypothesis formation and reformation is still problematic in that it encourages an attempt to select among specific cues as either right or wrong when in fact all of the cues are both right and wrong, depending on the context in which they are embedded. This is finally the most critical hurdle for the learning animal. The inadequacy of simple extrapolation of a one-to-one cue-response relationship based on past experience alone fosters the emergence of a new process. From Week 4 onward we see evidence that the dog has begun to attend to the horizontal aspects of context. He begins to integrate various elements occurring at the moment as a means of inferring the trainer's desires. This process is encouraged in Finnegan's case by the onset of contradictory messages. The data suggests that he faces this challenge by first attempting again to rely on vertical context within trainer and by separating social context to a greater extent, giving different responses to the same cues with different trainers. This is finally not adequate, since Finnegan must continue to deal with Trainer P. and her contradictions. Integration of elements within-event becomes a new tool. Once this process has been activated by experience, the animal is potentially beyond specific stimulus–response control. Contextual variation was instrumental in structuring the course of events toward behavioral flexibility.

The relationship between consistency and change as a description of the natural world is a classic and ongoing philosophical paradox, captured in its unsolvability by the cliche "everything changes and nothing changes." The natural environment is both stable and unstable; there is some degree of sameness and some degree of change. The suggestion raised by the NCTS is that this natural combination is ontogenetically critical for active organisms in that it assures a mixture of failure and success of behavioral assumptions based solely on past events. It is this paradoxical evolutionary result that co-evolved: flexibility in the environment, and flexibility in the developmental capabilities of organisms that inhabit that environment. Though the current study does not deal with Finnegan's ability to problem solve or display a general intelligence beyond the come and stay tasks, it does suggest that contextual variation triggers a developmental progression in cognitive function by forcing the animal to expand its repertoire in ways that rote consistency would not. This results in a more plastic and "intelligent" organism, able to utilize more of the cognitive capabilities at its command. While the use of contradiction in training Finnegan was an artifact of the study environment and might not normally occur, it served to highlight the process by which inconsistency can force the utilization of cognitive skills. Laboratory manipulations of "contextual variation" fall far short of the nature and degree of complexity evidenced in the NCTS: multiple behavioral options for the animal, stimuli with multiple signalling power and variability in consequences, all during the course of acquisition. Moreover, the complexity of the interactive processes at work when learning occurs at the hand of social others is critical to any theory which attempts to explain human development and learning. The learning processes activated by social encounters with all their inherent variabilities will not be easy to simulate with automated manipulation of variables. The interactive nature of social learning distinguishes it as a unique contextual problem for the study of learning.

REFERENCES

American Kennel Club. (1985). *The complete dog book* (17th ed.). New York: Howell Book House.

Fox, M.W. (1975). Pet-owner relations. In R.S. Anderson (Ed.), *Pet animals and society.* London: Balliere Tindall.

Galef, B.G., Jr. (1984). Reciprocal heuristics: A discussion of the relationship of the study of learned behavior in the laboratory and field. *Learning and Motivation, 15,* 479–493.

Hirsh-Pasek, K., & Treiman, R. (1982). Doggerel: Motherese in a new context. *Journal of Child Language, 9,* 229–237.

Krechevsky, I. (1932). The genesis of "hypothesis" in rats. *University of California Publications in Psychology, 6* (4), 45–64.

McIntire, R.W. (1968). Dog training, reinforcement and behavior in unrestricted environments. *American Psychologist, 23,* 830–831.

Pfungst, O. (1911). *Clever Hans: The horse of Mr. von Osten.* New York: Holt. (1965 edition, edited by Robert Rosenthal).

Piaget, J. (1970). Piaget's Theory. In P.H. Mussen (Ed.), *Carmichael's manual of child psychology* (3rd ed., Vol. 1, pp. 703–732). New York: Wiley.

Piaget, J. (1985). *The equilibration of cognitive structures* (T. Brown and K.J. Thampy, Trans.). Chicago: University of Chicago Press.

Pinkwater, J. & Pinkwater, D.M. (1977). *Superpuppy.* New York: Seabury Press.

Rosenthal, R. (1964). The effect of the experimenter on the results of psychological research. In B. Maher (Ed.), *Progress in experimental personality research, Vol. 1.* New York: Academic Press.

Rosenzweig, M.R., Krech, D., Bennett, E.L., & Diamond, M.C. (1962). Effects of environmental complexity and training on brain chemistry and anatomy: A replication and extension. *Journal of Comparative Physiology and Psychology, 55,* 429–437.

Scott, J.P., & Fuller, J.L. (1965). *Genetics and the social behavior of the dog.* Chicago: University of Chicago Press.

Sebeok, T.A., & Rosenthal, R. (Eds.). (1981). *The Clever Hans phenomenon: Communication with horses, whales and people.* New York: New York Academy of Sciences.

Smith, S.M., Glenberg, A., & Bjork, R.A. (1978). Environmental context and human memory. *Memory and Cognition, 6,* 342–353.

Timberlake, W. (1984). An ecological approach to learning. *Learning and Motivation, 15,* 321–333.

Tolman, E.C. (1932). *Purposive behavior in animals and men.* New York: Appleton-Century.

Valsiner, J. (1987). *Culture and the development of children's action: A cultural-historical theory of psychology.* Chichester, UK: J. Wiley and Sons.

Wolters, R.A. (1978). *Kid's dog—a training book.* New York: Doubleday.

CHAPTER 11

The Language of Animal Learning Theories: A Radical Behaviorist Perspective*

Steven M. Kemp

The University of North Carolina at Chapel Hill, U.S.A.

Everyone talks about stimulus–response psychology, but no one seems to do anything about it. This chapter constitutes a proactive effort to build a foundation for animal learning theories based upon an alternative to stimulus–response psychology, *the psychology of action.*

Disenchantment with traditional stimulus–response formulations in psychology has recently led a number of researchers (e.g., Harré, 1982; von Cranach, 1982; Lee, 1988; Oppenheimer, 1991) to advocate a view of psychology based on the notion of action. Among these, Lee's (1988) approach is distinct in that she begins from the radical behaviorist perspective of B. F. Skinner (1974).

Mandler and Kessen (1959) point out that various metatheoretical perspectives can be thought of as various languages used by psychologists in describing and explaining psychological phenomena. Thus, stimulus–response psychology can be understood as the linguistic practices of psychologists in describing and explaining psychological phenomena in terms of functional input–output relations. Alternatively, action psychologies involve the description and explanation of psychological phenomena in terms of things done by

---

*Thanks to Dave Eckerman, Bill Lycan, Danna Cornick, Stella Sutter, Jaan Valsiner, Bill Knorpp, Eve Segal, George Skelly, Dick Smyth, Dan Hunter, and others too numerous to mention, who have patiently listened to my mutterings on this topic for the last fifteen years or so. And to the even better friends who have refused to listen. The reader should also note a less personal, but equally important debt that I owe to the writings of Gregory Bateson and C.S. Peirce. Thanks most of all to my mom, Mrs. Edie Kemp, for her support during my long illness, said support making this paper possible.

the organism. In this chapter, I will expand upon Lee's (1988) framework in order to see what using this new language to reexamine the phenomena of animal learning can tell us about the structure of learning.

This chapter will consist of three sections: First, I will show what sorts of structure are made evident by a radical behaviorist view of action. Second, I will argue that the action theory perspective brings into question the usual choice of the basic unit of analysis in animal learning theories and suggests an alternative. Finally, I will describe a typical example of operant learning phenomena, operant conditioning of the pigeon, in the action-theoretic language.

ACTION AND STRUCTURE

Stimulus–response psychologies, including methodological behaviorism and cognitive psychology, are notorious for failing to define their terms, including such basic terms as *stimulus* and *response* (Gibson, 1960; Koch, 1954; Mandler & Kessen, 1959; Meehl, 1978; Turner, 1967). In attempting to define the basic terms of action theory, a number of authors (Austin, 1962; Brand, 1984; Davis, 1979; Goldman, 1970; Hamblin, 1987; Lee, 1988) have chosen to examine, to some degree or another, the structure of action. I will explore that structure in detail in this section.

Lee's Metatheoretical Approach

Given the wide variety of action theories cited above, it is important to summarize the particular view followed here, that of Vicki L. Lee (1988). Lee comes from the perspective of radical behaviorism offering a language for psychology based on the notion of action. She contrasts her view with the traditional stimulus–response terminology of contemporary psychology as well as with other views of action. She suggests that the best language for treating behaviors as actions is a language based on a basic vocabulary of action verbs.

Basic terms. Lee avoids the word *behavior* as it "is ambiguous between activity, moment, and action" (p. 42). For instance, Ziff (1958) argues that the behaviorist inevitably means action when he or she uses the term *behavior.* However, Harré (1982), not a behaviorist, uses the term *behavior* to mean mere bodily moment.

Lee prefers the term *conduct* to describe the general subject matter of psychology. She begins her inquiry by pointing to the sorts of events described in common English using action verbs, for example: "running, reading, writing, touching, holding, sitting, and driving" (p. 38). Unique, individual, particular event-tokens of this sort, Lee calls *acts.* General, broad classes of acts, Lee calls *actions.*

It is important at this point to note that Lee's terminology is quite distinct from the terminologies adopted in other action psychologies. Harré (1982), for instance, has a tripartite taxonomy of behavior/action/act. As noted above, Harré uses the term *behavior* to indicate mere bodily movement. He uses the term *action* to indicate action in the context of the person acting along with a supposed *intention*, possessed by that person, that is the proximate antecedent efficient cause of the action. He uses the term *act* to indicate action in the context of its broader social and cultural setting.

The problem of classification. Lee's argument also stands out from other psychologies of action due to her focus on the problem of classification. Lee (1988, chap. 4) details the *type–token distinction,* also known as the *species–individual distinction,* or the *class–particular distinction.* Lee prefers the last terminology. She defines a *concrete particular* as "anything we can regard as a single entity." By way of example, Lee specifies two sorts of concrete particulars: objects and events. She points out that concrete particulars are unique.

The other side of the distinction is exemplified by collections of particulars. Lee refers to these collections as *classes.* An older term for "particular" is *token,* and for "class" is *type.* I will be using this older terminology in this chapter. The notion of classes allows the introduction of abstract entities into Lee's explanatory scheme.

Lee follows Skinner (1969, p. 131) in using the notion of a class as the basis for theoretical explanation in psychology. This strategy points up the motivation for Lee's focus on the problem of classification. At the same time, it points up an important distinction between Lee's view of action and other related views.

The differences in focus between Lee (1988) and Harré (1982) reflect—to some degree—the theoretical prejudices of the two authors. Harré focuses on the breadth of the context of interpretation as the primary distinction between levels of explanation in part because he believes that antecedents (i.e., intentions), as well as consequents, play a part in the explanation of conduct. Lee focuses on the token–type distinction in part because she does not believe it essential to assume the existence of intentions, mental states, or mental events in order to offer explanation of conduct.

If individual act-tokens are caused by unique, particular mental events or mental states (for example, intention-tokens), then types-of-action (action-classes) can be explained in terms of types-of-intentions in straightforward fashion. Thus, a detailed examination of the problem of classification is not necessary for the mentalist. As a radical behaviorist, Lee will not assume the existence of unseen mental entities such as intentions as part of an a priori scheme for explanation. As we will see later, in order to construct an explanatory strategy without postulating mental entities, the radical behaviorist uses a more intricate model of psychological explanation, relying centrally on the token–type distinction.

Awareness and action. Another difference is that Lee takes *action* as having very broad scope. She contrasts her own view with von Cranach's (1982) narrower view of action as "goal-directed, planned, intended, and conscious behavior" (p. 36). For Lee, beginning as she does with the language of action verbs, any sort of conduct describable using an action verb is to be considered an action until shown otherwise. In order to claim a measure of generality for his definition of action, von Cranach goes further, claiming that this specific, narrowly defined type of conduct is "the more common form," with other forms "found only in rare cases." I will have more to say on the rarity of non-conscious conduct later on.

Despite the fact that Lee (1988) wishes to de-emphasize the distinction between conscious and non-conscious action, she agrees with Harré (1982) that the a priori elimination of verbal self-report from psychology on methodological grounds is an arbitrary practice and harmful to psychological inquiry. On the views of all these authors, self-awareness is a legitimate part of conduct.

Similarities to other action psychologies. There are other important similarities between Lee and other psychologists of action. Lee (1988), Harré (1982), and von Cranach (1982) all take it as essential that actions be construed as means–ends pairs. Harré (1982, p. 10) expresses this sentiment quite eloquently: Action psychologies "depend upon the use of a single, overriding principle, namely that action should be seen in terms of a basic means–ends format. Every action points beyond itself, and, it seems, must be regarded for scientific purposes as a means towards some end."

Both Lee and Harré emphasize the importance of the distinction between bodily movement (by whatever name) and action. Both insist that action consists in *doings* and not in *happenings*. As Harré puts it (1982, p. 12): "Action is what people do as opposed to what happens to them." (See also Hamblin, 1987, p. 140; Davis, 1979, pp. 4–5; Goldman, 1970, pp. 16–17; Brand, 1984, pp. 3–6, for various views on the doing–happening distinction.)

Thus, while explanatory strategies differ, a focus on the essential differences between actions and events, along with a commitment to a holistic specification of action, make these psychologies of action quite distinct from more traditional stimulus–response psychologies. Indeed, even Lee's neglect of Harré's distinction between personal action and action-in-social-context is due to her commitment to the notion that all action must be individuated in terms of its environmental consequences. Lee's position is, in this small regard, even more holistic than Harré's, as she groups together all the environmental consequences, whether personal or social.

The language of psychology. One last, unique aspect of Lee's view is her concern with the language of psychology. As noted above, by beginning her inquiry with ordinary action verbs, she avoids a reductionistic, essentialist definition of action in terms of other, putatively more basic, notions. By focusing on verbs such as *remembering,* rather the nouns, such as *memory,* she avoids too-early imputation of unobservable internal mental events or states. This keeps her taxonomy parsimonious. For instance, actions are defined without introducing the concept of intentions. (Note that a sentence like: *Sally intends to hit Joe* suggests that *intending,* itself, on Lee's view, very well might be an action.)

Stimulus–response psychologies, including methodological behaviorism and cognitive psychology, focus on nouns. In the study of learning, *lights* and *bells* lead to *lever*-press and *key*-peck, rewarded by *food* and *water.* Lee feels that this sort of language leads away from the true causes of conduct.

An Action Terminology

In order to get at structure by examining action, I propose a specific terminology for describing action, based on Lee's (1988) metatheoretical framework. Wittgenstein (1953) raised the question of the difference between an event, such as the raising of an arm, and an action, such as someone raising her or his arm. I begin with this question, hoping to specify a sequence of terms, beginning with *event* and concluding with *action,* that will clarify the nature of the difference between event and action.

I follow Lee (1988) in understanding *events* as entities extended in time: events begin and end. As Lee (1988, p. 29) puts it: "Events are concrete particulars that occupy time, and objects are concrete particulars that occupy time and space."

Movements are a specific sort of event that involve objects. An event specified in terms of the motion of some object or objects through space for some finite period of time is a *movement.* When at least one of the objects involved is the body of some animal or a part of that body, we call the movement a *bodily movement.*

Now, bodily movements are not the whole of the story. If my arm is at rest and is struck by some falling object, then my arm moves, but I did not move it. If I wire up the leg of a frog and send an electric current into the nerves, causing the frog's leg to jerk, then the leg moved, but the frog did not move it.

In order to deal with this further distinction, we need to add a new concept, that of *person.* Consider the behaving organism, not as an input–output device, not as an S–R automaton, but as a creative, active individual constantly acting upon its environment and being acted upon by it: a locus of behavior, its dispositions to act shifting constantly, changing, growing, and altering to cope with the changing environment around it. It is not an organism at odds with its environment, but a person integrally a part of an ecosystem. The logical structure of this collection of dispositions is what Lee calls a *person.*

A *deed,* or doing, is a specific sort of bodily movement done by some person. It might be clearer to say that a *deed* is an ordered pair, consisting of a bodily movement and a person, where the person is the do-er or actor, who moves her or his own body. In either case, a deed or doing is *that which a person does,* in contrast to a happening, which is *that which happens to a person.* Lee (1988) uses the term *activity* (p.48) to refer to deeds.

Again, this is not the whole of the story, for actions, according to Lee, are more than mere doings. An action consists of a means and an end. A deed or activity is just the means. As Lee (1988, p.49) puts it: "Postural activities and movements provide the means by which we act upon the world and produce end results."[1]

If deeds are the means, what are the ends? Lee (1988) is not too clear, but seems to suggest that ends are consequent states of the environment. Harré (1982) claims that ends must be understood in terms of intentions possessed by the person. My hypothesis is that ends are further actions. *We perform deeds in order to gain the opportunity for further action.* The preceding sentence expresses my central claim as to the basic nature of the means–ends structure of action.

I do something (action$_1$) in order that I later may do something else (goal = action$_2$). I go to dinner (action) in order that I may eat (goal). I turn on a light in order that I might read a book.

Thus, an action is an ordered pair consisting of <deed,action> where the deed is the means and the action is the end. In computer science and linguistics, this sort of definition, where the term defined (*action*) also appears as a part of the definition, is called a *recursive definition.* Recursive definitions allow for an infinitely expansible structure. A disadvantage is that infinite regress is possible and should be avoided.

Explaining Action

As I mentioned earlier, the token–type distinction plays a crucial role in a radical behaviorist view of psychological explanation. The proposed recursive definition of action provides a starting point for this explanatory strategy.

Two problems. Consider first of all that the definition is given in terms of types, not tokens. Action is defined, but not act. The specification of the type to which a particular token should be assigned, is called *individuation.* The individuation of acts is a difficult problem. On my view, an individual act-token is explained only in terms of the action-type(s) of which it is an instance. Thus the proper individuation of act-tokens is prerequisite to the explanation of individual acts.

Second, there is a venerable criticism of the individuation of acts in terms of their consequences. What of acts that do not result in their intended consequences? If I go to a restaurant in order to eat and the restaurant is closed, where is the act-of-eating that is the essential end of the means–end pair? The answer to this criticism is that the act-of-going-to-the-restaurant can only be understood *as* an act of going-to-the-restaurant by means of specifying that act-token as an instance of the action-type, goings-to-restaurants. The individual

---

[1] V.L. Lee (personal communication, August 19, 1991) comments that "means can be actions . . . and not just bodily activities." This constitutes a difference between my view and Lee's.

act-of-going did not result in an individual act-of-eating, but the individual act-of-going *did* belong to the general class of actions-of-going and the general class of actions-of-going has, as a *general goal*, the class of actions-of-eating.

Explanation in action terms. An act is an individual, concrete, particular event. Hence its *consequences* are also individual events. However, *goals* are generals. When an individual consequence is an instance of some goal, we call that consequence the intended *result* of that act. When a consequence is not an instance of any goal, then that consequence is an unintended *side-effect* of that act. (Recall that goals are further actions. This suggests that consequences are acts.)

I believe that it has been a fundamental mistake in psychology and philosophy to claim that actions can be individuated by identifying all the individual act-tokens that comprise them. If acts are collected according to the kinematic similarity of the physical bodily movement, the act-class or act-type is called a *deed*. Actions, like deeds, are type-level phenomena; but this does not mean that actions, like deeds, are mere collections of individual acts.

I wish to build a formal barrier to that reductive mistake into the action language itself. Let us say that individual acts (act-tokens) are *members* of deeds (act-classes) in the usual set-theoretic sense, but that acts are *instances* of actions, in the following sense:

An individual act is an instance of some action if (a) the act is an element of the deed-class (type of bodily movement) that is the means of that action, and (b) the goal of that act is the end of that action. How a goal (a general) may be a goal of some particular act is a matter for the particular psychological theory. In cognitivist terms, the goal might be a part of the plan in the mind of the actor. In Skinnerian terms, the goal is the action-class of which previous consequences have been instances. In either case, the *structure* of the relation is the same. The instance-relation between act and action is dependent upon other instance-relations between consequences and goals. Hence, this definition is also a recursive one.

Individual acts are mere doings. Action, properly understood, always involves some notion of purpose. Purpose can be modeled only with respect to action-classes, not individual acts. This is the technique by which the radical behaviorist explains purpose.

The Macrostructure of Conduct

The recursive definition of action allows for the individuation of actions, though not acts. This individuation is determined with respect to what I call the *macrostructure of conduct*. Lee (1988, p.57) says that any action "is embedded in a network of overlapping and interlocking actions." This suggests that the structure of conduct can be explicated using a language based on action verbs. Various relations between persons (actors), actions, and bodily movements (deeds) can be used as models of various ways that people behave.

The organization of conduct. A single act (e.g., Ned crooks his finger) may have many goals (having the finger bend, pulling the trigger, firing the gun, shooting the King, killing the King, starting the revolution, etc.) and thus may be part of many simultaneous actions. Thus, many actions may be *nested* together by virtue of including the same deed as the means to each, but with each action having a different goal (end). These goals may be partially ordered as to being more or less proximal or distal to the deed in question. In the philosophy of action, this ordering is considered to be central to the problem of individuating action (Anscombe, 1963; Austin, 1962; Brand, 1984; Davidson, 1963; Goldman, 1970). W. G. Lycan (personal communication, November 1990) refers to this ordering as the *rich–thin continuum.*

Another way actions may be ordered is as proper subparts or *components* of one another. I walk to school (action$_1$ = <walking, arrive at school>). In order to achieve this, I step forward (action$_2$ = <put one foot forward, step with the other foot>). Here two actions are nested having no parts in common, but one subgoal (step with other foot) is a precondition to a superordinate goal (arrive at school).

A third way actions may be related is that their component deeds may *overlap in time.* While walking to school, you chew some gum. The actions are not functionally related: Either goal may be achieved (or abandoned) before the other. One deed may start before (or after) the other.

Fourth, a single goal might be achieved by any number of deeds (or deed-sequences). I may go to school by walking along any of a number of paths. I may take a car or a bus. The deeds vary drastically, but the goal is the same. This relation is usually called *equifinality.*

Finally, the component subaction of a larger action may be performed by a different actor than is the larger action. This is most common in social action. The team wins the game, due in part to John's scoring a goal. Another possible application involves Lycan's (1988, chap. 1) notion of homuncular functionalism. The homuncular functionalist espouses the view that proper subparts of a person, say, that person's visual system, or dynamic balance subsystem might be considered capable of belief or action. The *homuncular* relation is one between actors; one actor is a proper subpart of another actor.

All of these structural relations among actions and the components of actions have been described elsewhere. The point here is that the notion of an action as the pairing of an event (or, more specifically, a deed or activity) with a further action is a formal way of characterizing all of the above relations.

The Microstructure of Actions

Lee (1988) concentrates on molar description in psychology. However, in order to address my specific concerns about the language of animal learning theory, we need to examine things at a molecular level as well. This raises the question of microstructure.

The notion of microstructure has received a good deal of attention of late, if only because the word *microstructure* appears in the subtitle of the new "bible" of the newest wave in cognitive science, *connectionism* (Rumelhart, McClelland, & The PDP Research Group, 1986; McClelland, Rumelhart, & The PDP Research Group, 1986). In philosophy, related issues are discussed under the rubric of *subdoxastic states* (Stich, 1978).

The essential notion of microstructure is that larger units, of whatever sort, seem to be composed of smaller units that act as functional intermediaries in the processes involving those larger units. As trivial as this notion may seem, we shall see that it has been ignored in many reputable theories of animal learning. By examining the microstructure of action, we will find a candidate for the basic unit of analysis for learning theories.

Types of microstructure. Cognitivists, of course, worry mostly about cognitive units: thoughts and beliefs and the like. If we wish to examine the structure of learning, we need to look at behavioral units: actions. Roughly speaking, the notion of microstructure can be modeled using the macrostructural relation of one action as a component subpart of another.

Consider the microstructure of response. A prototypical response such as a lever-press consists of a sequence of microactions, each subordinate *components* of the whole action—atomic or molecular activities (deeds), each with the goal of making the next microaction possible. (This is what behaviorists call *precurrent responding,* or *chaining.*) Just as I step forward now with one foot in order to step again immediately afterward with the other—my eventual (superordinate) goal being my arrival at school, so the rat must step up to the lever, raise its paw, lower its paw, etc., etc. Mechner (1992) distinguishes between an operant, such as a lever-press, and the sequence of *suboperants* of which the operant is composed.

Further, the expression "the rat pressed the lever" is ambiguous as between the richer description of the entire sequence of activities culminating in the paw actually moving against the lever and the thinner description of that ultimate micromovement alone. When does Ned's action of killing the King begin? When the trigger begins to move? When the finger begins to move? When Ned raises the gun? When he steps forward to shoot? When he plans the assassination?

In the real world, however, the environment constantly shifts. The cat chasing the rat in order to obtain food will find the rat far less cooperative than the rat finds the lever. Indeed, in the wild, the rat only occasionally finds grain or garbage in the same location and never finds it in exactly the same location as does the rat finding the lever in the cage.

Even in the laboratory, it is easier to press a fixed lever with one's eyes open. Choose an object in front of you, just slightly out of easy reach. Reach out and touch it. Withdraw your hand. Now, close your eyes and repeat the procedure. Even simple actions are easier when we rely on sensory information.

The reason that the sensory information is helpful is that hand and eye are never in exactly the same position relative to the external object. Even with a fixed environment, the organism's body constantly shifts its orientation. The exact positional relation between the actor's body and the object(s) acted upon is never repeated. Action must be understood in this context. This is a principal argument for equifinality (Brunswick, 1955).

The dynamics of microstructure. In general, we do not blindly execute subactions followed by further subactions, repeating until the superordinate goal is achieved. Rather, we act (i.e., perform a microaction) and then, depending upon sensory feedback, choose among a small set of possible next microactions. In short, we use sensory information to make microscopic mid–course corrections as we head toward our goal.

In his book, *Cybernetics,* Wiener (1947) gives the classic picture of the microstructure of action:

> When we desire a motion to follow a given pattern, the difference between this pattern and the actually performed motion is used as a new input to cause the part regulated to move in such a way as to bring its motion closer to that given by the pattern. For example, one form of steering engine of a ship carries the reading of the wheel to an offset from the tiller which so regulates the valves of the steering engine as to move the tiller in such a way as to turn these valves off. . . .
>
> Now, suppose that I pick up a lead-pencil. To do this I have to move certain muscles. However, for all of us but a few expert anatomists, we do not know what these muscles are; and even among the anatomists, there are few if any who can perform the act by a conscious willing in succession of the contraction of each muscle concerned. On the contrary, what we will is to pick the pencil up. Once we have determined on this, our motion proceeds in such a way that we may say roughly that the amount by which the pencil is not yet picked up is decreased at each stage. This part of the action is not in full consciousness.
>
> To perform an action in such a manner, there must be a report to the nervous system, conscious or unconscious, of the amount by which we have failed to pick the pencil up at each instant. If we have our eye on the pencil, this report may be visual, at least in part, but it is more generally kinaesthetic, or to use a term now in vogue, proprioceptive. (pp. 13–14)

It may seem odd that I quote from this hoary old text. But there are important lessons in this particular passage.

First, behaviorists of all stripes have been reluctant (for a number of reasons) to incorporate cybernetic notions into their work. A principal reason is that concern with microstructure is thought to be a step backward to the molecular behaviorism of Watson. I believe that there is an essential role for molecular analysis in the explanation of conduct.

Second, despite an initial flirtation with cybernetic structure (Miller, Galanter, & Pribram, 1960), cognitive psychologists have ignored the holistic, cyclic, dynamic, interactionist implications of that structure and continued in the "linear" tradition of stimulus–response psychology. Indeed, one of von Cranach's (1982) main interests is to reestablish concern for hierarchical cycles in the study of cognition.

Von Cranach's effort is laudable. However, he, like most contemporary advocates of a cybernetic approach, misses a key point of the above passage. As noted earlier, von Cranach (1982) restricts his study of action to conscious acts. He claims that other sorts of acts are "found only in rare cases" (p. 36).

In the above passage, Wiener claims that every "goal-directed, planned, intended and conscious behaviour" (to use von Cranach's own phrasing), even one so simple as the picking up of a lead pencil, *is composed of many microacts,* many of which, if not all, *are not conscious.* On Wiener's account, for each conscious act, there are dozens, if not hundreds, of non–conscious acts.

A serious consideration of the microstructure of action leads one to the conclusion that it is *conscious* acts that are proportionately rare. If such is the case, an explanatory strategy that does not make overmuch of the issue of awareness, such as Lee's, may be preferred to an explanatory strategy that requires introspective access, such as Harré's (1982, p. 18) or von Cranach's (1982, pp. 47–48).

Most importantly, as we shall see in the next section, a proper consideration of microstructure will point out the appropriate basic unit of analysis for the study of animal learning. Traditional theories of learning, both behavioral and cognitive, have failed to explain learning by taking their basic unit at the wrong level of organization.

IDENTIFYING THE BASIC UNIT OF ANALYSIS

The argument that a unique, basic act–description exists and that the specification of such actions is essential to proper explanations of learning will depend in great part upon an analogy between action and perception. In particular, the argument depends upon an analogy to Stich's (1978) distinction between beliefs and subdoxastic states. I claim that an equivalent distinction exists between actions and what I call *subintentional acts.*

Stich's Distinction

It may be useful to examine how subdoxastic states differ from beliefs in order to get an idea of how subintentional acts might differ from actions. One of Stich's (1978) examples is that of a person perceiving objects as being at different distances, the process of depth perception. Many different features of the changing visual field, many different stimulations of the retina, are involved in the process that results in the person's belief that object A is behind object B.

Stich argues persuasively that none of these subcomponents of belief-producing processes are themselves beliefs.

Intuitively, this makes sense. Suppose Sally believes that the lamp is further from her than the chair. It may very well be that, somewhere deep in her visual subsystem, the disparity between the image of the lamp on one retina and the image of the lamp on her other retina, is calculated. Further, her ultimate belief about the closeness of the lamp may be due, in part, to this calculation within her visual subsystem. Indeed, a proper understanding of the microstructure of perception may require an understanding of those sorts of calculations. Despite all this, it makes little or no sense to say that Sally *believes* that there is a binocular disparity between the two images on the two retinas.

Subdoxastic states differ from beliefs in two ways, according to Stich. They are inaccessible to consciousness and they are less "inferentially integrated" with the rest of the beliefs (other than the beliefs actually produced). Stich also mentions that the process from one doxastic state to another, or to a terminal belief, lacks the usual equifinality associated with the more ordinary sort of inference.

I suggest we can add a linguistic distinction to the list. We are distinguishing here between the claim that Sally believes *the lamp to be behind the chair,* and the claim that Sally believes that *there is a binocular disparity between the pattern on her left retina and the pattern on her right.* The terms *lamp* and *chair,* which refer to the objects about which Sally has a belief, are, grammatically speaking, the *predicate objects* of the belief sentence. Those two terms refer to things outside Sally's body. In contrast, 'pattern on the retina' is an expression that refers only to things within the body, or, more properly, to states of the body. I call this linguistic distinction the *predicate-object distinction.*

As Dan Hunter (personal communication, July 1991) points out, this distinction suggests that subdoxastic states are epistemologically more basic than perceptual beliefs, since we come to knowledge of the outside world through the acquisition of subdoxa regarding states of our own bodies.

Furthermore, from an evolutionary standpoint, knowledge about the nature of external objects cannot be hardwired into the brain to the same degree as knowledge about the nature of internal bodily states. Lamps and chairs have been around far too short a time for human brains to have evolved specific processes for recognizing them. We must *learn* about lamps and chairs.

However, the stimulation of rods and cones in the retina, and the reorientations of eyeballs, have been around for as long as retinas and eyeballs. There has been plenty of time for the brain to evolve so as to discern important differences in these bodily states. From an evolutionary perspective, an important difference is one that provides an evolutionary advantage. The evolutionary advantage of the ability to acquire knowledge of the outside world is obvious. Hence, it is quite reasonable to assume that brains would evolve to be able to detect exactly those changes in bodily states that provide information about the outside world.

In sum, it appears to matter a good deal whether or not the predicate object of a belief sentence makes reference to something outside the subject's body.

Are Microactions Actions?

All in all, dividing actions into functional subparts seems less of a problem than dividing the process of belief formation/acquisition into the processing of subdoxa. However, just as Stich (1978) raises the question of whether those cognitive intermediaries are truly beliefs, the analogous question needs to be considered. Are these behavioral intermediaries, the microactions, actually actions? Or do we need to distinguish a separate classification, that of subintentional act, for some of these microactions? If so, where do we draw the line between the two?

Austin (1962) makes the clearest statement of this problem. In discussing the rich–thin continuum of action noted above, he concludes (with some fervor) that, at some level, we must decide that such an intermediary is, in fact, not a proper action in some sense:

> With physical actions we nearly always naturally name the action *not* in terms of what we are here calling the minimum physical act, but in terms which embrace a greater or less but indefinitely extensive range of what might be called its natural consequences (or, looking at it another way, the intention with which it was done).
>
> We not merely do not use the notion of a minimum physical act (which is in any case doubtful) but we do not seem to have any class of names which distinguish physical acts from consequences. (p. 112)
>
> Note that if we suppose the minimum physical act to be movement of the body when we say 'I moved my finger', the fact that the object moved *is* part of my body does in fact introduce a new sense of 'moved'. Thus I may be able to waggle my ears as a schoolboy does, or by grasping them between my finger and thumb, or move my foot either in the ordinary way or by manipulating with my hand when I have pins and needles. The ordinary use of 'move' in such examples as 'I moved my finger' is ultimate. We must not seek to go back behind it to 'pulling on my muscles' and the like. (p. 112, footnote)

In the above passage, Austin makes two important points. In terms of the macrostructure of conduct, he notes that we have no usual way in common parlance English to identify a bodily movement distinct from its intended consequences. This supports Lee's view that the essential components of action are means and end. More importantly, in terms of animal learning, this lacuna in English has given rise to some confusion about what should count as a 'response' in learning theories.

However, it is Austin's second point that concerns us here. That point involves the microstructure of actions. Austin claims that the absence of any way (again, in common parlance English) of talking sensibly about a person as the do-er of microactivities (consider Wiener's "conscious willing in succession of the contraction of each muscle" above) means we must reject the notion that such *subintentional acts* are actions by the person.

Austin's conclusion leads to a problem. If subintentional acts are not proper actions, then they must, on my theory of action, lack some essential feature of being an action. On the analysis given, they certainly do not lack goals. And they certainly involve bodily movements. Just as Lycan (1988) suggests that the subdoxastic states of the person may be the beliefs of one of that person's proper subparts, I claim that subintentional acts are not proper actions because they are not performed by the person. Rather, they are performed by some subpart of that person. Returning to Austin's example above, I am the one who crooks my finger, but it is not me, rather it is some motor-control subsystem of mine, that pulls on the muscles.

Finally, consider the predicate object distinction. It seems to make sense for both beliefs and actions. Austin makes use of precisely this distinction in defining the "minimum physical act." In Austin's view of *a minimum physical act,* we note that the "thinnest" construal of the action, the limiting case, that of crooking the finger, is describable solely in terms of the body, whereas pulling the trigger, firing the gun, shooting the King, and killing the King (etc., etc.) all involve the body in relation to external objects.

I claim that the distinction regarding predicate objects is the crucial one both for determining what is an action (in the behavioral case) and for determining what is a belief (in the cognitive case). Other distinctions have merit, but a critical comparison will have to wait for another time.

The Basic Atomic Action

The way is now paved for the promised specification of a basic unit of analysis, a basic atomic action. The basic atomic action we are searching for should be the sort of microelement that composes the microprocesses that Wiener speaks of in the quoted passage. In order to find these basic elements of microstructure, we begin with the macrostructure and work our way down the most likely looking continuum, the richness–thinness continuum.

Travelling down this continuum, we find a sudden barrier to common sense. For the very next thinner act-description, the person does not appear to be the actor, the performer of the act. Taking this as our cue, we search nearby for a unique sort of act-description. We discover that the thinnest proper description of an act has three unique characteristics: (a) The predicate object of the action sentence (the thing done *to*) is always a part of one's body. (b) As Austin notes, the sentence describing the act is thoroughly ambiguous, admitting of two interpretations. Either the body part is moved "in the ordinary way," or by means of manipulation (directly or indirectly) by another body part. (c) When we isolate the first of these two alternatives, that is, moving one's body part "in the ordinary way," we discover a final mark. "The ordinary way" is only *one particular way*. Unlike almost any other act-description, it admits of almost no equifinality.

Returning to our recursive definition of action as a means–end pair, we see that, in the new formulation, the thinnest action looks mighty strange:

"Ned crooked his finger" (action$_1$) =
<"Ned's finger crooking" (deed), "Ned has his finger crooked" (action$_2$)?>

This is the most extreme example of what Lee (1988, p. 59) refers to as "end results bound closely to behavior." In short, Ned crooked his finger in order that his finger be crooked. It is exactly the strangeness of this formulation that tells us that we have found the elemental act. (More precisely, this is how we can use the action theoretic notation to specify an act as elemental.) Further, it is a way of eliminating the threat of infinite regress, a problem for any formulation using a recursive definition.[2]

The most important moral we can take from Austin is that English leads us astray at a critical moment. In English, we have no ordinary way of distinguishing the action wherein Ned crooks Ned's finger from the bodily movement that instantiates that action. The closest we can come is to designate the expression *Ned crooks his finger* as the action and the expression *the crooking of Ned's finger* as the bodily movement (deed).

However, this transformation between present indicative active and gerund is more notational convenience than genuine ordinary English usage. The language remains unclear. As does Lee, I begin with common parlance distinctions. But grammar alone cannot determine the nature of psychological phenomena. Theoretical commitments are unavoidable.

The Inadequacy of Molar Terms

It remains to show that not only are the usual act-descriptions of molar behaviorism and cognitive psychology not basic, but that those descriptions are inadequate for the purpose of psychological explanation.

---

[2] Actually, the problem of infinite regress is quite a bit more complex than this. For instance, in response to a question: *Why did Ned crook his finger?* a legitimate answer might be: *In order to start the revolution.* Thus, reasons and intended consequences might lead us outward to the richest description instead of inward to the thinnest. The problem of infinite regress is, I believe, soluble, but a detailed exposition of this must wait for another time.

Molar terms. The molar behaviorist takes the normal distal description of an act, like a rat's *pressing a lever* or a pigeon's *pecking a key,* as both the basic unit of empirical measurement and as the basic unit of theoretical analysis. This unit is called the *molar response.* Mainstream cognitivists have accepted molar specification of basic terms. The contemporary learning theorist takes the rate of occurrence for some molar response as the empirical measure of learning. This measure is called *response rate.* The basic theoretical construct said to correlate with response rate is called *response strength.*

Molar behaviorism, so-called, is the thesis that the normal distal description of an action is the only one that need concern the psychologist. By restricting descriptions of stimulus and response to a single position along the richness–thinness continuum, the neobehaviorists hoped to establish a more or less unambiguous language for recording the behavioral regularities they hoped to discover in the laboratory. The claim was made that the appropriate position along the richness–thinness continuum could always be distinguished in terms of the precise degree of equifinality just broad enough to encompass all the bodily movements of interest and to exclude all those not of interest.

However, molar responses are not basic actions. As Austin (1962) notes above, the normal distal description of an act all but inevitably involves reference to physical objects outside the animal's body. The rat presses a *lever* and the pigeon pecks a *key.*

The problem of response strength. Just as humans have not had time to evolve mechanisms for recognizing lamps and chairs, neither have we had time to evolve mechanisms for turning on lamps or sitting in chairs. We *have* had time to evolve mechanisms for extending our arms, crooking our fingers, bending our legs, adjusting our balance, etc.

What we have not evolved to do, we must perforce *learn* to do. On the structural view advocated here, what we learn must be composed of new relations amongst those things we already know. Hence, learned actions are composed ultimately of basic innate actions, that is, minimum physical acts.

In short, molar responses are themselves learned entities. Whatever the true nature of molar responses, any theory that purports to be a theory of *learning* must explain where molar responses come from. That is something that traditional learning theories do not explain. From this perspective, any learning theory that makes predictions solely in terms of increases or decreases in rates of molar responding is not a theory of learning per se, but rather a model of one aspect of learning.

The traditional reply of the molar behaviorist to the above criticism is that all of behavior is ultimately understandable in terms of changing rates of responding across all behaviors. Even if this claim is true (as I believe it is), the molarist reply fails. The examination of microstructure, above, indicates that molar responses are quite unlike minimum physical acts. We have no reason to assume that rates of molar responding are governed by the same laws as rates of basic actions.

Molar responses are highly structured complexes consisting (at least in part) of basic actions. Hence, the rates of basic actions we are concerned with are rates conditional on the occurrence of previous basic acts. Molarists might claim that rates of molar responding conditional only on the occurrence of stimuli can tell us about rates of basic actions conditional upon other basic actions as well as stimuli. Any such claim should be supported by mathematical argument. Presently, it is not.

Given these assumptions, proper explanation of any psychological phenomenon consists in showing how microactional sequences of basic atomic actions account for that phenomenon.

Indeed, the molarist case is in worse shape than the above suggests. Consider the collection of all possible microaction sequences. We might think that a specific molar response class, such as a lever-press, consists of a specific group of such microsequences. This is not the case. If the rat is located at one particular spot, say to the left of the lever, there does exist a specific (albeit large) group of microsequences, any of which could effect a successful lever-press. On the other hand, if the rat is located elsewhere, say to the right, none of those microsequence will do. A distinct group of microsequences is required. Further, as was noted above, in the wild, a rat is never in exactly the same place twice.

Finally, if we refocus our attention on the notion that behavior is that which the subject does, there is a sense in which a molar response is not something done by the subject at all. Molar terms describe basic actions taken in the context of specific environmental affordances. Said affordances are produced, in part, by previous basic actions. Despite this, environmental affordances are simply not anything the subject *does*.

All of the above makes for a rather discouraging picture of the prospect of explanatorily adequate theories of learning. Nevertheless, I am optimistic. A detailed proposal for a computational theory of learning must wait for another time. However, the example of the pigeon given below should both help to clarify the above issues and suggest the eventual form of such a computational theory.

THE CASE OF PIGEON LEARNING

In this section, I will take a specific set of well-known data and reformulate it in terms of the new language proposed. This reformulation will show why certain problems have arisen in prior treatments of the phenomena. It will also give a practical illustration of the new problems that come with the new language.

I have chosen the specific case of the operant conditioning of the pigeon. I choose this data because it is, in some sense, straightforward and well understood. (I hesitate to describe *any* behavior as "simple.") Despite its apparent simplicity, a good theoretical account is unavailable at present.

The Experimental Paradigm

To begin with, a description of the procedure is in order. For the experiment, the pigeon is taken from its home cage and placed in the operant chamber. There is usually a light that can illuminate the entire chamber. Typically, one wall of the chamber contains the apparatus—usually, one or more keys and a food-dispensing tray.

A key is a button on the wall that covers an electrical switch. Contact is made when the key is pressed. The button is usually made of a translucent material and can be lit from behind. By action of a mechanism behind the wall, a food pellet can be dropped into the food-dispensing tray.

All of the apparatus described, buttons, chamber lights, key lights, food dispenser, etc., are operated by a mechanism behind the wall of the cage. A fixed logical procedure or program is set up in that mechanism to operate each part of the apparatus under specified conditions. For instance, food might be dispensed on every third peck of the key; or one for every peck, given that the key is lit from behind with a red light; or only when the chamber is lit throughout.

The various logical relations in the program or procedure are called *contingencies*. They are intended to model the contingent demands and opportunities of a real-world environment. In practice, the procedure or program, called a *schedule,* often becomes very complex. The basic result, however, is simple. The pigeon comes to conduct itself so as to acquire the food. Within the limits of its capacity for learning, it can adapt to a wide variety of complex contingencies, learning to cope with those demands and thus gaining access to food provided by the food dispenser.

Finding the Basic Unit of Analysis

As in the general case, I believe that it is an essential first step to the construction of any theory to identify the basic unit of analysis. As a means of finding the basic unit, my current prejudice is for what I have called the *predicate object test*. The predicate object test involves finding the richest act-description wherein that which is acted upon, is a part of the actor's body. That description is the description of the basic action.

Applying the predicate object test. In the case of pigeon learning, traditional learning theories take the keypeck as the basic unit of analysis. The rate of keypecking is the principle empirical measure. The strength of the keypeck response is the fundamental theoretical construct. By *keypeck,* I take these theoreticians to mean the pigeon thrusting its head forward so that the beak depresses the key, closing the electrical circuit behind. Of course, the action sentence: *The pigeon pecks the key.* has a predicate object, the key, *outside* the pigeon's body.

Herein lies the dilemma. The critical measure of the pigeon's conduct, as well as its learning, is the closing of the electrical switch behind the key. The precise, and indeed, the *only* molar action description that captures exactly the right portions of the pigeon's behavior is the keypeck. The keypeck is the bit of behavior, the action, that the experimenter has experimented upon. Predictions about the keypeck are the *only* sort of predictions in which the theoretician could have the slightest interest. Yet the keypeck is not a basic act description.

The solution is simple. Examine the microstructure of the keypeck. Decompose it into basic acts. Only two types of action are needed. (a) *The pigeon reorients its head.* (b) *The pigeon pecks.* (That is, the pigeon thrusts its head forward.) Both of these actions are basic by the predicate object test. The predicate object in both cases is the head. Every keypeck can be thought of as a sequence of head orientations (until the key is directly in front of the beak) followed by a peck. In Mechner's (1992) terms, the keypeck is an operant with the peck as its *terminating sub-operant.* The microstructure of behavior is revealed by analysis of the sub-operants.

In the process of uncovering the basic actions underlying the keypeck, we have described the sequence leading up to the actual pecking of the key in terms of Wiener's (1947) cycle of alternations between micromotion and environmental assessment. This picture also corresponds to Gibson's (1972) view of vision as an active process: retinal inputs leading to ocular adjustments leading to altered retinal inputs, etc. Each reorientation of the head also moves the eyes with respect to the external environment, thus altering any subsequent retinal input. Any new information from this altered retinal input is available for the pigeon to use in the determination of the next microaction, be it another head reorientation, a peck, or some other act irrelevant to the experiment. Each bit of new information constitutes a new opportunity for the pigeon to reach the key.

The goals. Now, consider the macrostructure of this conduct. Due to the peculiarity of English, noted earlier, in individuating the minimum physical acts, we have also picked out the basic bodily movements involved. These are the deeds, the means. At the thinnest level of analysis, each head orientation is done so that the head be reoriented and each peck so that the beak move forward.

The head orientations are also done in order to provide new retinal inputs (information opportunities) to the pigeon. They are also done in order to move the beak into a position in front of the key. The peck probably is done to satisfy some innate propensity to peck in the pigeon as well as another to peck bright (or brightly lit) objects. (This propensity is revealed in the phenomenon of animal learning known as autoshaping.) However, as learning progresses, the peck is done in order to press the key, in order that food be provided, in order that the pigeon may eat. (We may stop with the eating as this may be treated, for our purposes here, as a terminal, irreducible goal.)

Simply put: every keypeck is a peck, but not every peck is a keypeck. In order for a keypeck to occur, at least the following must be true: a key must exist, the animal must be capable of pecking (a snail just will not do), the animal must be positioned with its beak in front of the key, the key must be peckable by the animal. *Peckable* means that the key is not held rigid by a clamp or covered by a peck-proof shield, and that the animal is not harnassed so as to be unable to thrust its head forward, etc. Peckability is an *affordance*.

The Question for Action Theories of Learning

In stimulus–response psychology, the question to be answered by any learning theory is clear. What is the functional relation between environmental events and the rate at which molar responses appear? Since I claim that a theory based on these molar responses is necessarily inadequate, the question must be respecified for the new sort of theory proposed here.

Linguistic issues. As suggested above, there is a sense in which the keypeck is not something the pigeon *does*. In English, we use terms such as keypeck to describe the pigeon's conduct. As Austin's analysis shows, terms such as keypeck inevitably confuse the subject's deeds per se with those same deeds understood in the broader context of action. Logically speaking, a keypeck occurs if and only if two things are true: a) the environment provides the appropriate affordance, and b) the pigeon pecks. While the environmental affordance is due, in part, to the previous conduct (i.e., precurrent responding) of the pigeon, the environmental affordance is, notwithstanding, not anything that the pigeon *does*. The keypeck is an interaction between organism and environment.

Learning, in essence, is the process by which the organism is changed by the demands of the environment. Our only measure of the state of the organism and, thus, our only measure of any change in that state, is the *doings* of the organism. If common-parlance descriptions of conduct cannot distinguish between the doings that measure learning and the interactions that cause further learning, then those self-same common-parlance descriptions cannot serve in theories of learning.

In sum, normal distal act descriptions (NDADs) pick out molar responses, which are, or should be, the basic empirical unit of measurement. Molar responses and the rates thereof are our only data for the study of behavior and learning. Toponymic act descriptions (TADs, expressions making reference only to parts of the body) pick out basic actions, which are, or should be, the basic theoretical unit of analysis. Basic actions are the only true measure of the underlying process we call learning. Basic actions explain molar responses.

As with all psychological processes, the relevant phenomena provide only an indirect measure. The challenge to psychological theory is to analyze the underlying processes given only the available data.

Psychometric issues. The intuitive appeal of traditional learning theories is the same thing that renders those theories useless as psychological explanation: NDADs are powerful linguistic devices that capture behavior with respect to the precise context of interest. Traditional learning theories, expressed using NDADs, appealingly suggest that all of conduct can be segmented neatly into molar responses and their rates. They do this at the cost of conflating environmental affordances and organismic deeds. That conflation leads the molarist to perpetually misattribute the environmental contributions to conduct to some source within the organism. This fundamental attribution error (Jones & Nisbett, 1972) is the mistake of mentalist and cognitivist alike.

All the same, to the degree that traditional learning theories can be said to explain learning at all, they do so using a powerful language *unavailable* to the proponent of a microstructural approach like the one advocated here. The molarist is obliged to show why laws governing molar responses also apply to other sorts of behavioral units. Similarly, a proponent of the present approach is obliged to show how the weaker language based on TADs can explain conduct understood within the broader contexts of personal goals, social settings, and cultural surroundings (Harré, 1982).

The solution is to consider learning as akin to a process of statistical approximation (Dennett, 1981). Assume that, for any organism, there is an ideal behavioral function, expressible in molar stimulus-response terms, that best allows the organism to cope with its environment. Learning is best understood as the processes whereby the behavioral propensities of the organism, espressed in terms of microsequences of basic actions, come to approximate that ideal.

In the new view of learning, conduct is a constant cyclic interaction between environment and organism. The environment is disposed to react in various ways to various acts. These environmental dispositions are called contingencies. The organism is also disposed to act in various ways to various environmental events. These organismic dispositions are called *propensities* or *repertoire.*

The question for learning theorists is to see what function can model the changes in repertoire actually occurring in the animal. Modeling the function must begin with a realistic model of the environment–organism interaction along with a realistic model of environmental contingencies. The function must gradually alter the model organism's repertoire in such a manner that the pattern of changing conduct matches, in all of the manifold ways possible, the pattern of changing conduct of animals in the laboratory and ultimately in the real world.

CONCLUSION

In conclusion, I am a molar behaviorist as regards description and observation, but a molecular behaviorist as regards theoretical explanation. To require the specification of a particular sequence of microacts in explaining composite action is to abandon equifinality in a futile search for reductive explanation of action. Instead, the proper account of action involves postulating a *probability distribution* of alternative microaction sequences that could account for acts within the given action class in principle.

The potential for Lee's action theory extends far beyond the application made here. Planned directions include arguments for the elimination of the stimulus–response distinction in theoretical accounts of learning, and a computer-simulation technique for solving the psychometric problem of comparing competing theories of animal learning.

REFERENCES

Anscombe, G.E.M. (1963). *Intention.* (2nd ed.). Ithaca, NY: Cornell University Press.

Austin, J.L. (1962). *How to do things with words* (2nd ed.; J.O. Urmson & M. Sbisà, Eds.). Cambridge, MA: Harvard University Press.

Brand, M. (1984). *Intending and acting.* Cambridge, MA: MIT Press/Bradford Books.

Brunswick, E. (1955). The conceptual framework of psychology. In O. Neurath, R. Carnap, & C. Morris (Eds.), *International Encyclopedia of Unified Science, 1,* (pp. 655–760; also published separately, 1952). Chicago: University of Chicago Press.

Cranach, M. von (1982). The psychological study of goal-directed action: basic issues. In M. von Cranach & R. Harré (Eds.), *The analysis of action* (pp. 35–73). Cambridge, UK: Cambridge University Press.

Davidson, D. (1963). Actions, reasons, and causes. *Journal of Philosophy, 60,* 685–700.

Davis, L. (1979). *Theory of action.* Englewood Cliffs, NJ: Prentice Hall.

Dennett, D.C. (1981). Three kinds of intentional psychology. In R.A. Healey (Ed.), *Mind, psychology, and reductionism.* Cambridge, UK: Cambridge University Press.

Gibson, J.J. (1960). The concept of stimulus in psychology. *American Psychologist, 15,* 694–703.

Gibson, J.J. (1972). A theory of direct visual perception. In J.R. Royce & Wm. W. Rozeboom (Eds.), *The psychology of knowing* (pp. 215–232). New York: Gordon and Breach.

Goldman, A.I. (1970). *A theory of human action.* Englewood Cliffs, NJ: Prentice Hall.

Hamblin, C.L. (1987). *Imperatives.* Oxford: Basil Blackwell.

Harré, R. (1982). Theoretical preliminaries to the study of action. In M. von Cranach & R. Harré (Eds.), *The analysis of action* (pp. 5–33). Cambridge, UK: Cambridge University Press.

Jones, E.E., & Nisbett, R.E. (1972). The actor and the observer: Divergent perceptions in the causes of behavior. In E.E. Jones, D.E. Kanouse, H.H. Kelley, R.E. Nisbett, S. Valins, & B.W. Weiner (Eds.), *Attribution: Perceiving the causes of behavior* (pp. 37–52). Morristown, NJ: General Learning Press.

Koch, S. (1954). Clark L. Hull. In W.K. Estes, S. Koch, K. MacCorquodale, P.E. Meehl, C.G. Mueller, Jr., W.N. Schoenfeld, & W.S. Verplanck (Eds.), *Modern Learning Theory* (pp. 1–176). New York: Appleton-Century-Crofts.

Lee, V.L. (1988). *Beyond behaviorism.* Hillsdale, NJ: Erlbaum.

Lycan, W.G. (1988). *Judgement and justification.* Cambridge, UK: Cambridge University Press.

Mandler, G., & Kessen, W. (1959). *The language of psychology.* New York: Wiley.

McClelland, J.L., Rummelhart, D.E., & The PDP Research Group. (1986). *Parallel distributed processing: Explorations in the microstructure of cognition, Volume II: Psychological and biological models.* Cambridge, MA: Bradford Books/MIT Press.

Mechner, F. (1992). *The revealed operant: A way to study the characteristics of individual occurrences of operant responses.* Cambridge, MA: Cambridge Center for Behavioral Studies.

Meehl, P.E. (1978). Theoretical risks and tabular asterisks: Sir Karl, Sir Ronald, and the slow progress of soft psychology. *Journal of Clinical and Consulting Psychology, 46,* 806–834.

Miller, G.A., Galanter, E., & Pribram, K.H. (1960). *Plans and the structure of behavior.* New York: Henry Holt.

Oppenheimer, L. (1991). The concept of action: A historical perspective. In L. Oppenheimer & J. Valsiner (Eds.), *The origins of action: Interdisciplinary and international perspectives* (pp. 1–35). New York: Springer-Verlag.

Palya, W.L. (1989). *Research methods lecture notes.* Unpublished manuscript, Jacksonville State University, Southeastern Behavioral Analysis Center, Jacksonville, AL.

Rummelhart, D.E., McClelland, J.L., & The PDP Research Group. (1986). *Parallel distributed processing: Explorations in the microstructure of cognition, Volume I: Foundations.* Cambridge, MA: Bradford Books/MIT Press.

Skinner, B.F. (1969). *Contingencies of reinforcement: A theoretical analysis.* New York: Appleton-Century-Crofts.

Skinner, B.F. (1974). *About behaviorism.* New York: Alfred A. Knopf.

Stich, S.P. (1978). Beliefs and subdoxastic states. *Philosophy of Science, 45,* 499–518.

Turner, M.B. (1967). *Philosophy and the science of behavior.* New York: Appleton-Century-Crofts.

Wiener, N. (1947). *Cybernetics: Or control and communication in the animal and the machine.* New York: John Wiley & Sons.

Wittgenstein, L. (1953). *Philosophical investigations.* (G.E.M. Anscombe, Trans.). New York: MacMillan.

Ziff, P. (1958) "About behaviorism." *Analysis, XVIII.* (Reprinted in *Philosophical turnings: Essays in conceptual appreciation* by Paul Ziff, pp. 155–160 Ithaca, NY: University of Cornell Press, 1966.)

Epilogue.
The Structure of Learning: Phylogenesis, Ontogenesis, and Microgenesis

Hans-Georg W. Voss and Jaan Valsiner

The concepts of *structure* and *process* surely belong to the most frequently used technical terms in the discipline of psychology and beyond. Ironically, much contradiction in definitional attempts can also be found—and the concepts share this fate with such other well-known terms as *stimulus* and *behavior*. There was even a comment by a colleague from the psychological institute who complained about a "logical error" when lumping structure and process: structure would refer to something static, like the skeleton of an organism or the raw construction of a building, whereas process would mean goal-oriented, systematic change, most basically meaning movement in time and space.

How, then, can process have a structure? In music, the individual notes (the elements) of a melodic phrase, or a theme, may be totally replaced by new ones, and nevertheless there can be a constancy in structure, which, in this case, would mean that transposition has occurred. Transposition is coupled with change, but there will be no process involved, unless change is governed by a superordinated compositorial principle such as the sequencing of accords in pursuing the overall structure of the musical piece. The reader may be well aware that transposition in music was claimed by Gestalt psychologists to represent an outstanding example for the "invariance against change" of Gestalten, in this case, of *Sukzessivgestalten* (successive, or temporal Gestalten; von Ehrenfels, 1890). The term *process* may therefore be used for characterizing systematically changing structures in terms of relations being established among elements. We think that this applies to morphogenetic change as well as to developing psychological functions in general, such as perceiving (rather than perception), memorizing (rather than memory), and learning (rather than knowledge acquisition).

It has become widely accepted among psychologists to conceptualize psychological phenomena in terms of processes rather than in terms of ontological givens. Thus, the "structure of learning" implicitly involves a process of learning that is to be characterized in terms of an ordered, or structured, sequence of steps (the *Sukzessivgestalt*). There is a dialectical relationship between the concepts being discussed here, in that in order to understand the structure of an event one has to come to know more about the process of its formation, and vice versa, any account of the processual character of events must include some considering of structure. This kind of circularity has led phenomenologically oriented authors to conclude that the structure of an event (for example, perceiving, learning) can only be understood (rather than explained) in *statu nascendi,* that is, by comparing successive stages or segments in the process of its formation (Merleau-Ponty, 1945). Process, like change in general, cannot be observed directly; it must be inferred from a comparison of successive snapshots as movement is produced in cinematography.

The cinematographic metaphor is often used to make the distinction between the static and dynamic perspectives, as those are complementary components in world's ontology. However, it is misleading, since it replaces the mechanisms that generate the movement in the shadow of the movement as an outcome. In this respect, the contrast between static and dynamic (moving, cinematographic) pictures is that between two outcomes, whereas the two mechanisms (the cinema projector on the one side, and systemic organization of the organism's visual and conceptual systems on the other) that actually generate the dynamic outcome remain without attention.

Furthermore, the processes of learning (as these unite microgenesis with ontogenesis) and development (as those relate ontogenesis with phylogenesis and cultural history—see Cole, 1992; Gottlieb, 1992) have characteristics that do not fit the cinematographic metaphor. A sequence of film frames is a finished, well-defined product, the effects of which are predetermined by the synchronization of the projection speed with the processing parameters of the human visual system. In contrast, phenomena of learning processes entail the active participation of the organism in its given state in the creation of the next stage. If we were to apply this notion to the film analogy, we would get a film in which (in the beginning of the projection onto the screen) it is not yet clear which frames may be projected next, and in which the previous and presently projected frames are probabilistically determining the nature of the next frames to come. If such a film were ever possible, it would amount to a highly uncertain experience for the viewer, who could not predict what the next experience would be like. Last (but not least), the simple physical system of static images projected in a time sequence would never fit as the model for open-systemic processes. In this respect—the nature of temporary states that characterize the sequencing of learning processes, as well as of the principles that govern its evolution—remains after all an open question, for which nonmechanistic models are mandatory.

Throughout this volume, authors have shared some effort in giving an answer to this question. For example, Goodyear (Chapter 4) was trying to uncover the states of mind, characterized as interpretative plateaus, in the construction of the learning process, and Kemp (Chapter 11) went down to the basic atomic actions and their microstructure, which may become involved in "constant cyclic interaction between environment and organism." For Christman and Groeben (Chapter 2), learning may be triggered and indeed become optimized by thoughtful reflexive choices. Notwithstanding the broad overall orientation exemplified by the chapters in this volume, we have learned that characterizing the structure of learning processes entails circumscriptions of a variety of theoretical concepts such as *dynamic learning system, productive learning activity, task specific development,* and *genetic growing system.*

Two general conclusions can be drawn from the chapters in this volume. First, *learning bears cultural meaning,* and there is a *sociohistorical dimension in the structure of learning processes.* Second, learning processes evolve in social context that is *mediated by acts of co-construction.* The process of co-construction is largely self-determined, or self-organized.

Cultural Meanings and Learning

There is wide acceptance of learning (as a process) to represent a basic factor in cultural transmission of values, skills, beliefs, or knowledge. Learning environments of children are organized according to the systems of activity that in a given culture are organized to form the cultural practices that assure an optimal functioning of culture's inhabitants (Laboratory of Comparative Human Cognition, 1983). Taking a worldwide view of the culture-specific construction of learning environments, it may be noted that formal schooling is more an exception than a rule to the large array of informal, ordinary learning contexts, the vital feature here being described by Heron as "the unintentionality, the day-by-day usualness, the taken-for-granted assumptions about what is and what is not important in life" (Heron, 1974, p. 97). The establishment of the formal school, with its reliance on formal instruction, designed to transmit the cultural-societal value of individual competition in achievement and performance, represents in itself a value and may be understood in sociohistorical terms (or even sociobiological ones) as a kind of optimal strategy for cultural and societal reproduction. If there is structure in learning processes of the kind Heron has described, the unstructured, or rather chance-determined nature, of "natural" learning undermines the priority given to starting the analysis with an exhaustive survey of "what" has to be learned (Johnston, 1981); rather, one would ask what makes the situation function as a learning event, or, "How will organism and environment/context coact together in order to produce a learning opportunity?" This brings us to the next point mentioned above.

Co-construction

A learner's context is another learner. A simple statement such as this may be provocative, since it may express neglect of the hierarchical structure of student–teacher relationships. Nevertheless, there may be reciprocity, with both participants being jointly involved in structuring the learning process according to some general organizing principles such as gaining rhymicity and synchrony in turn-taking behaviors or co-constructing the dialogue (see chapters by Voss and Christman & Groeben). It may be taken for granted that in adult–child interaction, the more competent adult owns a higher amount of responsibility for structuring the learning process. Co-construction therefore does not mean symmetry with respect to both quality and quantity of the activity being "invested" in the interaction. Van Oers (this volume) has given a neat demonstration of a co-constructivistic process in (formal) classroom learning relying on a "discursive activity" of participants, which also may considered to relate to a social (and cultural) practice of text making. This view also fits the dialogical perspective taken by Ramirez Garrido, Medina, and Santigosa in describing the "making of literacy" in adult education. Last but not least in this section's list of contributions to this volume, the evidence of children's creation of "discursive structures" in their minds, reported by Oliveira and Rossetti-Ferreira, throws some light on the co-constructive efforts of young children of less than about five years of age. Discursive structures, such as like taking the role of the adult or attributing the role of a baby-to-be-taken-care-of to a peer, may be seen here as instruments, or process structures, that have to be learned and that guide further learning.

The examples given here, which are extensively discussed throughout this volume, also underscore the high level of autonomy in the organization and regulation of the actions of a person who is involved in a dynamical learning system. The learner and his or her co-learner, or the learner and the learning environment, are synergistically linked. Their development may be characterized in terms of the evolution of dynamical systems in general. Self-organization includes self-reference of the system, with the emerging structures a nonlinear function of preceding states. This kind of recursive process, in which a large quantity of variables may be involved (depending on the overall complexity of the system), is often governed by a much smaller number of order parameters (for example, the frequency of turn-taking behavior in a dyad) and thus may become intelligible when expressed in mathematical equations.

Finally—would psychology lose much if we got rid of the umbrella term *learning*? As can be seen from various contributions to this volume, the use of this term as an easy attribution of causality for some phenomenon of organizational change has been rampant in psychology. It is our hope that our scrutiny of this very widely used (but poorly understood) term would lead us all to reconceptualize the processes that underlie its structure. Or in other terms—psychologists may need to unlearn the easy use of the term learning, and to replace it by carefully rethinking their conceptual understanding of psychological functions.

REFERENCES

Cole, M. (1992). Context, modularity, and the cultural constitution of development. In L.T. Winegar & J. Valsiner (Eds.), *Children's development within social context. Vol. 2. Research and methodology* (pp. 5–31). Hillsdale, NJ: Erlbaum.

Ehrenfels, C. von. (1890). Über Gestaltqualitäten. *Vierteljahresschrift für Philosophie, 14,* 249–292.

Gottlieb, G. (1992). *Individual development and evolution.* New York: Oxford University Press.

Heron, A. (1974). Cultural determinants of concrete operational behavior. In J.L.M. Dawson & W.J. Lonner (Eds.), *Readings in cross-cultural psychology.* Hong Kong: Hong Kong University Press.

Johnston, T. (1981). Contrasting approaches to a theory of learning. *Behavioral and Brain Sciences, 4,* 125–173.

Laboratory of Comparative Human Cognition (1983). Culture and cognitive development. In P.H. Mussen (Ed.), *Handbook of child psychology* (W. Kessen, Vol. ed) (4th ed., Vol. I, pp. 295–356). New York: Wiley.

Merleau-Ponty, M. (1945). *Phenomenologie de la perception.* Paris: Gallimard.

Author Index

Subject Index

343